1,000,000 Books

are available to read at

---◇---

www.ForgottenBooks.com

---◇---

Read online
Download PDF
Purchase in print

ISBN 978-1-330-37332-3
PIBN 10043241

1 MONTH OF
FREE
READING
at
www.ForgottenBooks.com

By purchasing this book you are eligible for one month membership to ForgottenBooks.com, giving you unlimited access to our entire collection of over 1,000,000 titles via our web site and mobile apps.

To claim your free month visit:

www.forgottenbooks.com/free43241

English
Français
Deutsche
Italiano
Español
Português

www.forgottenbooks.com

Mythology Photography **Fiction**
Fishing Christianity **Art** Cooking
Essays Buddhism Freemasonry
Medicine **Biology** Music **Ancient
Egypt** Evolution Carpentry Physics
Dance Geology **Mathematics** Fitness
Shakespeare **Folklore** Yoga Marketing
Confidence Immortality Biographies
Poetry **Psychology** Witchcraft
Electronics Chemistry History **Law**
Accounting **Philosophy** Anthropology
Alchemy Drama Quantum Mechanics
Atheism Sexual Health **Ancient History**
Entrepreneurship Languages Sport
Paleontology Needlework Islam
Metaphysics Investment Archaeology
Parenting Statistics Criminology
Motivational

Constantinople.   In the high offices which he had filled he
had acquired a smattering of French and some European
culture.   He photographed his aides-de-camp with a kodak
when there were no *mollahs* about, and he kept locked up
in a cupboard a French encyclopædia and a bottle labelled
" Koniak," with the second of which he was wont to refresh
his researches into the first.

Perhaps I ought to introduce myself to the reader.   I
am so well known in Turkey that no one would ever think
of asking me what my business is, and yet, now that I want
to describe it, I feel some difficulty in doing so, for my
occupations are very diverse, though I think that at bottom
they are all much the same.   I suppose I might be described as a concession hunter or a commission agent.   The
essence of my trade is to make Orientals buy what they don't
want—anything from matches to railroads.   I bribe them
to purchase my wares and they bribe me to put down in the
bill (which the Ottoman Government pays) a much larger
sum than I have actually received.   So we both make money.
I now proposed to complete one of these advantageous transactions.   Among other things I am agent for the Company
which has patented the Antiseptic Dynamo, an almost
miraculous application of electricity to hygiene, and equally
indispensable in the hospital and the nursery, as the adver-
tisement says.   As a new military hospital had been established at Karakeui, for the reception of wounded soldiers
from Thessaly, it seemed an excellent opportunity for
supplying a large quantity of this invaluable apparatus.

In the prosecution of this object I found myself alone
with the Vali that rainy evening, sitting on the edge of my
chair with my hands crossed over my stomach as a sign
of respect.   It is no doubt humiliating to show this deference to a Turkish functionary, but practical contempt
for the Turk exists mostly outside the Ottoman dominions
and, had the late Mr. Gladstone ever crossed the charme

frontier, I have no doubt he would have been as polite to the Sultan as any Ambassador.

After profuse salutations and compliments I addressed myself to business. "Your Highness," I said to the Vali, 'my chief object in coming here was to inquire after your sacred and amiable health, and to water my parched soul with the agreeable springs of your sublime conversation. But there was also another object. We, as you know, are one of those who strive to benefit the Exalted Government by the introduction of useful inventions, and my methods of business are familiar to your penetrating intelligence. As I had the honour to explain to your Highness in a humble letter, I am anxious to instal in the military hospital a system of Antiseptic Dynamos. My firm are so persuaded of the incalculable advantages to humanity which would accrue from the introduction of this invention that they would be willing to advance £1000 to meet any initial expenditure which might be incurred by the Sublime Local Authorities."

But I saw there was something wrong. It is a mistake to suppose that money will do everything in Turkey. It will do much, but there are occasions when it is as powerless as logic, and I already began to fear that this was one of them; for though the Vali had said nothing at all, his face preserved an expression of austere and virtuous dignity, and he showed no signs of extending an itching palm. At last he said gravely: "Certainly the Imperial Government is desirous to introduce and profit by beneficial inventions, but in the present case I cannot see any need for what you propose. The Imperial Ministry of War, in its unremitting attention to the wants of its troops (with a magnificent disregard for facts, he waved his hand in the direction of the starving soldiers standing in the rain), has provided all necessary medical appliances, and, besides, there is hardly anybody in the hospital. The wounded who are brought

over the mountains from Thessaly either die on the way or
else get well.   The 10,000 machines you want to sell would
stand in empty rooms."   "But still," I said, "they might
be useful another day, and the sale would always be advantageous—mutually advantageous."   "Perhaps," said the
Vali, "but your invention itself is dangerous.   Dynamo is a
most violent explosive, and is on the list of articles whose
introduction into Turkey is absolutely prohibited."   "Your
Highness is thinking of dynamite.   Dynamo is quite a
different matter, and not an explosive at all."   "Dynamo
and dynamite are all one," said the Vali, with an authorita-
tive air.   "Nothing would ever induce the Imperial Custom-
House to pass a single case of such articles, and they would
report to Constantinople that I was endeavouring to import
explosives."   "Perhaps," I said, with gentle emphasis, "we
might get over that difficulty.   For our own practical
purposes the point is not how much is *delivered*, but how
much is *ordered and paid for*.   If it was confidentially understood that the Imperial Custom-House would place insuperable difficulties in the way of the entry of the articles, I am
sure that my firm would be ready to make a great reduc-
tion—of even one-half—in the price, and nothing at all
need be imported into the Sublime dominions."   This idea
seemed to please the Vali, but, in a minute, he said decidedly,
"No, but still we could never get rid of the name.   It
would appear in the Government accounts as dynamite, and
if no dynamite was forthcoming, so much the worse.   I
should be supposed to have applied it to some secret and
evil purpose.   No, Effendim, Olmaz; it cannot be."   "But
if it is only the name," I said in despair, "we can omit it.
Let us leave out the dynamo altogether and describe the
apparatus merely as the Antiseptic."   "I don't like that
either," said the Vali, "'anti' is a bad word.   The Greeks
call insurgents *antartis*."   "But Antiseptic has nothing to do
with insurgents.   It means 'against rottenness,' the enemy

of corruption, so to speak," I added, striving to make things plain. "Exactly," said the Vali, "and that will at once be understood as a seditious allusion to the Sublime Ottoman Government. No, it cannot be." And to show that his decision was irrevocable he again assumed his virtuous air, and said, "All civilised countries are governed by law, and I am surprised that one who has lived in the Ottoman dominions as long as yourself should suppose that Turkish officials can be induced by hopes of personal advantage to neglect the regulations issued for their guidance. Law and obedience are the foundation of the State."

This from a man with whom I had done business for twenty years! Did he really think dynamos and dynamite were the same? His cursed encyclopædia might have taught him better than that! But whatever the depths of his ignorance might be, he was clearly convinced that any connection with dynamos would cost him his post, and perhaps his life. I saw my commission and pickings vanishing. In other words, industry and commerce were thwarted and repressed by the crass stupidity of a tyrannical Government, and progress turned to stagnation and decay. I felt honestly indignant. "Obedience to *good* laws," I said, "is no doubt the foundation of the State, but when the laws are bad and senseless, such as those that prohibit the introduction of electrical appliances, no advantage can come from obeying them. Every friend of Turkey knows how excellent are the qualities of the Turks, but they are neutralised by your government. You will not adopt the most elementary principles of civilisation and commerce. You are turning a fertile garden into a desert: you are sitting on a heap of gold and starving because you will not coin it. You are a splendid horse spoiled by an unskilful master." "No, no," said the Vali anxiously, scenting treason in this last metaphor; "you must not say that. The orders of our master are

entirely for the good of his people. The only trouble is
when they are not executed." "At any rate," I said,
"your Highness will hardly maintain that the present
Grand Vizier is a suitable person to direct the affairs of
a great country." I knew he would be caught by that
bait. Since his own dismissal from the office he hated all
subsequent Grand Viziers. "The Grand Vizier!" he repeated ironically. "Whenever I think of the Grand
Vizier, it reminds me of— Well, did you ever hear
the story of Hassan Effendi, the camel-driver of
Konia ? " I felt inclined to say "Yes," for I knew too
well the Vali's fondness for telling interminable Oriental
apologues, but I said resignedly, "No. Did they make
him Grand Vizier ? " "Not quite that," said the Vali;
"but he was the biggest camel-owner in all Anatolia.
One day the time came for him—as it must come for
us all—to die, and he lay in bed gasping in his death
agony" (the Vali gurgled horribly in his throat to imitate
a dying man), "but could not die. The bystanders perceived there was something wrong, and that the Angel of
Death could not take his soul. They concluded that he
had wronged some one, and that until he had been forgiven his soul could not enter into Paradise.[1] So they
sent for all the friends and even the enemies of Hassan
Effendi to come and bless him and assure him of their
forgiveness if they had any old scores against him. All
day long they came to give and receive forgiveness, and
never was there a more affecting scene of reconciliation
and mutual benediction. But it availed nothing. The day
and the night passed, but Hassan Effendi still lay gasping
on his bed with the death-rattle in his throat, and the
Angel of Death could not take his soul. His friends saw

---

[1] It is a Turkish custom for the friends of a dying man to assure him that
they have nothing against him, and to receive a similar assurance in their
turn. A Turk does not die happy if he thinks that any other Moslim has " a
right over him"—that is, a just claim or complaint against him.

that this was no ordinary case; and said among themselves, since all mankind have forgiven him, it must be
that he has sinned either against the Jinns or against
the beasts. He is a great camel-owner; maybe he has
wronged the camels—we had better get their blessing
and forgiveness. So they sent for the oldest camel-driver,
and asked him to consult the camels and arrange the
matter. The answer was not very favourable, camels
being notoriously the most disagreeable and unfriendly
creatures in the animal kingdom. They demanded a
holiday for the whole of the next day and permission to
hold a meeting on the plain outside Konia in order to
thoroughly discuss the matter and arrive at a decision.
There was nothing to be done but to accept the terms;
and all the next day the camels debated on the plain,
and there was such a grunting, groaning, wheezing, and
puffing as had never been heard in the world. And
all this time Hassan Effendi lay gasping on his bed,
and the Angel of Death could not take his soul. At last,
towards evening, the chief of the camels returned slowly
to the city and strode through the streets to Hassan
Effendi's house. He was as huge as an elephant and
the ragged hair hung down from his sides like streamers
of grey moss. He was too big to enter by the door,
and they suggested that he should deliver his benediction through the window. But he replied arrogantly that,
if they had no room for him in the house he would not
trouble them, and was going away. So they took down
the side of the house and the old camel entered Hassan
Effendi's room and knelt down by his bed. After salutations, he said: 'Hassan Effendi, I have come in the
name of the camels to give you our blessing and assure
you of our forgiveness, but before pronouncing the benediction I am charged to tell you what is the wrong which
we find it hardest to forgive. We do not complain that

we have to walk while you ride; that we carry burdens
and you whips; that the labour is hard and the food
short—God has made you men and us camels, and we
are of those who accept the decree of God. But there
is one thing which we find it hard to understand or
acquiesce in. It is that when our caravans go marching
across the plains they are always led by a little ass'[1]—and
whenever I see the Grand Vizier," said the Vali, coming
with sudden spitefulness to the point of this long anecdote, " I think of that little ass marching at the head
of the string of great camels."

"Your Highness's comparison is very just," I said;
"but though you have not the commanding position which
your talents deserve, you could yet do much in your province if you would show a greater readiness to introduce
civilisation and liberal institutions." " Institutions and
constitutions are no good," said the Vali. " How is Bulgaria better for her constitution? Formerly we flogged
the Bulgarians; now they flog one another, and any poor
Turks they can catch. Do you think that the Armenians
have not learnt the value of constitutions? Go and take
a basket and put into it constitutions and reforms, and cry
in the wilds of Armenia, as the hawkers cry in the streets
of Constantinople, ' I am the reform-man; I am the con-
stitution-man. I have reforms for sale; I have constitutions
for sale.' How many do you think will come to buy or to
bargain or take as a gift? Not many, my friend; for they
have learnt how little reforms are worth, and how dear
they cost in blood. When you can get a Turk to obey a
Rayah (native Christian), then you may begin to talk of
reforming the Turkish Empire, and of introducing any
system but that which we have now."

"But that," I replied, "is not at all what I mean.

[1] A string of camels is always led by an ass on which the leader of the
caravan sits.

Doubtless an abrupt political change is undesirable, and the wholesale adoption of European institutions in countries which are not prepared for them is productive of more evil than good. But some modification of the present system would be an undoubted benefit. Your Highness would probably be glad if there were fewer spies about" (the Vali groaned assent); "and a fair and open administration of justice would afford a protection to Turks as well as to Christians." "It would not protect me from being named Governor-General of Tripoli or the Yemen," said the Vali; "and it is necessary to deal firmly with our Christians. It may not always be possible to find legal proof of their machinations; but we know that they are engaged, or ready to engage, in conspiracy against the Ottoman Empire. With the sword we took these countries, and with the sword we must hold them. We do not want to ill-treat the Christians, and we show them nothing but kindness as long as they are gentle and unassuming. But of late years they have all had their heads turned, and want to become independent. Such a business can only end in blood. If we do not kill them, they will kill us and our wives and children."

"I cannot quite agree with your Highness about that," I said. "It appears to me ridiculous to suppose that these poor down-trodden Armenians can think of massacring Turks. If they arm themselves, it is only because they are afraid of your soldiers and Zapties and wish to have the means of self-protection. If you would only develop the commercial and material resources of your Empire, Christians and Turks would have a common interest. The Christians would want to support your Empire as the source of their prosperity. You do not find the big Greek and Armenian bankers at Constantinople disloyal to the Sultan It is the little people who have nothing to lose and who suffer daily that are disaffected. Instead of making common cause with the Christians, you run the risk of forcing all

Christians to make common cause against the Moslim."
"We are not afraid of that," said the Vali. "They are a
mob of curs. If one of them runs forward to bark against
his master, some other will bite him in the tail and pull
him back. All Christians, big and small, like making
money. We Turks don't know how to make money; we
only know how to take it. You want to introduce a
system in which Christians will be able to squeeze all the
money out of us and our country and keep it. Who profit
by all these concessions for railways, harbours, and quays?
Franks, Jews, Greeks, and Armenians, but never a Moslim.
Do you remember that railway I helped you to build from
Durograd to Moropolis? Franks travel by it, Greeks and
Armenians sell the tickets, and in the end all the money
goes to the Jews. But what Turk wants the railway, and
how much has any Turk made out of it?"

I might have said, "Exactly as much as passed into
your Highness's pockets when the concession was arranged,"
but I forbore from this obvious retort and let the Vali
go on. "This country is a dish of soup," he said, "and
no one has any real intention except to eat it. We eat
it in the good old-fashioned way with a big spoon. You
bore little holes in the bottom of the soup-bowl and draw
it off with pipes. Then you propose that the practice of
eating soup with spoons should be abolished as uncivilised,
because you know we have no gimlets and don't understand this trick of drinking through pipes."

"But surely your Highness has had experience yourself of the advantages which Osmanlis may obtain from
commercial enterprises and——"

"Oh, I have had a suck at the pipe," said the Vali,
"but, after all, I prefer eating with the spoon."

"And the spoon," I said furiously, for I had now got very
angry, "means murder, rape, and robbery. It means that no
man's life and no woman's honour are safe. It means that

in the name of taxation your soldiers make annual plunder-
ing expeditions and take, not what is owed, but what they
can get.   It means organised brigandage, and stupid brigand-
ages too, for if you would adopt the elementary principles
of civilised government you would get twice as much with
half the trouble."

"Once," said the Vali, calmly and irrelevantly, "I was
a very young man, and went a ride with my old father.
I was foolish then, and my head was stuffed with silly
notions and liberal ideas.   I spoke much as you have
spoken.   I told my father we ought to reform our constitution, systematise our administration, purify our family
life, educate our women, introduce liberal ideas, and imitate
Europeans.   And my old father answered never a word.
So we rode on along the banks of the Bosphorus.   At last
we came to a Christian village, and round the Christian
village were many pigs.   Then my father said to me, 'My
son, what seest thou?'   I replied, 'Pigs, my father.'   'My
son,' he said, 'are they all similar in size and colour, or
do they differ?'   'They differ, my father.   There are big
pigs and little pigs, white pigs and black pigs, brown pigs
and mottled pigs.'   'But they are all of them swine, my
son?'   'All, my father.'   'My son,' he said, 'it is with the
Christians even as with the pigs.   There are big Christians
and little Christians, Russian Christians and English Christians, French Christians and German Christians; but they
are all of them swine, and he who wishes to imitate the
Christians, wishes to wallow with the swine in the mire.'"

"But surely," I said in astonishment, for the Vali was
generally polite—"surely your Highness does not mean
to say that you think us all swine?"

"Well," he said, "I was very young then, and my
brain was full of nonsense—so I thought my father was
a fool.   But now that my own beard is getting grey—
by God, I think the old gentleman was right!"

CHAPTER I

HISTORICAL

BEFORE THE TURKISH CONQUEST

THERE is nothing in the form of the word Turkey to distinguish it from such names as England, France, Germany, or Russia, but it may be safely said that many of the errors which have been committed by politicians and others in dealing with the nearer East are due to the fact that Turkey has been treated as if it were like other countries, whereas the first requisite for an elementary knowledge of the Eastern question is to understand that Turkey is quite unlike any other country in Europe.

Whatever mixture or variety of races they may contain, England, France, Germany, and Russia may for practical purposes be defined as areas inhabited by Englishmen, Frenchmen, Germans, and Russians respectively; but in the south-east of Europe geographical designations must be differently interpreted. It would be no definition of Austria to say that it is a country inhabited by Austrians, and still less would it be true to say that Turkey is a country inhabited by Turks. Not that Turkey can be compared to Austria. Making all allowance for such conflicts as Germans against Czechs, and Hungarians against Roumanians, in which two races claim preponderance in one district, it may be said, on the whole, that the Austro-Hungarian Empire consists of a number of territories, German, Bohemian, Polish, Hungarian, Servian, and what not, each with their own population, but united under a central Government. But in Turkey, not only is there a similar medley of races, but the races inhabit not different districts but the same district. Of three villages within ten miles of one another, one will be Turkish, one Greek, and one Bulgarian, or perhaps one Albanian, one Bulgarian, and one Servian, each with their own language, dress, and religion. Under favourable circumstances, eight races and languages may be found in a large town: Turks, Greeks, Jews, Armenians, Bulgarians, Servians, Vlachs, and Albanians.

Why do these remain each with their own language, customs, and ideals, not as survivals interesting to the learned, but as living realities whose bickerings and jealousies supply the daily round of Eastern politics? The answer to this question is given only by history, and it therefore will be well to sketch the past of South-Eastern Europe before the arrival of the Turks. The latter are usually thought of as a destructive force, and rightly; they have destroyed a great deal and constructed nothing. But in another sense they have proved an eminently conservative force, for they have perpetuated and preserved, as if in a museum, the strange medley which existed in South-Eastern Europe during the last years of the Byzantine Empire. Their idea of government has always been simply to take tribute and secure the paramount position of the Osmanli. This once recognised, they do not care to interfere with the manners and customs of their subjects, but treat them with a contemptuous toleration. Further, they gained their first footing in Europe in consequence of the dissensions of Europeans. They have always been numerically inferior to the aggregate of their subjects, and could hardly have maintained their rule had the latter ever been able to unite against them. They have thoroughly learned, and still daily put into practice with admirable skill, the lesson of *divide et impera*; and

B

hence they have always done, and still do, all in their power
to prevent the obliteration of racial, linguistic, and religious
differences.

I. Sketch of Byzantine History

Though our object is to sketch the past, not of the
Byzantine Empire, but of the populations of South-Eastern
Europe, it will be well to bear in mind the great epochs
which mark the history of Constantinople. No city in
the world, not even Rome, has more personality. To her
belongs the Empire of the East; and, from Constantine
onwards, he who has possessed her, whether his territory
was shrunk to a few miles beyond the city walls or extended
round the shores of the Mediterranean, has always been
Emperor. In the West of Europe, history is called upon to
deal with many centres, states, and civilisations. In the
East of the Continent, until the rise of Russia, we have
but one centre in an incoherent flux of barbarian invasions
and ephemeral chieftainships; the Imperial City, which, like
a living thing, struggles, triumphs, fails, and triumphs
again, crowning in turn the Roman, the Greek, and the
Turk, and even in the hour of collapse and decay imparting to the House of Osman, as she imparted to the Palæologi, a mysterious strength, which supported the Greek
Empire for a hundred years when it was apparently at
the mercy of the Turks, and which supports the Turkish
Empire now. The difference between Eastern and Western
Europe is due mainly to the fact that civilisation and
political strength were in the former concentrated in one
city, and were not the property of races or districts. Races
invade and retire; districts are conquered and lost, reconquered and lost again; there is no fixity in the boundaries
or composition of the Empire; little which has character
or permanence except Constantinople herself, round whom,

century after century, the subject territories expand and contract with an almost rhythmic movement.

The first epoch—that from the foundation of the city to the reign of Justinian (325–527)—is an epoch of contraction. The Empire was invaded by Goths and Huns, and though the former were successfully removed from the East, they founded kingdoms in Spain and Africa, while in Italy the German general Odoacer deposed Romulus Augustulus, Emperor of the West, in 488. Before this date, the Empire, though theoretically one and indivisible, had been generally, for convenience of administration, split into two parts, ruled by two princes who had their capitals at Rome and Constantinople respectively. Henceforward, until the coronation of Charlemagne in 800 introduced a new order of things, there was but one Emperor, who resided at Constantinople but claimed a theoretical, though more and more shadowy, sovereignty over the West. The successes of Justinian (527–565) and his general Belisarius in Italy, Spain, and North Africa, and the assertion of the Imperial power over the Bishop of Rome, who was beginning to make himself felt as a political factor of importance, produced a movement of expansion, and made this sovereignty a reality for a brief period. But it was the peculiar destiny of the Eastern Empire to be allowed no rest : throughout its history no sooner was one enemy disposed of than another appeared. The Lombards succeeded the Goths, and made considerable conquests in Italy, while the Emperors were engaged in fighting the Persians in Asia and the Slavs in Europe ; so that when the next epoch-making Emperor, Heraclius, came to the throne, his western possessions were merely the extreme south of Italy and a narrow strip from Ancona and Ravenna to Rome.

The energy and ability of this Emperor enabled him to crush the power of Persia in the East, though distracted by simultaneous attacks from the Avars in the West, but his reign (610–641) is peculiarly remarkable as forming "the best dividing point between ancient history and the Middle Ages."[1] It presents three interesting features. Firstly, the Empire, which was Roman in origin, now becomes definitely Greek. Secondly, paganism vanishes and the Emperor and his subjects appear as the champions of Christianity. Thirdly, it is in this reign that the great antagonist of Eastern Christianity enters on the scene. In 628 the prophet Mohammed summoned both Heraclius and his adversary Chosroes, king of Persia, to embrace Islam, and from this time till the capture of Constantinople by Mohammed II. the Empire had to struggle against the races which professed the new faith. In the first stage of the struggle Constantinople twice successfully resisted sieges by the Arabs, first in 673–677, and secondly in 717–718; and, though the Moslems made progress in Asia, Leo the Isaurian (717–740) may be considered to have reasserted the supremacy of Christianity in what is now called the Levant. Meanwhile the separation from the West was becoming more decided. The struggle against the Arabs left the Emperors no time to resist the Lombards, who, in 750, captured Ravenna and the other possessions of the Empire in Italy. The iconoclasm of Leo III. and Constantine V. alienated the religious sentiment of Rome, and the Pope first invoked the help of Pepin, king of the Franks, to protect him against the Lombards, and finally, in 800, crowned Charlemagne Roman Emperor. Henceforward the separation between Rome and Constantinople was complete as far as secular matters are concerned, though the final breach between the Churches did not occur for some time.

The ninth and tenth centuries marked, on the whole, a period of prosperity for the Empire. Constantinople attained a unique commercial importance and enjoyed long spells of peace. At the beginning of the ninth century

[1] Oman, "The Byzantine Empire."

a somewhat humiliating arrangement had to be made with Harun-ar-reshid, and the Saracens took Crete and subsequently Sicily. But the Moslems became divided against themselves; the Buhawids broke up the Caliphate of Bagdad, and the Emperors Romanus and Nicephorus Phocas recovered Crete, Cilicia, and North Syria; while in Europe, Basil, "the Bulgarian-slayer," made the Danube the frontier of the Empire, which it had not been since the reign of Heraclius, and established his rule over the Balkan Peninsula.

The eleventh century is marked by two important phenomena—the appearance of the Seljuk Turks and the final separation of the Eastern and Western Churches (1054), which left a Christianity divided and weakened by internal dissension face to face with a united Islam. In 1071 Alp-Arslan defeated and captured the Emperor Romanus IV. at Manzikert, and, amidst the chaos and anarchy which ensued, the Seljuks advanced unopposed in Asia Minor. At last, in 1081, Alexius Comnenus forced himself to the front and founded the house of the Comneni, which ruled a hundred years. They were relatively successful in keeping back the Seljuks, but they were harassed by new Western enemies, first the Normans and then the Venetians. Byzantine commerce declined and Italian influence in the Levant rapidly increased. But the most important feature of this period was the Crusades, which, like most acts of intervention by Western Europe in the affairs of the East, were doubtful blessings to those whom they were designed to assist. The first of these expeditions did indeed aid Alexius to recover Western Asia Minor, but the Emperor and the Crusaders subsequently fell out, and, as a consequence of the quarrel, the latter founded the Latin states of Syria. It was reserved for the fourth Crusade, in 1204, to inflict on the Eastern Empire a deadlier blow than any yet received from Saracen or Turk. The House of Comnenus had then been succeeded by the feeble Angeli. Military and financial disorganisation led to the loss of Bulgaria and Cyprus and to a disastrous Seljuk war. The Emperor Alexius Angelus involved himself in foreign quarrels; Venice and the Italian Republics were bitterly hostile to Constantinople, and the Pope regarded the Emperor and his Church as schismatics. In these circumstances the Crusaders, instead of fighting the Moslems, attacked and captured Constantinople, where they established Baldwin as Latin Emperor, while Montferrat was made king of Salonica and the Venetians took many islands and part of the mainland of Greece. For fifty years the Greek Emperors lived in exile at Nicæa in Asia, and Eastern Europe was in a strange state of confusion created by a patchwork of Greek, Latin, and Slavonic states. The Latin Empire was merely an enterprise of military adventurers. It reposed on no sound national or political basis, and it made no friends in the East. It was naturally the enemy of everything Greek, and it was unable or un-willing to combine with the Slavs, who, as desiring an expansion of territory at the expense of the Greeks, would have been its natural allies. It came to an end in 1261, and Michael Palæologus recaptured Constantinople, where his house reigned until 1453.

But the Latin conquest had permanently reduced the Empire. During the half-century that Baldwin and his successors held Constantinople, Slavonic kingdoms had been firmly established in the Balkan Peninsula. Albania had become the Despotate of Epirus, the greater part of Greece had been divided among Latin states, and most of the Ægean Islands had passed into the hands of Venice. In Asia the Seljuks advanced again, and a crew of European adventurers called the "Grand Company," whom the Emperor Andronicus II. hired to defend him, proved as great a curse as the Turks themselves. Bad as things were, they were to become worse. In the first half of the fourteenth century appeared the Ottomans, who rapidly swallowed up what scraps of the Empire remained in Asia, and were most unwisely invited over to Europe by the Regent John Cantacuzene to assist him against the Servians. Their conquests were as rapid on this side of the Strait as they had been on the other. In the middle of the fourteenth century the Emperor had nothing left but Salonica and a portion of the Peloponnesus, and became a vassal of the Sultan. The appearance from Central Asia of Timur, who attacked and defeated Sultan Bayazid, gave a little breathing space, and Manuel Palæologus recovered parts of the European coast. Had Christendom been able to form any coalition against the Turks at the moment when they were attacked by Timur, the case of the Empire would not have been desperate; but the opportunity was allowed to slip. Mohammed I. again united the Turkish power. Salonica was captured in 1430, and Constantinople in 1453.

II. Invasions and Settlements of the Slavs

Let us now leave these high imperial politics and briefly consider the various races who invaded the Balkan Peninsula in the period between the foundation of Constantinople and the coming of the Turks, as well as the states which were founded by them. The history of the Balkan Peninsula is so little known that it may be convenient for purposes of reference, if not exactly interesting, to recount here its main features. We have to explain how countries which were inhabited by Greeks, Romans, and Thracians became in the main Slavonic, and to relate how the Slavs formed three states—the first and second Bulgarian Empires and the Servian Empire—each of which seemed at a given moment likely to become the dominant power of Eastern Europe, and each of which collapsed mysteriously in turn.

The earliest known inhabitants of the Balkan Peninsula

were the Illyrians on the West and the Thracians on the
East. The former were doubtless the ancestors of the modern
Albanians, and it has been conjectured that the latter are
to be identified with the Vlachs now found in Macedonia.
Both established independent states in ancient times, the
former the kingdom of Epirus under Pyrrhus (about 300 B.C.),
and the latter the more important Macedonian Empire. But
the civilisation of both states seems to have been entirely
Hellenic, and neither art nor literature throws much light
on the indigenous substratum. Probably in general characteristics they resembled the modern Albanians, a race
who, as individuals, are brave and capable, but with little
political instinct or power of combination, and, though not
wanting in individuality, so given to borrowing both words
and customs that it is hard to say what parts of their language and institutions are original. In any case, before the
foundation of Constantinople, the whole Peninsula underwent
a strong Hellenic influence, and, after the Roman conquest
of Macedonia, an equally strong Latin influence. There was
also, no doubt, in the population a large admixture of Hellenic
and Italian blood; along the coast were considerable colonies
peopled by emigrants from Greece, and naturally the Italian
troops and Italian officials were alike numerous.

North and north-east of the Danube lies a region which
is not perhaps well known to the majority of educated people
nowadays, and which was utterly unknown in the early centuries of this era—a land of darkness, mystery, and trouble,
from which swarm after swarm of strange and hateful barbarians poured upon the civilised world. The people called
Huns seem to have started this Western movement. Many
of them settled near the Ural Mountains or on the Volga,
others pushed on beyond the Don until they came in contact with the Gothic Empire, which occupied parts of South
Russia and Roumania, and probably extended to the Baltic.
The word Empire is commonly and conveniently applied to

the power of such races as the Goths, Huns, and Avars, but must not be understood to imply any real comparison with the Roman Empire. It merely means that the people in question was the dominant race in a heterogeneous collection of tribes, who were held together, some as serfs, some as allies, in a loose and generally ephemeral organisation. The Huns subdued the Ostrogoths, but the more civilised Visigoths retired before them, and ultimately obtained permission to cross the Danube and settle in Moesia. We need not make any detailed examination of the Goths or their movements, as they eventually departed from South-Eastern Europe without leaving any traces of their sojourn. Suffice it to say that the Visigothic influence became very strong in Constantinople, until their power and unpopularity provoked a massacre in 401—the first of many such massacres which the Imperial city has witnessed. In the early part of the fifth century, Attila the Hun founded an empire and forced the court of Constantinople to pay tribute; but the power of the Huns was disorganised by his death, and the Ostrogoths, who were now set free from their yoke, invaded the Balkan Peninsula, which they ravaged for twenty years, until the diplomacy of the Emperor Zeno induced them to depart in 488 by promising their chieftain the government of Italy if he could conquer Odoacer. After this, we hear no more of the Goths in the East.

As the disappearance of the Huns had set free the Ostrogoths, so the removal of these latter set the Slavs in motion, and their movements form the most important feature of the sixth and seventh centuries. It has been said of this people that they occupy a larger space on the map than in history, and the observation is not unjust. At the end of the seventh century the territory comprised between the Baltic on the north and the Ægean on the south, the Dnieper on the east and the rivers Elbe and Saale on the west, was almost entirely peopled by Slavonic tribes whose languages and customs showed a similarity which is very remarkable if we consider the enormous area over which they extended. Subsequent events destroyed this homogeneity. The western tribes were either assimilated by the Germans, or at least, like the Poles and Bohemians, carried off by the general current of Western history. The occupation of Hungary by the Magyars in the ninth and tenth centuries displaced many more, while those in the east were subjected to strong Scandinavian and Asiatic influences, and destined to a late but very important development under the name of Russians. We are here concerned with the group commonly known as Southern Slavs—that is, those who dwell south of the Danube. They are known to ancient writers by various names, which must not be interpreted too strictly as applying to definite territories or nationalities. They are most commonly called by Greek chronicles Σκλάβοι, Σκλαβηνοί, or Σθλαβηνοί, a word which is apparently the same as Slovene, the designation now borne by the inhabitants of Carniola and Carinthia, and which is akin to Slav, Slovak, Slavonia, and other names variously referred to roots meaning "speech" or "glory." A second name is Antai ("Ανται), apparently identical with the words Wend and Venäjä applied to Slavs by the Germans and Finns respectively, and now not used in the East, where, however, another national appellation, Serb, still survives. It exists in the modern forms Serb,[1] Servian, as well as in Sorabian and Sorbian,[2] Servia, and in the ancient Σέρβλοι and probably Σπόροι (used by Procopius), and is now applied in a restricted sense to the inhabitants of the kingdom of Servia, and in a more extended one to all who speak the Servian language. This use of the word, however, brings us into collision with the name Croatian (Hrvat, Χρωβάτοι). The Croatians speak a

---

[1] The natives write the word Srb, the r having attached to it a dull vowel sound not unlike our own pronunciation of Serb.

[2] A language spoken on the river Spree in Prussia and Saxony.

language practically identical with Servian, but they belong to the Roman Church and use the Latin alphabet, differences which have been sufficient to create a feeling of hostility between them and their kinsmen, who cling to the Eastern Church and Cyrillic letters.[1]

All these Slavs, whether called Antai, Slovenes, Serbs, or Croatians, seem to have possessed at the time of their irruption into the Eastern Empire certain common characteristics. They were free peoples, without either slaves or kings, and impatient of all authority. Their institutions were democratic, and their social organisation founded on a system of family communism. Their pursuits were mainly agricultural, and they built villages rather than towns. Their religion was a simple form of Nature-worship, and they had no priesthood. These characteristics go far to explain another—their remarkable want of political cohesion and tendency to break up into mutually hostile tribes and factions. This description will sound strange to those who, regarding the Russian Empire as the principal product of Slav civilisation, associate that name with autocracy and hierarchy; but there is no doubt that the Russians are a mixed race, and that much of their success is due to the fact that they have got rid of many Slavonic weaknesses.

Nor did the Southern Slavs remain a pure race. In the eastern half of the Balkan Peninsula their blood and destinies were mingled with those of the Bulgarians, an Asiatic people akin to the Finns, Huns, Avars, and Pechenegs, and forming part of what is often called the Finno-Ugric stock. Starting, no doubt, from the same regions as the Huns, they first settled on the Volga, where a kingdom known as the Greater or Black Bulgaria continued until the fifteenth century, but part of them passed farther west and came in

---

[1] It should be mentioned that some authorities think that the Croatians were, like the Bulgarians, an originally un-Slavonic, Hunnic people, who became Slavised.

contact with the Slavs. Nothing is known of their original
language and religion, but their dress, manners, and institutions distinguished them sharply from their Slavonic neighbours; for while the latter were governed by many chiefs to
whom they paid but scant obedience, the Bulgarian Khan
was an absolute monarch, isolated from his subjects by a
rigid system of Oriental etiquette, and obliged even to eat
alone. They also possessed slaves and a well-disciplined
army, and probably had most of the characteristics which
rendered the Turks so formidable a power. But their most
remarkable characteristic was receptivity. They adopted the
language and, to a certain extent, the manners of the Slavs,
and a considerable mixture of blood took place, modifying
the original physical type. It is not known at what period
the Bulgarians became completely Slavised, but it was clearly
before their conversion to Christianity in 864, as Saints Cyril
and Methodius were able to preach to them in a Slavonic
language. There is, I believe, nothing to prove that they
had not already come under the influence of the Slavs at
the time when they dwelt north of the Danube and had not
yet invaded the Empire.

Of the other non-Aryan tribes the Avars are of some
importance, for, though they do not appear to have contributed to the population of modern Europe, the rise and
fall of their power was one of the chief influences which
determined the movements of the Slavs and Bulgarians.
Little is known of them, but it would seem that they were
a destructive and barbarous horde, without any civilisation
of their own or any disposition to adopt that of others.
The only object of their wars was to pillage and carry off
booty, and they were celebrated for their "rings," enormous
circular fences with which they surrounded the prisoners
and plunder they had taken. In conjunction with the
Lombards, a Germanic people who had replaced the Ostrogoths, they destroyed the power of the Gepids, another

Germanic people; and when the Lombards invaded Italy they occupied the territory vacated by them, which was apparently the modern Hungary.

It is not difficult to explain the series of invasions which swept into the Balkan Peninsula, if we remember that the withdrawal of the Goths to Italy brought the Empire into direct contact with a seething mass of Slavs and Bulgarians, who were kept in motion by the pressure of the Avars on the north-west and of obscurer Asiatic tribes on the east. 577 is fixed as the date of the first considerable Slav invasion, but it is clear that for a century or more before this date there had been a considerable infiltration of Slav blood into the Empire. But after the end of the sixth century, the new-comers appear by tens and hundreds of thousands, sometimes alone and sometimes accompanied by Avars. In either case the permanent result was the same, for the Avars always retired and only the Slavs settled. In the reigns of Maurice, Phocas, and Heraclius no serious effort was made to check these incursions, for the first two Emperors were incompetent, and the third too much occupied with his struggle against Persia to protect any part of Europe except Constantinople. It is even said that he invited the Slavs to make settlements in his dominions; but this can hardly mean more than that he thought it prudent not to oppose them. The result was that by the middle of the seventh century the bulk of the population in the modern districts of Bulgaria, Macedonia, Albania, and Greece had become Slavonic, except in the large towns, for the military methods of both Slavs and Avars were exceedingly primitive, and unsuccessful in attacking fortified places. Salonica in particular withstood several sieges, and remained a centre of Hellenism. But in general the Hellenic element was driven to the coast, and the Albanians (or Illyrians) confined to a narrow strip of territory about the modern Mirditia. It is true that both Greeks and Albanians, or at least their languages, subsequently spread again over the country and reasserted their influence, but the testimony of geographical names shows conclusively that Epirus, Northern Greece, and the Peloponnesus must all have been occupied by Slavs at some period. It was also during the reign of Heraclius that the Serbs and Croats advanced in the West. The latter occupied Bua, Ragusa, and Zara, driving the Roman inhabitants of Dalmatia into the islands and promontories, and founded a kingdom which perhaps included Bosnia. To the south of this Croatian kingdom, which was the first Slavonic state in the East, and was most powerful from the seventh to the ninth centuries, were four tribes, called " the maritime Serbs." If we identify the Sklavinoi, who were already established in the Balkan Peninsula, with the Slovenes, who now inhabit Carniola and Carinthia, the effect of this movement was to split the Slovene race into two divisions and drive a wedge of Serbs and Croats between them. The successors of Heraclius were, like him, unable or unwilling to seriously grapple with the Slavs. Constans II. (642–668) was occupied in the earlier part of his reign with wars against the Saracens, and, when he was free from his enemies on the East, turned his attention to the far West and organised an expedition to Italy. The Slavonic invaders were merely obliged to pay tribute and do homage, but were otherwise left to their own devices. The reign of Constantine IV. (668–685) is remarkable for the repulse of the first Arab attack on Constantinople, and it is not surprising to read that, while all the military strength of the Empire was concentrated to repel this danger, the invasion of the European provinces from the North continued, and that Salonica was besieged by Slavs.

It is at this period, too, that we first hear of the Bulgarians as an independent Power, though they are mentioned as accompanying the invasions of the Slavs as early as the reign of Anastasius (491–518). In the third quarter of the seventh century they settled in the district of Onglos (Bujak), and subsequently in 679 subdued what are called " the seven Slavonic tribes " of Moesia, and occupied that province under their chieftain Isperich or Asperuch.[1]   The boundaries of this kingdom were approximately those of the modern Principality of Bulgaria, and the capital, Peristhlava or Preslav, was near Varna.   Constantine, exhausted by his efforts against the Arabs, submitted tamely to the establishment of the new state within his dominions, and his son, Justinian Rhinotmetus, at one period courted the aid of the Bulgarian chieftain Terbel.   By the beginning of the ninth century the Bulgarians had grown so powerful that they threatened Constantinople itself.   Their king, Krumn, appeared before the gates of the Imperial city, and might, perhaps, have taken it, had not the Greek army, conscious of the critical situation, deposed the incompetent Michael I. and proclaimed Leo the Armenian as Emperor.   Adopting a method which was beginning to become characteristic of Byzantine politics, Leo first endeavoured to assassinate Krumn at a conference; but, when this plan failed, proved that he was a soldier as well as a diplomatist, by inflicting on the Bulgarians a defeat so crushing that we hear little more of them for fifty years. These conflicts with the Empire naturally brought the Bulgarians into contact with Christianity.   In the middle of the seventh century, King Boris was baptized; and, after some hesitation between the rival claims of Rome and Byzantium, ended by acknowledging the spiritual authority of the latter.   This and all other questions affecting the history of the Orthodox Church are more fully dealt with in Chapter VI.

[1] From this variety in the orthography one is tempted to suppose that the name must have been pronounced Ispirikh with dull vowels like Yildirim in Turkish.

III. SLAVONIC AND OTHER STATES BEFORE THE
TURKISH CONQUEST

The transition from invasions and settlements to political organisations was first made by the Bulgarians. As soon as they accepted Christianity their advance was rapid and conspicuous. Simeon, the son of Boris (892–927), founded the first Bulgarian Empire, which extended from Mesembria on the Black Sea to the Adriatic, including the greater part of modern Macedonia, Albania, Greece, Servia, and Dalmatia, and leaving to the Byzantine Empire little besides Constantinople, Salonica, and Adrianople, with the territory immediately surrounding them. To mark clearly the position which he claimed, he assumed the title of Czar or Tsar,[1] which was thus used in Bulgaria when the Russian nation hardly existed. It is doubtless an abbreviated form of Cæsar, and indicated that he who bore it thought himself the equal of the Byzantine monarch. Simeon also did his best to introduce Byzantine civilisation among his people. The civil and ecclesiastical institutions of the new state were carefully copied from the model of the Empire, and numerous translations from Greek ecclesiastical works attest the existence of a certain degree of religious culture. But the first Bulgarian Empire was short lived. When we contemplate its sudden creation and wholesale adoption of Byzantine institutions, we are forcibly reminded of those modern states in the East which have chosen, or been supplied with, ready-made constitutions of the most advanced European type. We may doubt if Simeon's rule was really effective in his

---

[1] The correct pronunciation of this name in Russian is Tsar, with the *r* very soft and followed by a slight *y* sound. The spelling Czar seems justified by long use in English, like Caliph for Khalifah. It is due to the etymology from Cæsar, and perhaps to the Polish orthography Car. In modern Russian the words Tsar, Tsaritsa, and Tsezarevich are rarely used except in the Church prayers, and are replaced by Gosudar, Gosudarynia, and Naslednik. Czarine or Tsarina is not a Russian word at all.

remoter provinces, or exercised a lasting influence on many of the populations who owned his sway.   At any rate, his successor was not strong enough to keep the fabric together. The warlike Emperor Nicephorus Phocas invited the Russians (who now appear for the first time in the Eastern question) to assist him in invading Bulgaria.   Internal dissensions broke out in that country, and a noble called Shishman founded a dynasty of his own in the Western provinces. John Zimesces, the assassin and successor of Nicephorus, found, as many other rulers of Constantinople have done, that the Russians were awkward neighbours, but by his prompt and decisive action drove them out of Bulgaria and back from the banks of the Danube.   He also entirely destroyed the Eastern Bulgarian Empire.   The western part, however, remained independent under Samuel (993–1014), the son of Shishman, whose capital was at Ochrida, and whose dominions extended from the Danube at least as far south as Janina.   This state was finally conquered in 1018 by the Byzantine Emperor Basil II., generally called Bulgaroktonos, or "the Bulgarian-slayer," who, after a desperate struggle of thirty-four years, annihilated Bulgaria and brought the whole of the Balkan Peninsula under the direct rule of Constantinople.   According to the story, he took 15,000 Bulgarians prisoner, and blinded all except 150, whose sight was spared in order that they might lead the eyeless host back to their master.   When Samuel saw them he died of grief.

It was a hundred and fifty years before Bulgaria recovered from this blow and emerged again as an independent Power.   The new state was founded by the dynasty of the Asens, and is often spoken of as the Vlacho-Bulgarian Empire. The name Vlach is applied not only to the inhabitants of Roumania, but to the tribes scattered over Macedonia and Thessaly—particularly in the Pindus range—who speak a Latin language.   I propose to treat in another place of this interesting people, and will here merely say that one way of

explaining their present distribution is to suppose, not that
they have migrated from Roumania, but that they are the descendants of the Latin-speaking population which occupied
the Peninsula before the Slav invasions. This does not mean
that they are necessarily of Latin race, but it seems probable that, in the period preceding the Slav invasions, Latin
was the language of the Peninsula except on the Ægean
coast. The Slav invaders overran the valleys, and the Latin-
speaking tribes took refuge in the hills. At any rate, the
Vlachs are at present scattered in a manner which accords
with this theory, and almost invariably inhabit mountains,
while the plains around are occupied by other races. This
geographical distribution explains the double character of
the second Bulgarian Empire, for in the same district there
might be a double population—the Vlachs of the hills and
the Slavo-Bulgarians of the plains. At this period the Vlach
element seems to have been particularly important, for Thessaly was known as the Great Wallachia (Μεγάλη Βλαχεία),
although the centre of the Vlacho-Bulgarian Empire was not
in Thessaly or South Macedonia, but at Trnovo. Though it
is probable that the founders of this new state were Vlachs
rather than Bulgarians,[1] the Bulgarian element was in the
majority among their subjects, and the Empire of Asen II.
has as good a right to the title of Bulgarian as the Empire
of Simeon. The earlier princes of the dynasty contracted
alliances both political and matrimonial with the Kumans,
a tribe allied to the Turks, who, together with the Pechenegs
(or Patzinaks), appeared on the Danube in the eleventh and
twelfth centuries, and made incursions into Bulgaria which
in some cases resulted in permanent settlements.[2]

[1] Nicetas relates that a Vlach priest who had been taken prisoner threw
himself at the feet of Asen, and made a personal appeal to him for pardon
"since he spoke Vlach;" and at the beginning of the thirteenth century
Kaloyan, in his correspondence with Innocent III., speaks of his Roman
descent, which is apparently admitted by the Pope.

[2] There is reason to think that a great part of the population round
Sofia is descended from these tribes.

The outbreak which originated the second Bulgarian Empire was occasioned by the exactions of the Emperor Isaac Angelus, who collected taxes with extraordinary rigour in order to meet the expenses of his court. The two brothers Asen and Peter, having in vain demanded redress, proclaimed a revolt, and announced that St. Demetrius had left his shrine in Salonica, and, as a sign of special favour, taken up his abode in Trnovo, where they established the capital of their new state. The superstition and grievances of the peasantry assured them a favourable hearing; the Bulgarians rose against Isaac Angelus and successfully resisted his attempt to subdue them. But the national tendency to dissension asserted itself. Asen and Peter were both assassinated, and were succeeded by their younger brother, Joannitza or Kaloyan (Good John) whose natural abilities and exceptionally favourable opportunities enabled him to put the Bulgarian state on a firmer footing. He was shrewd enough to derive considerable advantage from the breach between Eastern and Western Christianity, which was rapidly widening, and carried on an exceedingly curious correspondence with Pope Innocent III., which ended in the despatch of a Papal Legate to Trnovo, who crowned him as *Dominus Blacorum et Bulgarorum*. As soon as he heard of the capture of Constantinople (1204), he offered his arms and assistance to the Latin Empire. But his overtures were met with a rude and most unwise rebuff, and he was even told to give up to the Latins the territory which he had taken from the Greek Empire. On this he made an alliance with the Greeks, and defeated the Latins at Adrianople. The Latin Emperor Baldwin himself was taken prisoner and perished mysteriously in captivity. But when he had avenged the insults of the Latins, Kaloyan turned against the Greeks. At the head of his barbarous Kumans, he massacred the Greek inhabitants of Thrace and Macedonia, and finally besieged Salonica. But here his eventful career came to an end. He died in his camp of the family complaint of assassination (1207), and chaos succeeded. Bulgaria seemed about to disappear from the map, when Kaloyan's son Asen, who had fled to the north, returned with a band of Russians and seized the throne.

The reign of Asen II. (1218–1240) was the most prosperous period of the second Bulgarian Empire, and perhaps of all Bulgarian history. The weakness of both the Latin and Greek Empires rendered him the strongest potentate in Eastern Europe. Like his father, he wished to be on good terms with the Latin Empire, and was a candidate for the post of Regent during the minority of Baldwin II. But he was not elected, and, angry at what he considered a slight, formed an alliance with the Greeks. His Empire comprised the modern Bulgaria and Servia (including Belgrade), Macedonia and Albania, and, according to his own boast, he left the Latins nothing but Constantinople and the cities round it. Considering how troubled were the times and how blood-stained the annals of his predecessors, his reign was marked by extraordinary peace and material prosperity. He was a warm patron of architecture and the Church. He filled his capital, Trnovo, with magnificent buildings, which made it second only to Constantinople in beauty and splendour, and also built and endowed a large number of monasteries in different parts of his dominions. Yet his Empire was not more stable than those which preceded it, and broke up immediately after his death in 1241.

It is hardly profitable to follow in detail the complicated intrigues and insurrections which compose the remainder of the mediæval history of Bulgaria. Rent by internal dissensions, the unhappy country was attacked by Tartars from the north and overshadowed by the growing power of Servia to the west. The two Slavonic states came into collision at the battle of Velbuzhd. The Bulgarians were utterly defeated, and may for some time be considered as the vassals of Servia, until the decline of the latter re-established equality. It is an inglorious feature of this period that the Bulgarians were allies of the Turks and assisted them against the Greek Empire. Corps were formed, called Voinik, composed of Christians who, in consideration of their taxes being remitted, served under the Ottoman standard against their co-religionists. The last Bulgarian Czar became the vassal of Sultan Murad and gave him his daughter in marriage. But, in spite of such concessions, Bulgaria was doomed. The power of the Southern Slavs was annihilated in 1389 at the battle of Kossovo, and four years later the Ottomans burnt Trnovo and destroyed the last vestige of Bulgarian independence. These events have, however, a closer connection with Servian history, to which we must now turn. For the sake of clearness we have treated Bulgaria separately, but in the fourteenth century Servia was the strongest Slav state in the Balkans, and it was mainly the failure of Servia to resist the advance of the Turks which destroyed the power and almost the name of the Southern Slavs during so many centuries.

In considering the history of the mediæval Servians, we must not make the mistake of thinking of them as the inhabitants of the modern kingdom of Servia. That kingdom is a creation of the Treaty of Berlin, and does not coincide with the boundaries of any of the older states which have borne the same name, or with any ethnographical division. As we have seen, the Greek historians do not call the Slavonic invaders of Macedonia Serbs, and the early use of the name connects it distinctly with the west of the Peninsula. The Servian advance seems to have been directed, in the first instance, towards Bosnia, Montenegro, and the Adriatic coast, whence it spread eastwards, and the most brilliant epochs of the nation are connected with " Old Servia " and North Macedonia, which are now Ottoman territory. Practically nothing is known of the history of the Servian tribes before the middle of the twelfth century. They were from time to time subject to the early Bulgarian rulers, but had no political union or central organisation of their own. Their territories were divided into districts or counties, called Zhupa, at the head of each of which was a chief, apparently elective, called Zhupan. These chiefs met together and elected a leader called the Grand Zhupan; but the titles of King and Czar belong to a later period. The Servians were converted to Christianity about the same time as the Bulgarians, in the middle of the ninth century. Though they ultimately adhered to the Eastern Church, their earlier ecclesiastical relations seem to have been chiefly with the West, and in 1050 Gregory VII. sent a consecrated banner to the Grand Zhupan.

About 1150 the darkness which envelops the early annals of Servia begins to lift a little with the appearance of Stephen Nemanya. He was originally merely Grand Zhupan of Novi Bazar, but he increased his possessions by such considerable conquests in Croatia and Dalmatia that he attracted the attention of the Emperor Manuel, who marched against him in person, and forced him to make a humble submission. During Manuel's reign Nemanya had to restrain his ambitions, but on the Emperor's death in 1180 he recommenced his activity. He captured Nish, and ruled over a territory comprising the western part of modern Servia, Montenegro, Herzegovina, and the vilayet of Kossovo. His capital was at Prishtina, and he assumed the title of King of Servia. He cultivated friendly relations with Frederick Barbarossa, and entertained him hospitably at Belgrade when he passed through Eastern Europe on his way to the third Crusade. In 1195 he apparently became weary of power, abdicated in favour of his second son, Stephen Urosh, and retired to Chilendar, a monastery which he had founded on Mount Athos, and which is still the centre of Servian hopes on the Holy

Mountain.   His successor is commonly known by the epithet of First Crowned,[1] because he was the first ruler of Servia whose position was recognised by a public coronation.   In his case the ceremony seems to have been performed twice—first by a Papal Legate in 1217, and subsequently by his brother, the monk Rastko, canonised under the name of St. Sava, and rightly venerated in Servia; for he appears to have been the real creator of the Servian kingdom and to have disposed of its destinies, though he never reigned.   Profiting by the strife between the Latins and Greeks at Constantinople, which had been so propitious to the second Bulgarian Empire, he succeeded in inducing the Pope and the Greek Emperor, as well as Baldwin, to recognise his brother as independent sovereign of Servia, Dalmatia, and Bosnia, and secured peace both at home and abroad.   Andrew II. of Hungary, alarmed at the growth of the new Power, which, by incorporating Bosnia and Dalmatia, had become conterminous with his own possessions, incited Stephen's elder brother to revolt against him.   This incident gives us in a nutshell the two weaknesses which mark the whole history of the Servian kingdom—the enmity of Hungary, and the extraordinary propensity towards family dissension and intrigue.   Servia was never able to concentrate her powers against the Greeks or the Turks on account of the necessity of defending herself against her jealous neighbour, who, until the advance of the Turks alarmed all Christendom, was always ready to attack her when she was in difficulties.   The gravest national crises, when the existence of the country was at stake, were insufficient to secure for the king the loyal cooperation of his nearest relatives.   In the present case the tact and ability of Sava brought about a reconciliation between his two brothers, but the danger recurred repeatedly when there was no one to remove it.

[1] Prvovenčani.

The next century and a half of Servian annals are filled with the domestic tragedies and military exploits of a series of monarchs called Stephen.   Nearly all Servian kings bore this name, its signification in Greek (a " crown ") having led to its use as a royal title, like Cæsar.   The middle of the thirteenth century is occupied by Stephen IV., surnamed the Great, and with his second son, Stephen VI., begins the period of national glory.   For more than fifty years—when the strength of Bulgaria had declined, when the restored Byzantine Empire, hopelessly weakened by its struggle with the Latins, had ceased to be a terror, and the Ottomans had not yet a firm footing in Europe—Servia was not only the most important power in the Balkans, but seemed capable of resisting the Turkish advance.

Stephen VI. quarrelled with Michael Palæologus, and took from him the whole of Macedonia north of the Vardar, including Mount Athos; but subsequently he adopted the wise and honourable policy of making an alliance with the Byzantine Empire against the Turks, whom he defeated both in Asia and in Thrace.   Stephen VII. crushed the power of Bulgaria, and thus prepared the way for the triumphs of the greatest of all the Stephens, commonly known as Dushan, or " the Strangler," because, according to one story, he killed his father in this way.[1]

His brilliant reign of twenty years was destined to make this unenviable epithet the most distinguished name in Servian history.   Dushan not only extended the frontiers and influence of his country to an unparalleled extent, but also made a code of laws which is still extant (the Zakonik), and protected literature and the Church.   This legislation and civilisation, however, appear to have been entirely an imitation of Byzantine models, and to have contained hardly any original elements.

---

[1] Some patriotic Servians who do not like this story try to derive Dushan from *dusha*, a soul.

He opened his reign by invading Thessaly, besieged the Emperor Andronicus III. in Salonica, and by a treaty concluded in 1340 was recognised by him as possessor of almost the whole Balkan Peninsula except Salonica and Durazzo. The death of Andronicus in 1341 was followed by the accession of the infant John V. Palæologus and the regency of the ambitious Cantacuzene. Dushan began by making an alliance with the latter; but amid the domestic dissensions which rent the unhappy Empire a rupture soon occurred. Dushan sided with the Empress Anne against Cantacuzene, and the latter called in the Turks to assist him. At first Dushan was entirely successful, and in 1346 he had himself proclaimed " Emperor of the Greeks and Servians " at Üsküb; his son received the title of king, and the head of his Church was made a Patriarch. But subsequently Cantacuzene, through his infamous alliance with the Turks, was able to win back parts of Macedonia and Thrace.

In the West, Dushan was even more fortunate than in the East. His victories over Louis the Great of Hungary gave him Belgrade, Bosnia, and Herzegovina, and his coins were minted at Cattaro. In the twentieth year of his reign he planned and started a vast expedition against Constantinople. This enterprise was of the nature of a Crusade, and was inaugurated with solemn religious ceremonies. He appears to have thought, not without reason, that a fresh and vigorous Power might be able, if possessed of the enormous strategical and geographical advantages of the Imperial city, to hold Eastern Europe against the Turk, and we can hardly blame him for making war on a Christian prince, for the Byzantine Empire, though it lasted another century, was apparently at its last gasp and in the hands of the usurper Cantacuzene, the ally of Orkhan.

Perhaps few but students have heard of Dushan's expedition against Constantinople, but it was certainly one of the most critical moments of European history. Unprofitable though it be to speculate on what might have been, it is interesting to realise that an exceptionally talented and energetic prince, representing a still rising Power, came within forty miles of Constantinople at the head of an army of 80,000 men. It is said that the inhabitants were ready to open the gates, and at any rate there were no military obstacles sufficient to prevent him from capturing the city and undertaking the task of defending Christendom against Islam. If the strength of Constantinople was able to preserve the Palæologi another hundred years, we may suppose that it would have been put to better use in stronger hands. But *Dis aliter visum*. Dushan died suddenly in camp on December 18, 1356. It was thought he had been poisoned.

The collapse of his Empire was astonishingly rapid, even if we take into consideration the characteristic instability of Slavonic kingdoms. Its frontiers had been somewhat fluid during his life, and he had adopted the bad policy of dividing it into provinces ruled by quasi-independent chiefs. The moment that he was dead these mostly revolted, and the Turks advanced amidst a confused mass of petty princes. Belgrade passed to Hungary; Thessaly, Albania, Bulgaria, and Bosnia became independent, and the last named seemed for a brief period to be the centre of the Servian power under Tvrtko, who proclaimed himself king of Servia, Bosnia, and the sea-coast. The Turks established themselves at Adrianople. The Servians, alarmed by this advance, allied themselves with the Greeks, but both together were defeated by the Osmanlis near the new capital of the Sultan. This defeat disorganised what little remained of Dushan's Empire. A usurper called Vukashin seized the throne. In imitation of Dushan, he organised a sort of Crusade against the Turks, but was utterly routed in a second battle on the Maritsa near Adrianople, and killed by one of his own followers during the flight which ensued.   In this emergency of the Servian people all dynastic ideas were abandoned, and Lazar, a distinguished soldier, was chosen as Czar.   The difficulties occasioned by the Turks were increased by the attacks of the Hungarians, and Lazar had no alternative but to allow the greater part of Macedonia to pass under the dominion of the Sultan without opposition.   The fall of Southern Servia derives a certain interest from the stories which have gathered round the figure of Marko Kralyevich.   For history he is little more than an unimportant vassal of the Sultan, but popular sentiment has made him the centre of a whole cycle of romantic legends, and credits him with a heroism for which there does not seem to be much foundation in fact.

In 1386 the Turks took Nish, and Lazar found himself obliged not only to pay tribute to the Sultan, but to furnish him with an annual contingent of a thousand mercenaries. The humiliation of Christendom at last made itself felt. When it was too late, an attempt was made to reconstitute the Empire of Dushan in the form of an alliance.   Servians, Bosnians, Albanians, and Bulgarians opposed the Turks together at the battle of Kossovo in 1389 and were together defeated.

This battle of Kossovo Polye (" the field of blackbirds ") produced an extraordinary impression on the Southern Slavs. In memory of this remote but fatal day the Montenegrins still wear a black mourning border on their caps, and the most pathetic of the Servian national songs are consecrated to the task of casting a halo of romance round the national disaster.   One of these ballads has been adapted in English by the late Lord Lytton,[1] and relates how the Mother of God appeared to Lazar before the battle and asked if he would choose an earthly or a heavenly kingdom—a somewhat unreasonable alternative, if one considers how much the victory of Lazar would have benefited Christianity.

[1] " Serbski Pesme," by Owen Meredith, 1860.

The Czar chose the kingdom of heaven, and set out to sacrifice himself and his army. Sultan Murad, moved by similar religious enthusiasm, begged his God that he might fall as a Moslim martyr fighting against the infidel. Both commanders obtained the crown of martyrdom, and, let us hope, went to their respective paradises. But the victory remained indubitably with the Turks, and seems to have been due to a very ugly piece of treachery; for, at the most critical point of the battle, Vuk Brankovich, a rival of Lazar, deserted him with 12,000 men.

With Kossovo ends the importance, but not altogether the interest, of mediæval Servia. The disaster was followed by a wholesale emigration of Serbs to Montenegro, Bosnia, and Hungary, especially the country round the Theiss; but for the moment the lot of those who elected to remain, though ignominious, was not particularly hard. Bayezid, the new Sultan, recognised Stephen Lazarevich, the son of Lazar, as a vassal prince and married his sister. In return for these honours the Prince or Knez, as the ruler of Servia was now called, paid an annual tribute to his brother-in-law, and rendered him important military services as his ally. At last the progress of the Turks and the collapse of the Slavonic states alarmed Sigismund of Hungary and obliterated the old enmity between that kingdom and Servia. He appealed to the Western Powers and organised a Crusade against Bayezid. But his army was routed at Nicopolis on the Danube in 1396, a date as fatal for Eastern Europe as the battle of Kossovo or the capture of Constantinople; for Oriental Christendom was now at the mercy of the Turks, and Hungary, the extreme outpost of the West, discouraged by a defeat. This victory of Islam was to no small extent due to the Servian troops fighting on the Turkish side. The Servians recovered Belgrade, but in the long run this gain hardly compensated them for the disaster which they were preparing by strengthening the Ottoman power. | Stephen was succeeded by George Brankovich, who built the famous castle of Semendria, the ruins of which are visible on the Danube to this day. Sultan Murad, thinking that he was becoming too powerful, demanded the surrender of this fortress, and, when it was refused, invaded Servia, drove out Brankovich, and left Turkish garrisons in the principal towns with a Turkish Pasha as governor. In 1440 Servia seemed to be annihilated, when a new champion appeared and procured her a respite of twenty years. This was John Corvinus Huniades, or Hunyady Janos, " the White Knight," of mysterious origin, who devoted his whole life and brilliant military talents to a Crusade against Islam and the endeavour to unite Eastern Christendom. He now advanced against Murad, and in a brilliant campaign drove him from the Danube, raised the siege of Belgrade, and forced the Turks to sue for peace. A treaty, which included a suspension of hostilities for ten years, was signed in June 1444, and the Turks evacuated Servia. A little repose would have done no harm, but Vladislav, the young King of Poland and Hungary, was incited by the Papal Legate to break the peace almost immediately. This act of certain perfidy and doubtful policy was not successful. Vladislav was utterly defeated and killed at the great battle of Varna in November 1444. But Murad, who was a strange combination of recluse and warrior, and who twice abdicated during his thirty years' reign, did not seem disposed to follow up his success.

His son and successor, who became Sultan in 1451, was a man of different temper, and at once directed all his energies to the attainment of the end which he had in view—the capture of Constantinople. It is not amiss that he was called Mohammed, for, after the Prophet whose name he bore, no man's life and exploits were of such supreme importance for Islam and Christianity, for

Asia and Europe. But, in spite of his intense personal desire to take Constantinople, he is not so much a personality as the representative of a nation, an instrument of Allah executing a divine decree which had already been published. When we contemplate the careers of Alexander or Cæsar, we feel that had they not been born, the course of history might have been otherwise. The assertion of Greek influence in Asia and Roman influence in Western Europe might have been considerably postponed, and perhaps never have taken place. But in contemplating the career of Mohammed we feel that, though he was worthy of the task before him, the task would have been performed without him. The strength of the Turks, the weakness of the Empire, and the absence of any other element of strength on the Christian side, formed a combination which could not hold together, and which in breaking up could rearrange itself in only one way. But, no doubt, Mohammed himself saw things differently, and overestimated the strength of Byzantium. The Empire was still a great name, and inspired an almost superstitious respect out of all proportion to its material power.

The young Sultan, though confident, was not rash. In order to have his hands free he made treaties of peace with the various princes of Eastern Europe, including Brankovich and Hunyady, who stood by and looked on at the duel between him and Constantine Palæologus. It is a wonder that the latter defended himself so long. He was an Emperor only in name, for the entire territory of the Empire had fallen into the hands of the Osmanlis, with the exception of the capital and one or two seaports on the Black Sea and Marmora, and in 1452 Mohammed occupied Roumeli Hissar on the Bosphorus. But in those days it was no easy task to take a fortified city, and the Sultan only accomplished his object by dragging a fleet over land and casting pieces of artillery which were considered marvels.

As soon as he was established in Constantinople, Mohammed proceeded to deal with the various Christian princes
with whom he had made treaties, and took Servia in hand
first.   Hunyady again came to the Servians' assistance, and
Mohammed, finding greater difficulties than he had antici-
pated, temporarily recognised Brankovich in return for the
payment of an annual tribute, but in 1456 again returned
to the charge and besieged Belgrade.   The Pope implored
Hunyady to prevent the progress of the Moslims, and, obe-
dient to the summons, the unwearied Crusader succeeded
in saving the city[1] and routing the Turkish army.   This was
his last and most glorious exploit.   Both he and Brankovich
passed away the next year, the latter aged ninety-one, and ignoble family quarrels terminated the independence of Servia.
The widowed daughter-in-law of Brankovich made the fatal
mistake of invoking the aid of the Pope and offering to
make Servia a dependency of the Papacy.   As in Constantinople, so in Servia, the people declared they preferred the
Sultan to the Pope, and opened their cities to the Turk.
The independence of Servia came to an end in 1459, and,
by a strange irony of fate, Mohammed was welcomed as a
deliverer.   Much the same thing happened in Bosnia.   The
Catholic King Stephen had persecuted the Bogomiles at
the instigation of the Pope, who wished to see this heresy
exterminated, but the sectarians were numerous and fanatical.   When Mohammed invaded Bosnia in 1563 they
refused to fight for Stephen and handed over their fortresses
to the Sultan.   Herzegovina was occupied a year or two
later, and thus the whole Balkan Peninsula became subject
to the Turks, except Montenegro and a few fortresses in
the Morea held by Venice.   The rest of the Frankish and
Greek Principalities which had sprung up in the period
succeeding the fourth Crusade were swept away, though

---

[1] Belgrade subsequently passed into the hands of Hungary and was taken
for the Turks by Suleiman.

Crete, Cyprus, and other islands were not conquered until later.

We must, however, say a few words of two peoples with whom the Turks now came in contact, and somewhat imperfectly subdued — the Albanians and the Roumanians or Wallachians. The Albanians are first heard of by that name in 1334, when the Emperor Andronicus appears to have directed against them a punitive expedition accompanied by Turks; but for several centuries the notices of them are rare and obscure. Even more than the Slavs they were devoid of cohesion and political sentiment, and have at no time in their history been more than an aggregate of tribes, mostly occupied by internal quarrels, but sufficiently protected by their own bravery and their impregnable mountain homes to resist all attempts at effective conquest, and to preserve a real though not a nominal independence. Early in the thirteenth century, soon after the Latin conquest of Constantinople, Michael Angelus, a member of the Imperial family, proclaimed himself Despot of Epirus, but it does not appear that the state so founded had any national or ethnographic connection with the Albanian people. In the middle of the fourteenth century we hear that Dushan received the homage of the Despot, and was lord of nearly all Albania.

Albania, or rather an Albanian, for the interest of the story is personal more than national, again attracts attention in the fifteenth century. George Castriotis, better known as Skanderbeg,[1] ranks with Hunyady as a determined and successful opponent of the Turks; but though our materials for judging him are scanty, it seems probable that a love of military adventure, rather than any national or patriotic sentiment, was his dominant impulse.

[1] His name was Alexander, which, with his title of Bey, became in Turkish Iskender-Bey, and in Albanian Skender Beg.

This want of great motives in an otherwise great career is characteristic of the Albanian race.

He was the son of the chief John Castriotis, but was brought up at the court of Murad II. as a Moslim, and served in the Turkish army until he was about forty years of age. He appears to have carried on a secret correspondence with Hunyady, and when the Turks were defeated at Nish in 1443, he revolted, and forced the Sultan's secretary, under threats of death, to give him an order instructing the Ottoman commandant of Kroya, in Albania, to deliver that fortress to him. He established himself there, and during eight years carried on a continual and successful struggle with the Turks, defeating Vizier after Vizier, and his old master Murad himself. The entire resources of the Turkish Empire,. and even the treachery of Skanderbeg's nephew, were unable to contend successfully with the geography of Albania and the bravery of its inhabitants, and the Sultan was obliged to retreat with an army which he commanded in person. Mohammed II., in pursuance of his usual policy, made peace with Skanderbeg until he had leisure to deal with him singly. But he was not more fortunate than his father in subduing the stubborn mountaineer, and was in his turn defeated at Kroya in 1465. Though this campaign was a victory for Skanderbeg, the struggle had been hard, and left him in great distress. He visited Pope Paul II. in 1466 to implore aid, but, though he was received with all honour, he was unable to obtain any practical assistance, and returned to his own country, where he died next year (1467). His work perished with him, and whatever unity he had given Albania disappeared between the quarrels of rival chiefs, and the encroachments of the Sultan on the one side and Venice on the other.

The Roumanians or Wallachians fall into two divisions,

the northern and the southern. What little is known of the early political history of the latter has been mentioned in speaking of the Vlacho-Bulgarian Empire. The northern division inhabit the two Principalities of Moldavia and Wallachia,[1] and a large proportion of the population of Transylvania, Bukovina, and Bessarabia belong to the same stock. The history of these lands is, in its early stages, as obscure as that of Albania, but after the fourteenth century the Roumanians appear as the bravest and most progressive people of South-Eastern Europe. This late and sudden development is easily explained. The districts immediately north of the Danube not only lay in the highway of the barbarian immigrations, but they formed the basis from which each invader made inroads on the south and west. Hordes of Goths, Huns, Gepids, Lombards, Avars, Bulgarians, Uzes, Pechenegs, and Kumans succeeded one another, but the last-comer always occupied some part of Roumanian territory. But when the flood of invasion finally ceased, Roumania was in a more favourable condition than the other Balkan kingdoms. The barbarian invaders had either moved on or lost their identity. The country did not lie in the line of the westward advance of the Turks, and was not liable to be overrun by Ottoman soldiery unless directly attacked. No Frankish states were established within its border, nor was there any struggle between the Eastern Church and the Papacy. It is true that the division into the two Principalities of Wallachia and Moldavia was a source of weakness and disunion, but even with this disadvantage the record of Roumania from 1400 to 1800 is, both in peace and war, more glorious than that of any of the other countries which we have considered.

Roumania when first heard of was inhabited by the

---

[1] The two Principalities are collectively termed Roumania. The name is not perhaps officially correct before the union of the Principalities in 1859, but I use it before that date for brevity and convenience.

people called Getæ or Dacians, who, after prolonged wars with Rome, were subdued by Trajan in 101 A.D. The invasions of Goths and other barbarians compelled the Romans to evacuate the province in 274, and from that date until the thirteenth century it was a barbarian camp, although in the tenth century it may have enjoyed a measure of peace and order under the first Bulgarian Empire, of which it was a dependency. At this period there was a close connection between the north and south banks of the Danube. The Roumanian civilisation seems to have been Slavonic rather than Byzantine in its origin, and the liturgy of the Roumanian Church was celebrated in Slavonic. Early in the thirteenth century the Kumans, the last of the invaders, were converted to Christianity; and at its close Radu Negru and Dragosh, both immigrants from Transylvania, founded the Principalities of Wallachia and Moldavia respectively. The fourteenth century was occupied in campaigns with Hungary and the extension of Moldavia towards the Black Sea. The first remarkable name of which we hear is that of Mircea, called the "Old," or the "Great," who fought at Kossovo. That defeat was disastrous for him as well as the other Christian princes. The Turks crossed the Danube, and Wallachia was made a vassal state of the Sultan, but allowed to retain practical independence in return for the payment of an annual tribute. Mircea lost no opportunity of resisting the Turks; he fought against them at Nicopolis, and utilised the defeat of Bayezid by Timur to consolidate and strengthen his country. But on the recovery of the Turkish power under Mohammed I., he had again to pay tribute. His death, in 1418, was followed by anarchy and dissension; but, shortly after the Turkish conquest of Constantinople, two remarkable men, Vlad (1456–1462) and Stephen (1457–1504), reigned in Wallachia and Moldavia. The extraordinary cruelty of the former, which aroused the astonishment of Mohammed the

conqueror, procured for him the name of Vlad the "Impaler."
In his defence it can only be said that his energy and
courage equalled his barbarity. He refused to furnish the
stipulated contingent of Janissaries to the Turks, and routed
Mohammed, who invaded Wallachia with the intention of
chastising him. Moldavia had hitherto lain outside the
Turkish sphere, and been subject to the influence of Hungary
and Poland, but the ambition of Stephen brought her into
relations with the Ottoman Power. This adventurous and
warlike prince began by making war on Vlad, and driving
him from Wallachia—an act of doubtful policy, like all other
dissensions between Christian states at this period—and then
defeated the Turks at Racova. He was hailed by the Pope
as the defender of Christendom, but, like most such Eastern
heroes, obtained no substantial aid. Until his death he
continued the struggle against the Turks with varying success. In spite of severe defeats, he succeeded in driving
them from his country; but at the end of his long reign
saw that Moldavia could not continue the struggle, and
had better make terms with her powerful but happily
somewhat distant enemy. It is said that his dying advice
to his son was in this sense; and at any rate, in 1513 the
latter made a treaty by which he promised to pay tribute
and assist the Sultan in time of war, but received in
return important privileges. Moldavia was to elect her
own rulers, and no Turks were to be allowed to settle in
the country.

The development of Roumania is thus chronologically
and geographically independent of the Greek Empire. The
various Slavonic and Frankish states, which had been carved
out of the territory of the Empire, collapsed with its weakness and extinction. But as the Greek Empire had never
had any effective or continuous control in the districts north
of the Danube, its death-agony did not disturb them, and
the period of their first achievements is precisely the period

of its fall.   But though, by exception, the capture of Constantinople is not literally the turning-point of Roumanian history, it is an event of such paramount importance for all Eastern Europe that it must be regarded as dividing and marking the two great divisions of history, and naturally suggests a pause in any general survey.

CHAPTER II

THE countries which have at one time or another formed part of the Ottoman Empire include Hungary, Roumania, and parts of Southern Russia, but for the last half-century, at any rate, the expression Turkey in Europe may be restricted to the countries south of the Danube. It is true that many of these countries do not politically form part of Turkey any longer, but for all of them the presence of the Turks in Europe has been the most important fact of the last five hundred years, and their history is the record of a struggle, more or less successful, against the Sultan.

This region south of the Danube is often called the Balkan Peninsula—a convenient though vague expression, which is sometimes loosely used so as to include Roumania, though, geographically, this extension of the phrase is hardly defensible. The word Balkan means mountain or mountain-pass, and is justly applied to a peninsula almost the entire surface of which is crumpled up into a series of ridges so numerous and irregular that it is difficult to reduce them to mountain systems or give a general description of their topography. This natural confusion is increased by the fact that much of the country is imperfectly surveyed, and indeed imperfectly known, while popular names are often applied to more than one locality, and are not very precise. The Peninsula may be roughly divided into three mountain regions, the Western, the North-Eastern, and the Central. The Western or Dinaric mountains are more or less parallel to the coast of the Adriatic, and are broken only by a few small rivers, which with difficulty force their way through the rocky barrier to the sea. This region comprises Bosnia, Montenegro, Albania, Epirus, and Western Greece. The mountains of Albania are sometimes known by the sonorous epithet of Acroceraunian, and the range which crosses the Turco-Greek frontier near Janina in a south-easterly dirce-tion is called Pindus or Agrapha. In the north-eastern region are the spacious plains of Bulgaria, Eastern Roumelia, and Adrianople, bounded by the ranges of the Balkans, strictly so called (also known as Koja Balkan or Stara Planina), and by the Rhodope or Despoto Dagh.[1] In the west the moun-tain masses of Rilo Dagh and Vitosha above Sofia form a sort of connection between the two ranges.

The central region of the Peninsula, from Western Servia to Greece, consists mainly of short mountain ridges, some running north and south, others north-east. Between them are enclosed fertile valleys, sometimes broadening into plains, sometimes (as at Ochrida, Prespa, and Castoria) contain-ing lakes. Among these mountains may be mentioned the Kopaonik range, dividing the kingdom of Servia from the Turkish province of Old Servia, the Shar Dagh lying to the south of the plain of Kossovo, and Mount Olympus, now called Elymbos, south of Salonica, and connected with the mountains which separate Greece from Turkey. Four con-siderable rivers, the Maritsa, the Mesta or Karasu, the Struma, and the Vardar, all having a south-easterly direc-tion, run into the Ægean Sea, the coast of which forms, near Salonica, a remarkable three-fingered peninsula. The northernmost of the three promontories is the celebrated monastic territory of Mount Athos, containing more than twenty monasteries, and inhabited exclusively by monks, all women, and, as far as possible, female animals, being rigorously excluded.

With such a configuration, it is easy to understand that communication, especially in an eastern or western direction,

[1] Dagh, like Balkan, means mountain in Turkish.

is very difficult throughout the whole of the Balkan Peninsula. For instance, a journey, even approximately as the
crow flies, from Adrianople to Skutari in Albania, through
Üsküb, presents almost insuperable obstacles. The Romans
kept up communication with Macedonia by the Via Egnatia,
a road which proceeded inland from the Adriatic by Elbasan,
but, in modern times, the insecurity as well as the difficulty
of this route have caused it to fall into entire disuse. At
present there are two main highways across the Balkan
lands, followed by two lines of railway. They both start
from Belgrade on the Danube, and follow the valley of the
Morava to Nish. Thence one of them proceeds south-east-
wards through mountain defiles to Sofia, and descending
into the plains of Eastern Roumelia, follows the Maritsa
to Philippopoli and Adrianople, whence it proceeds to the
Bosphorus. The other line goes more directly south from
Nish to Üsküb, and follows the valley of the Vardar down
to Salonica.

If we exclude these great lines of communication and
also the coast towns, it will be found that the greater part
of Turkey in Europe remains a blank, not only to the
"general reader," but to most Europeans resident in the
East. The plains of Northern Bulgaria are more or less
accessible from the Danube, and Monastir is now connected by rail with Salonica and through that port with
the rest of Europe, but Albania is an almost unknown
country; and much the same may be said of the more
eastern districts. If the reader, however well acquainted
with the East, will look at the map, and draw a line from
Salonica to Rodosto through Seres, Drama, and Dedeagatch,
and another line from any point on the northern slopes of
the Rhodope to Burghas on the Black Sea, and then ask
himself how much he knows of the geography and pepulation of the country between these two lines, his knowledge must be very exceptional if it extends beyond a few

towns such as Dimotiko and Adrianople.   Natural barriers,
insecurity, diversities of language and religion, have shut
off large portions of the Balkan Peninsula from one another
as well as from the rest of Europe, and rendered them inaccessible to the influence of such civilisation as prevails
at Constantinople and Salonica.

The existing political divisions, which are generally
called Balkan states, are about six in number.   North of
the Danube, but possessing some territory called the
Dobrudja, on the southern bank near the mouth, is Roumania, a kingdom formed by the union of the two older
Principalities of Wallachia and Moldavia.   Immediately
south of it, on the other bank of the Danube, is the Principality of Bulgaria, which is under the suzerainty of the
Sultan, and also formed by the union of two provinces,
Bulgaria, strictly so called, and Eastern Roumelia, which had
been separated by the Treaty of Berlin.   West of Bulgaria,
and, like it, bounded on the north by the Danube, is the
kingdom of Servia.   A Slavonic-speaking population, whose
language is either Servian or closely akin to it, occupy the
various Austrian provinces about the head of the Adriatic
and between the river Drave and the coast—Slavonia,
Croatia, Dalmatia, Istria, and even more northern districts;
but, as a rule, only the territories known as Bosnia and
Herzegovina are considered as Balkan states.   They are
officially described as Turkish provinces administered by
Austria-Hungary.   Below them lies the little independent
Principality of Montenegro.   The extreme southern part of
the Peninsula is occupied by the kingdom of Greece, and the
space between Greece and the countries enumerated above
is filled by the territories which still form part of the Turkish Empire.   They are officially divided into six provinces
—Skutari, Janina,[1] Kossovo, Monastir, Salonica, and Adrianople, besides Constantinople and its environs, which have

[1] Pronounced Yanĭna.   For some reason J, not Y, is the accepted orthography.

a separate administration; but, in ordinary language, other and older geographical designations are frequently used. The northern part of the Adriatic coast-lands below Montenegro is called Albania, and the southern part above Greece, Epirus. The district immediately south of Servia is called Old Servia, and that between Adrianople and the Ægean, Thrace. The name of Macedonia is most correctly applied to the country west and north of Salonica, but often receives a more extended sense, so that the phrase Macedonian question is used to mean all the problems created by the existence of Turkey in Europe.

The materials collected in the previous chapter explain why the population of this Balkan Peninsula is so mixed. On the top of the original Illyrians and Thracians, whoever they were, came an influx first of Greeks and then of Romans, which resulted in the creation of considerable Greek-speaking and Latin-speaking elements. Into this already somewhat mixed population poured a series of Slavonic and Bulgarian invasions, to say nothing of obscurer and more transitory tribes. The Slavs and Bulgarians tended to become confounded, for the Bulgarians became Slavised in language and customs, though they were long politically stronger than the Slavs, and the same districts are called Bulgarian or Servian at different epochs, according as one state or the other was superior. The Albanians also, who had been driven into a small space by the early Slav invasions, began to expand over Slav territory. Finally, the Turks gradually worked their way to a paramount position, not as a sudden avalanche of conquerors, but sometimes as settlers (as in Macedonia and Thessaly), and generally as the leaders of warlike expeditions. Often they were the allies of some Christian state, and their armies nearly always contained a large European element. Though persevering, they were excessively cautious, and, in consequence perhaps of their ignor-

ance of Europe, showed for a long time little disposition
to follow up their successes and a readiness to recognise
the position of any prince who would pay tribute.

In one sense the Empire continued after the fall of
Constantinople; that is to say, a Turkish Empire succeeded a Greek one, and the general methods of government remained nearly the same. The later Greek Government was, like the Sublime Porte, mainly a tax-collecting
organisation: it took tribute from its provinces and did
nothing for them; it employed foreigners and mercenaries; it had an official nobility and a ruling race.
" Financial rapacity," " venality and sale of offices," " de-
solation of rural districts," and " depopulation of provinces," are phrases which recur in Finlay's " History of
Greece," previous to the Turkish conquest, as regularly
as in modern Consular Reports.

The Byzantine Empire has met with various fortune at
the hands of its critics and historians. It was long the
fashion to speak of it with unmitigated contempt; and
this disparaging estimate, though often dictated by ignorance, seemed confirmed by the sarcastic tone which marks
the work of Gibbon. A natural reaction made Freeman
and other writers of this century dwell on the merits of
the Byzantine state and its rulers, and point out that
a system of government which lasted nearly 1300 years
must have had some characteristics beyond weakness and
superstition. This is no doubt true, and there is no reason
why we should not bestow all the praise which we justly
can on the Byzantine Empire and other Christian states
of Eastern Europe, provided that we do not thereby un-
justly disparage the Turks, as many literary crusaders
have done. The evils of Turkish rule are undeniable;
they exist at the present day, and are much the same
as they always were. But anti-Turkish writers speak of
the entrance of the Turks into Europe as if a barbarian

invasion had suddenly overwhelmed the industrious Slav and the cultivated Greek, and destroyed a peaceful and orderly civilisation. But this is hardly true. For centuries before the fall of Constantinople the history of South-Eastern Europe is one long record of blood and disorder: φόνοι, στάσεις, ἔρεις, μάχαι — murder, discord, strife, and battle. The crimes with which the Turks are frequently reproached, such as treachery, fratricide, and wholesale cruelty, are characteristic, not of them, but of the lands which they invaded. It would be hard to produce from the annals of the Sultans anything worse than the quarrels, treachery, and misgovernment of Andronicus and the Angeli, or than the cruelties of Vlad the Impaler. Neither can we praise the Byzantines at the expense of the Turks in the realm of art and literature. If Constantinople contains beautiful churches, it also contains beautiful mosques, and must thank the Turks for what is now the most picturesque and characteristic feature of its landscapes—the minarets which crown Stamboul or emerge more modestly from the groves which fringe the Bosphorus. Ottoman and Byzantine literature may fairly be compared; neither have had any influence or importance for Western Europe, and no one would ever read either except for the purpose of extracting information. But Ottoman poems may be set against Greek romances, and Ottoman chroniclers against the Scriptores Historiæ Byzantinæ. In criticising either the Byzantine or the Ottoman Empire at any epoch except their zenith, we must remember that we are dealing with sick men, and be gentle. As consumptive patients who would die under normal conditions may live for years with a fragment of a lung in a mountain sanatorium, so does Constantinople preserve states which have lost all organic strength, and whose weaknesses are the more apparent because they are nominally responsible for large and disorderly territories over which they have little real control. In the fourteenth and fifteenth centuries the Turks cannot have been regarded as "unspeakable" barbarians far below the standard of Christian Europe; for we find that Christians, who must have had ample information respecting them, were ready to invite them into the lands of the Empire, and after the fall of the Empire they were welcomed in Servia and Bosnia. In morals, humanity, and civilisation they were much of a muchness with the motley throng of Greeks, Slavs, Albanians, and Roumanians; in energy and union they were superior.

But it does not follow that, in the sequel, the Turkish Empire was as good for its Christian subjects as a continuation of the Byzantine might have been. Soon after the conquest it developed two characteristics in which it was distinctly inferior to its predecessor. Firstly, the Sultan, who had been a comparatively modest military chief, became an absolute Asiatic despot, surrounded by all the pomp and luxury which the classical writers call Persian, and also hallowed by an idea of special sanctity. It is true that the Byzantine Basileus possessed the germs of both these peculiarities; in fact, the Sultan derived them from him. But European taste kept the pomp of the Basileus within bounds, and his religion was the religion of his subjects. But there were no bounds to the lavish extravagance of the Sarai, where the revenues of a province were unhesitatingly squandered on an Imperial pageant or passing whim, and the Sultan's sanctity and divine right to power reposed on Arabic and Turkish ideas which were wholly repugnant to the beliefs and traditions of Christians. Secondly, the Turkish Empire tended to take the form of government by a crew of adventurers. It may seem that this is incompatible with a despotism; but it is not, particularly if the despot is indolent and indisposed to interfere in details. From their first appearance the Turks displayed a strange power of collecting together apostates, renegades, and people who had more ability than moral qualities. Their most formidable troops were composed of the children of Christians, taken from their parents at an early age, and brought up without any of the ordinary ties of family or citizenship. Similarly, the Imperial harem, which often exercised a powerful influence in politics, was filled with a crowd of women and eunuchs gathered from every country, but taken, like the Janissaries, in childhood, and ignorant of all the world outside the palace walls. With such elements as these, and a Sultan who associated mainly with such elements, it is not surprising if the Ottoman government often seemed to lose all system and order, and to mean nothing more than a permission given to certain cliques to plunder the rest of the Empire. The Turks had little feeling respecting such abuses, but they were sensitive to external defeats, and whenever these were occasioned by internal anarchy, the real power was generally entrusted to some capable Vizier who patched things together again.

We must draw a distinction between the history of the Turks and the history of their Christian subjects. The former is a purely military record. Modern writers are unwilling to regard history as a mere catalogue of reigns and battles, and pay more attention to the various movements, political, religious, intellectual, social, and commercial, which the life of each nation presents. This is very just in the case of nearly all nations; but the peculiarity of the Turks is at once apparent when we observe that their history is almost exclusively a catalogue of names and battles. For instance, for the Hungarians the Turkish occupation of Hungary had many important consequences, social and political. Hungary would not be what she is now if that occupation had never taken place, or had continued longer. But the same occupation had no social or political consequence for the Turks; they remained after it as they were before it; its importance for them is accurately measured by the military gain and loss.

The history of the Turkish Empire falls into four periods. The first is a period of advance and expansion, culminating in the conquests of Selim I. (1512–1520) in the East and of Suleiman (1520–1586) in the West.   This last reign is the zenith of the Ottoman Empire.   Suleiman ruled from Buda-Pesth to the Persian Gulf, and his navies threatened the coasts of India and of Spain.   The most important feature of this period is that the Turks were a central European power; they occupied Hungary and menaced Austria.

The second period, extending from the end of the sixteenth to the beginning of the eighteenth century, is marked by continual wars of varying success with Austria, Hungary, Poland, and Venice.   Of the many Sultans whose reigns it witnessed, few have any personal importance.   The sovereigns were no longer either generals or statesmen, and the Grand Viziers not only wielded the real power, but conducted in person the principal campaigns.   At the end of the seventeenth century fortune deserted the Turks.   They were driven back from Vienna, and out of Hungary, Transylvania, and Podolia.   After the Treaties of Carlovitz and Passarovitz, Turkey becomes definitely an Eastern state, menacing neither Western nor Northern Europe, and bounded by the Carpathians, the Danube, and the Save.

What a change had come over her military position in the third period (roughly 1720–1820) may be seen from the fact that twice in the eighteenth century Austria and Russia discussed the possibility of dividing the Sultan's Empire between them.   This period is marked by the Russian conquest of the northern shores of the Black Sea, and by repeated Russian invasions of Moldavia and Wallachia with the avowed object of protecting the Christian inhabitants of those provinces.   By the Treaty of Küchük Kainarji (1775), Russia was expressly recognised as the protector of the two Principalities, and as having " the right to speak in their favour, the Porte promising to listen with the attention due to friendly and respected Powers." This right of intervention is one which has since been much extended and practised by other Powers than Russia, and in other parts of the Ottoman Empire. Another interesting feature first appears in this period. The Porte, when pressed by Russia, appealed to the Western Powers, and the latter, especially France, gave their moral and diplomatic support to the Turkish side, receiving in return commercial advantages.

The last period of Turkish history (1820 onwards) is marked by the curtailment of the Empire, caused by the creation in its territories of a series of independent states, sometimes admittedly and sometimes practically, but not nominally, detached from the central administration. Mahmud II., one of the ablest and most energetic of the Sultans (1808–1839), though he attempted many reforms, was unable to preserve the integrity of his Empire. Greece successfully asserted her independence and Mohammed Ali established his dynasty in Egypt. Servia was recognised as a Principality, and the Roumanian Hospodars were as much under the influence of the Czar as of the Sultan. The Russians, thinking that the final collapse of Turkey was near, tried to force the Sultan to recognise them as the protectors of all orthodox Christians in his dominions, which was tantamount to the abolition of the Ottoman Empire. The Sultan was supported in his resistance by England, France, and Sardinia, who, with the Turks, defeated the Russians in the Crimean War (1853–1855). The Treaty of Paris, which closed that war, restored both banks of the Lower Danube to the Porte, but could not impart strength to retain them, and the Principalities first united under one prince and subsequently became independent. The Slavonic provinces had hitherto shown a more submissive spirit than the Greeks and Roumanians, but in the seventies insurrections broke out in Herzegovina and Bulgaria which eventually brought about a Russo-Turkish war in 1877. The Treaty of Berlin, which embodies the results of the contest, recognises the independence of Roumania, Servia, and Montenegro, constitutes Bulgaria an autonomous vassal state, entrusts Austro-Hungary with the administration of Bosnia and Herzegovina, and holds out prospects of reform to Crete and Macedonia, which have been realised in the first-named country but not in the second. In 1886, Eastern Roumelia, which had been separated from Bulgaria by the Treaty of Berlin, was united to it, and the two districts now form one country. The present dominions of Turkey in Europe correspond roughly with the ancient provinces of Thrace, Macedonia, and Epirus. Ethnographically they comprise the frontier districts of the Greek, Servian, and Bulgarian areas. Hence all the racial and linguistic elements are represented in them.

I have said that Turkish history is purely military. Of course, no nation can exist 450 years entirely without change, yet the statement that the Turks are unchanging requires very little qualification. Any one can see their impenetrability by thinking of what has occurred in Turkey in his own lifetime or at least in this century. The reforms of Mahmud and Abd-ul-Mejid, the Hatt-i-Sherif of Gülhane, the Hatt-i-Humayun of 1856, and the establishment of parliamentary government by the present Sultan were measures which would have revolutionised any ordinary country, but they have simply collapsed in Turkey without result and without fuss. Despite all statutes to the contrary, religious equality does not prevail, nor is Turkey constitutionally governed. The only important changes which have taken place since 1453 and really affected Ottoman society have a military character, for they concern the institution of Janissaries and military fiefs (*timar*).

The corps of Janissaries was, in its original constitution, one of the most remarkable bodies which the world has seen, and goes far to explain the unique character of the early Ottoman Empire—that wild brilliancy and vigour in which no ordinary ideas of humanity, morality, or economy find a place—and the strange contradictions presented by a government which seemed to possess all the sterner virtues, energy, discipline, and perseverance, but to be at the same time capricious, wayward, corrupt, and ignorant of the ideals which most states have at least professed to follow. Orkhan introduced, and Murad I. perfected, the system of slave soldiers. The Christian rayah had to pay to the Sultan a tribute of children, as of all other possessions. Every four years the Sultan's agents visited the Christian villages under Turkish rule, and took a fifth part of all the male children between the ages of six and nine, carefully choosing the strongest and most intelligent. They were regarded as the Sultan's slaves, taken to Constantinople, educated as Moslims, and entirely separated from their families and early associations. Some were ultimately used for civil employments, but the majority were destined for military service and drafted into one of the 165 ortas or companies of Janissaries. They were forbidden to marry or engage in trade; they were fed, clothed, and paid by the Sultan, and they could only be punished by their own officers. Haji Bektash, the founder of one of the most popular but least orthodox Dervish sects, blessed the new soldiers (*yeni-cheri*), who adopted his mystic and antinomian tenets, though they naturally found practical antinomianism more congenial than theoretical mysticism. The Janissaries were thus a religious military order composed of men selected for physical or mental excellence, divorced more completely than any monk from all worldly ties of birth, marriage, or profession, and encouraged to give their vigour full and unscrupulous play, subject to no law save that of unques-

tioning obedience to their superior officers. Such a body
was the most efficient and formidable arm ever possessed
by any despot as long as he knew how to wield it; but the
primitive constitution of the order lasted about a century
after the conquest of Constantinople. The first change
was that they were allowed to marry; the second, that they
were allowed to introduce their children into the service;
the third, that the children of other Moslims were enrolled.
The levy of tribute-children ceased in the seventeenth
century, the last recorded instance being in 1676. The
original character of the Janissaries was thus wholly obliterated, and they became simply Turkish troops, distinguished
from other troops by the fact that they were paid and
enjoyed certain privileges. These advantages enormously
increased their numbers as soon as the corps was open to
all-comers; but this increase and the depreciation of the
currency rendered the salary inadequate, and another change
took place. The Janissaries were allowed to engage in
trade and to provide substitutes for foreign service. The
result was doubly evil. Those in Constantinople became
the most turbulent and disorderly part of the populace of
the capital, and those in the provinces a reckless and in-
subordinate crew. At the beginning of this century they
defied and killed the Turkish governor of Servia, and
massacred and ravaged the province until they provoked a
popular movement strong enough to quell them. In 1826
Sultan Mahmud tried to reform the corps, but finding
that impossible, exterminated them and burned the quarter
where they resided.

The history of the Janissaries is chiefly important for
the social conditions of the capital; the analogous degenera-
tion of the military fiefs affected those of the provinces.
The institution of these fiefs dates from long before the
conquest of Constantinople, and some of the earliest are
said to have been granted by the Seljuks. In the valley of

the Vistritza one can still find Turkish country gentlemen who live surrounded by feudal retainers, and claim that their lands have been in the possession of their ancestors for more than six hundred years. Such old country families were by no means favoured by the earlier Ottoman Sultans, whose plan was to give distinguished soldiers fiefs for life; but, as among the Janissaries, the principle of heredity asserted itself, sometimes directly, sometimes through the subterfuge of *vacouf* or religious property. The life-holder of a fief nominally made over his interest to the Mohammedan Church, but the Church in return recognised the right of himself and his heirs to control the property. This fact accounts for the extraordinary number of *vacouf* lands in Macedonia. But the fiefs not only became hereditary or *vacouf*. About the same time that the Janissaries were allowed to marry, began the practice of giving them to court favourites who had no pretensions to military distinction, and who did not succeed in maintaining a military following. The feudal landholders (it would be erroneous to call them a feudal aristocracy) became less and less important as a military element, and at the present day Turkish country gentlemen, as distinguished from Albanian chiefs, are comparatively rare in Europe.

The history of the conquered peoples under the Turkish domination can be best treated of in subsequent chapters when we consider each race separately, but it may be well to indicate here its general lines. Until this century it is mainly a history, not of events, but of social conditions, and is concerned with such questions as, How the European subjects of the Porte were able to acquire political power either by becoming Moslims or by being employed by the Turks without changing their religion; how they found a certain national expression in religious and educational institutions; or how they acquired importance by concentrating commerce in their own hands. The lot of all was not equal. The happiest and also the most eventful history is perhaps that of the Roumanians. As already pointed out, their geographical position was favourable, and the arrangement made with the Porte after the death of Stephen the Brave (in 1504) not only left the country free to manage its own affairs, but forbade the settlement of Turks within its boundaries. Unfortunately the quarrels of the native nobility changed this state of things for the worse. The Roumanians were exceptional in South-Eastern Europe in having a society founded on aristocracy, for among the Greeks and Slavs Turkish dislike of hereditary rank did away with all distinctions except those arising from wealth or the Sultan's favour. The Roumanian Boyards, however, formed a powerful and privileged class, who did not admit the superiority of any one family, and fought among themselves for the dignity of prince. The more ambitious and unscrupulous could not resist the temptation of securing power by Ottoman aid. It thus soon came about that the prince was not only appointed by the Sultan, but maintained in his position by a Turkish guard, and at last the office was, like the Greek Patriarchate, openly sold to the highest bidder. At the end of the sixteenth century two remarkable princes, John the Terrible and Michael the Brave, ruled in Moldavia and Wallachia. Both revolted against the Turks and inflicted on them severe defeats, but both failed to permanently free their countries from Ottoman control. John, whose power rested on the peasant classes, was hated by the nobles and betrayed to the Turks, and Michael, who represented the party of the nobles, was weakened by the want of popular support. Though his talents and bravery enabled him to unite at one moment Moldavia, Wallachia, and Transylvania under his personal rule, the state thus formed was ephemeral, and the chief result of his brilliant career was that after his assassination in 1601, the Turks thought it safer to send foreign governors to Roumania instead of allowing natives to be elected. Nevertheless, the national spirit did not entirely die out in the seventeenth century, which produced such native rulers as Basil the Wolf of Moldavia and Matthew Bassarab of Wallachia. They were contemporaries (about 1634–1654), but unfortunately also enemies, and this enmity prevented them from doing much for the independence of their people. After their deaths, the appointment of foreign governors by the Sultan became more and more the rule. The two Principalities were indeed never administered by Mohammedan Pashas, like other districts of the Turkish Empire, but from 1716 to 1822 the governorships of Jassy and Bucharest were regularly conferred on Phanariot Greeks, who bought the offices from the Sultan, and naturally recouped themselves from their subjects. They were constantly changed, in order to re-sell the office as often as possible, the average duration of their tenure being little more than three years, so that they had rarely any knowledge of the country or sympathy with its inhabitants, while their luxury and indolence were proverbial even in Turkey. It is in this period, too, that the Russians began to interest themselves in Roumania, but their intervention does not appear to have been very welcome to the population or very successful. Austria was unwilling to see Russia increased by a considerable accession of territory, and the Roumanians did not feel sure that it was better to be incorporated in Russia than to be a dependency of Turkey. Nor had they much reason for enthusiastic gratitude towards their Christian neighbours, seeing that the military and diplomatic work of the century resulted in the cession of Bukovina to Austria in 1777, and of Bessarabia to Russia in 1812.

The Phanariot rule ended with the revolt of Greece from the Porte. When the War of Independence broke

out in 1821, the Greek Ypsilanti started an anti-Turkish
revolution in Jassy. But the Roumanians had no desire to
increase the power of the Phanariots, and a national insurrection by no means favourable to the Greeks broke out
in Wallachia under Vladimirescu. The Porte, thinking it
injudicious to continue the appointment of Greek governors,
named two native Hospodars; and during the next thirty
years Roumania was the scene of a long struggle—military
as well as diplomatic—between Russia and Turkey for paramount influence, and more than one complicated system of
dual control was introduced and abandoned. A national
party, led by Rosetti and Bratiano, and desirous to be free
of the Muscovite as well as the Ottoman, brought on an unsuccessful revolution in 1848, which for the moment curtailed the liberties enjoyed by Roumania; for the reign of
the Hospodars was limited to a term of seven years. But
the Crimean War weakened Russian influence in the Principalities and was favourable to the native element; for the
power of the Turks, though confirmed by the Treaty of
Paris, remained merely nominal. In 1859 Moldavia and
Wallachia elected the same man, Alexander Couza, as Hospodar, and the union of Roumania was thus accomplished,
though the suzerainty of the Sultan continued. But the
government of Couza proved unsatisfactory. He was deposed in 1866, and Prince Charles of Hohenzollern–Sig-
maringen, a young Prussian prince, was elected in his
stead, and ultimately, though not without much opposition, recognised by the Sultan and the Powers. In 1878
Roumania was declared entirely independent by the Treaty
of Berlin, and in 1881 she proclaimed herself a kingdom.
Such in outline is the story of the country which fared best
under the Turkish Empire.

The Albanians, also, did not suffer much from the Ottoman rule. They had no national government to lose, and
they were not deprived of their practical independence. At

the end of the fifteenth century, after the death of Scander-
beg, many of them emigrated to Italy and Sicily, and a large
number of those who remained sought security in another
way by becoming Moslims.   Conversions to Islam took
place on a still larger scale at the end of the sixteenth and
the beginning of the seventeenth century.   In the period
between the decay of the Janissaries and the rise of the
Phanariots, these Moslim Albanians played quite a considerable *rôle* in the military and civil services of the Porte,
and furnished many celebrated Viziers, among others the
Kyöprülüs, who for seventy years were the real rulers of
Turkey.   It is excessively difficult to disentangle the history
of the Albanians, particularly of such as remained Christians,
from that of the Greeks and Slavs by whom they were surrounded.   They penetrated as far south as the Morea, where
they formed a considerable percentage of the population.
The Moslim and Christian Albanians, though they quarrelled among themselves, seem to have united to keep the
Turks out of the western half of the Balkan Peninsula
south of Montenegro.   They were for ever fighting, either
with one another or with the Turks, or on the side of the
Turks against the Greeks or other enemies; but as fighting,
brigandage, and vendetta appear to have been in all ages
their favourite occupations, the Turks can hardly be held
responsible for the wild and turbulent state of the country,
though, of course, they did nothing to improve it.   At the
end of the eighteenth and beginning of the nineteenth centuries, Albania attained a certain political importance under
the celebrated Ali-Pasha of Janina, who, like Scanderbeg,
temporarily united by his personal influence the various
tribes of his countrymen.   In the course of a long, bold,
and dexterous but singularly unscrupulous career, he succeeded in concentrating in his own hands the principal
Albanian Pashaliks, and inducing the Porte to recognise
his rule.   But at last Mahmud II., fearing that he had

grown too powerful, ordered his deposition in 1820, and sent an Ottoman army against him to execute the sentence. Ali, having now nothing to hope for from the Porte, endeavoured to obtain support from the Greek revolutionary element, with whom he had long had relations, and encouraged and advanced the cause of Greek independence, but was killed in 1822.

In reviewing the fate of the Greeks under the Turkish dominion, we must keep distinct two categories. The inhabitants of the present kingdom of Greece and the Greek peasantry in Macedonia bore a yoke nearly as heavy as that which pressed on the Bulgarians and Servians. But the educated Greeks of the larger cities, and particularly that class at Constantinople known as the Phanariots, were happier in their destiny. In the period immediately following the conquest, the Turks were anxious to conciliate them; in the sixteenth century their position was less assured, but they gradually acquired the confidence of the Turks, and by the eighteenth century had won what may be called a Vice-Imperial status. I mean that the Greek Empire, though it had ceased to exist as a political force, continued to exist as an intellectual, ecclesiastical, and commercial force. The Greeks could not display the same local vigour as the Roumanians or Albanians, but, under the Turks, they retained an influence which was not provincial, but almost co-extensive with the Turkish dominions. This influence made itself felt in three spheres: Firstly, in matters ecclesiastical, which included literature and education and a large part of civil law; for the Turks allowed the ecclesiastical tribunals to decide cases involving such questions as marriage, divorce, and inheritance when they concerned Christians only; Secondly, the Greek was pre-eminent in commerce, for which the Turk had no aptitude, and the other races but moderate abilities; Thirdly, the Phanariots finally attained real political importance. During the eighteenth century the Dragomans of the Porte and Fleet, and the Hospodars of Moldavia and Wallachia, who were four of the most important officials in the Turkish Empire, were invariably Greeks. But though during this period the Greeks had almost more influence on the social, religious, and economic condition of the Balkan Peninsula than the Turks, they were only an influence, and not a nationality. Both collectively and individually, they possessed riches and power; but the Greek State vanishes from history between 1453 and 1821, and no index or chronological table records any actions of Greece in that period. It was only natural that the Southern Greeks, as being the most oppressed portion of the most intelligent subject race, should be the first to revolt from the Turks. The Phanariots, whose position depended on the maintenance of the Turkish supremacy, were in doubtful sympathy with the movement; and the War of Independence, though successful, secured less advantages for the Greeks as a whole than might have been expected. On the one hand, only a small portion of territory was made independent; and, on the other, the Greeks who remained Ottoman subjects lost the privileges which they had enjoyed. After the establishment of the kingdom of Greece, the Turks conceived a natural distrust of the Greek element, put an end to the Phanariot domination in Moldavia and Wallachia, and favoured the efforts of the Slavs to free themselves from the Greek clergy.

With the exception of the Montenegrins, who maintained in their mountain fastnesses an independence analogous to that of the Albanians, the lot of the Slavs under Turkish rule was indeed pitiable. The nobles of Bosnia and the Pomaks of South-Eastern Bulgaria secured a better position by turning Mohammedans, but the mass of the people remained true to their Christian faith, and as their reward endured centuries of martyrdom at the hands of Ottoman Pashas and Greek priests. For three or four centuries Servia and Bulgaria simply ceased to exist, and the countrymen of Dushan and Simeon became a helpless, friendless, nameless peasantry whose only function was to supply taxes and plunder, and who were not allowed to hold the smallest office. Servia being farther west and attracting from time to time the attention of Austria, was less deeply sunk in the slough of despond than Bulgaria, but the distance of the country from Constantinople created peculiar evils. The Janissaries, who could not be controlled from the Porte, refused to obey the local Turkish governors and established a sort of military rule under four Agas which practically meant organised brigandage and massacre. In 1804 their excesses provoked a successful rising under Kara George, and perhaps the Porte was not sorry that the insurgents got the better of the Janissaries. But the Servians now aimed at freeing themselves not only from the Janissaries but from Turkish control. The Porte was able to suppress Kara George, but a second rising under Milosh Obrenovich was more successful. In 1830 the Sultan was obliged to recognise him as prince, and his dynasty reigns in Servia to this day. At first they were vassal princes of the Porte, but the Treaty of Berlin recognised their independence, and in 1882 the Prince Milan was proclaimed king.

The chains of Bulgaria were heavier and her awakening later than those of Servia. Towards the end of the eighteenth century a remarkable Moslim chief, half-patriot, half-brigand, somewhat after the pattern of Ali of Janina, named Pasvan-Oglu, succeeded in establishing himself at Widdin and defying the Porte. He levied taxes and coined money in his own name, and actually threatened to march against Constantinople. The Porte on this granted him a firman as a Pasha, and he died as a vassal of the Sultan. During the middle of the nineteenth century the national feeling in Bulgaria became sufficiently developed to attempt to oust the Greeks and restore the national Church. The Turks were not unfavourable to this movement, and in 1870 the Sultan issued a firman creating a Bulgarian Church independent of the Patriarch of Constantinople. But, naturally, Bulgarian patriotism was not only anti-Greek but anti-Turkish. An insurrection in 1876 was crushed with a cruelty which attracted the attention of Europe, and brought about the Russo-Turkish War and the recognition of Bulgarian independence in the Treaty of Berlin.

It will be observed that, apart from the conditions which determined the lot of the conquered races separately, there were certain circumstances of general application which affected them all alike. These were chiefly connected with the decay of the Janissary system and of military fiefs. It is a strange paradox that, though the Turks conquered and ruled South-Eastern Europe, they were not of themselves sufficiently numerous to conquer and hold it, or possessed of sufficient political skill to administer their conquests. At every stage of their career they required the military and political assistance of other races, and the wonder is that it was always forthcoming. For some hundred years after the conquest of Constantinople the tribute of Christian children supplied them with their best soldiers and most capable officials. When that tribute ceased to be levied, at the end of the seventeenth century, their military glory was no longer in the ascendant and the necessary administrative talent was found among converts from Christianity to Islam. This occasioned a wholesale change of religion in many provinces, particularly Albania. But in the eighteenth century, when the old Greek Empire had been forgotten and the new Greek kingdom had not inspired distrust, the address and servility of the Greeks made them the governing class in the larger part of the Empire.

The abolition of the tribute of children was equally

important for the provinces. As long as it lasted, the country districts were naturally submissive, for the strongest element was continually removed from them. But when the flower of provincial youth, instead of being carried as slaves to Constantinople and forcibly converted to Islam, were allowed to grow up as Christians in their native villages, this uncomplaining meekness naturally disappeared. Bands of insurgents, called Haiduds among the Slavs and Klephts among the Greeks, made their appearance all over the Balkan Peninsula, and led a life of desperate but somewhat aimless opposition to the Turkish Government. They can be represented according to taste either as bloodthirsty brigands or as romantic but somewhat eccentric apostles of liberty. The Sublime Porte, which has always loved the maxim "Set a thief to catch a thief," counteracted these bands by authorising the formation of other bands called Armatoles. These were a sort of Christian militia, who were on good terms with the authorities, but also not oversevere to the Klephts.

The national movements of the nineteenth century have inspired the Porte with a general distrust of Christians. None of them in Europe are allowed to bear arms except Albanians; few hold civil posts. There are probably at the present moment more Turkish officials than there have been at any previous period of Ottoman history, and it will be interesting to see if the Turks will be able to provide from their own race the necessary number of administrators, who have never been forthcoming before. The very number of the national movements, though it inspires continual anxiety, is a source of strength to the central Government. Greeks, Serbs, and Bulgarians, to say nothing of Vlachs and Albanians, have each their peculiar aspirations, and by playing off one against the other and consistently supporting whatever may happen to be the weaker party, the central authority maintains its power.

CHAPTER III

THE TURKS (I)

IN the previous chapter we have seen how swarm after swarm of barbarians poured out of Asia into the civilised world. Let us now observe the same phenomena from the Asiatic side, and, looking westwards from the East, endeavour to form some idea of the course of these invasions and of the character of the invaders. The task, though interesting, is peculiarly difficult; for, owing to the paucity of records, it is often hard to distinguish fact from legend or theory, and the loose employment by Easterns and Westerns alike of national designations is a constant source of error.

At the present day large parts of Eastern Europe and most of Asia north of the Hwang-Ho, of Tibet, and of the Hindu Kush (that is to say, the districts vaguely, but very inadequately, described as Mongolia, Turkestan, and Siberia) are inhabited by people for whom it is not easy to find a common designation, but who may be most conveniently treated as forming a linguistic unit. Their languages may be divided into four families—the Manchu, the Mongol, the Turkish or Tartar, and fourthly a more miscellaneous group comprising Finnish, Magyar, and a number of less known tongues. The resemblances between these four families, though definite, are of a general kind, and lie in the structure rather than in the vocabulary; but all the languages are sharply distinguished from those of the Chinese or Aryans, by whom the speakers are surrounded. As I propose to recur to this subject, I will not treat of it further now.

It is clear that at the present day there is no racial unity corresponding to this linguistic group, and it is not clear that there ever was. Many Finns are physically undistinguishable from Swedes. The original Huns are always spoken of as a peculiarly hideous race, but the Magyars are some of the best-looking people in Europe, and show no trace of the physical type commonly called Mongol or Tartar. Very many Osmanlis exhibit a Caucasian type, for which there are good reasons. Since their arrival in Anatolia and Europe they have continually intermarried with Arabs, Kurds, Greeks, Slavs, and Albanians, and the practice of contracting unions with foreign slave girls has still further mixed their blood, especially in the wealthy families. But even before they appeared in Anatolia, they had long been in contact with the Persians or closely allied races. The earliest known inhabitants of the modern Bokhara, Ferghana, and the adjoining districts were apparently Iranians, and we can hardly doubt that the westward-bound Turks took out with them a considerable admixture of Iranian blood.[1]

We have seen that a great medley of races was covered by such names as the Avars. The idea which underlies the formation of the corps of Janissaries—that of creating a military organisation, the members of which had severed all their natural ties of language, country, and family, and were united only by discipline to their chiefs and by a secondary acquired language—was evidently a natural product of the Turkish mind. Probably similar things were done in Central Asia. Military Powers of one kind or another were for ever rising and falling; confederations took the name of their most important tribe; the van-

---

[1] I would, however, observe that one is apt to generalise too widely from observing the physique of the Turks of Constantinople. In June 1897, I saw many thousand Turkish soldiers together in Thessaly, collected from all parts of Anatolia, and was much impressed by the strongly non-Caucasian type of many.

quished lost their name and were merged in the victors. The name Osmanli is a clear instance of what may have happened in many obscurer cases. It is now applied loosely to any Moslim in the Turkish dominions, and those who use it most strictly would never hesitate to give it to all Turkish-speaking Moslims. Yet many of the latter must be descendants of the Seljuks, and many of Christians, whereas the original Osmanlis were merely the tribe or dependents of Osman, and for a long period not only distinct from, but at war with, the Seljuks. At the present day the name Turk or Tartar generally denotes a Moslim speaking a Turkish language, and Mongol a Buddhist speaking a Mongol language. But in earlier centuries it is not so easy to draw the distinction. Timur has been called both a Mongol and a Turk. Jenghiz Khan was apparently a Mongol, but his son was called Jagatai, and Jagatai in Turkish is the recognised expression among the Turks themselves for the Eastern dialects of their language. A still more remarkable transfer of names is exhibited by the word Kazak,[1] or Cossack, originally the designation of a section of the Kirghizes, but now hardly known except as applied to the military organisations of South Russia, which, though they perhaps originally contained Tartar elements, have long been purely Russian.[2]

If we consider these people—Turks, Mongols, Magyars, Manchus, and the rest—as a whole, the part which they have played in history has been a large but strange one. Their contributions to the art, literature, science, and religion of the world are practically nil. Their destiny has not been to instruct, to charm, or to improve, hardly even

---

[1] The word appears to mean properly an animal separated from the herd.

[2] Another instance of national and linguistic, but not racial unity, which in some ways illustrates the formation of these Turkish societies, may be found in the United States. The population is drawn from every country in Europe, yet for all practical purposes they have but one language, and are not only homogeneous, but are developing a special physical type.

to govern, but simply to conquer. The sterility of their authors has deprived them of the fame which the scale, if not the grandeur, of their exploits deserves. When one tries to piece together these obscure and fragmentary records, what a catalogue of terrible names passes through the memory: "The scourge of God," Huns, Avars, and Turks; the Ghaznevids, the Mamluks, the Golden Horde, the Great Mogul, Jenghiz Khan, Tamerlane, Mohammed the Conqueror. Who can reckon the tribute they have taken, the cities they have sacked, the blood they have spilled? They have ruled from the north of Africa to the shores of the Pacific; they have sent expeditions against Vienna and Japan; they have ruled in Russia, in Persia, and in India; and, though their empires have mostly been ephemeral, a Turk still sits on the throne of Constantinople, and a Manchu on that of Peking.

The earliest information respecting these races comes chiefly from Chinese sources, which describe, under the general name of Hiung-nu, the tribes to the north of the Hwang-ho, against whose incursions the Great Wall was built. We have no record of their early westward movements except the appearance of the various hordes in the West; but it is clear that in the fourth and fifth centuries a movement to the north-west, that is, towards the Urals and Volga, did take place. It is marked by the settlements still existing of Samoyedes and Ostiaks on the Asiatic side of the Northern Urals, by the Finns, Lapps, and other races in North Russia, and by the Mordvinians and Cheremissians on the Volga. But a subsequent movement, of whose causes we are equally ignorant, drove the more important part of these tribes—the Huns, the Bulgarians, and the Avars—south-west from the Ural and Volga, against the frontiers of the Roman Empire.

The name Turk appears in Chinese as Tu-kiu, and in Greek as Τοῦρκοι, as early as the fifth and sixth centuries,

F

and in the last ten years monuments have been discovered on the Yenisei and Orkhon which throw a light on the pre-Islamic civilisation of the Turkish people. The most important of these is an inscription found near the latter river and erected in 733 A.D. to the memory of Kül-Tegin by his brother Bilge Khagan. The Turks appear to have had two occupations, pasturage and warfare, the latter either on their own account or as mercenaries of the Chinese. They were excellent horsemen,[1] and the spirit of military adventure was specially favoured by their peculiar institutions, by which the youngest son usually inherited his father's property, while the elder brothers went out into the world to seek their fortune. Among them was already noticeable that special instinct for discipline and order which characterised the followers of Jenghiz Khan, Timur, and the Osmanlis, and which has unhappily nothing to do with good government, but merely makes every man render implicit obedience to his military or official superior. They possessed an alphabet,[2] but they had no written law or sacred

---

[1] It is interesting to notice that the inscription, in recounting the exploits of Kül-Tegin, always gives the names of the horses he rode in his various campaigns.

[2] This alphabet has a superficial resemblance to runes, due to the fact that, unlike most other alphabets, it is composed exclusively of vertical and oblique strokes without any horizontal lines. It has been acutely suggested that this peculiarity is due to the fact that both runes and the old Turkish alphabet were commonly carved on wood, on which material it was not convenient to cut horizontal lines following the grain. V. Thomsen (*Inscriptions de l'Orkhon:* Helsingfors, 1896) thinks that this alphabet is derived from the Aramaic through its Pehlvi and Sogdian variations. If so, it is remarkable that written Turkish has from the first fallen under the influence of Semitic letters, and had to struggle against their inability to express vowels. Old and modern Turkish meet the difficulty in the same way, namely, by not writing the vowel, but by indicating its quality by the preceding or succeeding consonant, *e.g.* in Osmanli the terminations *mak* and *mek* are distinguished not by their vowels, but by their consonants, and are written in an orthography which may be transliterated as *mq* and *mk.* Similarly, in the Yenisei and Orkhon inscriptions, the letters *k, g, t, d, b, j, r, l, s* have each two forms according as they are pronounced with hard or soft vowels. Subsequently Nestorian missionaries introduced into Central Asia the Estrangelo alphabet, from which are derived the Uigur, Mongol, and Manchu systems of writing.

books. Their religion seems to have consisted of the worship of the sky and the five elements, earth, water, fire, wood, and metal or iron. The old name, Tangri or heaven, is still used in Osmanli Turkish for God, but the ancient religion seems to have had little lasting effect on the national character. Its most important characteristics are negative; there is no trace of any organised priesthood or other institutions tending to settle and control these soldiers of fortune. They came, however, into contact with both Christianity and Buddhism. The former was introduced into Central Asia by Nestorian missionaries through Khorassan, and in the fourth and sixth centuries we hear of Bishops of Merv, Herat, and Samarcand. Buddhism was apparently introduced rather later in the sixth century.

From the third until the end of the sixth century these Turks played a considerable part in the affairs of China, which need not detain us here. It is more to our purpose to notice that they came into collision with the dynasty of the Sassanids in Persia (215—639 B.C.), and pressed persistently westwards towards the southern extremity of the Caspian, waging a continual war, described by Persian writers as the contest of Iran and Turan. As the Byzantine Empire was also at war with Persia, they seem to have thought they might make an alliance with Byzantium against the common enemy. In 562 the Turkish Khan, called Dizabul by the Greeks, and identified with the Bumin Khagan of the inscription of Bilge Khagan, sent an embassy to the Emperor Justin. He had certainly large views of foreign policy, for he proposed to act as an intermediary for the silk trade between China and Byzantium, and in return asked the Emperor to denounce the fifty years' peace which he had made with Chosroes, and attack Persia on the western frontier, while the Turks attacked it from the north. Justin refused his overtures. He probably had not the slightest idea of the importance of the Turks, but perhaps his decision was right. The subsequent examples of those who accepted their help are not encouraging. But an unexpected Power swept away the Sassanids, and opened to the Turks ' the south-western route, which they had blocked. The Prophet Mohammed died in Medina in 632, and one of the first lands to feel the power of his successor was Persia. The country was conquered, and made an appanage of the Caliphate in 639. The earlier Caliphs resided chiefly at Damascus, but the Abbasides fixed their capital at Bagdad, and Persia tended to become the centre of the eastern Moslim state, Egypt and Spain having a separate history. The Abbaside Caliphs gradually became weaker, and at last retained little but their spiritual authority, the temporal power having passed into the hands of Persian Viziers. This circumstance, strangely enough, was the cause of the next great forward step taken by the Turks. They entered the service of the Abbaside Caliph, rid him of his Persian masters, reasserted in name his temporal power, and, as a matter of fact, assumed it themselves.

From this period we may divide the Turks into two sections—those who moved south-west, and who, as they were drawn towards Anatolia and Europe, sought more or less definitely the conquest of what they called Rûm, and those who remained in Central Asia, and ultimately tended to fall within the Chinese sphere. The latter, or a part of them, were known as Oigurs or Uigurs. Their princes reigned at Kashgar; they were converted to Islam, and attained a certain civilisation, deeply affected by Chinese influences. They employed a form of the Syriac alphabet, which had been introduced among them by the Nestorians, and a book is still extant called *Kudatku Bilik*, "The Art of Government," composed at Kashgar in 1065, in the reign of Boghra Khan.

The first step westwards is marked by the Samanids, a dynasty in which both Iranian and Turkish elements were combined, and which ruled in Transoxiana, Khiva, and Khorassan under the Abbaside Caliphs. As this dynasty broke up and the Abbasides became gradually weaker, a struggle ensued between the Caliphate, supported by Turkish troops, and various popular Persian parties. During this period of confusion a Turkish adventurer founded the power of the Ghaznevids in Eastern Afghanistan. Mahmud of Ghazni, who subdued a great part of Northern India, was scrupulously correct in his relations with Bagdad, and reported his victories to the Caliph as the head of the military state of Islam, but his successors tended towards greater independence. The Seljuks, whose original home was apparently the modern Dzungaria, first appear in the middle of the eleventh century, under their leader, Toghrul, as fighting against Masud, the son of Mahmud of Ghazni. They drove the Ghaznevids eastward into India, and made themselves masters of Khiva, Khorassan, and Irak. The Caliph Kaim requested Toghrul's assistance, and at a solemn ceremony which took place at Bagdad in 1055 made over to him the temporal power. Toghrul died soon afterwards, but his son, Alp Arslan, who succeeded him, performed even greater feats in the name of the Caliph. He won back Syria from the schismatical Fatimite Caliphs of Egypt; he conquered Georgia and Armenia, and finally defeated the Byzantine Emperor Romanus at Manzikart in 1071. Though the Crusades and other events complicate the history of the next two or three centuries, Asia Minor was from that time practically lost to the Empire and given over to the Turks. Alp Arslan was succeeded by his son, Melik Shah, under whom the Seljuk Empire reached its greatest extent and glory. He ruled from Transoxiana to the borders of Egypt, and counted among his provinces Syria, Mosul, Khorassan, and Khiva. It is said that during his reign he ten times travelled from one extremity of his vast dominions to the other. This reminds us of the

captain of a roving Turkish band; but in other respects he
marks a transition from the organisation of a warlike
nomad tribe to a permanent anti-Christian Mohammedan
state, just as his name contrasts with Toghrul and Alp
Arslan. Nizamu-'l-Mulk, who was Vizier both of Alp
Arslan and Melik Shah, wrote a work called *Siaset-name*,
or " The Science of Government," which shows that this
Seljuk state had already developed the most striking
features of the modern Ottoman Empire. We see from it
how the religion of Mohammed came to these wild soldiers
of fortune as a stricter discipline, but not as a new moral
law; and when the astute Vizier counsels the free use of
espionage, and recommends that provincial governors and
agents should be often moved and not allowed to become
too powerful, one feels that the Turk is indeed unchanging.
The Empire of Melik Shah became dismembered after his
death. The history of the eastern provinces becomes connected with that of the Mongols and China, and the history
of Syria and of the south with that of the Crusaders and
of Egypt. The power of the Turks as a race advancing
westwards at the expense of the Byzantine Empire was
centred in the Seljuk Sultanate of Konia (or Iconium). The
capital was established there by Masud in the first half of
the twelfth century, but only after a troublous period in
which the Anatolian Seljuks contended with the Danish-
mends of Sivas, and other obscure chieftains. Among the
more celebrated Sultans of Iconium were Kaikhosrau, Kai-
kavus, and Alau-'d-din Kaikobad, who built many beautiful
mosques and gateways, which are still in existence.

At the end of the twelfth and beginning of the thirteenth
centuries occurred another extraordinary ebullition of the
Turanian [1] races. A Mongol of the country near the river

[1] It appears to me that the word Turanian, though most undesirable if
used as a designation of all languages which are not Semitic or Aryan, is convenient and appropriate as a name for the languages mentioned at the beginning of this chapter, and for the people who speak them.

Onon called Temujin, but better known by his title of
Jenghiz Khan, or "the Inflexible Lord," swept over Northern
Asia at the head of his heterogeneous hordes, and conquered
and destroyed from China to Moravia and the Adriatic.
His personal exploits hardly touched either Byzantium or
Konia, but his successors were the bane of the Seljuks. Of
the heirs of his kingdom, one, Khubilai Khan, founded the
Yuen dynasty in China; another, Batu Khan, established
the camp on the Volga, generally known as the Golden
Horde, which ruled over Central and Southern Russia for
a hundred and fifty years; and a third, Hulagu Khan,
invaded Persia and Syria, massacred the inhabitants of
Bagdad, including the Caliph, and thus made an end of the
Abbaside Caliphate (1258). The Seljuk Sultan Kaikhosrau II. was defeated by the Mongols at Kuzadag in 1243,
and it seemed, towards the end of the thirteenth century, as
if the Turkish power in Anatolia was likely to succumb
before them, when a new name appears in history.

It is during these struggles of the Seljuks and Mongols
that we first hear of the people to explain whose origin this
long story has been recounted—the Ottoman Turks. Viewed
from Europe, they appear like the matador in the bull-fight,
appointed to slay an animal maddened and weakened by
the attacks of numerous foes. Viewed from Asia, they are
merely another instance of the sudden rise of a small clan to
eminence and empire, which we have seen too often to feel
any surprise. It is said that Suleiman, the first ancestor of
the family, came from Khorassan. He clearly belonged to
one of the many Turkish tribes who poured into Anatolia
after the battle of Manzikart, and were subsequently driven
west by the pressure of the Mongols. His son, Ertoghrul,
established himself first near Erzeroum, and then moved
westward with the idea of entering the service of the Seljuk
Sultan of Konia. According to the legend, fate favoured
this intention. During his journey he saw from a mountain

height two armies fighting on the plains below, chivalrously
determined to aid the one which seemed to be outnumbered,
and by his intervention decided the fortune of the day.   It
proved that he had aided the Sultan Alau-'d-din to defeat a
horde of Mongols, and as a recompense he received from the
grateful monarch the fief of Eskishehir.   His son Osman
(whence Osmanli, and by corruption Ottoman [1]) and his
grandson Orkhan took Broussa, Nicæa (Isnik), and Nicomedia (Ismid) from the Greeks, and when, at the beginning
of the fourteenth century, the Empire of Iconium broke up
into ten provinces ruled by Khans or Emirs, the Ottoman
chiefs were lords of the province of Khudavendigiar, which
is still the official name of the vilayet of Broussa.   It is
worth while recapitulating the names of the other nine
states, as they are still occasionally used as territorial designations by both Turks and Europeans: (1) Kastamuni, the
ancient Paphlagonia; (2) Karasi, the ancient Mysia, with
Bergamo (Pergamus) as the capital; (3) Sari-khan, the
ancient Lydia, capital Cassaba (Sardis); (4) Aidin, the
ancient Ionia, with Aya-soluk (Ephesus) as the earliest
capital; (5) Menteshe or Caria; (6) Tekke, Lycia, and
Pamphylia; (7) Kermian, the ancient Phrygia, with
Kutahia as capital; (8) Karaman, Lycaonia, and Cappa-
docia, with the towns of Konia and Cæsarea; (9) Hamid,
Pisidia, and Isauria.   The most remarkable activity of the
first Osmanli sovereigns was perhaps that manifested in
Europe, but Orkhan and Murad I. subdued three of these
nine Khanates, and, though the remaining six conspired
against Bayezid, he disposed of them all.   But at this point
his progress was stopped and the young Ottoman Empire
nearly overthrown by another great Turanian movement
similar to that of Jenghiz Khan and directed by Timur or
Tamerlane, a native of Samarcand.   After conquering the

---

[1] The name Osman is borrowed from the Arabic, and correctly written
'Uthmân or 'Othmân.   But the Turks could pronounce neither *ain* nor *th*.

Golden Horde and Northern India, Timur turned his arms first against Syria and then against Asia Minor, where he utterly routed Bayezid's army and took the Sultan himself prisoner in 1402. His campaigns had three results. They led to the establishment of the Mogul Empire in India; they broke the power of the Golden Horde and thus enabled the Russians to free themselves from the Mongol yoke; and they broke, at least temporarily, the power of the Osmanlis. But the Byzantines could not use the opportunity; Timur went off east with his armies and died in 1405; the Osmanlis recovered from the shock, and, fifty years later, took Constantinople.

The pre-eminence of the Osmanlis among the Turks seems to be the result mainly of geographical position. Their story is typical of the national life of which we have been speaking. The family histories of the Ghaznevids and early Seljuks closely resemble the beginning of the house of Osman. But no previous Turkish states had severed their connection with Eastern Asia sufficiently to become a permanent danger to Europe. Even Konia was a long way from Constantinople, and the Seljuks when established there were already in their decline. But in the case of the Osmanlis, the first impetus, the new fountain of vigour, burst forth in Western Anatolia, comparatively close to Constantinople. Their victorious arms advanced early into Europe, a stride which the Seljuks could never have made. They incorporated European recruits in their armies, and by the conquest of Constantinople received first a stimulus which sent them on victorious as far as Vienna, and secondly an unparalleled national citadel, possessed of a strength far more lasting than any which mere fortifications can give, and capable of holding together a decaying Empire which would have soon decomposed if centred in Konia or Samarcand. Yet it would be unjust not to recognise the personal merit of the Osmanlis. They no doubt possessed in their highest form all the Turkish virtues — courage, energy, obedience, discipline, and temperance: and it is truly remarkable that they did not collapse after the defeat inflicted on them by Timur. It may be urged that Timur made no attempt to destroy their power or lay waste Asia Minor, but merely humbled Bayezid and went away. This is so; but Bayezid was the fifth from Ertoghrul, and feebler Turkish dynasties collapsed of themselves in a shorter period.

The Osmanlis are still in Constantinople, and, though they have ceased to be a terror, are still a preoccupation to the West. They have become, under the force of circumstances, less actively warlike than they were, but otherwise they seem exempt from those laws which tend to produce a measure of uniformity among European nations. They have done little to assimilate the peoples whom they have conquered, and have still less been assimilated by them. In the larger part of the Turkish dominions, the Turks themselves are in a minority. Only in the vilayet of Konia and the interior portions of Broussa and Aidin is the mass of the population Turkish, in the sense in which it is English in England or Russian in Russia. In the Armenian provinces about one-third is Turkish, one Armenian, and one Kurdish. Going farther south, the proportion of Arab blood becomes larger and larger, till at last in Syria, Palestine, and Arabia only the officials are Osmanlis, and not over-willingly obeyed by the natives. Everywhere on the coast Greeks abound, and in the interior of European Turkey the Turkish race is certainly of all numerically the weakest. To a limited extent the Osmanli fuses with other Mohammedan races, such as Kurds and Albanians, particularly in the negative form of being unwilling to openly quarrel with them; but, on the whole, the Turks are now what they were when the first Seljuk adventurers seized on Asia Minor—an army of occupation. The expression Turkey in Europe means no more than would the expression England in Asia, if used as a designation for India. Indeed, in many respects, though not in all, there is a great similarity between the two Empires. In both cases a large extent of territory, comprising the most diverse races, is administered by a comparatively small body of invaders, who, owing to difference of language, can only communicate imperfectly with their subjects. In both the ruling race has an overweening sense of its own superiority and remains a nation apart, mixing little with the conquered population, whose customs and ideals it tolerates, but makes little effort to understand. In both there is in practice a religious distinction between the native and the governing race, though, of course in India the theory is widely different from that prevalent in Turkey. Naturally the parallel is only true in its most general outline, but it will enable the reader to realise the isolated position of the Turk in his own country.

Perhaps one fact which lies at the root of all the actions of the Turks, small and great, is that they are by nature nomads. It is their custom to ornament the walls of their houses with texts instead of pictures, and, if they quoted from the Bible instead of the Koran, no words would better characterise their manner of life than " Here have we no continuing city." Both in the town and in the country they change their dwellings with extreme facility, and think it rather strange to remain long in the same abode. The very aspect of a Turkish house seems to indicate that it is not intended as a permanent residence. The ground floor is generally occupied by stables and stores. From this a staircase, often merely a ladder, leads to an upper storey, usually consisting of a long passage, from which open several rooms, the entrances to which are closed by curtains, not by doors. There are probably holes in the planking of the passages, and spiders' webs and swallows' nests in the rafters. The rooms themselves, however, are generally scrupulously clean, but bare and unfurnished. The walls are plainly whitewashed, and ornamented only by one or two *yaftés* (the illuminated texts alluded to above). Chairs and tables there are probably none, and the cupboards let into the wall are usually of rough unplaned deal. The general impression left on a European is that a party of travellers have occupied an old barn and said, " Let us make the place clean enough to live in ; it's no use taking any more trouble about it. We shall probably be off again in a week." All houses are constructed entirely with a view to the summer, and the advent of winter, despite the fact that it lasts about six months and is often severe, seems a constant source of surprise. The inhabitants huddle into one room heated by an iron stove or open brazier, and leave empty the rest of the house which cannot be warmed. The same rough-and-ready arrangement is seen in the disposition of the rooms. They are not assigned to any special purpose. You sit in a room and write on your hand ; when you are hungry, you call ; a little table is brought in and you eat ; when you want to go to bed, a pile of rugs is laid in a corner and you go to sleep on it. The same thing may be witnessed in a more striking form at the Imperial Palace of Yildiz. I have seen a number of secretaries and officials working in a room decked with red plush and the ordinary furniture of European palaces. Some were sitting curled up in armchairs, with their inkpots poised perilously on the arms, the idea of having a writing-table never having come into their heads. Some were squatting on the floor, eating with their fingers off broad dishes placed on a low table. One was taking a siesta in the corner. Nothing could have more vividly suggested the idea of a party of tent-dwellers who had suddenly occupied a European house, and did not quite know how to use it.

It is not only in such details that this characteristic occurs, but in the whole economy of the state. The Turks certainly resent the dismemberment of their Empire, but not in the sense in which the French resent the conquest of Alsace-Lorraine by Germany. They do not use the word Turkey, or even the Oriental equivalent ("the High Country") in ordinary conversation. They would never say that Servia or Greece are parts of Turkey which have been detached, but merely that they are tributaries which have become independent, provinces once occupied by Turks where there are no Turks now. As soon as a province passes under another government, the Turk finds it the most natural thing in the world to leave it and go somewhere else. In the same spirit he talks quite complacently of leaving Constantinople some day: he will go over to Asia and find another capital. One can hardly imagine Englishmen speaking like this of London, but they might conceivably so speak of Calcutta.

Perhaps it is to this spirit that most of the vices of the Turks should be attributed. Travelling generates an immoral habit of mind; that is to say, you do many things in a place where you are going to stop only a few hours which you would not do in your permanent residence. Observe the undisguised selfishness and greed of ordinary railway travellers, the brutal violence with which they seize eligible seats or other comforts, the savage gluttony with which they ravage the buffet and carry off their food. Explorers apparently go further, and deal very lightly with the lives and persons of the natives through whose country they pass. So the Turk pays no attention to the inhabitants of the territory he occupies: he makes himself comfortable in his own way in whatever shelter he finds; knocks a hole in the finest fresco if he wants to run a stovepipe through the wall, or pulls down a Greek temple if he wants stones. He builds nothing but what is immediately necessary, and repairs nothing at all. Why should he? He will pass on somewhere else and take another house.

To continue the metaphor of the Turk as a travelling nomad—and indeed it is only half a metaphor—we may say that he brings surprisingly little luggage with him. By an apparent contradiction he is the most and the least assimilative of mortals; he borrows religion, clothes, language, and customs, but remains profoundly Turkish in spite of all. In fact, when one comes to reflect, there is hardly anything which is Turkish and not borrowed. The religion is Arabic; the language half Arabic and Persian; the literature almost entirely imitative; the art Persian or Byzantine; the costumes in the upper classes and army mostly European. There is nothing characteristic in manufactures or commerce, except an aversion to such pursuits. The Turk makes nothing at all; he takes whatever he can get as plunder or pillage; he lives in the houses which he finds or which he orders to be built for him. In unfavourable circumstances he is a marauder; in favourable, a grand seigneur who thinks it his right to enjoy with grace and dignity all that the world can yield, but who will not lower himself by engaging in art, literature, trade, or manufacture. Why should he when there are other people to do these things for him? The palace of Dolma Baghche, built by Abdul Mejid, is a striking example of Turkish method—one cannot say style—in art. The Imperial author evidently said, " Build me a palace as palaces are generally built in Europe, but bigger than any other king's, and put a collection of pictures in it, since that is a suitable thing for a king to have." Externally the result is not unpleasing; the great hall is impressive on account of its size, but marred by the strange device of having painted columns on the walls; the collection of pictures is instructive.

Hence it is that when the Turk retires from a country he leaves no more sign of himself than does a Tartar camp

on the upland pastures where it has passed the summer—
fire-holes, marks of tents, and rubbish, which perhaps render
cultivation difficult, but do not affect the landscape.   Even
as slight are the traces shown at Belgrade, Sofia, and Athens
of the Turkish times, which have left little effect externally,
though they may have retarded the development of the
people.

In fact, all occupations except agriculture and military
service are distasteful to the true Osmanli.   He is not much
of a merchant: he may keep a stall in a bazaar, but his
operations are rarely conducted on a scale which merits the
name of commerce or finance.   It is strange to observe how,
when trade becomes active in any seaport or along a railway line, the Osmanli retires and disappears, while Greeks,
Armenians, and Levantines thrive in his place.   Neither
does he much affect law, medicine, or the learned professions.   Such callings are followed extensively by Moslims,
but they are apt to be of non-Turkish race.   The true Turk
has three spheres of activity.   First, he is a Government
official, a class of which I shall speak elsewhere.   Secondly,
he is an agriculturist and a breeder of animals.   He does
not rejoice in reclaiming barren land or in turning the
mountain-side into fruitful vineyards.   On the contrary, he
has turned wooded countries into deserts by his improvident
habit of cutting down trees for firewood and making no
attempt to plant others in their place.   But he has a keen
appreciation of the simplest and most material joys of
country life.   He likes fine horses, fat sheep and cattle,
good corn and olives, rich grass.   He willingly goes out
shooting, and some of the Sultans were mighty hunters.
But more than all, he likes a good kitchen-garden, where he
can grow fruit and vegetables, succulent pumpkins and
cucumbers, and perhaps regale a party of friends with roast
lamb in a little summer-house under the shade of his mul-
berry and walnut trees.   Thirdly, the Turk is a soldier, not

in the sense that Germans or Russians "make" good
soldiers, but in the sense that the moment a sword or rifle
is put into his hands, he instinctively knows how to use
it with effect, and feels at home in the ranks or on a
horse.   The Turkish army is not so much a profession, or
an institution necessitated by the fears and aims of the
Government, as the active but still quite normal state of the
Turkish nation.   Hence its equipment and commissariat
must not be judged by European standards, nor does the
incapacity or corruption of its officers impair its efficiency as
much as might be supposed.   Every Turk is born a soldier,
and adopts other pursuits chiefly because the times are bad.
When there is a question of fighting, if only in a riot, the
stolid peasant wakes up and shows a surprising power of
organisation and finding expedients, and, alas! a surprising
ferocity.   The ordinary Turk is an honest, good-humoured
soul, kind to children and animals, and very patient; but
when the fighting spirit comes on him, he becomes like the
terrible warriors of the Huns or Jenghiz Khan, and slays,
burns, and ravages without mercy or discrimination.

It is clear that people of such strangely limited activity
can only form a state or society with the help of extraneous
elements.   Of late years the efforts, in many cases successful, of the subject Christian races to throw off the Ottoman
yoke have created a feeling of jealousy and distrust, which
makes the Turk anxious to employ them as little as possible
in the public service.   But this was formerly not the case,
and in the earlier Ottoman history, as has been truly said,
the Sultan was often the only important person of Turkish
race.   Not only the commerce and financing, but the work
of administration was done by foreigners.   One of the most
extraordinary features in the history of this strange people
is the manner in which they were able to make use of other
races, just as the old chieftains in Central Asia collected
round their standards Turks, Mongols, Iranians, and any

one else who was useful. The capture of Constantinople was due in a large measure to the artillery and other contrivances of European artificers: the corps of Janissaries, as well as that of the Palace pages, who often rose to high rank, was composed of the sons of Christians forcibly taken from their parents: many of the greatest naval and military commanders were Italians or other European renegades: many of the most eminent Grand Viziers, Arabs or Albanians: most of the Imperial consorts, foreign slaves. Even the Turkish state, when closely examined, proves to be no more really Turkish than the prose of Saad-ud-Din or the Mosque of St. Sofia.

Yet clearly there must be something Turkish, and that something a force of no mean magnitude, seeing the part that Turks and Turkey still play in the history of the world. The something in question is the Turkish nation itself, as seen best in the provinces of Anatolia, but also in some parts of Turkey in Europe. And here let me say, if I seem to have had little praise for the Turks up to now, that the reason why most people blame them is because they know so little of them. As already explained, the ruling classes of Constantinople are one of the most mixed breeds in the world. The true Turk must be sought in the provinces. Those who have passed even one night in a Turkish village cannot but have been struck by many characteristics of the inhabitants. One is their dignified courtesy and beautiful manners, due no doubt to the consciousness that every Turk, as a member of the ruling race, is an aristocrat. Ragged soldiers and rough shepherds have often an air which makes it impossible for the stranger to feel that they are socially his inferiors. Another characteristic is their hospitality: they will rarely accept money, and when it is proffered merely reply, " I am not an innkeeper." The Eastern Christian, on the contrary, after receiving his guest with effusion, and dwelling on

G

their common religion, often presents an exorbitant bill. In industry, honesty, and truthfulness the country Turk usually compares favourably with his Christian neighbours, and may be trusted implicitly when he has given his word. Alas! that one must add another salient characteristic—his extraordinary stupidity, or rather the extraordinary limitation of his knowledge and interests. Even this expression is not quite accurate, for the Turk has no interests in our sense of the word. Few things throw a more instructive light on the character of a nation than an examination of the ideas which cannot be expressed in their language. Now the Turkish language, copious as it is, contains no equivalent for "interesting." You can say this is a useful book, or a funny book, or a learned book, or a book which attracts attention, but you cannot precisely translate our expression, "This is an interesting book." Similarly you cannot render in Turkish the precise shade of meaning conveyed by the phrase, "I take an interest in the Eastern question or the Mohammedan religion." The various approximate equivalents imply either a more active and less intellectual participation than that denoted by interest, or else suggest that these serious subjects are something queer and funny which it is amusing to hear about.

This *lacuna* in the language has its counterpart in the brain. The ordinary Turk does not take an interest in anything, and his intelligence seems incapable of grappling with any problem more complex than his immediate daily needs. A natural want of curiosity, and a conviction that their own religion contains all that man knows or needs to know, keep the provincial population in a state of ignorance which seems incredible and fantastic. There are thousands, perhaps millions, of people in the Ottoman Empire who believe that the Sultan is suzerain of Europe, and that all other monarchs pay him tribute. There were people in the time of the last Russo-Turkish war who, when they saw shells falling and bursting, thought they were stars brought down from heaven by enchantment. There are Mollahs and Kadis who seriously discuss how near to a mosque a telegraph wire can properly pass, seeing that it is a means of conveying the voice of Satan from one place to another. Most extraordinary of all, there are people who have never seen gold coins, and refuse to accept them in payment. It is well to remember the existence of such people when one hears allusions to the influence and effects of European public opinion in Turkey. But perhaps the characteristic which has been of most vital importance in forming the destiny of the Ottoman race, and has raised to the status of a great nation a Siberian tribe which might otherwise have remained as obscure as the Tunguses, is the feature which was noticed by the old Chinese chroniclers, and which can be observed to-day—the innate sense of discipline. It is the only cement which keeps together the apparently tottering fabric of the Turkish Empire. It makes the half-fed, half-clothed soldier ready to endure every privation, and prevents the corruption and incapacity of the officers from producing the anarchy which would be inevitable in any other country. Probably the lot of the Mussulman peasant is in ordinary times worse than that of the Christian, Armenian or other, yet anything like sedition is unknown, and even complaints are rare. Were a holy war proclaimed, not a man but would be prepared to die in defence of the system of extortion which grinds him down.

Perhaps I ought to allude to another characteristic of the Turk—his laziness. In some ways the popular European idea of Oriental indolence is unjust; for the Turk, as a peasant, is the most laborious and industrious of men, and as a soldier the most enterprising. But clearly many of the qualities which we have already reviewed tend to produce inertia. The Turk is too proud to do many things; too stupid to do others. His religion—

of which more anon—inculcates a fatalism which leads to a conviction that effort is useless. But perhaps what gives more than anything else the impression that the Turk is fundamentally indolent is the fact that all his recreations consist of repose. When the nomad halts, he does not wish to sing, or dance, or distract himself with games after the European fashion, but merely to rest quietly. He has a power of sitting still, doing nothing, and wanting to do nothing, which seems to us animal rather than human. His idea of bliss—what he calls *keif*—is to recline in the shade, smoking and listening to the soothing murmur of running water.

In this essay I am endeavouring to give an account not so much of the organisation and administration of the Ottoman Empire in Europe as of the elements imported into the Eastern question with the arrival of the Turks. One of these is the Turkish language. As the modern Turks are a composite race, so is their speech, especially in its written form, a composite language; that is to say, its vocabulary and, to a limited extent, its grammar are derived not from one stock, but from a combination of several. It may in this respect be compared with English, which is the result of blending Anglo-Saxon with Norman French; only in the case of Turkish the mixture is far more incongruous, as the three languages thus united, the original Turkish, Arabic, and Persian, have nothing in common and belong to absolutely different families.

I have already briefly enumerated the divisions of the linguistic group to which Turkish belongs, viz., the Magyar-Finnish, the Manchu, the Mongol, and the Tartar-Turkish. The last-named group comprises many languages. Their classification is a matter of some difficulty, and I will here merely enumerate the principal divisions and the tribes who speak them, in order to give an idea of how wide is their distribution.

In the extreme east are the Yakuts on the river Lena, a harmless tribe of nominal Christians, whose language is of great interest and importance for philology. To the south-west of them come the various tribes of Eastern Turks in Kashgar, Kulja, Yarkand, and Khotan, who apparently represent the remains of the Uigurs. In the Russian provinces of Fergana and Turkestan, in Bokhara and Khiva, we meet with the names Sart, Uzbek, and Kirghiz. Of these, Sart, though now commonly used as a name for the Jagatai Turkish spoken in those provinces, is, strictly speaking, not a linguistic designation, but denotes a dweller in cities and a merchant, as distinguished from a country-man and agriculturist, called Tajik. But it is also true that the latter word denotes a person speaking a Persian dialect, and presumably of Iranian extraction. Uzbek also is not strictly a linguistic name, but political, and denotes the Turks who are, or were, the ruling faction in the Khanates of Khiva, Bokhara, and Kokand. Kirghiz is the name given to the tent-dwellers who extend from the Pamirs, across Turkestan north of the Sea of Aral to Oren-burg. Their language—at any rate in Central Asia—does not differ materially from the Sart except in being rougher.

In European Russia are two Tartar settlements—one having Kazan as its centre, and one in the Crimea. Both as political powers arose from the Golden Horde, who were Mongols, but the languages of both are now Turkish and closely akin to Osmanli. It is probable that among these Tartars are incorporated many Turanian tribes akin to the Mordvinians and Cheremissians. Tartar settlements extend west as far as Poland, and the Nogai kingdom (Crim Tartary) was an important power in the fifteenth, sixteenth, and seventeenth centuries. South of the Kirghiz, but north of Persia, and between the Caspian and Bokhara, dwell the Turcomans or Turkmens, whose language is intermediate between Sart and the Western Turkish, and who are divided into numerous tribes. Some of the best known are the Yomuts, the Tekkes of Merv, the Sariks of Penjdeh, and the Salors, most of whom have played a political *rôle*. Going farther west, we come to Azerbaijan, a name given to North-West Persia and to the Turkish spoken there and in the adjoining districts of the Caucasus. This language is perfectly intelligible to one who knows Osmanli, but is rougher and employs fewer Arabic words. One of the Azerbaijan families called Kajar has furnished the reigning Persian dynasty. There are also numerous Turkish tribes in South Persia. In Turkey itself it is impossible to say who besides the Imperial family have any claim to be considered as members of the tribe of Osman, but it is clear that there are several classes of Turks who can be at once distinguished from the main body that has taken the name of the leader. Such are the Tartars of the Dobrudja; the Kizil Bashs;[1] Turkish immigrants from Persia, who are hardly Mohammedans; the Yuruks or nomad Turks, who wander about in Asia Minor, particularly in the vilayets of Adana and Aidin; and many settlements in Turkey in Europe who are known as Koniots or Konariots. They are found in the north of Thessaly, in the valley of the Vistritza and north of Salonica, and there seems no reason to reject their own tradition that they are isolated bodies of Seljuks who emigrated to Europe in the pre-Osmanli times.

All the Turanian languages are characterised by the fact that they have no grammatical gender, and that their method of word-formation consists exclusively in appending suffixes to roots and stems. Prefixes and infixes of any kind are unknown. The root, which can often be used as an independent word, is invariable, or nearly so, but its significations may be modified in various ways by the

---

[1] Apparently the Kizil Bashs are Turks, whereas the Kurds, with whom they are often confused, are not.

addition of a syllable or string of syllables. Further, a common but not universal characteristic is what is called vowel harmony—that is to say, the vowels of the root are of the same quality, and the vowels of the suffixes are more or less assimilated to the vowels of the root—an arrangement which undoubtedly facilitates pronunciation. Thus the Turk says *Achajaghiz*, but *gidejeyiz ; pederiniz*, but *kulunuz ; györdüyü, gitdiyi, oldughu,* all of which are analogous formations from the three roots *györ, git,* and *ol.*

In addition to these general features, the Tartar-Turkish languages, all of which are closely allied to one another, have many very distinct characteristics. They have a common phonetic system and vocabulary: they all possess four or five case forms and an elaborately developed verb, which, however, never incorporates the pronominal object. In all of them the negative is not a separate word, but a part of the verbal inflexion, and they none of them form compounds.

There is, of course, nothing in the principle of suffixing alien to an Aryan language. Latin and Greek employ the process to a large extent, but other processes as well, and they differ from the Turanian languages in their variety and irregularity. Turkish formations are monotonous and regular, whereas *mensæ, domini,* and *consulis* are all genitives, and the formations of the Greek verb are so copious that it is impossible to give any rule as to the derivatives in use from a particular root. This diversity is the result of selection from an immense variety of forms. The wealth and inventive power of the Aryan languages provided the materials for at least twice as many formations as are actually in use for any particular noun or verb. Euphony and other causes suggested the retention of some and the rejection of others, so that each word becomes, so to speak, a personality whose idiosyncrasy has to be studied before one can tell with what grammatical forms it would be suitable for it to associate. In Turkish all this is unknown; a grammar is, strictly speaking, a convenience, and not a necessity. The Turkish verb, when displayed in all its details, is a spectacle of appalling complexity, and yet if a person ignorant of the language were given a list of suffixes and half-a-dozen simple rules, he could work out the full paradigm as if it were an algebraical sum. This is possible because in Turkish words the suffix never becomes confounded with the root or stem. It is always possible to divide the word up into its component parts—by strokes of the pen if you will: *chichek-ler*, flowers; *györ-dü-nüz*, you have seen. *Györdü* means he has seen, and *gyor* is the imperative, see. You cannot treat forms like *domini, monui*, in the same way, for if *i* is called a suffix, that which remains when it is removed, *domin* or *monu*, is not a word, and the forms in question imply a long series of changes. This is, in fact, the heart of the matter: multiplicity and irregularity mean that a language has had a history—that it has passed through changes and developments—that it has been the battlefield of various principles, some of which have lost, and some won. They may be compared to the wrinkles and other marks on a face, which tell of the eventful experiences through which the owner has passed. It is noticeable that irregularity, though not confined to Aryan languages, is more universal in them than in any other family.

The agglutinative languages, if compared with one another, show a gradual approximation to the Aryan type. The most perfect specimen of the original state (or at least what we suppose to be the original state) is Manchu, where the suffixes are actually written separately from the word to which they are appended. Finnish, on the other hand, is nearest to the Aryan type, as it presents considerable variety of formation, and owing to the operation of highly complicated rules (which can, however, be worked out with mathematical regularity) the fusion of the root and its suffixes is almost as complete as in Latin. Osmanli stands midway. Such forms as *Istamboldan, Istambolda* (from or in Constantinople), might just as well be written as two words, but case forms like *Kyöpeyin, Kyöpeye* from *Kyöpek*, show an approach to real declension. Also the symmetry of the verb is not absolute, as there are two sets of personal suffixes, one for the past and conditional tense, and one for all the others; but, with a few such slight exceptions, the regularity is complete.

One of the main peculiarities of the Turkish language is that it seems to express thought in exactly the opposite order to our own. In translating any sentence, however long, it is almost always necessary to begin with the last word and work directly backwards to the first. For example—

Der-saadet ile Varna beininde ishleyen Loid Kompaniasinin
Capital and Varna between running Lloyd of Company of
Vulkan vaporina rakiben Istambola gelioruz
Vulcan Steamer on Stamboul to coming are we.

That is, literally, We are coming to Stamboul on the steamer Vulcan of the Company of Lloyd running between Varna and the capital.

The difference between such an idiom and our own is, that whereas we endeavour to make plain the main drift, or at any rate to sketch the form of our sentences in the first few words and then to fill in the detail, the Turk keeps the main point to the end. Just as he accentuates the last syllable of words, he metaphorically accentuates the last word of a sentence, and till he has pronounced it his meaning is doubtful. It is plain that a language with this principle ought to avoid long sentences. Popular Turkish does so: it is terse, vigorous, and clear. But Turkish writers, in their desire to express in their own language all that can be said in Arabic and Persian (which, roughly speaking, place words in the same order as European tongues), fall into the error of constructing sentences of inordinate length. This fault is aggravated by the fact that Turkish possesses no relative pronouns of its own, and, more than this, no words like " when," " where," " because," " that," " if," &c. It is true that equivalents of these useful words have been borrowed from Persian, and that the Turkish interrogatives are used as relatives, but these words and phrases at best hold their own in approved Turkish, and have by no means supplanted the older method. If a Turk wishes to say, " When I was in Constantinople, the man whom you have seen to-day begged that I would write to Ahmed," he probably expresses himself somewhat as follows : " In the time of my being at Constantinople, the to-day seen by you man requested my writing to Ahmed." With such idioms, it is easy to understand how sentences can be swollen out by the insertion of any number of participial and gerundival constructives until they surpass the longest efforts of Greek and German writers.

The admixture of Arabic and Persian has not simplified Turkish grammar, but has merely complicated the vocabulary. Three Turanian languages, Finnish, Hungarian, and Turkish, have been carried from Asia into Europe, and, unaccustomed to express anything but the daily wants, the popular songs and traditions of simple nomads, have been called upon to translate a whole political and religious vocabulary for which they had no equivalent. Hungarian and Finnish have solved the problem by literally translating European ideas in the terms of their own vocabulary. For instance, " spirit " means breath ; it is therefore rendered in Finnish by *henki*, which also means air or breath, and " spiritual," in the sense of religious, is rendered by the corresponding adjective *hengellinen*. In the same way the Germans say *Geist* and *Geistlich*. English proceeds differently, and borrows from Latin without translating. We do not say breath and breathy, but spirit and spiritual. The method of the Turks is the same. They have borrowed wholesale from Arabic, and the transformation of their language has been more striking than the changes undergone by Finnish or Magyar. There are several reasons for this. First, Arabic was regarded as a holy language, therefore the more of its words could be used the better. Secondly, all Orientals, and particularly Arabs, have an idea that fine writing and fine speaking should not be too intelligible. No Turk is in the least astonished if he does not understand a composition written in Turkish. He merely respects the author as having a command of choice expressions. He hardly regards literature or writing as a normal part of life. He expects to understand a story when it is told him, or a business transaction when it is explained to him verbally, but he regards a book or a letter much as an Englishman regards a technical legal document, as a thing he could not possibly write himself, and of which he can only be expected to understand the general drift. Thirdly, the Turks, like most Mohammedan nations, have adopted the Arabic alphabet ("the letters which brought down inspiration") to write their own vernacular. This alphabet, which fate has made cosmopolitan in the Old World, is of all systems of writing least fitted to be so. It is specially adapted to the Arabic language, which has a multiplicity of strange consonants and a peculiar grammatical system which renders it unnecessary to write the vowels fully. Turkish having few consonants and many vowels, cannot be adequately represented by a system of transcription, which, for instance, has only one sign to express *o*, *ö*, *u* and *ü*; one cannot distinguish in writing *oldu*, he was, and *öldü*, he died. Further, the single letter *kef* is used to express *k*, *ky*, *g*, *gy*, *y*, *v*, *w*, and *n*, and the dictionary authorises one to pronounce the word spelled by the three letters *elif*, *vav*, *kef*, as *avin*, *evin*, *evg*, *ün*, *ök*,

and *ön*. In fact, pure Turkish written in the Arabic alphabet
gives rise to so many doubts and uncertainties that it is
hardly suitable as a means of written communication, and it
is usual to employ Arabic words as much as possible in
writing, because there is no doubt as to how they should
be read.

Besides the Arabic element, modern Turkish contains a
considerable amount of Persian.   While Arabic has come to
be regarded in the East as the proper language for religion,
law, and serious discussion generally, Persian is the accepted
tongue for poetry and belles lettres, and the introduction of
Persian words in Turkish is thought a peculiar beauty.   A
number of quite common every-day Turkish words are purely
Persian in their origin, but still the language has never been
so thoroughly incorporated in Turkish as Arabic; and the
free use of Persian words in prose is generally a sign that
the author thinks he is writing literature to be read for the
sake of its style.

The result of this enormous borrowing from two foreign
languages is that there are many Turkish books in which
only the terminations and auxiliaries are Turkish. Johnsonian
English gives one but a faint idea of the real old Stambouli
style, to realise which we must imagine an English work
filled not only with the choicest *sesquipedalia verba*, but with
such phrases as *mutatis mutandis, primus inter pares*, κατ᾽
ἐξοχήν, introduced in every line, the whole welded together
in sentences of enormous length, each with only one finite
verb for its last word.   This style was perhaps intensified
by Byzantine influences.   Linguistically, the effect of Greek
on Turkish is not obvious, but the conquerors of Constanti-
neple adopted many usages from the Byzantine court, and
no doubt the pompous and inflated language of the chrysobulls confirmed all their notions as to what constitutes dignity
in literature.   Poor Turkish language ! Smothered under
a mass of foreign words, its powers of terse and vivid

expression and its wonderfully copious methods of word-formation have been deliberately stunted and neglected, and nothing developed except its capacities for being long-winded and obscure. In popular songs and stories we find a language expressive, harmonious, and forcible, but if we turn to works supposed to be written in fine Turkish, we see poetry which may be compared to the Latin verses of talented scholars, and prose by the side of which Euphues seems unaffected. Such things cannot be dismissed contemptuously, because they represent the taste of a nation. The Turk looks upon writing as a special art, in which it would be highly inde-corous to employ ordinary language. In every town writers may be seen sitting at the street corners or in their little shops. The man who has decided on the grave step of writing a letter communicates the substance of what he has to say to the writer, and the latter embodies it in suitable language, according to his own powers of composition and the rank of the person addressed, for it would be a want of étiquette to address a high official in a style which every-body can understand. If the recipient of a letter is himself not a literary character, he may require to have the document explained to him. It is said that during the Turco-Greek war many Turkish soldiers wrote to their families in Anatolia, saying that they were wounded and requesting remittances, but that these requests, when written down by a professional letter-writer and deciphered by the village sage, were thought to be a statement that the sender of the letter was well and saluted his friends.

I will not here enumerate the Stambuli chroniclers and poets. The curious reader will find their names in any history or encyclopedia. But if I pass them by in silence, it is not from distaste, but from diffidence in recommending a study which can appeal to few. Their writings may be compared to the gateways of Dolma Bagche, or some triumph of calligraphic skill in which the letters and dots are arranged not in the positions which facilitate comprehension, but in those which produce the best artistic effect. Of late years it has become the custom to compose in a comparatively simple style, but the old ornate language can still be read in that column of the newspaper which has the felicity to contain the Court circular or the orders which have come forth from "the centre of Majesty" and which, "honoured in their exit and their issue," burst upon a delighted world. The combination of dignity and fatuity which this style affords is unrivalled. There is something contagious in its ineffable complacency, unruffled by the most palpable facts. Everything is sublime, everybody magnanimous and prosperous. We move among the cardinal virtues and their appropriate rewards (may God increase them!), and, secure in the shadow of the ever-victorious Caliph, are only dimly conscious of the existence of tributary European powers and ungrateful Christian subjects. Can any Western poet transport his readers into a more enchanted land?

There is another kind of Turkish literature, if indeed that name can be given it, consisting of popular songs and stories, which is more natural, more interesting, and perhaps more important than the works of the Court historians and poets. A collection of them has been published by Dr. Ignacz Kunos,[1] together with some plays and riddles, of which latter the Turk, like many other Turanian tribes, is peculiarly fond. Unlike the "Tales of a Parrot" and the "Forty Viziers," which are mostly mere translations, these stories have a peculiar flavour of their own. They are rude and coarse and smack somewhat of the barrack-room, or rather the camp-fire, but it is a camp-fire on some central Asian plain, and the soldiers gathered round it listen with pleasure to tales of miracles and magic, of kings who, at the

---

[1] With a mistaken patriotism he translated them all into Hungarian. Many of my readers will agree with me that it is just as easy to read the original Turkish.

recommendation of dervishes, go down wells, and find at the bottom gardens, dragons, and beautiful princesses. In the same way I have heard an old country Turk relate to an appreciative audience, who showed no signs of incredulity, a story of his youth in which a Kurdish magician, who had three eyes and was invulnerable, played a conspicuous part. The jins, peris, and dervishes certainly suggest the " Arabian Nights," but there is something dreamy and vast in the setting of the stories which reminds one rather of the " Kalevala " and Samoyede legends. It is peculiarly interesting to note how often the hero is some nameless adventurer, who, either by his own energy and intelligence, or by the timely intervention of some supernatural power, rises from nothing to the highest position. Such careers are characteristic of old Turkish life, just as the horseman who rides for ten years across a plain is characteristic of their ideas of physiography and the duty of man.

Perhaps the most original quality of popular Turkish literature is its humour. The average Turk is distinctly a merry man and loves a joke, particularly a practical joke. Wit he has little, and refinement less, but a genuine sense of the ludicrous, and a special fondness for that class of absurdity known as " a bull," and peculiar, as far as I am aware, to Irishmen and Turks.

The classical exponent of this species of humour is Khoja Nasreddin Effendi, the author or hero of a collection of stories known all over Turkey, and constantly repeated, if not exactly read. The Khoja is believed to have lived in Akshehir in the fourteenth century of our era, and is the type of the village Imam. In the printed edition of the stories he is represented as a stout man with enormous spectacles, riding on a donkey and carrying the saddle-bags on his shoulders, as he is said to have done on one occasion from a well-intentioned desire to relieve the animal of their weight. His mind is an extraordinary mixture of stupidity

and shrewdness ; the latter, however, is sufficiently predominant to generally secure him success in the end in
spite of his blunders, and besides, one is never sure how far
he is really dense and how far pretending to be a fool.

The following examples will give some idea of these
stories.

One Friday the Khoja's fellow-villagers insisted on his
preaching a sermon in the mosque, which he had never
done, not having any oratorical gifts. He mounted the
pulpit sorely against his will, and looking round at the congregation, asked in despair, " Oh, true believers, do you know
what I am going to say to you ? "   They naturally replied,
" No."   " Well, I am sure I don't," he said, and hurriedly
left the mosque. The congregation were, however, determined
to have their sermon, and next Friday forced him again
into the pulpit. When he again put the same question
they replied by agreement, " Yes."   " Oh then," he said,
" if you know, I needn't tell you," and again escaped. On
the third Friday the villagers made what they thought must
be a successful plan. They got the Khoja into the pulpit,
and when he asked what had now become his usual question,
replied, " Some of us know and some of us don't."   " Then,"
replied the Khoja, " let those of you who know tell those
who don't." After this the congregation resigned themselves to do without sermons.

One hot night the Khoja slept on the verandah to be
cool. He awoke, however, in a fright, and saw what he
took to be a robber dressed in white climbing over the
garden wall. He seized his bow and immediately sent an
arrow straight through the imaginary burglar. On calm
examination, however, he found that the white object was
one of his own night-shirts which his wife had washed and
hung on the wall to dry. The Khoja accordingly began to
call out " Praise be to God," and other religious exclama-
tions, which awoke the neighbours, who mistook them for

the morning call to prayer. Finding it still wanted several hours to sunrise, they surrounded the Khoja and indignantly inquired what he meant by his untimely piety. " I was thanking God," he replied, " that I was not inside my shirt when I shot an arrow through it."

The country Turk will spend hours in telling such anecdotes, and every new invention is fathered on Nasreddin Effendi. So great is his popularity, that it is said that one Sultan offered to maintain at the Imperial expense any of his descendants who would appear at Constantinople and prove their lineage. Many claimants presented themselves, but on examination were rejected. At last one evening came an uncouth figure with a Konia accent, mounted on an Anatolian pony. He dismounted at the Seraglio gate, and, not seeing clearly in the dusk, tied up his horse to one of the large drums used by the Janissaries, which happened to be lying there. The horse, however, soon found out that he was not attached to a fixed object, and began to drag about the drum, kicking it with his feet. The guard rushed out, the drumming continued ; the word spread in the palace that the Janissaries were in revolt ; among the Janissaries, that the Sultan was going to massacre them, and only after a general uproar was the cause of the disturbance discovered. The claimant for state support was brought before the Sultan and explained the object of his visit and his error. The Padishah and all his council were unanimously of opinion that no further evidence was needed, and that his action could only be explained on the principle of heredity. The allowance was granted at once.

The tomb of the Khoja may be seen to this day at Ak Shehir, in the vilayet of Konia. In the middle of a field or graveyard—I am not sure which, for I saw the site in midwinter when everything was deep in snow—is a small domed building, partly open at the sides ; under the dome is a tomb above which hangs the enormous green turban, about the size of an ordinary umbrella, which the Khoja wore in his lifetime. A small hole is left in the masonry of the grave, as he insisted on having a window through which he could look out on the world of men, and a slab which bears his name gives the year of his death as 1366 A.H., equivalent to about 1950 A.D., by which inscription he is said to have meant to puzzle future generations.

Somewhat akin to the humour of Nasreddin Effendi are the exploits of Karagyöz, a sort of Turkish Punch, During the month of Ramazan the people assemble about three hours after sunset (which gives them time to break their fast and perform the long prayers proper to the season), to witness some musical or dramatic entertainment. This often takes the form of a shadow-play ("the moving show of magic shadow shapes which come and go"), performed by the reflections of dolls about a foot high cast upon a linen screen. The chief characters are Karagyöz (Black Eyes) and his friend Haji Aivat, and though the Turkish police have done much to adjust their costume and reform their adventures, the latter are still either pointless or unsuitable for publication. A great part of the performance generally consists in imitating bad Turkish as spoken by Greeks, Armenians, Albanians, Franks, and others, and is a very salutary discipline for any foreigner who thinks he has mastered the Osmanli language.

CHAPTER IV

EVERY Friday in Constantinople is performed a ceremony called the "Selamlik" or public visit of the Sultan to a mosque for the mid-day prayer. Former sovereigns usually discharged this duty at St. Sophia or one of the principal religious edifices, in each of which is a Mahfil or Imperial pew. Abd-ul-Hamid II., however, has since the beginning of his reign shown a preference for the mosques in the immediate vicinity of Yildiz, and of late years has had one constructed for his special use, and to all intents and purposes in the palace grounds. From the gate of Yildiz descends a steep road bordered on one side by annexes of the palace, which terminate in two pavilions, one devoted to the reception of distinguished persons and ambassadors, while in the other are accommodated the common herd of sightseers. On the other side are a garden and a mosque, white, new, and unpretentious, but deriving a certain grace and dignity from the background, where the coast of Asia and Mount Olympus are seen rising from the Sea of Marmora.

Long before mid-day on Friday soldiers, and spectators, among which latter are hundreds of Turkish women, occupy all the available space. Cohort after cohort of muscular peasants, drawn from every district of this variegated empire, marches up to the clang of barbarous music and takes its place. As a military display the spectacle is remarkable ; as a pageant, disappointing. Turkish ceremonies lack order and grandeur. Detectives thread their way through the crowd. and now and then arrest some poor innocent. Dirty-looking servants from the palace, wearing frock-coats, no collars, and white cotton gloves, hurry hither and thither carrying dinners wrapped up in cloths, which are sent to various persons as complimentary presents from the Imperial kitchen. Fat men of great rank and girth drag about laboriously black Gladstone bags in which they have brought uniforms stiff with gold. Tourists in strange head-gear peep and gibber. Ultimately—for the Caliph avails himself of the letter of the law which says that the mid-day prayer must be said after the sun has begun to decline—ultimately a trumpet sounds. The troops salute and officials hastily confiscate the opera-glasses of the tourists, who are generally so surprised and indignant that they fail to notice what little they might have seen with their eyes. The trumpet sounds again, the soldiers shout " Long live our emperor ! " and a victoria with the hood up comes slowly down the steep road. An old man in uniform, Field-Marshal Osman Pasha,[1] the hero of Plevna, sitting with his back to the horses, speaks with deep respect to some one seen less distinctly under the hood. The carriage stops at a flight of steps leading to the private door of the mosque. The hood is lowered by a spring, and he who sat beneath it alights, mounts the steps, and, in a moment of profound silence, turns and salutes the crowd. He has not come as the chief of a military race should come, on a prancing steed or with any dash and glory. There is no splendour in his dress or bearing; but for the moment that he stands there alone a solemnity falls over the scene, the mean and comic details disappear, and we are face to face with the spirit of a great nation and a great religion incarnate in one man. Of all his subjects assembled there before him, there is not one whose life and fortune do not depend on his caprice ; of all those wild men gathered together from Albania, Arabia,

[1] Since dead.

and the heart of Anatolia, there is not one but would fall down and kiss the hem of his garment did he deign address them, or cheerfully die to preserve his tyranny; of all those women, there is not one but would account his slightest and most transient favours her highest glory; of all those Liberals and Young Turks, there is not one who, when the time for talking is over and the time for action comes, will not submit to his will: for all that the Osmanlis can do, all they may suffer, all the ideas they can form of politics or statecraft are centred in that one personality, and they who would depose him can think of no better expedient than to appoint another like him as his successor.

The power of the Sultan may be regarded under three aspects, which correspond to a triple historical origin. He is the chief of a warlike nomad tribe, the successor of the Greek emperors of Constantinople, and a religious ruler who claims to be the head of Sunnite Islam.

The first of these aspects is naturally the oldest. The early history of the Turkish race shows clearly the beginnings from which the Turkish Sultanate has been developed. The earlier sovereigns affected a military simplicity of life, took the field with their troops as a matter of course, and were regarded as essentially the commanders-in-chief of a nation of soldiers, and only secondarily as civil rulers. Much as subsequent Sultans, many of them timorous prisoners in their own palaces, have done to change the old idea of Imperial power, the unhesitating and unflinching devotion with which the modern Turk obeys the commands and supports the extortion of the Padishah is no doubt derived from former times when the army and nation were one. The earliest notices of the Turks speak of their extraordinary natural sense of discipline, and though this has been undermined by adverse influences, particularly of late years, it still remains a salient characteristic. This is one reason why it is difficult to conceive of a revolution in

Turkey.   Many Sultans have been deposed and assassinated, but invariably as the result of a rebellion of the Janissaries (who were not Turks), or of a palace intrigue, not of a popular movement.   That is to say, if the superior officers appoint a new commander-in-chief, the rank and file do not criticise but obey the new nominee; but they will not of themselves mutiny against their general.   Recent years in Turkey seem to be one long record of discontent, yet the most unpopular orders of the Sultan have always been obeyed; and though much has been talked and written about revolution by the so-called Liberal party, nothing has ever been done.

Among the purely Turkish features of the monarchy must be reckoned the law of succession, which is that the eldest male in the whole house of Osman ascends the throne.   This means that, in normal circumstances, a father is rarely succeeded by his son, but generally by a brother, nephew, or cousin.   Thus, the present Sultan succeeded his elder brother, Murad, who succeeded his uncle, Abd-ul-Aziz, and the heir to the throne is his Majesty's younger brother, Reshad Effendi.   Such a system was advantageous, and even necessary, for a wandering band of soldiers of fortune, who could not be governed by a child or by any one who did not possess real authority.   But its inconvenience grew clear as soon as the House of Osman ceased to be nomad chieftains and became the heads of a great state.   It must be accepted as an axiom that no Oriental potentate, however enlightened, can rid himself of the idea that the heir to the crown is his natural enemy.   The only chance of any community of interest existing between the possessor and the heir of power, or of the heir being allowed to receive an education in any way preparing him for his high destiny, is that he should be the son of the reigning prince.   Among the earlier Sultans the unamiable practice of fratricide practically made the crown hereditary from father to son. On ascending the throne, the first care of a prince was to put to death all his brothers, and most of his sons were kept in seclusion, and not allowed to participate in political or military activity. The progress of civilisation has rendered impossible the systematic murder, but not the incarceration of brothers; and the consequence is that the crown may devolve upon an elderly man who has been kept a close prisoner all his life, and who has no more experience of the world than a monk. Practice, though perhaps not theory, has often allowed a certain amount of freedom in the election of a sovereign—that is to say, if, when the throne is vacant, any prince can, with the aid of the army, seize upon the supreme power and put his competitors out of the way, his title has generally been accepted; but there is no trace in Ottoman history of any attempt to dispute the claims of the House of Osman or to establish a rival dynasty. This is clearly a great element of strength compared with the Christian kingdoms with which the Ottoman Empire contended during many centuries, and it doubtless did much to counterbalance the many weaknesses which have always been inherent in the Turkish state.

But while remaining unalterably faithful to the royal house, Turkish national sentiment clearly dislikes and distrusts the principles of aristocracy and hereditary rank. The connections of the Imperial family do not form a noble or privileged class. Male relatives of the Sultan tend to disappear or to lead very secluded lives; the publication of any list of the princes and princesses is strictly forbidden, and almanacks which have printed such information have more than once been suppressed. Mohammed the Conqueror expressly declared the offspring of princesses to be ineligible for the higher commands,

and the position of spouse to these Imperial ladies carries
no influence and entails most unpleasant domestic arrangements. The Sultan does not marry free women, but
cohabits with slaves, who, on bearing male offspring, are
advanced *ipso facto* to the position of princesses (one can
hardly call them queens). They have in most cases
been separated from their parents at an early age, and
are often ignorant of the country of their birth, so that
no family can become powerful through Imperial alliances.
How real is the danger thus guarded against can be seen
by the fact that, even under the present system, one of
the surest methods of preferment for individual Turks
is to have some connection through their wives with the
Imperial harem. Outside the Imperial family there is
practically no hereditary rank and few hereditary fortunes. The true Turks have no family name whatever;
and though many important clans of Albanian or other
non-Turkish origin possess and are proud of such designations, they are not used at Constantinople. The
Moslim law, by which an estate is divided between the
children, and the Oriental propensity of the Government
to seize and confiscate accumulations of money, discourage
parents from making any attempt to transmit their position to their offspring. In no country is there a more
open career to talent and to luck. The son of a peasant
may still become Grand Vizier, as in the " Arabian Nights ";
and if pliancy and subserviency are rewarded more than
real merit, it must at least be admitted that absolute
and democratic equality among Moslims prevails under
the government of the Sultan as completely as in the
United States.[1]

[1] Of the three chief Turkish titles, Pasha, Bey, and Effendi, the first only
has a definite meaning, inasmuch as it is conferred by the Sultan, and cannot
be otherwise assumed. The two latter are as indefinite as our Esquire. Bey
(the old Bek) is generally used by Government officials, officers, and the sons
of distinguished persons. Effendi (a corruption of the Greek Αὐθέντης) is

The capture of Constantinople transformed in many ways the Ottoman Sultanate. There had naturally been a steady increase in the pomp and state surrounding the sovereign from the time of Osman to that of Mohammed II., but until the capture he had been a chieftain and a general rather than an emperor. For the Turks Byzantium and its lord had long been the centre of the universe and the zenith of human grandeur. They felt that, in conquering it, they and their sovereign had for practical purposes become masters of the world, and had a right to demand the allegiance of all whom they could reach. True, there was the mysterious New Rome in the West—the conquest of which was planned by Mohammed II. and not abandoned by his earlier successors—but it was a long way off, and hardly entered into the sphere of Constantinople. As the Greek emperors had regarded themselves as the natural masters, by divine right, of all Christianity, *in suo orbe*, so the Sultans stepped into the same position, put forward the same claims with much greater vigour, and even took the Greek Church under their protection, as related in another essay. The pomp and ceremony which characterised the Sultan's court, and won for him in mediæval times the title of the " Grand Seignior," were Byzantine in their origin rather than Turkish, as many small points of resemblance show. When we read that there stood in the emperor's palace a golden tree with singing birds and golden lions which roared, we are forcibly reminded of the Turkish taste for costly toys. The humiliating obeisances exacted from European ambassadors at the Seraglio had their counterpart at Constantinople as early as the time of Nicephorus Phocas. The cry, " Padishahimiz chok

applied to the most diverse classes, to Mollahs, Sheikhs, and other learned persons, to native Christians, who rarely use the title of Bey, and to Imperial princes. It is also used with the title Bey, much like Monsieur in French. Thus, in correct Turkish, one should address a Bey as Bey Effendi. Aga or A'a (the old *Aka*) is applied to petty officers and elderly respectable men who have no claim to official rank.

yasha," with which the Sultan is saluted, recalls the " In multos annos " which was addressed to the Basileus in precisely similar circumstances, and the subjects of both monarchs describe themselves as slaves (δοῦλοι or *kullar*) in speaking to their masters. It is said that the Sultan's state barge has still Byzantine eagles carved on it;[1] red ink is still used in official documents, and their involved and inflated style is no doubt partly due to an attempt to imitate the Imperial chrysobulls. Polygamy was, of course, an Asiatic custom; but all that is known of the organisation of the harem shows that it is not merely a collection of wives and concubines for the Sultan, but also a female court, with an elaborate hierarchy and ceremonial. This, no doubt, was to a large extent modelled on the court of the Byzantine empress, who was attended by eunuchs, and, though not without influence, was, at least in later times, kept in a seclusion which we should be inclined to call Turkish if history did not show that the epithet is inappropriate.

To the Greek Empire, also, must be traced a most important peculiarity of the Sultan's power, namely, his limited authority over foreign subjects in his own dominions. In most European states a foreigner is subject to the law of the country in which he chooses to live, and enjoys no greater privileges or immunities than natives. Only foreign Embassies and Legations are exempt from this general rule. Their houses are extra-territorial, and regarded as forming part of the territory of the accrediting state; their members cannot be forced to pay taxes or to submit to the laws of the country where they reside. In Turkey all foreigners enjoy almost the same immunities as diplomatists in other countries. Their domiciles cannot be entered by the Ottoman police without the consent of their respective Consular authorities, and notice must be immediately given to those

---

[1] The present Sultan has not used this barge, at least of recent years, and I have had no opportunity of seeing it.

authorities if any foreigner is arrested. Whenever a foreigner is tried, the Consul of his country (or a representative) must be present, and can protest against the sentence and prevent its execution if he considers it illegal. All suits between foreigners are tried in their own Consular courts, and civil suits between foreigners and Ottoman subjects in mixed courts, at the sittings of which a representative of the Consul must be present. The taxes and dues which can be taken from foreigners are regulated by treaty, and cannot be increased or modified except with the consent of their Ambassadors or Ministers. This system is often described as the Capitulations, a name given to the older treaties concluded with Turkey (that of Great Britain bearing the date 1675), and is generally considered to be due to the fact that Christians cannot live under Mohammedan law. This argument is forcible and convenient, as it enables Europeans to claim similar privileges in other non-Christian countries; but, historically, it must be admitted that the present position of foreigners in Turkey is an outgrowth, not of any special arrangements made when Constantinople passed out of Christian hands, but of institutions sanctioned by the Byzantine emperors.

The Empire, embracing so many nations, each with its own religion, laws, and customs, was naturally inclined to be tolerant of national usages, and to allow a certain measure of autonomy even in the Imperial city itself. During the ninth and tenth centuries many Latins settled in Constantinople, and the authorities seem to have been quite ready to let them form communities and manage their own affairs. In the eleventh century this tendency was greatly strengthened by the policy of the Comneni and Angeli, who, in order to secure the alliance of the great Italian states, encouraged Italian citizens to form settlements, gave them commercial privileges, and allowed them to pay lower dues and taxes than the subjects of the Empire. Such concessions were granted to colonists from

Amalfi, Venice, Genoa, Pisa, and Narbonne. The colony was generally styled community, and consisted of a landing-place with a central commercial establishment (*emporion, fondaco, funduk*); it was under the authority of an official sent out from the mother city, and known as Podestà, Consul, or Exarch, who, with the assistance of a council, managed its religious, judicial, and administrative affairs. The Latin Churches were subject to the Pope, and did not acknowledge the authority of either the Empire or the Patriarch. The Genoese colony of Galata and Pera, √ on the other side of the Golden Horn, was allowed to erect fortifications, and became practically an independent re-public under the style of La Magnifica Comunità. After the conquest of Constantinople, the Turks put an end to the independence and the fortifications of Galata, but did not otherwise interfere with the foreign colonies. As they had always practised a contemptuous tolerance for other religions and customs, they saw no objection to Franks worshipping their own God and deciding their own lawsuits in their own way. As they had no commercial ambitions or aptitudes, they saw no objection to encouraging and protecting the trade of the Franks. In 1540 Capitulations were signed with Venice recognising again the Venetian "Bailo," who had been the head of the ancient community, and similar treaties with the Netherlands, Poland, England, and other Powers succeeded. As, however, the Turks have always been inclined to confuse nationality and religion, they were disposed to think there was one Frankish or Latin race belonging to the Frankish religion, a circum-stance which has often led to uncertainty as to the precise significance of the words Frank and French.[1] After the decline of Genoese influence in Galata and Pera the French

---

[1] The French themselves were partly responsible for this confusion be-tween French and Frank (= European). In the latter part of the sixteenth century their ambassadors constantly appealed to the capitulations granted √ by Suleiman to Francis I., as proving that all nations not represented by an ambassador *at that time* were under French protection in Turkey.

gradually assumed the protectorate of Latin religious establishments in that quarter, and the French Capitulations of 1740 seem to recognise (though not very expressly) the right now enjoyed by France of protecting the Roman Catholic religion in most parts of Turkey.[1] Those who gave the Capitulations doubtless thought they had merely made regulations about the superstitions and squabbles of unimportant foreign Christians, just as by the ecclesiastical and judicial liberty accorded to the Greek clergy they had regulated the position of the numerous body of Christian Ottoman subjects. But with the lapse of time a great difference appeared between the two cases. In the case of Ottoman Christians the Porte has always been able to follow the spirit of its original regulations, which is to keep the Christian in a subordinate position; but in the case of foreign Christians they are obliged to follow the letter of the Capitulations, which exempt from their immediate jurisdiction the most important commercial element in all the large towns, and create a series of *enclaves* of non-Ottoman territory in the Turkish dominions.

Thirdly, the Sultan styles himself Khalifatu-'r-rasuli-'llah, Caliph (or Vicar) of the Apostle of God, or, in Turkish, Khilafet-penahi, the refuge (or protection) of the Caliphate. This title has been borne by the Ottoman sovereigns since 1512, but, as a rule, has been little more than a title. It has, however, been the policy of the present Sultan to make a reality of the spiritual power, and to cause himself to be recognised as not only Emperor of Turkey, but as head of the Sunnite Mohammedan Church all over the world. In view of the great importance of this claim and the considerable success which has attended it, a somewhat detailed examination of the Caliphate will not be out of place. No one who has investigated the subject can fail to have noticed how contradictory are the statements made about the Sultan's claims. Nor is this surprising. There are at

[1] In Northern Albania the Catholics are under the protection of Austria.

least, three versions of every religion—the belief of the vulgar, the belief of the educated, and the real original teaching of the religion, known to few and generally believed by no one. When political considerations are added, the case becomes more complicated, and there may be a great difference between what ordinary persons say they believe and what foreign savants think they ought to believe. If the question were asked, Is the Emperor of Russia the head of the Christian Church? there would clearly be a great difference between the replies of a Russian peasant, a Greek priest, and an English Nonconformist. Now, the claims of the Sultan to be head of the Mohammedan Church are somewhat similar to those which the Russian Emperor might put forward to be the head of Christianity. Large sections of Mohammedans, *e.g.* all Shiahs and the inhabitants of North-Western Africa, reject his claim altogether; educated people in all parts of the world see that it is hardly scriptural; but the majority of his subjects accept his pretensions without question or reserve.

The word Khalifah means successor or deputy, and in the Koran is applied to Adam and David, as the vice-regents of God on earth. After the death of Mohammed, it was essential that some head should be appointed to rule the infant state, and Abu-Bekr, of the Prophet's tribe, was elected, with the appropriate title of the Successor. He was followed by Umar (Omar), Uthman (Osman), Ali, the son-in-law of Mohammed, and Hasan, the son of Ali. Hasan, and his brother Husein were killed, and a new dynasty, known as the Ommiade (Umaiyah) Caliphs, was founded under Muawiyah, son of Abu Sufyan of the Koreish, one of the leading companions of the Prophet. This dynasty made Damascus their capital, and numbered fourteen Caliphs from 661 A.D. to 749 A.D., when Marwan was defeated by Abu'l-Abbas, who was proclaimed Caliph

at Kufa, and founded the dynasty of the Abbasides. This
family were descended from Al-Abbas, the paternal uncle
of the Prophet, and were held in high esteem on account
of this distinguished descent. They subsequently made
Bagdad their capital, and used the title of Khalifah until
the sixteenth century. Their power, however, began to
decline from the middle of the tenth century. From 910
to 1171, a rival dynasty, known as the Fatimites, who
claimed descent from Fatma, the daughter of the Prophet,
ruled in Egypt and North Africa, and in 1258 the Mongols
took Bagdad, and made an end of the Abbaside power.
The uncle of the last Khalifah, however, fled to Egypt,
where his descendants asserted their claim to the spiritual
supremacy of Islam during three centuries. In 1517 the
Ottoman Sultan, Salim I., conquered Egypt, and the titular
Abbaside Khalifah, Mutawakkil Ibn-'Amri-'l-Hakim, was
induced to formally cede his rights and office to the conqueror.

It should also be mentioned that an independent
Caliphate was established in the West by the descendants
of the Ommiades who had been expelled from Damascus.
This dynasty reigned at Cordova from 755 to 1225, and
after the capture of that city by the Spaniards, there were
Sultans bearing the title of Caliph at Granada, until they,
too, fell in 1484.

Let us now turn to the theoretical qualifications of
the Khalifah as laid down by Moslim theologians. It is
agreed that there can only be one Caliph at a time, that
he must be the greatest Mohammedan prince of the age,
and that he must be elected by the Assembly of the
Faithful. Further, there can be little doubt that, according
to all the best authorities, he must be descended from
the Koreish, the tribe of the Prophet. This last qualification is, of course, fatal to the claims of the Sultan, who
cannot possibly be descended from the Koreish or any

other Arabian family, and it is therefore disputed, or rather passed over in prudent silence, by the established Church in Turkey. But the early history of Islam makes it clear that this dogma about the descent of the Caliph is not mere theological pedantry or theorising. From the death of the Prophet—nay, from the very birth of Islam—there was a struggle between two tendencies, the one wishing to spread a spiritual and world-wide religion, the other to establish a theocracy under a military oligarchy. The partisans of the first idea were known as Khawarij, and we are expressly told that they held that the Caliph might be of any tribe or country, and not necessarily of the Koreish. This was considered a heresy, and in the Caliphate of Ali the sect revolted from him, and were mostly killed. There is, therefore, every reason to believe that the tradition declaring that the Caliph must be of the Koreish reposes on historical fact, and there is at any rate no doubt that any one who follows the Sunna must accept this tradition.

For this reason there are probably few Mohammedan doctors, except those in the pay of the Sublime Porte, who are ready to state *ex cathedrâ* that they regard the Sultan as Caliph, or to go beyond the cautious declaration that since the welfare of Islam is the highest object for all good Mussulmans, they should support all arrangements which advance it. But accurate and dispassionate theology is a rare science, and since the Sultan possesses the most striking externals of the Caliphate—the kingdom, the power, and the glory—only the very learned or the very discontented see flaws in his title. In support of his Majesty's claims, it may justly be said that he has " the right of the sword," that is, he is the most powerful Moslim prince of the age; also, on his accession, a form of election is gone through by the Ulema, for it must be remembered that the Caliphate is essentially elective and not hereditary; also, he is the guardian of the sacred cities of the Hejjaz and of Jerusalem, and in his keeping are a fragment of the Prophet's mantle and other sacred relics. It may be doubted how far the ordinary Turk's respect for his sovereign is really due to the fact that he considers him to be the head of Islam. We have already observed that loyalty and obedience are characteristics of the Turkish race, and were seen in their fullest development in the reigns of the earlier Sultans, who had no pretensions to the Caliphate. On the other hand, no pains are spared at the present day to keep his Majesty's sacrosanct character before the eyes of his subjects, and to impress upon them that absolute obedience is a religious as well as a political duty. But the most important feature of the Caliphate is that it enables the Sultan to claim to be the chief, not only of the Turks, but of all Mohammedans of every race and nation. In so mixed an empire as Turkey, where a large proportion of the Moslim population consists of Albanians, Arabs, and Kurds, such a claim is very valuable to the sovereign, and it can also be extended beyond the limits of the Empire. It is difficult to say how far the Sultan's claims are respected outside Turkey among Sunnites; they are certainly absolutely rejected in Morocco and West Algeria. The Sultan of Morocco claims to be a descendant of Fatma, the Prophet's daughter, and in North-Western Africa is unquestionably accepted as the Caliph. The Sultan of Turkey is also not recognised by the various Dervish communities of Africa, including the powerful confraternity of Senoussi, and, as far as I know, no clear statement has ever been made as to the views of Mohammedans in Russian and British-Indian territory. Probably they vary according to the political circumstances of the time. It is said that, before the Russian conquest, the rulers of the Central Asian Khanates did definitely accept the supreme authority of the Sultan, though they were too distant for that authority to have any practical consequences.

Let us now pass to a consideration of the general working of the Turkish state. Every Sultan is a theoretical autocrat, but it depends on each individual sovereign how much he chooses to exert his powers. Practical autocracy is an absorbing occupation, and requires, not only an industrious and intelligent man, but also a system of communications sufficiently developed to enable the head of an empire to keep in touch with the more distant portions. The earlier Sultans who came to the throne after the conquest of Constantinople were not wanting in energy, but their successors soon degenerated. They ceased to lead their armies in the field, and then retired more and more from the business of government, buried in the seclusion of the palace, and engrossed by the enervating pleasures of the harem. But even for those who had the capacity and will for government it was physically impossible to exercise any detailed control over the more distant provinces. In days when there were neither railroads nor telegraphs the Sultan might boast that the governors of Belgrade or Van were his slaves, but as long as they were in their provinces they were necessarily independent in all matters concerning internal administration. The present reign, however, has witnessed a remarkable union of all the conditions required for real autocracy: an extension of the telegraph throughout the Empire; a prince who seerns delights, and is content to devote day and night to the examination of minutiæ which most heads of departments would leave to their subordinates; and, lastly, an absence or elimination of all elements capable of withstanding the Imperial will. Hence Turkey, in the reign of Sultan Abd-ul-Hamid, is probably the nearest approach which the world has ever seen to real autocracy—that is, a state where *everything* is directed by the pleasure of the ruler. It is not merely that all the acts of Ministers must receive the Imperial sanction; the Sultan can and does interfere directly in every department by sending orders to subordinates, and these orders are often contrary to the general regulations which the Government of the Empire is supposed to observe. This state of things is not, strictly speaking, illegal; all power is in theory delegated by the Sultan, and there is no constitutional reason why he should not, as he does, interfere with the exercise of this delegated power. The only restriction on the exercise of his absolute authority is that it must not be contrary to the religious law.

As we have seen, there is no distinction between Church and State in Islam, and the Sultan, as Caliph, is pope as well as emperor. A large part of his special religious duties, however, are discharged by an official called the Sheikh-ul-Islam,[1] who may be regarded as the spiritual counterpart of the Grand Vizier, and also, since there is no distinction between law and religion, as a sort of Lord Chancellor. The Sheikh-ul-Islam is strictly an official; he is appointed and dismissed by Imperial order, and usually changed whenever the Grand Vizier is changed. Although on occasions of ceremony he appears at the head of the clergy, he has in no sense the same sort of authority as an archbishop, and is indeed often somewhat despised by religious persons as a mere civil functionary generally chosen on account of well-tried subserviency. His importance comes rather from his legal than from his ecclesiastical character. He is a supreme court of appeal for cases which can be decided by the Sheri or religious law. In Turkey this law is applied to all questions of real property, even in the case of foreigners, and for the faithful it can be indefinitely extended to all spheres of human life. The decisions of the Sheikh-ul-Islam are known as *fetvas*, and generally consist of a laconic reply to a question framed so as to

[1] Or, more correctly, Sheikhu-'l-Islam.

be capable of being answered by the words *olur* ("it is permissible") or *olmaz* ("it is not permissible"). The question is always drafted in a quite general form, the plaintiff and defendant being called Amr and Zeid, like John Doe and Richard Roe in English law. What occasionally gives to these *fetvas* an extraordinary interest is the fact that the Sultan or Caliph is subject to them as much as any one else. The Sultan may stop the Sheikh-ul-Islam from issuing a *fetva* by dismissal, hanging, or any other process; but once a *fetva* authorising the deposition or death of a Sultan is issued, every good Mohammedan may and ought to obey it. Murad, the elder brother and predecessor of the present Sultan, was deposed in virtue of such a *fetva*.

It is obvious that it is of supreme importance to the Sultan to have a perfectly loyal official as Sheikh-ul-Islam, for he naturally is anxious that the holder of the office should not only issue no *fetva* against him, but also justify his policy. It is, however, difficult, even for a Sultan, to get a *fetva* which is not legally correct. The earlier sovereigns were more than once prevented from ordering a general massacre of Christians, and the present Sultan is said to have applied in vain for a declaration that any form of constitutional or parliamentary government is contrary to the law of Islam. This inflexibility is due, not so much to the high character of the Sheikh-ul-Islam, as to the fact that he has very little choice as to the answer he gives to the question asked of him. In the first place, he only countersigns the *fetva* which bears his name; the substance of the decision is prepared by an official called the Fetva-Emini, who consults the necessary authorities and drafts the document for his signature. But even the Fetva-Emini has no initiative. In the phraseology of Sunnite theology, "the door of free interpretation is closed." Not only is religion limited by the Koran and the Traditions, but the latter must be understood only according to the received

explanations, and no amount of learning or sanctity authorises any one to make use of the smallest particle of originality. The Sheikh-ul-Islam has thus little opportunity
for displaying initiative, but he can refuse to answer the
questions put to him, and if the questions concern "Zeid
the Caliph," this right, though negative, may become very
important.

The Grand Vizier is the Sultan's representative for
secular matters. Vizier (more correctly Vazir or Vezir)
means one who bears a burden, and is hence applied to a
Minister who takes up the burden of public affairs in order
to relieve the sovereign. The word is, however, little used
by the Turks, except to denote a rank as opposed to an
office, and the Grand Vizier is always known by the title of
Sadr Azam.[1]

He was originally the only recipient of the Sultan's
delegated power, and, as such, stood between the sovereign
and all the other officials of the Empire. He still nominally holds this position, and Imperial orders are made known
to the provincial authorities by a Vizirial letter. But his
real importance has been greatly diminished by the habit,
which has increased during the last few years, of sending
communications direct from the palace to other Ministers,
and even to quite small officials, so that it sometimes
happens that the Grand Vizier's instructions are met with a
respectful statement that contrary orders have been received
direct from the Sultan. The palace of Yildiz has become
almost a Government office. Among its officials are a large
number of secretaries, whose business is to convey his
Majesty's orders to their destination. It is not usual for
the Sultan to sign his commands, but no official would
venture to disobey a letter from one of the private secretaries making known to him the tenor of an Imperial

---

[1] A'zam means "greatest," and Sadr literally "breast," hence the foremost
part of anything, the seat of honour or the principal post in a state.

Irade. It is characteristic of the present state of Turkey
that one hears little of Hatti-Sherifs, Firmans, or Vizirial
letters, but that it is hardly possible to speak of any kind of
business without constant reference to Irades; that is, the
expression of the Sultan's will communicated by his secretaries.

There are at present twelve Ministers, namely, War,
Justice and Public Worship, Marine, Foreign Affairs, Interior, Finance, Evkaf (" pious foundations "), Public Instruction, Civil List, Commerce and Public Works, Police, Mines
and Forests. They all hold their office at the Sultan's pleasure, as does also the Grand Vizier. Sometimes the whole
Cabinet is changed, and sometimes single members of it.
In either case the change is generally sudden, and unac-
companied by any explanations. The importance of the
Ministry of War is somewhat diminished by the existence
of a special Military Commission which sits at the palace,
and by the independent organisation of the Artillery under
a Marshal at Tophane. Similarly the Ministry of Police
is entirely separate from the Ministry of Justice, and the
Custom-House is practically separate from the Ministry of
Finance. Such arrangements show a tendency to prevent
each Minister from having a real grasp of his department,
and to break the official world up into a number of artificial
divisions which have no point of union except the sovereign.

There are also two Councils. One is the Council of
Ministers, consisting of the Grand Vizier, the Sheikh-ul-Islam,
and most of the Ministers. This Council sits at the Sublime Porte, but is also frequently summoned to the palace,
where it meets in a room adjoining that occupied by the
Sultan, and during its deliberations communicates frequently
with his Imperial Majesty by means of messages, but without seeing him. Of all privileges enjoyed by Turkish
officials, the highest and rarest is the right of being allowed
to appear unsummoned in the Imperial presence and submit

one's views.   Any favourite who can do this becomes more important than the highest functionaries who have only the right of addressing the Sultan when called before him. The Council of State is a much larger body, somewhat resembling our Privy Council, and divided into a number of sections, such as the Legislative Section, the Financial Section, the Section of Appeal, and the Section of Cassation.   It does not correspond to the Senates or Parliaments of other countries, but is perhaps the hardest-worked body in Turkey, as it examines and sometimes decides upon a multitude of matters referred to it either from below by the various departments, or from above by the Sultan.   Turkey, though autocratic, is also a land of bureaucracy and circumlocution.   Cases are referred from one Ministry to another, from the central to the provincial authorities, or *vice versa*, from the Ministers to the Council of State, from the Council of State to the Council of Ministers.   What renders this process a peculiarly dreary farce is the knowledge that the decision in most cases does not rest with any of these bodies.   At any moment of the circumlocution process the Sultan may, if so disposed, settle matters by issuing an Irade, and if the case is of the smallest importance, after every one has had their say, it will be submitted to his Majesty, and remain an indefinite time until he has leisure to pronounce on it.   The palace of Yildiz is literally and metaphorically filled with appeals and dossiers on which the dust has gathered undisturbed while they await the Imperial attention.

Perhaps the best-known name in connection with the Turkish government is "Sublime Porte."   This phrase, like "The Sweet Waters," "The Golden Horn," and others which sound Oriental, is not really so, but European in its origin. It is never used by the Turks themselves as a synonym for the Ottoman Government, which styles itself officially "Hukyumet-i-seniye," or the "Glorious Government."

"Sublime Porte" is an imaginative translation of Bab-i-Ali, which means the "High Gate." There is some dispute as to what exactly was the gate originally so designated, but at present the name has a definite local signification, and is applied to the building in Stamboul which contains the offices of the Grand Vizirate, the Council of State, the Foreign Office, the Ministry of the Interior, and various Commissions; but, in diplomatic correspondence written in European languages, the phrase is used as equivalent to the Government of Turkey, much as the phrase Cabinet of St. James is applied to the British Government.

Turkish public offices have perhaps larger clerical staffs than those of any other country. Practically only two careers are open to a Turk of good family educated at Constantinople—the Army and the Civil Service; and almost every young man who is not an officer spends some time in one of the many bureaux of Stamboul. I say advisedly spends some time, for it would be inaccurate to imply that the majority of these Kiatibs or clerks do anything or receive any money. Entrance into a public office is for a young Osmanli much what entrance into Oxford or Cambridge is for a young Englishman. He becomes a man; dons a black frock-coat, and often assumes an additional name to be used by all the world, that which he has previously borne being reserved for the family circle and intimate friends. The higher officials have, of course, duties to attend to, and employ such of their subordinates as suit them best; but the number of the latter is much greater than is necessary, and a large proportion never do anything but smoke cigarettes and drink coffee. Turkish offices always seem full of people; ten or fifteen clerks will often be congregated in one apartment, and even those who have private rooms receive a continual stream of visitors and petitioners, and apparently never engage in any consecutive work. One result of this system is that there is little secrecy. It is nearly always possible to find out what is being done about a given matter, though the inquirer may sometimes be perplexed by the variety of versions which he will hear. Another natural result is that no private affair receives any attention unless the persons interested continually remind the officials concerned of its existence, request the heads of departments to order the necessary papers to be written, and, when the order is obtained, beg some friendly clerk to execute it as a personal favour. Yet one cannot accuse the Sublime Porte of sterility; few public institutions have produced so much imaginative literature, and most aspects of the Eastern question are periodically treated in circulars to the Powers, which generally present quite novel and original statements of the case.

Before I proceed any further I had better emphasise a distinction which has probably already dawned upon the reader—that between the real and the paper government of Turkey. If one takes as a basis the laws, statistics, and budgets as printed, it is easy to prove that the Ottoman Empire is in a state of unexampled prosperity. Life and property are secure; perfect liberty and toleration are enjoyed by all; taxation is light, balances large, trade flourishing. Those who have not an extensive personal acquaintance with Turkey may regard such accounts with suspicion and think them highly coloured, but they find it difficult to realise that all this official literature is absolute fiction, and for practical purposes unworthy of a moment's attention. Once in Russia, which is in many ways an Eastern country, I missed a steamer on the Neva owing to its having left a certain pier half-an-hour before the time advertised. I tried to appeal to the pier-keeper's sense of justice by pointing to the time-table displayed in his office, but he could not see the point of my argument and merely replied, " You should never pay attention to what is printed. " You never should, at any rate in Turkey.

No reform is clamoured for which does not already figure in the statute-book; no complaint is made which cannot be disproved by statistics. This is partly due to the Oriental idea of literature. Just as no one would use the language of everyday life in the most trifling letter, so everyday facts are felt to be inappropriate to literary composition. You cannot write a letter without describing yourself as a slave and ascribing all virtues to your correspondent. Similarly you cannot write a history without describing the Sultan as ever-victorious, and you cannot write of his country without describing it as well defended and prosperous. The natural divorce between literature and facts is so complete that the Oriental attaches little more importance to striking statistics or to declarations of the Imperial clemency than he does to epistolatory compliments. He feels that it would be rude and bad style to say anything else.

But there are other reasons for the difference between the real and the paper government. The true Turkish government is remarkably simple, for it consists of one principle, and of one only, namely, that Turks are a ruling race, and both individually and collectively superior to all Christians. The importance of this principle lies in the fact that it does not depend on the Sultan or any particular class, but that it is the intense conviction of the whole Turkish nation. Eastern peoples, not only in Turkey, but in many other countries, form a solid national conspiracy against foreign and Christian influence. They know when their Government is forced to give way against its will; they know when orders are meant to be obeyed, and answer the rein in a moment; they also know when they are not meant to be obeyed, but are what are called "watery commands," and then they do not obey them. It is an arduous task to make the Turkish Government issue a distasteful order; but the foreigner feels that the situation is indeed hopeless when he sees that the order obtained at the cost of such pains is not a victory, but merely a first step in the struggle. Unless the Porte are continually reminded of its existence, it is ignored. If they are so reminded, they probably reply by copious reports from the provincial authorities, proving that the proposed measures are disastrous and impossible of execution, and perhaps by petitions extorted from Christians begging that they may be left as heretofore to the clemency of the Imperial Government. And in the end this national conspiracy, this invincible inertia, nearly always wins the day. The Turk changes not; his neighbours, his frontiers, his statute-books change, but his ideas and his practice remain the same. He will not be interfered with; he will not improve; he will hear neither threats nor advice; he will not turn aside from his old path to please his friends or escape his enemies; he will follow it to the end, though he may see clearly where he is going. There have been many Turkish constitutions, laws, and ordinances elaborated by Mahomed II., Suleiman, Abd-ul-Hamid II., and many others, but it is unnecessary to examine them, because there is no growth in the Turkish state. The British state is only intelligible as the outcome of a long series of historical changes. The French state is only intelligible as a reaction against other forms of government, and a result of social convulsions. But the Turkish state is simply what it always has been; its written laws and institutions are merely temporary forms, almost disguises, which clothe for a time without really affecting the vital realities of Turkish rule. I will therefore not attempt to trace the development of Turkish institutions or examine the successive reforms, including Parliamentary government, which have been introduced, but will merely try to give some facts about the existing administration.

The internal organisation of the country is nominally subject to the Minister of the Interior. The Empire is divided into a number of provinces called vilayets, at the head of each of which is a civil governor-general called Vali. There are six such provinces in European Turkey, namely, Salonica, Monastir, Adrianople, Scutari, Janina, and Kossovo. The district of Constantinople has a separate jurisdiction. Each vilayet is subdivided into three or four sections (Mutesarrifats or Mutesarrifliks) under a governor called Mutesarrif. These subdivisions were formerly called Liva or Sanjak, both meaning " flag," and the latter word is still in common use. The Mutesarriflik is in its turn subdivided into Kazas, each under a Kaim-makam or Lieutenant, and each Kaza into a varying number of Nahies, or aggregates of from five to ten villages, under a Mudir. All these officials are civil servants. Except in rare cases the Vali has no control over the troops; and the central power, always fearful of provincial officials becoming too powerful, makes use of the antagonism which easily arises between the civil and military administrations.

The Judicial administration is also independent of the Executive, but the two branches understand one another very well when it suits their convenience, and, apart from this, the Executive has authority, if not to try, at least to arrest and imprison. So common is the exercise of this power that it is esteemed an act of Imperial clemency when the Sultan orders the release from prison of " all persons against whom there is no charge." Two, if not three, systems of jurisprudence coexist in Turkey. One is generally known as the Sheri, or religious law, which is based on the Sunna, and administered by Cadis, the supreme court of appeal being the Sheikh-ul-Islam. This law is religious only in the sense that it is derived from religious works. In the case of Mohammedans it may be applied to all transactions, but its peculiar importance depends on the fact that all questions respecting real property, whatever be the religion or nationality of the parties concerned, must be decided according to its principles. Real estate in the Ottoman Empire is of three kinds: *mulk* or private property, crown lands or *mirie*, and *vacouf* or property belonging to religious institutions. This last category is very extensive, and gives rise to most complicated cases. It is the custom among Turks not only to leave lands directly to mosques or other pious foundations, but also to devote part of the income arising from a piece of property to such purposes. In either case the property becomes *vacouf*, and its use and transfer are regulated by special rules, which, it need hardly be said, generally prove inconvenient to non-Moslims.

As a counterpart to the Sheri, native Christians are allowed to have ecclesiastical courts, which are empowered to decide cases affecting Christians of a particular sect in such matters as marriage, divorce, and inheritance.

The general civil law of the Empire is contained in a Code based on the Code Napoléon, and applicable to both Moslims and Christians, and (with certain modifications which I have mentioned in speaking of the Capitulations) to foreigners as well as to Ottoman subjects. It is administered by a series of courts and officials who are under the Minister of Justice, whereas the Cadis are under the Sheikh-ul-Islam.

The conditions of life in the capital and in the provinces are so different that it will be well to speak of them separately. The only town which can compare with Constantinople is Salonica. Though it has never been the Imperial residence, its long and eventful history, its polyglot and cosmopolitan population, and the strong European and non-Turkish influences to which it is continually subjected, are all points of resemblance with the greater city.

Constantinople has never been a national capital. It was not Latin under Constantine; it was not Greek under the Greek-speaking Emperors; it is not Turkish under the Turks. It is and always has been a meeting-place where the races of Europe and Asia gather together, and in so doing lose more or less their national peculiarities and tend to assume the type which is called Levantine. Nothing, perhaps, gives one a better idea of the character of its inhabitants than what is styled an *Almanach à l'usage du Levant*. Every leaf which is daily torn off is a museum for the chronologer, philologist, and student of comparative religion. It bears inscriptions in six languages: Turkish, French, Bulgarian, Greek, Armenian, and Spanish in Hebrew letters. It records the flight of time according to five systems. Thus, the same day is described as December 9, 1898, new style, or November 27, old style (followed by the Greeks, Bulgarians, and Armenians); or Rejeb 26, 1316, for the devout Mohammedan, who counts from the Hijra; or Teshrin-i-sani 27, 1314, for the official Turk, who follows the "financial year" (a remarkable invention of the Sublime Porte); or Kislev 25, 5659, for the Jew who does not pretend to be a Christian. Nay more, the *Almanach* extends the same large impartiality to all religions. It registers the disagreeable ends of Greek, Bulgarian, and Armenian martyrs, and bids the believer rejoice, according to his particular convictions, over the Immaculate Conception of the Blessed Virgin, the Prophet's journey to heaven on a winged steed, and the Dedication of the Temple of Jerusalem—all these exhilarating events being commemorated on the same date. Besides this, it informs us that the day in question is the 30th after Kassim,[1] that twelve o'clock Turkish or sunset is at 4.30 P.M. *à la franca*, and

---

[1] The peasantry as a rule use none of the calendars given above, but divide the year by two feasts, Kassim and Hidrelis, the former of which is regarded as the beginning of winter, the latter of spring.

that mid-day is 7.23 Turkish.[1] How unlike the narrowness of the almanack which hangs on the wall in front of me at present, and assumes that all decent people belong to the Established Church and are chiefly interested in knowing what are the lessons for the day! The little Levant almanack does, it is true, give a certain pre-eminence to Mohammed and his celestial tour; he sprawls over the middle in triumphant Arabic flourishes, crowding the Bulgarian and Armenian martyrs into corners, and casting vowel points and spots parlously near the Immaculate Conception. But though recognising the predominance of Islam, it addresses a public which has no one language, religion, or code of institutions. It wishes to be useful to the Pasha and the Rabbi; to him who speaks Bulgarian and to him who speaks French; to him who thinks the sun sets at 4.30, and to him who considers that mid-day is twenty-three minutes past seven.

The population of Constantinople is like the almanack One does not know whether to wonder most at the union between these heterogeneous elements or at the utter want of union and sympathy between residents in the same city. In some few quarters the various communities are found living together, but as a rule they inhabit separate districts. Turks live chiefly in Stamboul, Nishan Tash, and on the Asiatic shores of the Bosphorus; the Jews at Kuz-kunjuk and Haskeui; the Armenians, Greeks, and Franks in various parts of Pera, Galata, and the European shore of the Bosphorus. The separation is greatest between the Mohammedans and the Christians. The native Christian is generally at least bilingual, but many Turks are profoundly ignorant of all languages and customs but their own, and many inhabitants of Pera know little more of Turkish and

[1] Turkish time is based not on mid-day like ours, but on the sunset, which is always twelve o'clock. As sunset is a variable hour, a Turkish watch has to be regulated at least once a week. All the Bosphorus steamers and some of the railways keep Turkish time.

the Turks than do the dwellers in London. Men jostle one another in the streets, salute one another, cheat one another, kill one another, and at the end of the day retire into worlds as absolutely different as if they departed for homes in France, Athens, and Kurdistan. But yet these people do not really belong to different nations. Different though they be in speech, dress, food, and customs, they are not separated from one another by belonging to different governments with different problems and ambitions. They have mostly no political life at all, and their ideas as to nationality are eminently characteristic. Most of them are, of course, Turkish subjects, but nothing is valued more than the possession of a foreign nationality, because, as explained above, it withdraws the holder from Ottoman jurisdiction and entitles him to Consular protection. We naturally think of nationality as being a matter of birth and race, but in the Levant it is regarded as a kind of privilege which may be acquired, lost, or changed. No one sees anything incongruous in one brother being an Englishman, a second a Belgian, and a third a Turkish subject. On the outbreak of the Turco-Greek war, Hellenic subjects were placed under certain disabilities which affected their business. One of them came to me and asked if he could not be made then and there a British subject. He was distressed to find it was impossible; but a day or two afterwards I met him satisfied and smiling. He had become a Servian, and all was right again.

The word Levantine is not considered complimentary, and I use it reluctantly, but for the very good reason that it denotes a definite type, and that there is no synonym. The fact is that the name does not exactly suggest honest and honourable dealings. Courts and Imperial cities do not tend to develop the rugged and sterling virtues, but rather encourage diplomacy and the arts of pleasing. For many centuries before the Turkish conquest the Greeks had been characterised by astuteness rather than heroism, and probably the Byzantium of the Angeli and Palæologi was in essentials much like Pera to-day. But it cannot be denied that the Turkish conquest intensified all the faults of the inhabitants. They had to learn subserviency, not only to an emperor, but to a governing class of scornful aliens. The only road to power and prosperity lay in pleasing and flattering the Turks. The latter, with their incapacity for administration and commerce, required continual assistance; but they continually let the Christian know that, though he might be intellectually their superior, and apparently indispensable, he was but a dog in their eyes, who might be whipped or killed in a moment of caprice. Every Christian who served the Turk was working against his own religion and the traditions of his own race. Whatever ingenuity he might display, whatever rewards he might gain, he could not be stirred by a noble ambition or feel he was labouring for a great cause. The number of foreign colonies at Constantinople had doubtless always afforded employment for the characteristic Levantine profession of go-between, interpreter, dragoman, agent, or whatever it is called. The Turks increased this employment tenfold, for they understood neither the languages of their subjects, nor anything of trade and finance. As they farmed the taxes, so they farmed every sort of business. The agent who conducted any transaction was expected to produce a certain sum at the end. Of course, he had to make his profit; how he made it, how much he and his subordinates took, the Turk did not care.

This method of transacting business is ingrained in the Levantine nature. Their conduct cannot be justly compared to that of an Englishman who should take a bribe. According to their ideas, all the parties to a transaction, official or commercial, must make something out of it. How else should they live? The idea that they can live on their salaries is ridiculous; for the salaries are, firstly, inadequate, and, secondly, not paid. The Turk dislikes giving fixed wages of any kind, and if he has a European coachman or governess who want to receive their money regularly and put it in a bank, he regards them with unfriendly suspicion. He keeps and feeds his dependents, gives them a largess now and then, and lets them have plenty of opportunities for making money out of shopkeepers and petitioners. Though, in Constantinople, one is always hearing stories of vast bribes and vaster peculation, no one seems to get rich. In other countries such operations, if successful, produce show and splendour, but here not at all. This is partly because, as the proverb says, " Ill gotten, ill go." He who receives a bribe of £50,000 has probably to distribute £40,000 to various persons who must be kept in good-humour. But, also, no one dare draw attention to himself; and if any one did dare, it would be hard to find an occasion for display. You cannot keep racehorses or yachts, or give balls in Constantinople. This brings us to another feature of Levantine life—the extraordinary interference on the part of the police and Government with individual liberty. It is difficult to make the system of espionage which prevails at Constantinople seem credible. It is customary to regard it as a recent abuse, but it is doubtless of very old date. Travellers in the seventeenth century mention that no one dare leave his house at night for fear of the spies. For the last few years, at any rate, Constantinople has been overrun by them. All public gatherings, except those for religious purposes, have been forbidden, and even social and family festivities rendered impossible. No Turk dare associate with foreigners, or give a large dinner-party to his own people, and two or three Turks of eminence cannot safely meet in a private house. The whole city groans under the tyranny of the Minister of Police. It is inevitable that spies in their desire to show zeal should invent baseless accusations. The highest functionaries may be summoned in the middle of the night, and interrogated by persons much their inferiors in rank on utterly frivolous charges; and any one who should venture to oppose this régime would find his fortunes and perhaps his life imperilled. It is singular that the Turks should endure tyranny so aggravating and so unnecessary, for no doubt it is felt more by the Turks than by the Christian inhabitants. One can only reply that every nation gets more or less the government it deserves; and that, if the Turks submit to such an imposition, it is because both their good and bad qualities, their loyalty and obedience, as well as their inertia and want of ideas, contribute equally towards a passive attitude. Yet I doubt if the system is really kept up by secret executions and torture, as often reported. My scepticism does not result from lack of information, for I have heard the most detailed accounts from natives of midnight horrors and wholesale drownings in the Bosphorus; but, though no doubt many persons have been somewhat strictly interrogated, I do not believe that many have been tortured, in as far as highly uncomfortable detention can be distinguished from torture. If one considers the last five or six years in Turkey, it will be found that not more public men have died than in other countries; that the evidence on which their deaths are attributed to poison is very slight, and that those who are suspected of disloyalty and liberal views do not disappear more than the others. On the other hand, there is no doubt that people have been summoned in the night, placed on board a steamer, and sent off to distant parts of the Empire, nominally as officials, but really as exiles. The real evil is that all the joy of life, all freedom and originality, all political, intellectual, and social activity, are destroyed by the ubiquity of this espionage. A man is spied on by his colleagues, his subordinates, and his servants, who all write reports of his daily doings, and no one can tell what silly invention may attract attention. Spies are themselves spied on; and sometimes the spy and his victim are on friendly terms, and the latter revises the reports made on his own conduct.

There is no doubt that Christians are much better off in the great cities than they are in the provinces. In Constantinople they do not feel the evils of the present administration more than the Turks, and perhaps not as much. It is true that, since the attack made on the Ottoman Bank in 1896 and the subsequent massacre of Armenians, there has been a tendency to accuse native Christians of conspiracy, and no doubt a corresponding amount of blackmailing has taken place; but, on the whole, the Christian in Constantinople is at least as well off as the Moslim. In the first place, the great evils of provincial administration are absent. The taxes are light, and not farmed or collected by soldiers. The Greeks and Armenians have a natural genius for trade, which causes both communities to be in a flourishing condition; and, though they are hampered by restrictions which make both material and moral progress difficult, they are in an ordinary way left much to themselves. The business aptitudes of the Christian are so incomparably superior to those of the Moslim that they infallibly secure for him a better position unless the balance is redressed by the use of physical force. Before the massacres of 1895 and 1896 one would have said that their lives and property were safe. Certainly after these outbreaks this statement can only be made in a very qualified manner; but such massacres are exceptional eruptions, and if the Christians are living on a volcano, they are still living as people often do in such circumstances, quite comfortably. In the face of the fact that these outbreaks passed unpunished by Europe, it may seem paradoxical, but I think it is true, to maintain that the Christians in Constantinople have relatively little to complain of in the way of permanent oppression, because some Power or other is always ready to air their grievances. But there is no one to protect the Turks, and prevent their own Government from pressing on them. And very rightly too. I am no hater of the Turks, and think that in many ways they are better than the Rayahs. But they are the ruling race; they have only themselves to thank for whatever oppression they endure, and it is ridiculous to appeal to foreign Powers, as "Young" Turks often do, for aid in throwing off their self-imposed yoke.

Still, Turkish life in Constantinople is a gloomy business. The rigorous measures adopted by the police to prevent all assemblies stop amusement, whether public or private; the censorship has almost destroyed literature, and everything of human interest is carefully excluded from the press. Turkish papers revel in essays on Madagascar, and such-like distant topics, but dare not say a word respecting the politics of Turkey and the neighbouring countries. No foreign book which contains any criticism on the Ottoman Government or the Mohammedan religion is allowed to enter the country, and this prohibition is carried so far as to exclude from Turkish soil, not only authors like Dante and Shakespeare (who spoke disrespectfully of the Prophet), but even all encyclopædias and guide-books.

All life is regulated by Irades. Now an Irade is not so much a command as a permission. The standing order is, "Thou shalt do nothing at all," and every deviation from this negative attitude requires a special authorisation. Without such permission no Turk, especially if he be a man of rank, can leave the capital, frequent the society of foreigners, or conduct any sort of business. He cannot marry his children, or acquire property, or devote himself to any pursuit or study, without his actions being brought to the notice of the Government and interfered with. He probably finds himself obliged from time to time to contribute large sums to patriotic or religious funds, and is reduced to various subterfuges to hide the real amount of his fortune.

In contrast to the cosmopolitan life of the capital, it may be said that the provincial government is thoroughly Turkish. We naturally find everywhere an abundance of non-Turkish population and non-Turkish customs; but the whole system and spirit of administration are essentially Ottoman, and need not astonish us, if we consider the earlier Turkish states, such as the vast, loosely-connected Empire of the first Seljuks, reaching from Samarcand to the Persian Gulf. It was impossible that one government— that is, one man—could really control such an Empire; at the most, he could but receive a deputation from the distant portions, if they were loyal, or, in the contrary case, send troops to suppress a revolt. The Turkish mind has never outgrown this stage. Their notion of sovereignty is taking tribute, and gaining as much advantage as may be for Osmanlis out of a given territory; but they have no idea of uniting their provinces into a compact whole, or of establishing a community of interest between the rulers and the governed. In considerable districts of Turkey the population has never been really subdued, and the Government do not attempt to enforce their authority. Such are the Dersim, and large parts of Kurdistan and Arabia in Asia, and most of Albania in Europe. Other parts, such as Bulgaria, Crete, and Samos, have been detached from the Empire by the interference of Christendom, and are now connected with it by merely nominal ties. But the Turk does not notice this. If the Sultan confirms the appointment of a governor, if a Prince or Khedive pays a respectful visit to the sacred threshold of Yildiz, his notions of sovereignty are satisfied. Neither does he concern himself about the prosperity of the remoter districts of the Empire.

It was an old Turkish maxim that it is a good plan to keep the border districts in a state of devastation, because such frontier lands render it difficult for an enemy to penetrate into the Empire. This principle is not perhaps consciously followed by the modern Turks, but one is often reminded of it when one enters Turkey. One cannot logically expect the Ottoman Government to encourage the spread of trade and commerce, or to develop the material resources of their dominions, because they know that Christians will profit thereby at the expense of Turks, and, worse even than this, foreign companies, not amenable to Turkish jurisdiction or Turkish methods, will establish themselves in the Turkish dominions and curtail the Turkish power.

At Constantinople at least two Ministers and many important officials are Christians, but in the provinces hardly any considerable post is now held by a non-Moslim. There are no Christian Valis or Mutesarrifs, few, if any, Christian Kaim-makams, and only a small proportion of Christian Mudirs. The office of Christian vice-governor is not really an exception to this rule, as I shall subsequently explain.

In the chief town of every province or district is a building called the Konak, in which are the Government offices. It is not the residence of the governor, who usually arrives there every day after his morning meal, taken about 10 A.M., and departs in ample time to re-enter the bosom of his family before sunset, or twelve o'clock Turkish. At Salonica the New Konak is a magnificent structure which compares favourably with any public office in Europe; but this is an exception, and as a rule the Government buildings are whitewashed, barrack-like buildings devoid of all architectural pretensions. About the doorway hang fierce-looking soldiers with broken teeth and battered uniforms. In the centre is a muddy courtyard, and the ground-floor is devoted to stabling and stores. We

leave our goloshes at the foot of a somewhat rickety staircase of unpolished wood and arrive at the first floor, a
wooden uncarpeted corridor, thronged with soldiers, with
petitioners who object to being dismissed, and with people
who have been summoned and only wish they could get
away. Some wear frock-coats and some sheepskins. A
number of rooms open off the corridor, from which they
are separated not by doors but by heavy curtains. Over the
entrance of each is an inscription—such as " The Secretary,"
" The Guardian of Papers," " The Defterdar (Financial Agent)
of the Vilayet." Soldiers raise the curtain which closes the
most important of these apartments, and we are ushered
into the presence of " him who confers honour on the
governorship of the glorious Vilayet of ——, the prosperous
and successful Mehemet Pasha." His Excellency sits behind
a desk of quasi-European style, or, if he be one of those who
wish to emphasise that they are " Old " Turks, on a low divan.
The carpets and other appointments are fairly luxurious,
but there is almost invariably a spider's web in the window,
and the panes are broken. Round the room are many
chairs, on which sit several silent, impassive men, some
perhaps in turbans and flowing robes, but most in Stambouli frock-coats, an ungainly garment which buttons close
round the neck and shows no linen. Some of them are
certainly spies on the governor, and others friends who can
control the reports of the spies. Business seems to continue during the visit. Secretaries in frock-coats come in,
stand before the governor with their arms folded, and then
hand him immense strips of paper bearing a few lines of
writing. Some he endorses, and so refers them to other
authorities, and some he signs by dabbing his signet ring in
lamp-black and pressing it on the paper. A Turk attaches
no importance to a written signature, arguing with a logic
that seems strange to us that any one can write a man's
name but no one but himself can have his seal. If the

governor wishes to dictate, a secretary squats down on his heels and proceeds to write on a slip of paper held in his hand. The mass of verbiage scribbled every day in a Turkish office is appalling and would soon choke up all the pigeon-holes of Downing Street. But though the Turks write inordinately, they take no care of their papers, and as a rule merely stuff them into bags and throw them away after a month or two.

The careers of Turkish governors are so various that it would be misleading to sketch any as typical. Nominally, the country has a civil service entered by examination from the Government colleges and offering regular promotion. Practically appointments are made by favour, and in all important cases by palace favour. A year or two ago a body was constituted with the title of " Commission for the Selection of Functionaries," but it was never allowed to do more than *recommend* candidates, and its recommendations have generally received scant attention. The Government has always persistently refused to let any officials, even the most subordinate, be nominated except from Constantinople. There are good and honest officials in Turkey, and, if they were allowed to choose their own staffs, there would be a reasonable prospect of reform and decent government. But they are not. Whatever a governor's character may be, several spies are sure to be appointed as his subordinates, and, if he be a man of exceptional honesty and capacity, it is pretty certain that his colleagues or subordinates will be persons of the opposite character. Jealousy and suspicion are at the root of all Oriental administration. If a man is popular and well spoken of in his province, he at once creates an impression that he may raise some kind of revolt against the Central Government. But if he is unpopular and has obviously no object but to fill his own pocket, he is thought less dangerous. Some governors go through a long and regular career in the civil service, serving as

Kaim-makams, Mutesarrifs, and Valis in different districts, and one often meets officials who have had wonderfully varied experiences of Armenia, Mesopotamia, Arabia, Tripoli, and the uttermost parts of the Ottoman Empire. Others are promoted suddenly from other branches of the service, and all are liable to sudden dismissal. Others again have held high positions in the capital, attracted too much attention, and been sent away in disgrace.

Perhaps the greatest evil connected with Turkish posts in the provinces is that they are all underpaid. The most honest officials find that they cannot live on their salary, and private fortunes are rare. There is, therefore, no method of rubbing along except to supplement the exiguous remuneration of the Government by certain ancient and well-known methods. Of course, if an official is naturally dishonest and avaricious, he makes even freer use of his opportunities; and, strange as it may seem, a reputation for corruption and rapacity is not always unpopular even among the provincials. They like a man whose "eye is full" (*gyözü tok*), which means a man whose pockets are full and whose eyes are not always wandering after his neighbour's goods. Now a corrupt man, if of a certain standing, has probably made his pile, and though from habit he will go on taking a little, is less dangerous than a comparatively honest man with no money behind him, who, when pressed by any combination of circumstances, may squeeze hard in order to extricate himself.

It may seem that some Turkish salaries are sufficient for the position of the recipients; but here again we must remember the difference between reality and paper. No official figures on this subject can be taken, or indeed are meant to be taken, in their natural sense. The Turkish Government mostly pays its debts, whether salaries or sums due for contracts, &c., by means of orders on provincial treasuries known as *havalés*. After much petitioning, an official at last receives a *havalé* for say one thousand Turkish pounds, which let us hope for his sake is a much larger sum than is really owing to him. The paper as first given to him is probably a *kham havalé*, a "raw" or blank order, that is to say, the name of the provincial treasury which is to pay it is not inserted. The recipient takes this document to a professional discounter of such papers and obtains the best terms he can, probably about 50 per cent., or five hundred pounds instead of a thousand. The discounter is in touch with various provincial governors, and knows which of them are prepared to cash the orders of the Sublime Porte, and how much per cent. they will give. It is, of course, advantageous to a governor to cash *havalés* if his provincial treasury will stand it, because he is certain to make at least 10 per cent. off the transaction. The discounter then has the name of a suitable governor inserted in the *havalé*. The provincial treasury will be debited with a payment of a thousand pounds. The nominal recipient of this sum has received five hundred in satisfaction of his claims. There remains another sum of five hundred pounds (or, rather, as much of it as can be got from the provincial treasury) to be divided between the discounter, the Vali, and the financial authorities of the vilayet. The Vali's signature is necessary to authorise the payment of the money; but there is a difference in Turkey between having an admitted right to receive money from the Government and actually receiving it. The latter and comparatively rare transaction can be only accomplished when the Defterdar, in consideration of weighty reasons, writes on the back of the paper *Vérilé*—"Let it be given."

Finances conducted on this system evidently require to be judged by a special standard. In such circumstances we cannot be astonished at the application of public funds to private uses. In some ways bribery and corruption redress themselves; if everybody accepts *douceurs* the money circulates round, and it all comes to much the same in the end. But naturally the methods of Turkish finance lead to frightful evils. For instance, large sums granted for public works—buildings, roads, bridges, &c.—disappear mysteriously with little or no result to show. The traveller may propose to drive along a road marked on the *Carte des Communications Postales de l'Empire Ottoman* as a *route carossable* of the first class. The driver will object and say diffidently, " There are a great many bridges on that road." In case my reader has never made a journey in Turkey I should explain that a bridge is regarded as a natural obstacle to travelling. It is probable that it is either non-existent, broken, or unsafe. In any case, a detour of some length will be necessary to find a place where the river can be crossed. " There are many bridges on that road," repeats the driver. " I know there are," you reply; " the Vali told me that there had been a severe inundation a month ago and that he had sent a Commission to examine all the bridges. They made a very careful survey, and in fact spent £1500 in repairing them." The driver looks thoughtful and wonders how any one who talks Turkish can say such strange things. Being a man of few words, except when swearing at his horses, he does not argue, and merely asks an extortionate price for the hire of his carriage. When you come to those bridges (it would be incorrect to say when you go over them), you will know how the Vali and the Commission make their money, and admit that the coachman has not asked too much.

Still greater are the evils which arise in connection with taxation. The taxes on paper are moderate, and it can be proved that the payment per head is less than in any other country in Europe. But they are generally farmed. The farmer has to make his own profit and to arrange for the collection. If he employs his own agents, he has to pay them and find the wherewithal to do so. More often the collecting is done by soldiers (the fact that this is expressly forbidden has nothing to do with the matter), and the soldiers, ragged, hungry men, whose pay is months in arrear, have to keep themselves. When the practical business of collecting begins, the question is not how much a village ought to pay, but how much it *can* pay, and that much is taken. The very leniency of the Turks proves disastrous. Even tax-collectors are sometimes indolent or good-natured, and will take no money from a village because it is very poor or very distant. But when bad times come, the omission is remembered and arrears are exacted with unsparing rigour. The provincial treasury cannot tell what demands it may have to meet. When there is an emergency—and the Sublime Porte has an emergency once a year—peremptory commands are sent to every vilayet ordering money to be remitted to Constantinople. In favourable circumstances a Vali cannot think of improving or developing a vilayet, but merely of keeping sufficient to meet such immediate needs as paying the troops. In unfavourable circumstances he cannot think at all of local interests; the calls from the Porte are imperious; he knows that his official good name and promotion are at stake; and the more anxious he is to make a career, the more likely is he to send the contents of his treasury to the capital and leave a crowd of unpaid, half-fed men to live as best they can from what they can take. Yet the Ottoman Government will often allow itself to be cheated without protest. One of the most important sources of revenue is the sheep-tax. In estimating the budget, this tax is calculated according to the number of sheep known to exist in different districts, which *prima facie* seems plausible. But sheep on the Imperial estates, which are many and extensive, are exempt from the impost. Accordingly, when the time of collection comes, the owners of sheep around such lands pay the Sultan's bailiffs a small sum for

the right of driving their flocks on to the privileged territory, where they can defy the agents of the Ministry of
Finance. In other cases the authorities, in order to make
a small immediate gain, will weaken the resources of the
country, injure the public interest, and incur the dangers re-
sulting from scarcity of provisions. For instance, when the
tithe is taken in kind, the collectors often refuse to allow
the crops of olives or cereals to be gathered and stored, and
leave them so long that they are spoiled in the fields. The
reason of this is that the Government sells in the open
market the commodities taken as tithe, and, being anxious
to obtain as high a price as possible, diminishes the quantity
of the article in order to enhance its value.

In the early days of the Ottoman Empire successful
warriors were rewarded with the gift of conquered lands,
which they held as fiefs. Macedonia is still full of country
gentlemen who originally obtained their lands in this way,
and until 1867 the provincial administration was to a great
extent based on this arrangement. Districts were ruled by
Dere-beyis or local magnates. These were either Turkish
feudal holders as described or non-Turkish chiefs (such as
are still found in Albania and Kurdistan), who were best
conciliated by allowing them sufficient authority to preserve
their nominal loyalty to the Padishah. The country was
thus split up into a large number of districts which might
be called either principalities or estates, the possessors of
which were practically independent and had power of life
and death within their own boundaries. It was inevitable
that the Central Government should alter this state of things
as soon as improved communications enabled them to do so.
Little as the Turks like railways, they are great patrons of
the telegraph, because it is the most powerful instrument
for a despot who wishes to control his own officials. It is
no longer necessary to leave a province to the discretion
of a governor, and trust that he will come home to be

beheaded when that operation seems desirable. With the telegraph one can order him about, find out what he is doing, reprimand him, recall him, instruct his subordinates to report against him, and generally deprive him of all real power. As the Ottoman administration recks little of the public convenience, they frequently summon a governor to the telegraph office, and monopolise the wire for as long as they choose in communicating with him. But the old system was probably, on the whole, better. The Dere-beyi no doubt felt a pleasure in exercising his power of life and death, which seemed to others a superfluous activity; but he had a proprietor's interest in his estate, and was anxious to promote local interests and send as little money to Constantinople as possible. He was a centrifugal force, and in his way promoted independence, whereas the modern Vali is entirely centripetal.

I have alluded above to the office of Christian vice-governor or Muavin. These officials are an interesting and instructive study. They have long existed sporadically, but at the beginning of 1896 the Porte published a series of reforms for the "Vilayets of the Empire," which included this institution among others. In the preceding autumn the Sultan, under great pressure from the Powers, had sanctioned the so-called "Armenian Reforms," and by subsequently extending some of them to all districts, the Turkish Government hoped to avoid before the Moslim world the appearance of granting exceptional privileges to Christians. The appointments were actually made, not without some hesitation, of course, and pretence of making great concessions, and extraordinary ingenuity was shown in depriving them of all importance. First of all, the Christian appointed was never of the same race and sect as the population of the province, which was in itself sufficient to prevent him from seriously exerting himself for their welfare. Greeks were named to Bulgarian districts and Catholics to Greek. Secondly, as long as the governor was at his post, the vice-governor was not allowed to do anything or see any important papers. He was there, it was explained, to offer general advice, and to replace the governor if need be; but he was, to some extent, a fifth wheel to a coach, and the bureaucratic machine would be deranged ·if the routine work passed through his hands. Thirdly, when the governor went away he was temporarily replaced, not by the vice-governor, as was expected, but by the official highest in rank—generally the Defterdar. Now Turkish rank is peculiarly mysterious. It is not social, and it is not, strictly speaking, official—that is to say, it does not follow that he who has apparently the highest office has also the highest rank. It is granted independently of office, much in the same way as decorations in England. It can easily be imagined that the Christian vice-governor was generally found to be the lowest in rank of the superior officials.

The question of Christian functionaries presents many difficulties. It is often asserted that the only effective protection to Christians lies in the appointment of as many as possible. This would no doubt be true if it were possible to choose the functionaries from the inhabitants of the province where they are to serve and give them sufficient authority to secure their independence. But this the Mohammedans always succeed in preventing. Theory cannot be reduced to practice, and the faults of the Christians are the greatest obstacle to their employment. Their servility and timidity render them worse than good Moslims, and so ingrained are their mutual hostilities and suspicions that every one would rather be ruled by a Turk than by a Christian of another sect.

When one reads European reports on the condition of the Turkish provinces, or reflects on the wonderful things one has seen with one's own eyes, one is inclined to think that the system cannot go on. It is annually proved that the machinery of government is collapsing; that there is no money and no food; that no one can pay any taxes, and that everybody must starve. Yet it all goes on next year *eskisi gibi*—"the same old way." They that had been skinned are skinned again, and they that were starving are starving still, but not dead. The Porte which had no money to pay the soldiers last Bairam, has no money to pay them this Bairam either. This year, as last year, it is stated that there is positively no alternative but to sell a province to Russia. This year, as last year, when the inevitable pay-day comes round, it is found that the Porte has performed some mysterious operation, probably described as "converting" its debts, and has plenty of money again. It may safely be affirmed that if any European Power were to undertake to finance Turkey, the whole place would be bankrupt in a week, and need years of recuperation. But political economy seems to be one of those things which must be accepted or rejected as a whole. Partial and blundering acceptance means collapse, but if, like the Sublime Porte, you reject it *in toto*, if you discard such conceptions as the National Debt, and pay no regard to the theory of wages, the theory of demand and supply, and all other theories whatever, it seems to make no difference. Financially and economically the Turkish Government means simply taking money from its subjects with no intention of repayment. As long as Christians cannot resist the demands for contributions, as long as Moslims are content to serve with little or no return and under considerable hardship, there seems no reason why this system should ever come to an end. Its only limits are the limits of human endurance.

This state of things is not new. People in Turkey

often attribute their sufferings to the policy of the present
Sultan, and maintain that the world went better ten or
twenty years ago.   Some evils have, no doubt, become
peculiarly acute in recent times, but it is clear that the
disease is chronic and inherent, not sudden or adven-
titious.   Massacres, spying, and maladministration are not
peculiar to the reign of Abd-ul-Hamid II., but are prominent features all through Turkish history.   Neither are
predictions as to the speedy collapse of the Turkish Empire products of this century.   Ever since the Turks
occupied Constantinople almost every traveller and statesman who examined the condition of the country has
expressed the opinion that the whole state was unstable
and decadent.   One British Ambassador warned his Government in the reign of Sultan Ibrahim (1640–1648) that
the dissolution of the Empire was imminent; another,
when the Russians took Oczakow in 1735, expressed
the opinion that Constantinople was at the mercy of
Russia. Yet the Ottoman Empire has neither improved
nor disappeared.   For its continuance there are two obvious causes: first, and chiefly, the mutual antipathies
of the Christian Rayahs, who cannot combine against
the Turk; second, the divergent aims and interests of
the Christian Powers, who cannot agree on any successor
to him, though they recognise the exceptional and anomalous character of the Ottoman Empire by their continual
interference in its internal affairs.

  But one cannot help wondering why the Turks themselves let so strange a Government continue.   The majority
of them are, in their own way, honest, patriotic, God-fearing
men: some of them are intelligent and energetic.   Why
will they not reform ?   One answer is that no changes seem
to make the Turkish Government any better.   Perhaps the
greatest reform ever introduced into Turkey was the abolition
of the Janissaries.   Yet it has not altered the general char-

acter of the administration, and probably no change which
would alter it would be acceptable to the Turkish people.
Many, particularly of the younger men, profess to be
anxious for "reforms," and are commonly known as Young
Turks or *la jeune Turquie*. Their ideal is some form of
constitutional government, such as the Parliament of 1877;
but I do not know that any section of them are sufficiently
definite or practical in their organisation to have any detailed programme. They and their literature are the objects
of the special suspicion and severity of the Ottoman Government, and a Christian rising creates less alarm than a conspiracy among Ottoman schoolboys.

Now, it may be that this horror of reforms springs from
a correct instinct that any change in the present order
of things would endanger the rule of Moslims over
Christians. If we assume that it is desirable to continue
the Ottoman Government—an assumption which no one
but a Turk need make—we must admit that this implies
the superiority of Turks to Christians. It does not mean
the equality of Turks and Christians; that is a thing which
is talked of but never realised, for the very good reason
that it is impossible. As long as force rules, the Turks are
superior to the Christians. They are stronger, braver, and
more united. But when force does not rule, when progress,
commerce, finance, and law give the mixed population of
the Empire a chance of redistributing themselves according to their wits, the Turk and the Christian are not
equal; the Christian is superior. He acquires the money
and land of the Turk, and proves in a law-court that
he is right in so doing. One may criticise the Turkish
character, but given their idiosyncrasies, one must admit
that they derive little profit from such blessings of civilisation as are introduced into the country. Foreign syndicates
profit most, and after them native Christians, but not the
Osmanli, except in so far as he can make them disgorge

their gains.   Those who have associated with Turks will
have discovered a fact which it is difficult for the rest
of the world to believe, namely, that they are afraid
of Christians.   The periodical outbreaks formerly called
" atrocities," but now described as " events " (a beautiful
euphemism which the Sublime Porte has imposed on the
diplomatic language of Europe), appear to us as a cowardly
slaughter of unarmed men and helpless women and children.
But no doubt the average Turk regards these same events
as necessary measures of self-defence.   He is always ready
to believe that the Armenians and Bulgarians are import-
ing arms or planning to burn down Constantinople, and
says with sincere alarm that no Moslim's life is safe.   I
have met many liberal Turks who talked freely of liberty
and equality, but never one who did not approve of the
Armenian massacres of 1895–6 and attempt to justify
them.   The converse of this is, that the Christians in
Turkey do not feel any more sympathy for liberal or
" Young Turks " than they do for old and bigoted ones; for
young or old, radical or conservative, their complaints and
hopes are confined to their own race and religion, and
take no account of the majority of the population in their
dominions.

The Turkish reformer and the Christian have nothing
in common, and the mass of Turks mistrust the reformer.
Even in such a matter as military reform, where there can
be no doubt that improvements are in the interest of the
Moslim, and the Moslim only, the Turk will not take the
view which his friends think he obviously ought to take.
Foreign military instructors have again and again presented recommendations, and again and again they have
been rejected, sometimes openly, sometimes with a pretence
of acceptance, but always quite firmly.   The Turk has a
dim perception that even in military matters he cannot
understand and practise European methods.   If he tries

to do so, the control will pass out of his hands into those of people who are cleverer than himself. But though he may think them clever, he does not on that account feel any respect for them. He regards them as conjurors who can perform a variety of tricks, which may be, according to circumstances, useful, amusing, or dangerous; but for all Christendom he has a brutal, unreasoning contempt—the contempt of the sword for everything that can be cut, and to-day the stupid contempt of a blunt sword.

CHAPTER V

ON MOHAMMEDANISM

MOHAMMEDANISM was introduced into Central Asia by the Arabs, who, after conquering Persia, penetrated into Bokhara and Fergana in the first decade of the eighth century It effectually drove out before it Buddhism and all other forms of religion, and is now professed by all the Turkish races west of Kashgar, and by some farther east in Siberia and China. It is, as is well known, a religion which, perhaps more than any other, affects conduct as well as belief; it forces into its own peculiar mould every department of human life, and modifies profoundly the character of the nations which adopt it. It therefore merits some attention from a social and political point of view.

The creed of Mohammedanism is generally compressed into the well-known formula: "There is no god but God, and Mohammed is His prophet." But there is another and longer version which runs as follows:—

"I believe in God and His angels and His books and His prophets, and the last day, and the predestination of good and evil by God, and the resurrection after death. I bear witness that there is no god but God, and I bear witness that Mohammed is His slave and His prophet."

The tenets here enumerated comprise all that is most important in Islam, and perhaps the easiest way to obtain a clear idea of the religion in its theoretical and practical aspects will be to consider these doctrines, without binding ourselves to the order in which they are here enumerated, though we may well begin with the belief in God.

As is well known, Mohammed inculcated monotheism in its most uncompromising and fiercest form. More than half of the Koran is a polemic against polytheism or trinitarianism. "Say he is one God, God the eternal. He begets not and is not begotten, and there is none like to Him." So runs the chapter called *Ikhlas*, which is considered to be equivalent in value to two-thirds of the whole book, and which is recited by the devout many times a day. To clearly understand the Mohammedan conception of God, it must be remembered that Allah is an abbreviation of Al-ilah,[1] the God, that is, the one, true, only God, as distinguished from the minor divinities of the ancient Arabs. There is something controversial in the mere mention of Allah ; it is in itself a challenge to Christians and polytheists. The Koran is full of magnificent passages respecting the majesty, omnipotence, and omniscience of this Deity. It is He that has created and sustains us : in Him only we live and move and have our being. ✔

"With Him are the keys of the Unseen : none knoweth them save Him. He knoweth what is on the land and what is in the sea. There falleth not a leaf but He knoweth it. There is not a seed in the darkness of the earth nor aught that is moist or dry but it is (written) in the perspicuous book. He it is that taketh you to Himself by night (*i.e.* in sleep) and knoweth what you have earned during the day : then He raiseth you up again that the number of your days may be fulfilled. Unto Him shall ye return and He will declare unto you what ye have done." (*From the chapter of Cattle or* VI. 58.)

"What is in the heavens and what is in the earth sing praises to God, for He is the Almighty and wise. His is the kingdom of the heavens and the earth : He quickeneth and He slayeth and He is mighty over all. He is the first and the last, the seen and the unseen, and He knoweth all. It is He who created the heavens and the earth in six days ; then He sat down on His throne. He knoweth what enters into the earth and what comes forth from it ; what descends from the heavens and what ascends to them. He is

---

[1] *La ilaha illa 'llah*—"There is no god (*ilah*) except the true God " (*Allah*).

with you wheresoever ye be, and whatsoever ye do He regardeth it."
(*Beginning of the chapter of Iron or* LVII.)

"Blessed is He in whose hand is the kingdom ; who hath power
over all, who created death and life to prove you and see which of
you doeth well. He is Almighty and ready to forgive. It is He
who created the seven heavens, one above the other. Thou canst
not see any discord in the creation of the Merciful. Look again—
canst thou see a flaw ? Gaze again and again. Thy sight shall
return to thee dimmed and dazzled." (*The beginning of the chapter
of the Kingdom or* LXVIII.)

"God, there is no God but Him, the Living, the Eternal.
Neither slumber nor sleep taketh Him ; to Him belong what is in
the heavens and what is on the earth. Who is he that can inter-
cede with Him except by His permission ? He knoweth what is
before mankind and what is behind them (*i.e.* the future and the
past), and they comprehend nothing of His knowledge but what He
chooseth. His throne extends over the heaven and the earth, and
the care of both is not a burden to Him." (*The Heifer or* II. 256.)

Yet, in spite of these splendid passages, which in the
original send a devotional thrill through the reader, it must
be admitted that the Deity of the Koran is not, according to
our ideas at least, an altogether satisfying object of worship.
Alone in the terrible isolation of His unapproachable glory,
He is connected by no links with His creatures. There is
neither Son, Madonna, nor Saint to act as mediator. The
Prophet, though " the best of men," has no claim personally
to a supernatural character, and it would be the height of
impiety to address prayer to him. Though God is in the
Koran habitually styled the Merciful and Compassionate,
and described as ready to forgive the penitent, the general
conception of Him is that of a Being more terrible than the
jealous God of the Old Testament. He has for His own
inscrutable reasons created the world and predestined part
of its inhabitants to eternal bliss and part to eternal torment.
Everything, both good and evil, happens by His will and
permission. Thus, though He may prescribe a certain moral
law for His creatures, He himself is above all law and mora-

lity; piety cannot take the form of walking with God or of struggling to imitate some divine idea, but must content itself with acquiescence in the mysterious decrees of an irresponsible Potentate. The name Islam or " Resignation,' by which Mohammedans designate their religion, sums up its characteristics, and the same phrase may be translated either " Verily, we are Moslims," or " Verily, we are resigned." Obviously this conception of the Deity is really not far removed from pantheism, or the worship of an unknown and merciless force—Karma, fate, or whatever we like to call it. But the ordinary language of Mohammedanism tends to avoid such a view and to personify God as an Absolute Monarch.

"O God, King of the Kingdom,[1] Thou givest the Kingdom unto whom Thou wilt, and Thou takest away the Kingdom from whom Thou wilt; Thou exaltest whom Thou wilt, and Thou humblest whom Thou wilt. In Thy hand is good, for Thou hast power over all. Thou makest the night to follow the day, and the day to follow the night. Thou bringest forth the living from the dead, and the dead from the living." (*The chapter of the Family of Imran or* III. 25.)

This view of the Almighty as " the only Potentate, Lord of Lords and King of Kings," recurs all through the Koran, and is curiously illustrated by the Namaz or form of public worship ordained by the Prophet. There is no sacramental rite, such as the Mass; sacrifices, though not unknown, are never offered in mosques; properly speaking, there is no priest, for the Imam claims no sacerdotal functions, and it is merely for convenience' sake that he leads the prayers of the congregation, and, so to speak, keeps time. Still more remarkable, there are hardly any requests or supplications in these prayers. They consist almost entirely of stately

---

[1] It would, perhaps, be more accurate to translate *maliku-'l-mulki* as "Possessor of the Kingdom," but the words are evidently chosen because they come from the same root, and " King of the Kingdom " reproduces the literary effect.

formulæ, enunciating the Unity of the Almighty, ascribing to Him honour and praise, and blessing the name of His Prophet.   There is nothing which would satisfy a Western Christian congregation smitten with a sense of sin or craving for hysterical excitement.   The whole performance is a court ceremony and closely resembles an Eastern visit of politeness.   The Almighty has commanded that He should be recognised five times a day; five times a day the pious Moslim visits His house, performs his respectful salutations, pays the proper compliments, and goes away again.[1]   Such views of the Deity and of religious obligation are entirely suited to the Turkish character, which is neither sentimental nor speculative.   The ceremonial of the mosque is plain, sane, and dignified; it encourages neither superstition nor excitement, and it cannot be made ridiculous.   On the other hand, it is dry, narrow, and wanting in those elements of mystery, emotion, and poetry which mark the worship of Christians in their nobler temples and are typified by the dim splendours of a Gothic or Byzantine Cathedral, just as the Namaz is typified by the bare, whitewashed walls of a village mosque.   The only Mohammedan nation who have much taste for art, the Persians, are Shiites,[2] a sect which may justly be called heretical in the sense that they have made out of Mohammedanism something very different from the religion taught by Mohammed.

Let us now turn to the article of the Moslim faith expressing belief in the prophets of God.

From what has been said of Allah, it might be supposed that He is too far removed from mankind to take much interest in their doings.   If all things are predestined and written in a book, logic suggests that there is no more to be done.   Like the deities of Epicurus, the Creator should take His ease and watch the performance of the play He has pre-

---

[1] *Vide* Note I., p. 202, "On Mohammedan Worship."
[2] *Vide* Note II., p. 207, "On Sunnites and Shiites."

pared. But popular religions and popular logic never coincide. If some passages of the Koran suggest that God is a distant, unknowable, inexorable law, others, and they are perhaps the majority, preach the fear of a very present and personal Master, who hears, sees, warns, punishes, nay, even plots against the ungodly.[1] He who has pre-arranged the destiny of every soul cries to mankind through His prophets, " Fools, why will you go to hell ? " In all ages He has sent signs and messengers to His people, " If haply they would have sense and believe." Mohammedan tradition asserts that 124,000 prophets (*nabi*) and 314 apostles (*rasul*) have come from God, of whom six have attained special eminence—Adam, Noah, Abraham (the Friend of God), Moses (He who spoke with God), Jesus (the Spirit of God), and Mohammed (the Apostle of God). All Mohammedans have a sincere veneration for both Moses and Jesus, though perhaps antagonism to Jews and Christianity make them somewhat reticent in expressing it. The name of Abraham (Ibrahim) is often given to men, and he is mentioned in the daily prayers (" O God, bless Mohammed and his descendants as Thou didst bless Abraham and his descendants.") But Mohammed is " the seal of the prophets," the end and completion of the revelation. No message will come after him, and for the purposes of practical salvation the Moslim may disregard his predecessors. Mohammedanism is an ungainly word, but in one way more exact than Islam ; for the faith which it designates, though a development of Judaism and Christianity, bears in every tenet and practice the impress of the personality of Mohammed. Space does not permit us to give any adequate account of this remarkable man, but it may be well to briefly recapitulate the chief events of his life.

He was born in 570 or 571 A.D,. of the family of the

[1] "The Jews were crafty and God was crafty, for God is the best of crafty ones."

Hashimi, of the tribe of the Koreish, in Mecca. That city was a place of pilgrimage for the neighbouring tribes on account of the shrine of the Kaaba, which it must be remembered was pre-Mohammedan and the centre of a cultus respecting which we have little accurate information, except that it combined star-worship with the adoration of stones, notably the celebrated Hajaru-'l-aswad or "Black Stone," which is still an object of the deepest veneration to all Mohammedan pilgrims. Mohammed was left an orphan while still a child, and in early youth entered the service of a wealthy widow named Hadija, whom he married when he was twenty-five and she fifteen years older. Up to the age of forty he was apparently little more than an honourable and prosperous citizen of Mecca. He gained some experience of the world by accompanying Hadija's trading caravans to Aleppo and Damascus, but according to the Sunnite tradition he could neither read nor write. Doubtless he always took an interest in religious questions, and obtained both information and congenial society among the Hanifs or philosophic inquirers, of whom there were many in his native land ; for the Meccans were tolerant of speculation, and regarded their religion as an industry rather than a creed.

Mohammed had from childhood been subject to fits of a nervous malady. Towards his fortieth year these seizures increased in violence. He wandered in the desert and saw visions. According to some authorities, a few of the short Suras, now arranged at the end of the Koran, are to be referred to this period, in which he was as yet unaware that he had any definite mission. But orthodox tradition holds that the verses first revealed are those which now stand at the beginning of Sura XCVI. In a vision which he had on Mount Hira, the Angel of God appeared to him and said, " Read." He replied, " I cannot read." This command and answer were repeated, and the third time the angel recited to

him the Sura, " Read in the name of thy Lord who created." [1]
He confided this vision only to Hadija and a few relatives
and friends, and for two and a half years received no more
revelations, and fell into a state of despondency in which he
meditated suicide. One day he was seized with a violent
fit accompanied by fever, and was, according to his custom
when so attacked, wrapped up in a cloak. As he lay thus,
the angel again appeared and addressed him in the words of
Sura LXXIV., " O thou that art wrapped up in thy mantle :
arise and preach and magnify thy Lord." From this moment
rather than from the earlier revelation dates the commencement of his active mission. Visions and revelations followed
quickly; converts more slowly; but he soon achieved the
earliest stage of greatness—unpopularity. The Meccans
regarded the offertory as the essential part of religion. They
lived on idolatry, and denunciations of the practice struck
at the root of their prosperity. At one moment Mohammed
seems to have thought of making a compromise, and recognising in some way the existence of the pagan deities. It is
greatly to his credit that he withstood the temptation and
braved the general hostility. Nearly all his family were
put under a ban, and during two years retired from Mecca
and lived in a ravine to the east of the city. At last they
were allowed to return owing to the influence of Abu Talib,
Mohammed's uncle, who, however, died shortly afterwards, as
did also Hadija.

Mohammed was now some fifty years of age, and appeared
to have failed entirely. His uncle, who had protected him,
and his wife, who had consoled him, were both dead. He
had few adherents ; the mass of the Meccans regarded him
as a wild and dangerous radical, and, though his family
stood by him with Arab clannishness, they did not sympa-
thise with his ideas or like him any the better for the trouble
he had caused. In the next ten years all this was reversed.

---

[1] Chapter of Clotted Blood, XCVI.

He became a soldier and a statesman, a conqueror and a
legislator. His country accepted him as its civil and religious head. He called upon the neighbouring sovereigns to
obey his message, and not long after his death his followers
compelled them to do so.

This change in his fortunes was mainly brought about
by the flight of himself and his disciples to Medina, an
event which is commonly known as the Hijra, and appropriately chosen as the commencement of the Mohammedan
era. It was as useless to preach a new religion in Mecca
as in the Vatican. All the habits, associations, and interests of the inhabitants connected them with the worship
which Mohammed wished to overthrow. In Medina, on
the contrary, the conditions were in his favour. The city
had apparently no conspicuous temples or ·deities; it was
full of Jews, and the inhabitants were hence familiar with
the ideas of monotheism and the coming of the Messiah.
There was also an old hostility between them and the
Meccans, so they took kindly to the idea of a purer
religion which would destroy the idols and the importance
of their rivals. It is true that in the long-run blood
proved thicker than water: the Prophet assigned to his
native town a religious importance which can only be
explained by his early training. But on first arriving at
Medina it is clear that he sought support chiefly among
the Jews, and was ready to make his religion a sort of
universal Judaism. For a year or more he bade his
disciples turn towards Jerusalem when they prayed, but
in the end the pride and intractability of the Jews made
him see that he must build up his system on a broader
base. It is curious to observe how that stubborn people
have rejected two of the greatest religions of the world.
Had they been more pliant we might have seen a Jewish
Empire and Jewish Sultans.

The Hijra took place in 622. The followers of the

Prophet migrated gradually and secretly. He himself remained till the last, and fled somewhat suddenly owing to a plot against his life. Once established at Medina, Mohammed was soon recognised as the chief of the city. He built the first mosque and arranged its ritual. He also began a career of polygamy, contrasting strangely with his earlier life, in which he was scrupulously faithful and genuinely attached to the elderly Hadija. In the second year he declared a holy war against Mecca, and defeated the Koreish at Badr, but in the following year was defeated by them at Ohod or Uhud. They followed up this victory by the siege of Medina, but were repulsed, and from the fourth to the seventh year of the Hijra Mohammed extended his authority by a series of successful expeditions against the neighbouring tribes. The Meccans recognised his success by the pact of Hudaibiya, one of the provisions of which allowed him to visit the Kaaba at the season of pilgrimage. This he did in the next year with 2000 men, remaining three days. The eighth year of the Hijra was marked by an unsuccessful expedition against Muta in Syria, and by the final conquest of Mecca. Mohammed accused the Meccans of violating the pact of Hudaibiya, and advanced against them with a considerable force. He occupied the city almost without resistance, perhaps in consequence of an understanding with some of the principal men, and proceeded to destroy the idols in the Kaaba, but treated the shrine itself with great respect, and had it repaired. After a fortnight's residence in his birthplace he returned to Medina, and subsequently successfully conducted several warlike expeditions. The ninth year is often called "the year of deputations," on account of the number of embassies which came to the Prophet offering the submission of the various tribes. In the early part of 632 he paid his last visit to Mecca, and in June he died rather suddenly at Medina.

The salient feature which distinguishes this career from those of other great religious leaders is its ultimate success from a worldly point of view. Buddha renounced a crown: Christ's kingdom was not of this world. Not only did the manner of His death annihilate the aspirations of all who had hoped for a temporal Messiah, but it is clear from the silence or brevity of pagan writers that the whole series of events which culminated in the Crucifixion passed unnoticed by the Roman world, and were for the public of the day of no political importance. Christianity could never have attained its spirituality, its adaptability to all climes and races, had it been connected with any particular form of government or society. But in the history of Mohammedanism all these conditions were reversed. The temporal success of the founder has proved ultimately the failure of his system as a world-wide religion. He was not crucified. On the contrary, it is eminently characteristic of him that he declined to believe that Christ suffered this punishment, evidently considering that God could not have allowed a great Prophet to perish so ignominiously.[1] He triumphed over his enemies, and spent the end of his life as undisputed head of a theocratic state, a portly, elderly man, full of years and honours, revered by all with whom he came in contact as Pope and Cæsar in one. It is greatly to his credit that this position never turned his head. In the hour of his glory the epileptic visionary behaved like a prudent and cautious statesman, disclaimed all miraculous powers, and continually reminded his followers that he was but an ordinary man. Neither can any great fault be found with his private life. He would have been less open to criticism if he had not received special revelations authorising his irregular unions; but, on the whole, considering the state of public feeling in Arabia at the time, it cannot be denied that the ten

[1] *Vide* Note III., p. 208, "On Mohammed's Ideas of Christianity."

widows and one maid whom he espoused were a very modest allowance for a man with the opportunities of Solomon. But his success had a far-reaching and not a good effect on his religious system. Mohammed confounded the Church and the State, because he was himself the head of both; he established not so much a system of doctrines as a polity regulated by a vast number of complicated ordinances, which, though purely secular in their scope, have acquired a religious character and sanction. Unity has not been preserved in Islam any more than in Christianity, and it cannot be said that at the present day the Mohammedan Church is one body under one head; but in every country where it is the dominant faith, its members are held together less by common doctrines and observances than by the feeling that they all belong to a privileged political order, which confers certain rights, and exacts certain duties from its members. Perhaps we may even hazard the surmise that some of the first Moslims were attracted to the Prophet, not so much by devotion to monotheism, as by a liking for well-organised and successful military expeditions. Islam has never won for itself the position of a cosmopolitan expression of monotheism. Many Western philosophers have called themselves Theists or Deists, but none have become, or apparently thought of becoming, Mohammedans.

The Creed couples the books and the prophets of God, and we had better follow its example by treating of Mohammed and the Koran together, for the book cannot be separated from its writer. Theoretically Moslim theologians hold that the Almighty has revealed 104 sacred books: ten to Adam, fifty to Seth, thirty to Enoch, ten to Abraham, and one apiece to Moses, David, Jesus, and Mohammed. "This book," said Gabriel, in delivering the Koran to the Prophet, "is a guide to the pious . . . who believe in what was revealed to thee and what

M

was revealed before thee." The revelation to Moses is called the Taurat, from the Hebrew *Tora* or law. It is mentioned in the Koran (*e.g.* "He has sent down to thee the Book confirming what was before it, and has revealed the law and the gospel before for the guidance of men "), but it is related in the "Traditions" that when Omar proposed to read the Pentateuch to the Prophet, the latter looked annoyed. Well, *pereant qui ante nos nostra dixerint.* The Psalms of David are several times alluded to in the Koran under the name of Zabur, and once quoted. "We have written in the Zabur, 'My righteous servants shall inherit the earth.'"[1] The book revealed to Jesus is called Injil, a corruption of *Euangelion,* but is not identical with the Gospels, for it is a book given to Jesus by God, and not an account of his life and teaching. According to strict theology, Jews and Christians are called "People of the Book" (Ehlu-'l-Kitab), and enjoy a position superior to that of heathen polytheists. The courteous Mollah, who shows the intelligent stranger round his mosque, and hopes that the largeness of his views will find a counterpart in his gratuity, often lays stress on the fact that Christians and Moslims are alike "people of the Book." But, except on such occasions, I doubt if the respect paid by Moslims to our Scriptures is of any practical importance or effect.

As Mohammed superseded all previous prophets, so does the Koran obliterate and replace all previous revelations. Not even the learned make any pretence of studying them, and, indeed, all but the last four are purely imaginary. But the Koran is a living reality, and, within certain geographical limits, as important a phenomenon for the science of humanity as is the Bible. Never was there a religion more bibliolatrous than Islam. The Moslims lavish on a book that veneration which it is forbidden to accord to images or

[1] Sura XXI.; *cf.* Ps. xxxvii. 29.

symbols. Not only is the Koran believed to be inspired in our sense of the phrase, but it is held to be the *ipsissima verba* of the Almighty, created by Him from all eternity, and preserved in the highest heaven till the time of Mohammed, when it was sent down to the lowest sphere, and thence delivered to the Prophet piecemeal by the angel Gabriel. It is amazing that any Arabic-speaking people should accept this account of the Koran, for never was any work more clearly not a connected whole, but a collection of disjointed fragments. The Prophet dictated to various secretaries the thoughts which he considered as revelations, and these were subsequently collected into a volume under the direction of the Caliph Osman. The present arrangement of the work is purely arbitrary, the chapters being placed according to length, the longest first. The chronological order is rather the exact opposite, the short rhapsodical suras, many of them full of feeling and poetry, being the early utterances of Mohammed when the revelation first burst on him, whereas the long didactic and legislative discourses, which are comparatively tame and flat, are the work of a man with an assured position, much of whose early enthusiasm has died away. It is difficult for a Western to judge of the Koran fairly. Its faults as a literary production are certainly glaring. The style is loose and often ungrammatical; the author frequently repeats and sometimes contradicts himself,[1] and had no notion of telling a story clearly. Compare the histories of Abraham, Joseph, and other well-known characters as given in the Bible and as related by Mohammed, and it will be seen that the Arabic account is hardly intelligible to a reader unacquainted with the subject. It was perhaps the consciousness of a certain natural obscurity that caused the Prophet to so often reiterate his main doctrines in the most striking and definite form, and endeavour to make his work

[1] *Vide* Note IV., p. 212, "On Abrogated Verses in the Koran."

a plain and perspicuous book, which on all main points it certainly is. But what we cannot well judge of is the linguistic effect of the Koran as a rhetorical composition. There is no doubt that its rhyming periods have an over-powering attraction for the Arab ear, which is charmed and intoxicated by the resonant sound, so that it takes no notice of the imperfections of the sense—a phenomenon not unknown in the religious literature of other countries. Most Turks, however, though they know what their prayers mean, have no pretension to a knowledge of Arabic, and their attitude is similar to that of the old lady who found such comfort in " that blessed word Mesopotamia." Yet, however little they may understand the sacred book, it has an important influence on the life and general condition of the Turkish Empire.

Firstly, the unprogressive character of Mohammedanism is due mainly to the Koran. We have seen how the differ-ence between the lives of Christ and Mohammed is reflected in the differences between their religions. Not less marked has been the effect of the sacred books of Islam and Christianity. One of the most remarkable features of the Gospel is its indefiniteness, in the best sense of the word—that is to say, there is so little in it applicable to only one place or one epoch. If one thinks of what are usually considered the crying faults of the times in which our Lord lived—such as idolatry, slavery, and various forms of cruelty and lust—it is surprising to find that they are not denounced in the Gospel or even forbidden. A per-fectly general system of morality, applicable to all ages, is enunciated, which renders these and other sins impossible for those who practise it, but detail and local colour are conspicuous by their absence. The Koran is the opposite of all this. Mohammed denounces the idolatry, infanticide, and other evil customs of the Pagan Arabs, somewhat after the manner of the Prophets of the Old Testament, and conferred an inestimable boon on Arabia by changing the existing condition of religion and society. Unfortunately, he also thought proper to legislate in detail for the form of society which he preferred—a state of things certainly far superior to that which he abolished, but still not one to be forced upon all nations in all times and countries. He legalised polygamy, slavery, and other things to which objection may be taken, and it is impossible to detach his theological teaching from his legislation. The weakness of Islam is that a liberal interpretation of the Koran presents almost insuperable difficulties. The New Testament lends itself to many modes of treatment; both Roman Catholics and Broad Churchmen read it with approval; it was not composed by the founder of the Christian religion; it puts forward no claims on its own behalf, but appeals mutely to the succeeding ages to interpret it as best suits their need. The Koran, on the contrary, after an introductory prayer, opens with the notable words, "There is no doubt in this book," and throughout constantly asserts that it is a revelation sent by the Almighty. Its precepts are put forward, not only as injunctions of the Prophet, but as divine orders. Such coherency and thoroughness were, and still are, an enormous force for Mohammedanism as the Church militant. They give it an unequalled power of converting, drilling, and disciplining savage nations. But the same characteristics become a source of weakness in the religion of a great state in contact with European Powers. Much of Mohammed's legislation is wholly incompatible, not only with what is commonly called civilisation, but with commerce and other business which a nation must carry on, if it does not desire to be left behind. Yet there are no means of modifying the law of the Prophet, or of setting it aside as non-essential. No Western critic or Eastern heretic has ever disputed the genuineness of a single chapter, or even verse, of the Koran. The book announces itself as the Word of God, " a direction to the pious," and must be accepted as a whole, and unreservedly, or not at all. As the Prophet left his Church and State, so they are now, and so they must remain—austere, rigid, unalterable, with only a curse and a sword - thrust for those whose institutions do not harmonise with their prescriptions.

Such is the general effect of the Koran, and it is not a good one; but in another and special manner its teaching has proved disastrous in Turkey and other countries where there are Christians under a Mohammedan government. During a great part of his mission the Prophet was engaged in actual warfare with the Meccans or the tribes of the Hijaz. The suras composed during this period reflect his own feelings at the time, and contain violent denunciations of the unbelievers, and exhortations to his followers to slay them without mercy.

" Fight in God's way with those who fight with you. . . . Kill them wherever ye find them . . . for sedition is worse than slaughter. But fight them not by the sacred mosque until they fight you there ; then kill them, for such is the recompense of those that misbelieve. . . . Fight them that there be no sedition, and that the religion may be God's " (II. 185).
" And when ye meet those who misbelieve, then strike off their heads until ye have massacred them, and bind fast the bonds " (XLVII. or Mohammed, 4).

There is every reason to believe that such passages had reference to the particular occasions on which they were uttered, and were not meant to be specially applicable to Christians, whom Mohammed intended to treat with toler- ance. But Moslims, and particularly Turkish Moslims, are very uncritical. Their method of interpretation is exactly that of the devout Christian who said, " None of your contexts for me. Plain Scripture is what I go by." De- nunciations such as those cited are quoted in a detached form, and not only contribute to maintain permanently hostile feelings between the Mohammedan and Christian subjects of the Sultan, but are used to excuse, even if they do not provoke, deliberate massacre.

Of course these diatribes, even if read in their true sense, show how great is the difference between Moham-. medan and Christian ethics. The Prophet did not love his enemies or turn his cheek to the smiter. All his moods and vicissitudes, his struggles, anger, triumph, and prosperity are reflected in his book, and form part of the moral law of his followers. It may seem unjust to call the Koran worldly, for it insists continually and vehemently on the awful reality of the next life and the folly of those who attach importance to earthly things. The Prophet, of course, praises martyrs and self-sacrifice, but he seems to point to an ideal of dignified and prayerful, but distinctly mundane, prosperity. He enjoins alms; he bids his followers deal justly with widows, orphans, and the poor, but as men in a superior position creditably fulfilling their obligations. He did not consort with publicans and sinners, but with men of liberal views from the best families of Mecca. The quality on which he unconsciously lays stress, and which, doubtless, characterised him in his later years, as it characterises his followers now, is a certain grave dignity, hating, above all, anything frivolous and fussy, but not averse to discreet self-indulgence in private, and perhaps, according to our ideas, not entirely clear from the charge of hypocrisy.

Islam is the youngest of the great religions, and therefore has had less time to change. But even if full weight be allowed for this relative youth, it is remarkable how accurately the precepts of the founder are obeyed, how closely his example is followed. Could St. Peter or St. Paul enter the cathedrals which bear their names, could Buddha visit the temple of the Grand Lama at Lhassa, they would

probably be mystified and astonished by the religious services which they would witness. But were Mohammed to
be present at the Namaz in St. Sophia, there is no reason
to believe he would see anything to arouse his surprise
or criticism. The whole ceremonial, the gestures and the
language, come from Arabia, and are what he himself used
and prescribed 1300 years ago. This invariability is not
altogether due to the minuteness of the Koranic regulations.
The omissions of that work on some subjects are as remarkable as its prolixity on others, and it is by no means a
complete thesaurus of Moslim law and ceremonial, *e.g.*
circumcision, which is generally considered of binding obli-
gatien, is never enjoined. This and a host of other rules
which regulate the life of the individual and the community
are due to the example or verbal precepts of the Prophet as
reported in the " Traditions," often spoken of collectively as
the Sunna or Sonna.[1] They are not theoretically of the same
weight as the Koran, but they form for all intents and purposes a sacred book, and no orthodox Mohammedan would
dream of questioning their authority. The most remarkable
instance of the deep impression left by the local environment
of the Prophet is the Hajj,[2] or pilgrimage to Mecca. Every
Mohammedan is bound once in his life to visit the holy
city, and there perform a number of ceremonies, unique in
the ritual of Islam. It is clear that Mohammed, partly not
to offend his followers, partly in obedience to his own prejudices as a Meccan, felt bound to respect the ancient
ceremonies and sacred sites. By so doing he unavoidably
forged another link in the chain which connects his
religion with superstition and barbarism. During the Hajj
Islam has no pretensions to be cosmopolitan, but becomes
entirely Arabian, and adores not the Lord of all worlds
but old Meccan fetishes. The devout Haji cannot but

---

[1] *Vide* Note V., p. 212, " On the Traditions."
[2] *Vide* Note VI., p. 213, " On the Ceremonies of the Hajj."

return with increased prejudices against progress and civilisation.[1]

To return to the Creed. The belief in angels is perhaps the least important article of all. It contributes that element of mythology which no popular religion has ever been able to eliminate, and seems to consecrate the many stories respecting ghosts, witchcraft, and magic current among the superstitious peasantry. Just as in morals, the Moslim cannot escape from the antiquated prescriptions of the Koran, so in the intellectual sphere he is bound to believe in the existence of a whole pantheon of angels, devils, and jinns. The last named, who are repeatedly mentioned in the Koran, are supernatural beings, created from fire, not, like mankind, from the dust, and possessed of miraculous powers. They were the servants of Solomon, as recounted in Sura XXVII., and Mohammed himself is said to have preached to them near Taif.

The doctrine of the last day, or judgment of God and the resurrection of the dead, is so familiar to the Christian world that one is apt to forget that most pagan nations hold it either not at all or in an exceedingly fragmentary form. It is one of the greatest achievements of Mohammed that his words still succeed in implanting in rude converts from heathenism, as well as in educated Moslims, an intense conviction of the reality of the next world, and a readiness to sacrifice this brief life for the unending life to come. The joys of Mohammed's paradise have generally been stigmatised as coarse and sensual. The criticism is just; for though there are not wanting in the Koran passages which seem to point to higher and more spiritual ideas, they are rare and obscure, whereas the descriptions of the

---

[1] Mohammedan doctors say that Islam consists of the performance of five duties : (1) Bearing witness that there is but one God ; (2) praying five times a day ; (3) giving alms ; (4) fasting in Ramazan ; (5) making the pilgrimage to Mecca once in a life. It is noticeable that the Hajj is treated as of the same importance as the profession of monotheism.

material pleasures to be enjoyed by believers are many in number and explicit in detail. But it is worth while noticing that the houris, which have so struck Western imagination, are not the chief feature of the Koranic paradise, which is really the ideal of the dweller in the desert, and the opposite of the evils most familiar to him on earth. As the frozen Eskimo has been said to think of heaven as essentially a hot place, and to pain the missionary by his simple and outspoken desire to go to hell-fire, so the scorched Arab naturally connects bliss with coolness, shade, and running water, and an examination of the Prophet's words will prove that these are the joys of heaven on which he most insists.

But whatever we think of this heaven and hell, there can be no doubt of their reality for the Moslims. The Turkish soldier believes in paradise as firmly as did the followers of the Old Man of the Mountain, and exposes himself without hesitation to a death which will take him straight to eternal felicity. For it is to be observed that the award of the last judgment is not strictly in accordance with our ideas of right and wrong. All non-Mohammedans are doomed to eternal punishment, and all Mohammedans will reach heaven eventually after passing through a more or less lengthy purgatory. Martyrs, however, will go straight to bliss; and by martyrs are meant all who fall in battle fighting against the infidel—a characteristic definition. Such a doctrine harmonises admirably with the spirit of a military race, but is somewhat apt to make the Moslim think he has no moral obligations towards Christians, though it would be most unfair to say that this is the teaching of the Koran. We have seen elsewhere that the Turk has no definite equivalent for our word Turkey. He consequently draws no clear distinction between what we should call natives and foreigners. He speaks of Christians, Franks, and Moslims, but he would never talk of a Turkish Chris-

tian in the same way that we might speak of an English
Roman Catholic. Hence he sees no distinction in kind
between a war with Russia and an attack on Armenians;
both are *jihad*, or battle with the infidel. He has a tendency, and a tendency which is daily becoming more pronounced, to regard every Christian as an enemy of the
Moslim religion and the Moslim state, and to restrict the
most elementary moral duties to persons of his own creed.
In this restricted sphere Turkish morality is, no doubt, on
the whole satisfactory, particularly among the lower classes
and in the provinces. But it may be doubted if the most
liberal and tolerant Moslim is ready to punish a member of
his own creed for the worst excesses against Christians.

No doctrine of Islam has left a stronger impress on the
nations who have adopted it than the belief in predestination, or the decrees of God—*kadr* or *kismet*. It is the un-
doubted teaching of orthodox Mohammedanism [1] that all
the actions of mankind are absolutely predestined by the
Deity, who writes them down beforehand in a register ("the
preserved tablet"). It is popularly believed that on the
festival called "The night of decrees" (Leilatu-'l-berat) the
guardian angels receive from the Almighty a tablet on
which is inscribed the fate of their charges during the
coming year, and pessimistic fancy adds that he who listens
may hear them weeping as they read the lines of destiny.
Not only does the Moslim hold that the course of the
world is predestined, but he thinks of the will of God as
something external to himself, which máy mar his best

[1] It is natural that so energetic a man as Mohammed should occasionally
have used language inconsistent with fatalism. There is a remarkable passage
(Sura IV. 80) which, according to the commentator, contains no contradiction, though the infidel reader may feel less certain as to its coherency:—
"Wherever ye may be, death will overtake you, though ye were in lofty
towers. And if a good thing befall them they say, 'This is from God;' but
if a bad thing, 'This is from thee.' Say, '*All is from God.*' What ails these
people? They can scarce understand a tale. Say, '*What befalls thee of
good is from God, and what befalls thee of bad is from thyself.*'"

efforts or unexpectedly crown his supineness with unmerited prosperity. Such ideas paralyse the natural energy of the Turk, and reflect themselves in popular language. "The pestilence raged for forty years, and the people whose time had come to die did die," says a proverb. Why then take any sanitary precautions? It is irreligious to suppose you can avoid answering your name at God's roll-call by sprinkling yourself with carbolic acid or any other profane nastiness, and if your name is not on the list, you run no danger. All Turkish life, private and political, is permeated with this spirit. The people are in a way full of vigour, but no race has so little ambition in the sense of deliberately prosecuting a distant object. The early Sultans indeed cherished the idea of the conquest of all Christian Europe, and showed a fair amount of skill and perseverance in directing their absolute power to this end. But it is long since any plan other than merely negative can be traced in Turkish policy. "Sufficient unto the day is the evil thereof" (the saying, I admit, is not Mohammed's); let us adopt any temporary shift to procure money or get rid of the interference of foreign Powers for the next week, and leave the future to God. Doubtless He will "set the dog to worry the pig;" the Russians will probably fall foul of the English, and the servants of God will be able to repose again. The extraordinary thing is that the Empire which has practised this policy for so long is still, and, in spite of the prophecies of its enemies, alive and apparently able to obtain money whenever it is really required, and to show vigour when least expected.

We have thus enumerated the chief doctrines of Islam, and endeavoured to see what is their practical effect on the life of the nation which professes them. The result of our brief examination seems to be that this effect is, in the main, cramping, restrictive, and sterilising; and it is therefore necessary to point out that this religion has another and vivifying side. Probably no system has done so much to encourage individual liberty and responsibility, despite its formality, despite its despotism, despite the fatalism which it teaches. It is the most unsacerdotal religion in the world; it recognises no sort of priest, and calls on every man to save and justify himself before the Almighty. The most solemn ceremony performed by the Caliph as head of the faith does not differ in kind from the daily prayers of the most illiterate peasant. This sense of individual importance has its counterpart in daily life, for instance, in the Turkish soldier—the incarnation alike of Islam and of the Turkish race. According to military experts, he has not only the passive obedience of the Slav, but a readiness in finding expedients and an individual initiative which are rare in the armies of other countries. Islam has hallowed and strengthened the sense of discipline, the unquestioning submission to authority, which have always characterised the Turk; but, on the other hand, by inculcating on every man a feeling of his dignity and a consciousness of his responsibility, it encourages and enlivens individual effort in the few spheres in which those who profess it are able to show energy. The Sultan may be a Roman emperor; but every Turk is a Roman citizen, with a profound self-respect and a sense not only of his duties, but of what is due to him.

Islam also deserves all credit for the temperance which it preaches. No doubt the upper classes in Constantinople drink considerably, and drink with the deliberate intention of intoxicating themselves. But putting aside this section of society, which may justly be described as contaminated by European influences, it may be safely said that the great majority of the Turkish nation—soldiers, peasants, merchants, and the learned professions—never touch alcohol. Against the moral value of this abstinence may be set off the position assigned to women; but any just criticism of

Mohammed's legislation on this subject and its results must not lose sight of two points. Firstly, Mohammed did not invent the seclusion and subjection of women. He accepted, with some improvements, the current Arabian ideas on the subject. The system of the harem is in its origin not Moslim, but simply Oriental. The only reproach that can be made against the Prophet is that on which I have already dilated—namely, that by too definite legislation he rendered subsequent development and reform impossible. Secondly, those who talk of the degradation of Mohammedan women would do well to remember that in Mohammedan countries prostitution and illegitimacy are almost unknown. It is true that only the length of his purse and the temper of his lawful wives (both of them very effective restraints) limit the unions which a Moslim may contract with slaves, but the offspring of such unions are legitimate children, and inherit share and share alike with the children born in wedlock. A Moslim woman is never free, but, on the other hand, it is almost impossible to imagine any circumstances in which she would be cast on the world without a protector. A certain solidarity characterises, not only family relations, but all Moslim society. There are no paupers; giving alms is not a mere theoretical obligation, but an essential religious duty really discharged. It may be replied that there are many beggars. There are, and the spectacle is very unpleasant; but, from the beggars' point of view, could they, given their misfortunes, have a better life? If one has twisted limbs or any incurable malady, including laziness, is it not more healthy, interesting, and lucrative, to sit begging at street corners than to be the inmate of a charitable institution? One thing is certain—Moslim beggars never starve.

Nor is Islam wanting in more intellectual excellences. If we could only strip from it its bibliolatry, and sever the fatal connection between religious and secular law, the

manly simplicity of its cardinal doctrines, its calm acceptance of the existing order of the world, rising superior to
explanations based on emotion and sentiment, and its dignified resignation to the will of God, must command our
approval and sympathy. Those who have devoted adequate
and impartial attention to the life and work of the Prophet
of God will mostly admit that a feeling of admiration and
respect dominates their most critical estimates of him, and
will not refuse to join in the modest benediction which
generally accompanies his name, " God bless him and grant
him peace."

Any estimate of the influence of Islam in Turkey would
be misleading without reference to an important phenomenon on which we have not yet touched—the dervishes.
It may seem, and indeed it is, a flat contradiction of most
of the previous statements in this chapter to say that Islam
is so essentially a Semitic religion that it is hardly ever
held in a pure form except by Semitic races. But the contradiction exists in fact. Moslim law, politics, society, and
morality—above all, everything connected with mosques
and similar institutions—show a rigorous adherence to the
precepts of the Prophet. But in the domain of personal
religion, although the true Turk is more stolid than the
other races of the Empire, Turks as well as Aryans crave
for something more human than Allah, something more
emotional than the disciplined gymnastics of the Namaz.
The Persian and Indian Shiahs have modified Islam more
profoundly than they would care to admit, in order to satisfy
these cravings; and in Turkey, side by side with the rigid
orthodoxy of the Mollahs, we find that the dervishes supply
the element of mystery, ceremony, and excitement which
the populace love, and which Mohammed would probably
have disliked. They appeal to the highest and lowest
forms of religious sentiment. Educated minds find pleasure
in the poetical speculations of the Mesnevi, while wonder-

working saints, holy tombs, singing, dancing, and quasi-magical ceremonies please the vulgar.

The Persian word dervish appears to mean originally a begging monk, though not necessarily or usually a celibate, but is now often loosely applied to the members of any religious confraternity. Thus the followers of the Mahdi and of the Sheikh Senusi are often styled dervishes, although their peculiar tenets appear to consist chiefly in an attempt to return to the primitive conditions of the Moslim state and have nothing in common with those of the Turkish dervishes. It is only of the latter that I speak here. There are several orders of them, the most important being the Bektashis, the Mevlevis, and the Rufais (the two latter commonly known to Europeans as dancing and howling dervishes); but they all possess certain common peculiarities which may conveniently be treated of together. The peculiar ritual or method of imparting mystical doctrines practised by any order is called its *tariq*, or road, and the members are said to follow such and such a road.

As we have seen, the transition from the Moslim idea of God to pantheism is not difficult. The Semites, not being metaphysical, do not make this transition; but other races have a tendency to do so, and the dervishes give expression to this tendency. All things are created by God, and all things happen by His will and pleasure. "There is no power or strength," or, as we should say, force, "except in God." He alone exists, and the whole universe is an emanation of Him, and in fact is God. The distinction between the Creator and the creature, between thee and me, disappears; all is reduced to unity. For the fully initiated there are no personal pronouns. It is related in the Mesnevi that a lover—that is, the inquiring human soul—knocked at the door of his beloved, by which name the Divine Power is typified. The voice from within cried, "Who is there?" The lover answered, "It is I." "This house will not hold me and thee," replied the voice. The lover departed, and after a year of prayer and fasting returned, knocked again, and in answer to the question, "Who is there?" replied, "*It is thou.*" "Let myself come in," replied the voice, and the door opened.

This is, no doubt, an extreme specimen of dervish mysticism; one cannot arrive at such conceptions without considerable training; but they are the goal towards which all dervish and Sufi[1] teaching tends. These philosophers are far from believing, with Mohammed and his real followers, that God has revealed the truth in " a plain book." For them the religious man is not so much a believer as a seeker after truth, and his life a journey through several stages, of which the last is absorption into the Deity. Their religious terminology is full of such expressions as " the knowledge and love of God," which, however, bears a more mystical and less personal meaning than we attach to it. Mohammed would probably not have liked the phrase, and would certainly have explained it as signifying " Fear God and read the Scriptures."

Dervishes observe the Mohammedan forms of prayer, Ramazan, and other ceremonies; but they have also their own characteristic form of worship called Zikr, consisting of the repetition, sometimes continued during several hours, of some religious formula, such as " There is no God but God," or the ninety and nine names of the Deity. The formulæ used are almost all of unimpeachable orthodoxy; but the spirit of the performance is widely different from that of the Namaz, as its object is to distract the devotee's mind from earthly things, and finally to throw him into the state of trance or ecstasy, called *hal.* The repetition of such formulæ can, no doubt, be defended from the Sunna; but it is clear that the whole doctrine and practice of the dervishes

---

[1] A name of uncertain derivation given to the mystical and poetical philosophy of such Persian authors as Hafiz.

contain a large pre-Mohammedan element, which is perhaps Indian in origin. The connection with Persia is clear enough. Some of their most revered Sheikhs came from Persian-speaking countries and wrote in Persian; they are on good terms with the Shiahs and share their peculiar respect for the Caliph Ali. This personage is the great subject of contention between the Sunnite and Shiite sections of the Moslim world. The former consider that he was the fourth Khalifa, neither greater nor less than the others; the latter that he was the rightful successor of Mohammed. They reject the Sunnite Khalifas, and specially execrate the memory of the first three, who kept Ali out of his rights, and of those who were responsible for the murder of his sons Hasan and Husein. Somehow or other, Ali has become associated with mystical and heretical doctrines; his admirers are suspected of considering him not only the equal of the Prophet but an incarnation of the Deity, and monograms of his name are a conspicuous feature in most dervish Tekkes. Hence he has among rigid Sunnites a somewhat equivocal position, similar to that of the Virgin Mary among Protestants.

It is somewhat difficult to explain the position of dervishes in the Turkish Moslim world. They cannot be said to be unorthodox, for nearly every religious man is a lay member of one or other of their orders. They profess an ostentatious respect for the externals of Islam, and they have a great influence among the people. But, on the other hand, their esoteric doctrines, as expounded in such a work as the Mesnevi, cannot be reconciled with the natural meaning of the Koran, and there is a deep-seated animosity between dervishes and the officials of the established Mohammedan Church, such as Mollahs and Softas. The Mollahs are beneficed clergy in receipt of some small salary attached to mosques and other pious foundations, the Softas theological students. There are many thousands of them in such religious centres as Constantinople and Konia, but the reason why most of them have adopted this learned profession is not by any means a passion for theology, but a desire to escape military service, which can only be done by professing oneself a religious student. If once accepted in a *medresse*, or school, they are practically provided for during their lives, and can lead an existence of almost absolute idleness. Their chief occupation consists in learning by heart treatises on Moslim law, which they make no attempt to understand, and they are often unable to read or write. These large houses of fanatical and ignorant men, mostly between the ages of twenty and forty, without regular employment, are a constant source of danger, and are sometimes disbanded by the Government. It would, perhaps, be an illusion to imagine that the average dervish is less ignorant and superstitious than the average Softa, but he is certainly far more gentle and less fanatical; the authors whom he studies are, if more extravagant, less cramping, and the farther he travels on the road of pantheism the more tolerant does he become. But to pantheism is closely allied the dangerous doctrine that, as both good and evil come from God, there is no difference between them. Such a tenet can be safely held only by those few who have really mastered their passions and extinguished their desires; but it is to be feared that many dervishes find it easier to understand that the prohibition of such things as alcohol does not apply to the elect than to attain to the corresponding stage of self-control.

There is a certain external resemblance between Mohammedanism and old-fashioned Anglicanism, and it is curious to observe that some of the religious ceremonies of dervishes are superficially analogous to those of extreme ritualists. The ceremonial lighting of candles and the use of incense in public worship, both of which are practised by dervishes, are as hateful to the Mohammedan clergy as to the British Protestant. " It is never related in the Traditions," a Mollah once said to me, " that our Lord the Prophet went about lighting candles on the tombs of dead dervishes. Had it been necessary or useful we should certainly have heard that he did so." [1]

Of the orders mentioned above, the Bektashis were founded in the fourteenth century by Haji Bektash, a native of Bokhara. He also named and blessed the corps of Janissaries, which has always maintained a certain connection with the order. The Bektashis have a remarkable shrine and monastery—if, indeed, the latter word can be rightly used of them—at Aramsun, near Cæsarea, in the vilayet of Angora. They are very widely spread over Turkey, and are particularly influential in Albania. They have the reputation of being exceedingly antinomian both in theory and practice. It is said, though I have never been able to verify the statement, that the present Sultan is, or was, a member of the order.

The Rufais were founded by Ahmed Rufai of Baghdad, where his tomb still exists. They attempt, by the performance of their peculiar Zikr, to arrive at a state of ecstasy, in which they cut themselves with knives and apply red-hot irons to their mouths or other parts of their persons. They are generally known as " The Howling Dervishes," because the earlier stages of the ceremony, which are publicly performed at two Tekkes at Constantinople, consist of shouting some short formula, such as " Ya, Allah ! " until the vocalists fall on the ground exhausted, drenched in sweat. Many of them are negroes, and any one who has had an opportunity of seeing, in the Southern States of America, a negro service in a church sufficiently far removed from white influences, will be able to observe how congenial this form of ceremony is to the African, whether celebrated in the name of Juju, Mohammed,

---

[1] There is no objection to having lamps burning round a tomb or to large wax candles being lighted when light is required. The enormity consists in superfluously and ceremoniously lighting candles in the daylight.

or Christ. As far as I know, the later and severer stages of this Zikr are not performed in Constantinople, at least not publicly; but their existence is testified to by a collection of cutlasses and uncanny spiked iron implements suspended on the wall of the Tekke near the Mihrab. The Rufais claim miraculous powers; and in Scutari, at the conclusion of the Zikr, diseased children are brought in, and either breathed upon by the Sheikh or placed under his feet. I once walked back from the ceremony behind a father and his little girl who had sore ears, to cure which malady she had been breathed upon by the Rufai Sheikh. " Thanks be to God," said the father, " his blessed breath touched you, and the pain has gone." " But my ears hurt still," said the little girl. " Oh no, they don't," said the father, with the calm assurance of a dogmatic theorist. " They hurt more than ever," said the little girl, considerably nettled.

The Mevlevi, or dancing dervishes, have perhaps a greater historic and literary interest than the other orders, and their picturesque ritual makes them popular in every part of Turkey. They merit, therefore, some attention. The founder of the sect was Jelalu-'d-Din-er-Rumi, commonly called Mevlana, or " Our Lord," a native of Balkh, who came with his father to the court of Alau-'d-Din, the Seljuk Sultan who reigned at Konia in the early part of the thirteenth century. He there enjoyed an immense reputation for learning and wisdom, and is said by his biographers to have performed many miracles, and, in particular, to have often transported himself to distant places, and to have received similarly marvellous visits from foreign sages. He composed a celebrated poem, called the Mesnevi (Arabic, Mathnawi, or couplets), consisting of six books of Persian verse, in which the Sufi system of pantheism is inculcated with considerable elegance of expression through the medium of a series of legends and apologues. The generalship of the order is hereditary in his family, and the holder is commonly known as the Chelebi[1] of Konia, from the place of his residence.   He is a person of great importance, and it is the custom for him to gird each Osmanli sovereign, when he ascends the throne, with the sword of Osman.

The popular account of this practice is as follows:— When Osman was beginning his conquests, and had taken Broussa and other towns from the Greeks, he sent a polite embassy to Sultan Alau-'d-Din, who was then the most considerable Turkish sovereign in Asia, to explain his proceedings and his desire to remain on good terms with the greatest chieftain of his race.   Alau-'d-Din replied that he had no objection to the Osmanlis taking from the Greeks whatever they could get, and, as a proof of his goodwill, sent the celebrated Jelalu-'d-Din to give Osman a sword of honour, a ceremony slightly suggesting the investiture of a vassal.   But this story presents difficulties.   According to the ordinary chronology, Alau-'d-Din reigned from 1219 to 1236; Jelalu-'d-Din was born in 1202, and died in 1273; Osman reigned from 1288 to 1328.

I was once told by a Zaptie that when the Chelebi proceeds to Constantinople to gird on the sword, he does not go farther than Scutari himself, but sends a representative to perform the ceremony, because if he were to set foot in Constantinople, he would, *ipso facto*, become Sultan and Caliph.   This is probably pure fiction, but it shows how highly he is esteemed.

It is related of Mohammed that "when he heard the noise of a musical pipe, he put his fingers into his ears;" but Jelalu-'d-Din was passionately devoted to music, and, like Luther, did not see why the devil should have all the good tunes.   He instituted the practice of dancing, or rather whirling rapidly round to the sound of reed flutes, as a means of attaining spiritual ecstasy.   This exercise is called by the dervishes *sema*, hearing, or *muqabile*, meeting—the

---

[1] Chelebi means a refined or cultivated man.

idea being that the soul rises above all earthly things, and is alone, face to face with God, whose voice it can then hear. The services of the dancing dervishes at Constantinople have become little more than a show to make money out of tourists; but at Konia they are conducted on a larger scale and are seriously devotional, the public not being as a rule admitted.[1] Konia is, or was, a city of mud hovels, among which tower a few majestic but dangerously dilapidated gateways and minarets, dating from Seljuk times, white, chaste, and inscribed with the austere warnings of the Koran. In equal contrast to these and to the ignoble modern tenements, rises a blue dome above the tomb of " Our Lord " (Jelalu-'d-Din). The building beneath it consists of three parts—a mosque, in which are performed all the rites that can be required of devout Mohammedans; a dancing-room or *sema-khane;* and a gallery leading from it, in which is the tomb. The latter is protected by silver railings, and the rich stuffs with which it is covered—the lamps, candles, and other accessories—give it the appearance of a Roman Catholic altar. On the walls are mystic monograms, Persian inscriptions, and invocations to Sheikhs and Pirs. When a solemn *sema* is performed in this building at night, the strange costumes and tall head-dresses of the whirling figures, the blaze of light, the weird music of the moaning flutes, and the dimly descried glory of the altar-tomb, combine to create an impression of mystery and splendour which are often expected, but very rarely found, in what those who have never been there call the gorgeous East.

I have heard on good authority that, in the dangerous period in the winter of 1895–96, when religious and national feeling ran high in Turkey, it was mainly owing to the Mevlevis that the Softas of Konia were prevented from attacking the Christian population of the town. The whole

---

[1] I visited Konia before the railway reached the town. It may be changed now.

sect are certainly most interesting and often excellent people, and display a large-mindedness and receptivity to European ideas which seem incredible to those who have not talked with them. It is unfortunate that the same studies which produce this spirit also lead them to retire from the struggle of the world, and exert little active influence.

I once had an opportunity of conversing with a high functionary of the Mevlevi sect. By his request I visited him between 10 and 11 P.M., as the month was Ramazan, and the earlier hours of the night were taken up by the ordinary Mohammedan prayers. From his house, which stood in a large courtyard, there issued a rhythmical noise like the pulsations of a steam-engine, and I wondered if there could be a factory in the neighbourhood. As I went up the staircase the mysterious noise grew louder and louder, but I could not imagine whence it proceeded until I was suddenly introduced into a large room where at least a hundred dervishes were seated, some against the walls and some on sheepskins spread in the middle of the floor, dressed in flowing garments, blue or drab, and wearing tall felt hats shaped like flower-pots. The noise was produced by these all chanting "Ya Hú, ya Hú, ya Hú, ya Hú,"[1] in a low guttural voice, which spiritual exercise they intended to continue till morning. The expression of their faces was that of men in a mesmeric trance, and not one of them seemed to notice the arrival of a stranger. In the middle a stoutish man of about forty was walking up and down. He was dressed like the others, but his shaggy yellow beard and golden spectacles made him look more like a German professor than a dancing dervish. He apologised for receiving me so late, saying, with a tolerant but weary air, that he was obliged to attend the long prayers recited in

[1] Hú or Huwa, the third personal pronoun in Arabic, is often used in the sense of God.

mosques after sunset during Ramazan, and I thought he also seemed rather glad to .escape from his own religious ceremony. He then took me into another room which presented a very singular appearance, as it was lighted by ten silver candlesticks placed on the floor in the shape of the letter Y. There was no sofa or divan of any kind, and we sat on cushions placed on the floor. On the wall were hung some pictures of Mecca and of the Bektashi shrine at Aramsun, as well as some remarkably bad photographs which he had taken himself. He had obtained a kodak, he told me, from Paris, but with infinite difficulty, and he regretted that local prejudices did not allow him to use it freely. To my great surprise he offered me *raki,* and took some himself, though as a rule the laxest Mohammedan will at least pretend not to drink in Ramazan. He apologised for not speaking French, which he said he could read a little, and asked me if I could recommend him a good French newspaper of liberal views. Then he said that he had heard that Sir J. Redhouse had translated the Mesnevi into English. Had it produced much effect in London? He had heard that music was used in English services, as in those of the Mevlevis, and he seemed to think it would be natural that British congregations should take to dancing as well. I did not like to disappoint him by saying that I had not heard of the existence of any dancing dervishes in England, and therefore spoke of the Mohammedan Church at Liverpool. He said with some hesitation, and in a low voice, that this was not what he had meant. He did not care about the introduction of Mohammedanism into England, but he had hoped that people might have seen that the mystic principles enunciated in the Mesnevi were compatible with all religions, and could be grafted on Christianity as well as on Islam.

NOTES TO CHAPTER V.

I. On Mohammedan Worship.

The prayers offered by Moslims fall into two classes. The first, and by far the most important, is the form of prayer prescribed by the Prophet, called Salat in Arabic, but generally known in Turkey by the Persian name Namaz. The second class comprises all other supplications, which are often distinguished from the Namaz by the name of Du'a. Every Namaz consists of two or more repetitions of a ceremony called Rikat (literally " prostration "), which may be regarded as the unit of worship, a service being said to consist of so many *rikats*. A *rikat* is little more than the repetition in several prescribed attitudes of the formulæ Allahu akbar [1] ("God is most great ") and Subhana'llah (apparently meaning something like " We sing the praises of God ") and of a few verses of the Koran. These latter may vary, but need not do so; a pious Moslim fulfils the duty of prayer if he repeats the same gestures and formulæ some twenty or thirty times every day of his life. The Namaz should be performed five times a day : at sunrise, when the sun has begun to decline, midway between this hour and sunset, at sunset, and about two hours later. There is a further distinction of prayers into *farz*, or those believed to be prescribed by God, and *sunnet*, or those founded on the practice of the Prophet. Thus, the mid-day prayer consists of four *rikats* which are *farz*, but these are preceded by four and followed by two *rikats* which are *sunnet*. There are also three extra hours of prayer, and extra *rikats*, which may be performed at the ordinary hours, but these are only observed by the very devout. It is essential that the prayers should be said in Arabic, and that the worshipper should have performed his ablutions. Men may say them anywhere, but it is more meritorious if they attend a mosque. Women should pray at home. At public services the Imam alone prays aloud, the congregation repeat the words to themselves.

The word mosque is a corruption of Masjid (a place of prostration). The earliest form of these places of worship was apparently an open stone platform with a wall at one end, but in Turkey they are always covered buildings, pointing towards Mecca. The direction of the Holy City is marked by a Mihrab or niche, on each side of which stand two large candles, and over which is almost invari-

---

[1] Or, in Turkish pronunciation, *ekber*.

ably written, "Whenever Zacharias visited her in the Mihrab."[1] Near the Mihrab may usually be seen several Korans on wooden stands, and to the right of it is a pulpit called Minbar, ascended by a flight of steps. More in the centre of the building, but still on the right hand, is a platform raised on pillars, on which sit Mollahs who often read the Koran between the services. On the walls are generally large shields on which are written the names of God, Mohammed, and the first four caliphs, and pious artists are pretty sure to have painted on every convenient space caligraphic exercises which are often hard to decipher, but which generally prove to be "There is no God but God, and Mohammed is his Prophet," the verses of the Throne (Sura II. 256), the Fatiha, or some such sentiment as "God is the Light of the Heavens and the Earth," "God is He who sees and hears." Near the door are places for ablution, and in large mosques at Constantinople there is often on the left-hand side a sort of private pew called Mahfil, in which the Sultan can worship unseen at the Friday prayer.

With these explanations the reader should be able to follow any Namaz, say the mid-day Friday Namaz at St. Sophia.

A little before the time for prayer an official called Muezzin mounts the minaret and calls out a formula known as the Ezan, which is as follows: "God is most great (*four times*). I testify that there is no God but God (*twice*). I testify that Mohammed is the Prophet of God (*twice*). Come to prayer (*twice*). Come to salvation[2] (*twice*). God is most great (*twice*). There is no God but God." Inside the mosque the Mollahs sitting on the elevated platform repeat the same call, adding at the end, "Prayers are now ready." Meanwhile worshippers have been dropping in and take their places in long lines across the mosque. As they enter they put off their shoes and leave them at the door. This usage is not really ceremonial, but intended to keep clean the floor, which is covered with matting. Those who have not performed their ablutions at home wash their hands, feet, and faces in the mosque, and take water into their mouths. Before beginning his prayers each person repeats to himself a formula called Niyet : "I pro-

---

[1] This strange inscription is chosen simply because it contains the word Mihrab, which means here chamber. The passage comes from Chapter III. of the Koran, which gives an account of the youth of the Virgin Mary. Perhaps it is necessary to remind the reader that most Oriental inscriptions are pointless. If they come from a holy book and look ornamental, no one requires any more.

[2] In the morning he adds, "Prayer is better than sleep."

pose to offer up this day to God alone, with a sincere heart and my
face turned towards Mecca, prayers of" so many *rikats*. The Imam
stands alone in front of the congregation, facing the Mihrab. The
first part of the Namaz is not said in unison, but by each person for
himself, kneeling and rising independently of his fellows. This is
because the *rikats* in question are *sunnet*, and not *farz*. As soon as
the *farz rikats* begin the whole congregation perform the prescribed
gestures simultaneously with the regularity of soldiers at drill. The
movements of the Imam are the same as those of the congregation,
and, as already explained, all the *rikats* are similar. The worshipper
raises his hands to the side of his head, and, touching his ears with
his thumb, says, "God is most great." Then, with his hands folded
below his waist and looking at the ground, he says, "I extol Thee,
O God,[1] and praise be to Thee : blessed be Thy name and Thy greatness be magnified and Thy praise be glorified, for there is no God
save Thee." Then he says, "I seek refuge in God from Satan, the
accursed," and then recites the Fatiha, or first chapter of the Koran :
"In the name of God, the Merciful, the Compassionate. Praise be
to God, the Lord of the Worlds, the Merciful, the Compassionate,
the Ruler of the Day of Judgment. Thee do we serve, and of Thee
we ask aid : lead us in the straight way, the way of those to whom
Thou art gracious, not of those against whom Thou art wroth, nor
of those that err." After this he repeats as many verses of the Koran
as he thinks proper. As a rule the Ikhlas (LXII.) is used, "Say,
He is God alone : God the Eternal : He begetteth not, and is not
begotten : And there is none like unto Him." Then he bows down,
placing his hands on his knees, but still standing, and says, "God is
most great. I praise God" (Subhana 'llah), the latter thrice. Then,
still erect, but with his hands at the side of his body, "God hears him
who praises Him. O Lord Thou art praised."[2] Then he falls on
his knees and again says, "God is most great ; " and then prostrating himself, with his forehead on the ground, repeats thrice "Subhana 'llah." Then raising his body and sitting on his heels, he says,
"God is most great ; " and then prostrating himself again, again
repeats, "God is most great—Subhana 'llah." This ends one *rikat*.
The second *rikat* of a series omits the introductory formulæ and com-
mences with the *fatiha*. After every two *rikats* the worshipper sits
down with his left foot under him, and spreading his hands on his
knees says the following prayers : "Homage is due to God, and

---

[1] Subhanaka 'llahumma.
[2] A man praying alone says both verses. In a mosque the Imam says the
first and the congregation the second.

prayers and good works. Peace be upon thee, O Prophet, and the mercy of God and His blessing. Peace be upon us and on the righteous servants of God." Then holding up the first finger of the right hand, "I testify that there is no God but God, and I testify that Mohammed is His slave and prophet." Every two *rikats* end with this formula, which is called Teshahhud. At the end of the whole set of *rikats* which make up any set of prayers, the following is recited in the same sitting posture :—

" O God, have mercy on our Lord Mohammed and the family of Mohammed, as Thou didst have mercy on Abraham and the family of Abraham ; for Thou art worthy to be praised, and Thou art glorious."

" O God, bless our Lord Mohammed and the family of Mohammed, as Thou didst bless Abraham and the family of Abraham ; for Thou art worthy to be praised, and Thou art glorious."

" O Lord God, give us the blessings of this life and the blessings of life everlasting ; save us from the torments of hell."

Then turning the head first to the left and then to the right, he says twice, "The peace and mercy of God be with you."

The full mid-day prayer on ordinary days consists of ten *rikats*, four *sunnet*, four *farz*, and two more *sunnet* after the *farz*. On Friday two extra *sunnet rikats* are recited, and there is also a sort of sermon. A Mollah ascends the pulpit and pronounces an oration called *khutbe*. In St. Sophia, and other mosques which were once churches, he leans on a sword when preaching, and it is said that in time of war he holds a drawn sword in his hand. The *khutbe* is perhaps hardly a sermon in our sense of the word, for it is largely addressed to the Deity, and contains prayers for the protection and triumph of Islam. It also contains a commemoration of the early Caliphs and companions of the Prophet (after each of whose names the congregation respond, " May God·be pleased with him "), and a prayer for the present Caliph. In Afghanistan and other independent Moslim kingdoms I believe the sovereign of the country is prayed for. In Russia and India prayers are sometimes offered for the long life of the Czar or Queen, but this is a very different matter to mentioning their name in the *khutbe*. " God bless the King, God bless the faith's defender, God bless (no harm in blessing) the Pretender," as the old Scotch song has it. On solemn occasions it is usual for the Imam to offer up extra prayers, selected or composed as he thinks best, which are called Munajat. I believe they are always recited when the Sultan is present.

During Ramazan real sermons are often preached in the evening. At this season, too, a long service called Teravih, consisting of twenty *rikats*, is performed after the last Namaz, but the *rikats* do not differ from the ordinary type.

The Koran frequently enjoins the offering of sacrifices and the practice is considered meritorious. On the feast of Kurban Bairam every adult male is bound to sacrifice a sheep. A sacrifice may not be performed in a mosque, and is not, I believe, attended by any ceremony, except cutting the animal's throat with the words Bi-'smi-'llah ("In the name of God"). It is meritorious to give the flesh to the poor.

Apart from the Namaz, which is essentially a service to be recited at certain hours, Mohammedans are accustomed to say a prayer (Dua) on any solemn occasion, such as a departure, circumcision, opening of a new house, &c. The *fatiha* is often thought sufficient for such purposes, but sometimes other prayers are used which are generally a collection of phrases from the Koran strung together. Prayers for the dead are regarded as a sacred duty and Turkish epitaphs generally end with the appeal, "(Say) the *fatiha* for his soul."

The following are the principal religious seasons observed in Turkey. The dates are given according to the lunar months (which are always used for religious purposes), and, of course, vary every year when expressed in the solar reckoning :—

Ramazan : a month of fast in which neither food, drink, nor tobacco must be taken between sunrise and sunset. People consequently sleep through the day as much as they can and devote the night to amusement or devotion. I have already mentioned the Teravih services. Towards the end of Ramazan comes the Leil-ul-Kadr, or "night of power."[1] It is commonly observed on the 27th, but, according to strict tradition, the exact date is unknown, and it is only certain that it is between the 26th and 29th of Ramazan, for which reason it is the custom to spend as much of those four nights as possible in prayer, it being currently believed that there is one moment at which all the requests of those who are found worshipping are granted. Ramazan ends with the feast of Bairam (Sheval

[1] The highly mysterious chapter of the Koran (Sura XCVII.) which speaks of this night is as follows : "Verily we sent it (the Koran) down on the night of power. And who shall make thee know what the night of power is? The night of power is better than a thousand months. In it descend the angels and the spirit by permission of their Lord in every matter. It is peace till the rising of the dawn."

1), called in Arabic 'Idu-'l-fitr. The first morning prayer is performed with great ceremony and followed by a *khutbe* and special supplications; feasting continues for three days. About two months later (Zi-'l-hijje 10) comes a second feast of three days, called in Turkey Kurban-Bairam, but in Arabic-speaking countries Idu-'l-azha, commemorating the sacrifice of Ismail (whom Mohammedan tradition substitutes for Isaac) by Abraham. On the first day the morning Namaz is again performed with great solemnity and every adult male sacrifices a sheep on returning to his house.

Other festivals are the following:—Leilu-'l-berat (*vide supra*, page 187), on Shaban 15. Hirka-i-Sherif (Ramazan 15), the "Feast of the Prophet's Mantle." The Sultan proceeds to the mosque in the Old Serai in which this relic is preserved, and after performing the mid-day prayer, venerates it and shows it to a select company of high officials who accompany him. The relic is said to be a small fragment of greenish cloth wrapped up in forty silk handkerchiefs, each larger than the other. Mevlud, or birthday of the Prophet (Rebiu-'l-evel 12). Leilu-'l-Miraj (Rejeb 27), the night when Mohammed went up to heaven on a winged steed. On all these occasions, including the entire month of Ramazan, it is customary to illuminate the mosques and minarets at night with hundreds of small lamps. A Turkish festival always begins at sunset on the previous day—*e.g.* if the date of the Mevlud is given as July 30, the feast lasts from sunset July 29 to sunset July 30.

II. ON SUNNITES AND SHIITES.

The most important division of Mohammedans is into Sunnites and Shiites. The latter number some fifteen millions in Persia and India; to the former belong practically the whole of the rest of Islam, for the heretical sects are of little numerical importance.

The Sunnites believe in the office of Khalifa, Successor or Vicar of Mohammed, and accept Abu-Bekr, Omar, and Osman as the first three Khalifas. They accept the six books of traditions which are commonly designated by the name of Sunna. They are divided into four schools, all equally orthodox, and differing only in their interpretation of minute points of law and ritual—the Hanafiyas (Turkey, Central Asia, and North India), Shafi'iyas (Egypt), Malakiyas (Morocco and North Africa), and Hambaliyas (parts of Arabia).

The Shiites reject the institution of the Caliphate and hold that after the death of Mohammed the headship of the Mohammedan Church was vested in an Imam. The first Imam was Ali, whom they consider the successor and almost the equal of the Prophet, and the office continued to be hereditary in his family until the time of the twelfth Imam, commonly called Imam al-Mahdi, who mysteriously disappeared down a well, but is believed to be still alive. His reappearance will announce the coming of the day of judgment. The Shiahs have also a great veneration for Hasan and Husein, the two sons of Ali, of whom the first was poisoned and the second slain in battle near Kerbela. Their deaths are commemorated at the Persian festival of Muharrem. In distinction to the Sunnites, who hold that truth can only be found in tradition, and that no one at the present day is capable of forming a new and independent opinion as to the interpretation of the Koran or sayings of the Prophet, the Shiites maintain that certain learned doctors, whom they call Mujtehid, have a right to use their judgment and form such opinions. They reject the six books of the Sunnite traditions, but have other collections of traditions of their own. There are various small differences between their ritual and law and those of the Sunnites, the most important being that they are said to admit temporary marriages, and to allow that a man may deny his religion in order to save himself from persecution.

III. On Mohammed's Ideas Respecting Christianity.

Christ and Christianity are often mentioned in the Koran; and it is a matter of some interest but great difficulty to know what was the extent of Mohammed's acquaintance with the religion and what was his real attitude towards those who professed it. He clearly assumes that Christianity is a familiar reality to his audience, and we can hardly doubt that he did his best to learn its tenets; but, on the other hand, it seems to me plain that he had never discussed the religion with an even moderately orthodox Christian, and that he had never read, or rather had read to him, any of the Gospels, at least in their entirety.

In his own way the Prophet was a student of comparative religion, but it must be admitted that he was amazingly ignorant and uncritical. He could not read; he believed that all his utterances on religious questions were divinely inspired, and he slew those who criticised them. Such a method begets a habit of rash assertion, and it is instructive to observe some of his statements about

Judaism. It is clear that he had talked with Talmudists, and was acquainted with even the details of many Talmudic legends. Yet he accused the Jews of saying that Ezra was the Son of God,[1] though there is nothing in Hebrew literature to warrant this strange charge. He said that Pharaoh's vizier was called Haman, and that the Virgin Mary was the sister of Aaron. Many critics have been loth to admit that he was capable of confusing the two Miriams; but *litera scripta manet*, and no explanation has been offered more plausible than the irrefutable remark of the orthodox commentator that for all we know the Virgin may have had a brother called Aaron. Clearly the man who made such errors may have misrepresented what he heard about Christianity; but his remarks on the Crucifixion seem to me to prove conclusively that he had heard very little. In Sura IV. 155, he says that Christ was not crucified, and treats the statement that He was as a calumny of the Jews, similar to their aspersions on the virtue of the Virgin Mary. Had he been acquainted with ordinary Christian ideas respecting the Resurrection and Atonement, he would probably have denounced them, but he could not have made a passing allusion to the Crucifixion as a piece of Jewish scandal-mongering. No doubt, in the seventh century, Oriental Christianity was more occupied with discussions on the nature of Christ than with the doctrine of the Atonement; but still Mohammed could hardly have conversed with Christians without discovering that the Crucifixion was as integral a part of their faith as the Trinity or the sonship of Christ, and he would presumably have criticised it as seriously as he criticised those doctrines. It is often supposed that he came into contact with Gnostics, Ebionites, and other schismatics. Perhaps so. It does not seem to me to be proved that the theories of such people formed a natural part of the intellectual atmosphere which he breathed, but we are all at the mercy of linguistic hazard, and, maybe, the only Christian with whom he could communicate was some fantastic sectary.

Directly or indirectly he knew that the Christians believed in the Trinity and considered Christ to be the Son of God, and he directed a severe polemic against these doctrines. He thought that the Trinity consisted of the Father, Son, and the Virgin Mary. This misconception seems to me to be easily explicable, particularly if we suppose that his knowledge of Christian doctrine was second-hand. There is a venerable, but eminently probable, anecdote which

---

[1] IX. 30. "The Jews say Ezra is the Son of God and the Christians say that the Messiah is the Son of God."

relates that a Russian peasant, when questioned about the Trinity, said he considered that it consisted of God, the Madonna, and St. Nicholas. Perhaps the special title of Jesus, "The Spirit of God," arises from a confusion between the second and third persons of the Trinity. Mohammed's declarations regarding the nature of Christ are precise. He was miraculously created by God and had no father; but he was not the Son of God, because such an expression implies relations between God and a woman which are incompatible with the Moslim idea of the Deity. "When He decreeth a thing He only saith 'Be' and it is." He *ordered* the miraculous birth of Christ, but "He begetteth not and is not begotten." With this reservation the Koran speaks of Christ with deep respect and accords to him (Sura IV. 169) the title of "Rasulu-'llah," which is the peculiar designation of Mohammed himself, and generally translated "Prophet of God," but more accurately "apostle." It also contains long accounts of His nativity, which sometimes verbally recall the first chapter of St. Luke, and of his miracles, among which is that of making a clay bird live and fly, as recounted in some apocryphal Gospels. It is not clearly stated in the Koran what was the end of Christ's mission; but, according to the Sunna, when the Jews wished to crucify Him, He was taken up by God into heaven, whence He will come again "to break the cross and slay the swine." There is a curious passage in Sura V. recounting how Christ caused a table with food to descend from heaven, which seems to be a confusion of the Last Supper and St. Peter's vision as related in Acts x.

In Sura LXI. we read: "Jesus, the Son of Mary (Isa-ibn-Maryam), said, 'O children of Israel, verily I am the Apostle of God to you, confirming the law that was before me and giving you glad tidings of an Apostle who shall come after me whose name shall be Ahmad.'" Ahmad is a derivative from the same root as Mohammed, both meaning "praised" or "glorious," and the Prophet no doubt meant to say that Christ had foretold his coming. It is generally supposed that the passage is an allusion to the promise of the Paraclete, and that, in some corrupt Greek text, Παράκλητος had become changed into Περικλυτός, which might be rendered by Ahmad in Arabic.

The following are a few of the more remarkable passages from the Koran dealing with Christianity :—

Sura V. 76 ff. "They are infidels who say, 'Verily God is the Messiah, the Son of Mary.' But the Messiah said, 'O children of

Israel, worship God, my Lord and your Lord.' . . . They are infidels who say, 'Verily God is the third of three, for there is no God but one.' . . . The Messiah, the Son of Mary, is only a prophet : prophets before him have passed away. And his mother was a just woman. They used both to eat food" (*i.e.* were not supernatural beings who could live without nourishment).

IV. 169 ff. "O people of the Book, do not exceed in your religion or say of God aught but the truth. The Messiah, Jesus the Son of Mary, is but the Apostle of God and His Word, which He cast into Mary, and a spirit from Him. Believe in God and His Apostles, and say not Three (*i.e.* that there is a Trinity). Forbear : it will be better for you. God is one God. Far be it from Him to beget a Son. . . . The Messiah doth not disdain to be a servant of God."

V. 116 ff. "On the day when God shall assemble the Apostles and shall say . . . 'O Jesus, Son of Mary, didst thou say unto men, Take me and my mother for two gods beside God?' He will say : 'Glory be to Thee. It is not for me to say what is not true. If I had said it, Thou wouldst have known it. Thou knowest what is in my soul, but I know not what is in Thy soul. . . . I never told them aught but what Thou didst bid me : worship God, my Lord and your Lord.'"

IV. 155. (The Jews are accursed) for their unbelief, "and because they spoke against Mary a gross calumny, and because they said, 'Verily we have killed the Messiah, Jesus the Son of Mary, the Apostle of God.' But they did not kill him and they did not crucify him, but they had only his likeness. Those who differ about him are in doubt concerning him : they have no knowledge about him and only follow an opinion. They did not really kill him, but God took him up to Himself."

II. 59 (repeated in V. 74). "Verily they who believe (Moslims) and Jews and Christians and Sabæans—whoever of them believeth in God and the last day and doeth what is right, shall have their reward from their Lord. There is no fear for them, neither shall they grieve."

V. 85. "Thou wilt certainly find that the worst enemies of the believers are the Jews and idolaters, and thou wilt find nearest in love to them those who say, 'We are Christians.' This is because there are priests and monks among them, and because they are not proud." (This was evidently composed when he was disgusted at the stubbornness with which the Jews rejected his advances, but in many other passages he says more or less expressly that, as far as truth and error are concerned, the Jews and Christians are all much of a muchness.)

IV. ON ABROGATED VERSES.

The Koran contains an extraordinary number of contradictory statements, as the reader may have noticed even in reading the brief extracts which I have quoted. There is indeed an initial contradiction in the very account given by Mohammed of his revelation ; for, though he considered that a connected and pre-existing book was being revealed to him piecemeal, he was also aware that there were inconsistencies in this revelation. In Sura II. 105 we read : "Whatever verses we (that is, God) cancel or cause thee to forget, we bring a better or one like it." There is considerable difference of opinion among the orthodox as to what are the precise verses which are cancelled by God, but it is agreed that at least some twenty are abrogated by subsequent revelations. The Moslim divines show great faith and ingenuity in reconciling contradictory passages, and as a rule only admit abrogation where two different ceremonial or legal injunctions are found in the text. It is clear that the Prophet was not able to read and revise his own words as a whole ; and, as he was a ready speaker and something of an opportunist, the uncorrected reports of his discourses are less grammatical and less consistent than the published versions of modern oratory.

V. ON MOHAMMEDAN TRADITIONS.

The Traditions, called Sunna (custom) or Hadis (Arabic, Hadith, saying), are a record of the sayings and doings of Mohammed as handed down by his companions. They are contained in six collections, compiled about two and a half centuries after the Hijra, which mention the name of the persons through whom each tradition has passed. The "science of the traditions" consists in carefully scrutinising the continuity of the chain and the credibility of the various links. The most important collection is called the Sahibu-'l-Bukhari, compiled by Mohammed Ismail of Bokhara. He is said to have examined 600,000 traditions handed down by 40,000 persons, and to have accepted of them only about 7000 traditions and 2000 trustworthy authorities. Although the six collections are not believed to be the Word of God, as is the Koran, it is held by the Sunnites that no one at the present day is competent to criticise them, that they must be accepted without reservation, and that all Moslims are bound to follow the precepts and example of the Prophet. On these six collections is based the Moslim system of jurisprudence known in Turkey as Sheri (Arabic, Shar‘), but here again there is no freedom of interpretation, as it is held that since the four doctors Abu-Hanifa, Malik, Shafi‘i and Ibn Hanbal, no one is competent to form an independent judgment. Both the Sunna and Jurisprudence are now chiefly studied in digests such as the Multeka and Hidaya.

VI. On the Ceremonies of the Meccan Pilgrimage.

The pilgrimage to Mecca must be performed once in his lifetime by every Moslim who is in good health and has the money necessary to defray the expenses of the journey, and to support his family during his absence. It is said that the Sunna does not recognise the performance of this duty by proxy, but it is certainly the practice in Turkey for wealthy persons to send a substitute. The ceremonies of the pilgrimage must be performed in the first ten days of the month Zilhije (Arabic, Dhu-'l-hijja), but pilgrims usually start about two months previously and allow themselves ample time to repose in Jeddah on arriving, and to undergo the quarantine to which they are usually subjected. On reaching the last stage before Mecca they assume the pilgrim's dress, which consists of two seamless garments, one thrown over the shoulder and one worn round the waist. The head must be uncovered, and the feet shod only with sandals. As they go to the holy city they sing a song called Talbiya: "I am ready (labbaika), O God, I am ready. Thou hast no partner. Thine is the praise and the grace and the kingdom. Thou hast no partner." On arriving at Mecca they proceed at once to the building known as "the sacred mosque" (Masjidu-'l-Haram), which is not like an ordinary mosque, but consists mainly of an open square surrounded by marble colonnades. In the centre of this space is the Kaaba, said to have been first erected by Adam and rebuilt by Abraham. It is a square stone building covered with an embroidered black cloth. Set in the wall near the door is the celebrated black stone. The pilgrim walks round the Kaaba seven times and kisses the black stone. He then visits a spot called the "Station of Abraham," ascends Mount Safa, and runs seven times from the summit of this mountain to that of Mount Marwa. These ceremonies are accompanied by various special prayers and take several days. On the 7th of Zilhije a sermon is preached in the sacred mosque, and on the 8th the pilgrims proceed to the valley of Mina and remain the night. On the 9th they run to Mount Arafat, pray there, and proceed later to a place called Muzdalife, where they stay the night. On the 10th day, which is the climax and conclusion of the pilgrimage, the pilgrims go again to Mina, cast seven stones at each of three pillars in memory of Abraham's having treated the devil in the same way, and then each of them sacrifices an animal in the valley of Mina. They then repose for three days, but before leaving again circumambulate the Kaaba, kiss the black stone, pelt the pillars, and drink the water of the well Zemzem. It is said that the Kaaba is quite empty, but there appears to be some uncertainty as to whether the pilgrims may enter it or not. A Moslim who had made the pilgrimage told me that they can do so on condition they never tell a lie again, but that most of them find this restriction incompatible with their secular avocations and refrain. But as he admittedly had not entered the sacred building himself, I cannot vouch for his accuracy. The pilgrims suffer much from the bad sanitary condition of Mecca and the extortion of the inhabitants, but the Moslim world seems to think that such hardships enhance the merit of the pilgrimage, and to be unwilling to make any reforms.

CHAPTER VI

THE ORTHODOX CHURCH

THE title at the head of this chapter is used merely for convenience, and not as implying any judgment on the correctness of the doctrines taught by the Church of which it treats—the Church, that is, of Constantinople, Russia, and the greater part of the Balkan Peninsula. Eastern Church is too wide a designation, as it seems to include Armenians, Nestorians, and other bodies with whom the Orthodox Church is not in communion; and Greek Church is too narrow, and likely besides to give rise to serious misconceptions. It seems, therefore, simplest to describe this Church by the name she gives herself, Orthodox—or, in Russian, Pravoslavny—just as we call a certain style of religious belief Evangelical, without necessarily implying that we think it accurately represents the teaching of the Gospel.

The Orthodox Church, though intensely hierarchical, acknowledges no one head like the Pope. It is recognised that an assembly of bishops representing the Church can pronounce infallible judgments on matters of faith and discipline; but the Patriarchs possess no authority, as does the Pope, different in kind from that exercised by bishops. They enjoy a certain pre-eminence, but even in their own Sees are not autocratic, and only rule with the assistance of a Council. At the present day the Orthodox Church consists of some twelve Churches, using different languages and varying in points of detail, but united as equals in one communion or federation, united, too, in a particular detestation of the despotism of the Pope. These ecclesiastical federated states fall into two classes: first, the ancient historical Churches, mostly under Patriarchs; secondly, relatively modern national Churches. Of these latter, the Russian is the most ancient and by far the most important; but, as Greece, Roumania, and Servia were detached from the Turkish Empire, their respective Churches were recognised by the Patriarch of Constantinople, though not always without a struggle, as "autocephalous and isotimous."

Before the foundation of Constantinople in A.D. 330 there were three Patriarchates — Rome, Alexandria, and Antioch. Either as the See of St. Peter, or, more probably, as the Imperial city, Rome had an undisputed claim to the first place. In the East, Alexandria was the most important Church, and the bishop, who was originally styled Pope,[1] had some pretensions to universal jurisdiction. The dioceses of Pontus, Asia, and Thrace were governed by exarchs of their own at Cæsarea, Ephesus, and Heraclea, Byzantium being administered by a suffragan of the latter. When, however, Byzantium became Constantinople, and the residence first of a Christian emperor and then of the only Christian emperor, it was natural that the bishop of the Imperial city should acquire an exceptional position. The transfer of the seat of empire from Rome to Constantinople decided the character of Eastern and Western Christianity. The Pope, left free from civil control, was able to acquire temporal power, and gradually to develop into that most interesting and durable of potentates, the Sovereign Pontiff and Vicar of Christ upon earth. The presence of the emperor effectually prevented the bishop of Constantinople from even aiming at so high a destiny. Any idea of making the

---

[1] His present title is still "Pope and Patriarch of the great city of Alexandria and Œcumenical Judge."

Church an *imperium in imperio* was nipped in the bud by the banishment of St. John Chrysostom, which terminated the struggle between the rash prelate and the Emperor Arcadius (404) and once for all adjusted the relations between the Court and the Patriarchate.

But though the emperors were determined to teach the bishop of Constantinople his place, and see that he did not intrench on the prerogatives of the Crown, they had no objection to his being the first of bishops, and willingly aided him to assert his pre-eminence in the East; and, though they admitted that the bishop of " Old Rome " possessed a certain seniority, they constantly called that ambitious prelate to order. In this ecclesiastical struggle Constantinople was destined to be worsted; but the ecclesiastical conquest of the East was an easy matter, rendered easier by the fact that, comparatively early in the history of the Church, the mass of the population in the Sees of Alexandria and Antioch accepted the Nestorian or Monophysite heresies with hierarchies of their own, which left the orthodox Patriarchs little more than their title. The second Council of Constantinople (351) decided that the Patriarch of Alexandria was to direct the affairs of Egypt only; Pontus and Thrace were constituted independent dioceses, and the Patriarchate of Constantinople was declared to be second in dignity to Rome alone. Antioch seems to have acquiesced in this arrangement; but Alexandria and the Pope protested, without, however, producing any effect.

In the fifth century the power of the See of Constantinople increased by leaps and bounds. St. John Chrysostom asserted a claim to the dioceses of Asia and Pontus. Under Theodosius, the Patriarch Atticus claimed also Thrace and Illyricum. This enterprising prelate even caused the consecration of bishops to be forbidden unless the consent of Constantinople was obtained; and in the law which placed

Illyricum under his jurisdiction it was at first enacted that the See of Constantinople had all the prerogatives of " Old Rome," but the clamours of the Pope and of the bishop of Salonica caused this provision to be abrogated.   Finally, the Council of Chalcedon (451), in its canon No. 27, entrusted the Patriarch of Constantinople with the dioceses of Thrace, Asia, and Pontus, which made his power for the moment almost greater than that of the Pope.   The latter protested, and drew a distinction, never abandoned by the Roman Church, between the doctrines enunciated by General Councils and the disciplinary canons they might enact.   Alexandria and Ephesus also protested; but the latter, one of the most ancient and powerful Sees, and even now held in peculiar veneration, was reduced to submission by the Patriarch Acacius (471–489), who also claimed, and in some measure successfully asserted, the right of consecrating other Patriarchs.

Shortly after this we find the bishop of Constantinople beginning to use the title of Œcumenical Patriarch, which he still bears.   The epithet had previously been sporadically applied to the bishops of both Rome and Alexandria; and it is not surprising to find that the Emperor Justinian, with his vast ideas of Imperial reunion and extension, should have been the first to give to his Patriarch a designation which seemed to imply that Constantinople was the centre of the world for the Church as well as for the State.   Under the Emperor Maurice, in 582, the Patriarch John the Faster used the title in a more formal manner in summoning a General Council of the East.   The Pope, Gregory I., protested energetically, and induced Phocas, the successor of Maurice, to abolish the title; but it was soon resumed and not again abandoned.   It is difficult to say what is the exact meaning of the adjective.   Perhaps the See of Constantinople has never been devoid of a secret desire to exercise universal jurisdiction, but it has not been successful in executing this

wish.   At the present time the Patriarch is Metropolitan of
the Orthodox Church in Turkey, except in such parts as
come within the dioceses of Alexandria, Jerusalem, Antioch,
Sinai, and Cyprus.   Over these, and over the Russian, Hellenic, Roumanian, Servian, and Austrian Churches, he has no
authority, and is merely given a certain ceremonial and
honorary precedence as *primus inter pares.*

But when Antioch and Alexandria were on the wane,
and Rome and Russia had not yet assumed their present
importance, Constantinople had in some ways an œcumenical position.   During the fifth and sixth centuries it is the
centre, not only of Eastern, but of general Christian history ;
and this is perhaps the reason why the General Councils
of the Church, almost forgotten in England except by the
learned, are still familiar names to the laity and peasantry
of the East.

Of the first six Councils all were summoned by emperors, and five were held at or near the Imperial city,
of whose political life and activity they formed an integral
part.   From Constantine onwards every emperor consciously,
or unconsciously strove after what was both the highest
Christian ideal and the great desideratum of practical
statesmanship—the unity of the Church.   The convenient
laxity of paganism combined unity and variety—the fact
that some preferred to sacrifice to Apollo and some to
Venus did not hinder both from being members of the
same State religion.   When people took to quarrelling,
anathematising, and killing one another because they could
not agree as to the precise character of their deities,
the State seemed threatened with a new form of discord,
which clearly called for a calming and unifying treatment.
Such treatment the emperors endeavoured to apply in two
ways ; sometimes by summoning General Councils, to exchange and formulate ideas, sometimes by testy edicts,
forbidding what the Court regarded as tiresome and per-

verse wrangling. In the first case, they won the approba-
tion of the Church, and even the honours of canonisation;
in the second, they were anathematised for their pains
by the angry disputants. In formulating doctrine the
Church accepted the collaboration but not the authority of
the emperor.

Even before the Empire had been definitely transferred
to Constantinople, Constantine felt the necessity of putting
an end to the Arian dissension—that great controversy
about the nature of Christ which threatened to rend the
Church asunder. Arius, a presbyter of the Church of
Alexandria, taught that there had been a time when God
the Father existed alone, and that the Son only subsequently came into being, which seemed to deny the
divinity of Christ, and to make him a mere creature.
Constantine at first regarded the quarrel as a tiresome
dispute of clerics, but he soon saw that the case was
serious, and summoned a Council at Nicæa (Iznik), at the
sittings of which he was himself present. As is well known,
the Council, which drew up, at least in part, what is known
as the Nicene Creed, condemned Arius. Arianism, it is
true, died hard; but the verdict of the Council was final,
and the principle established that Catholic doctrine could
be defined in this manner.

The central doctrine of Christianity — the essentially
divine nature of Christ — was thus laid clearly down, but
doubt and confusion were still possible respecting the Third
Person of the Trinity; for it seems probable that the
Creed of the Nicene Council was shorter than the form
now in use, and concluded somewhat abruptly with the
simple formula, "I believe in the Holy Ghost." The
heresy known as Macedonian denied the personality and
co-equal Godhead of the Holy Spirit, but was condemned
at the second Œcumenical Council summoned at Constantinople by the Emperor Theodosius in 381. As already

mentioned, this Council was important in another way as establishing the position of the Patriarchal See of Constantinople.

The doctrine of the Trinity and the divinity of Christ being thus satisfactorily defined, it was natural that the Church should attempt the solution of the further problem of the nature of Christ—that is to say, the explanation of how Christ is both God and man. It was inevitable that, in the discussion, before the question was clearly posed and answered, many erroneous speculations should prevail. The most important of these was the doctrine of Nestorius, Patriarch of Constantinople, who brought matters to a crisis by publicly preaching against the use of the title " Mother of God " (Theotokos), applied to the Holy Virgin. He appears to have held that she was only the mother of a man, with whom the Divine Person united Himself. This doctrine was condemned both by Cyril of Alexandria and by the Pope; but the Patriarch of Antioch and the Eastern bishops generally disapproved of the anathemas in which Cyril formulated his criticisms, and the Church was divided into two hostile camps.

The third Council was summoned at Ephesus by Theodosius II. The Pope was represented by legates and the Patriarch of Alexandria was present. The emperor did not attend, but sent a high official to keep order, a necessary but inadequate precaution, as the proceedings of the Council, which was exceptionally turbulent; were a disgrace to ecclesiastical discipline. After much violence and vituperation, the doctrine of Nestorius was condemned; but, unlike the Macedonian and Arian heresies, did not disappear. Henceforth, though the General Councils define Catholic doctrine, their anathemas do not annihilate, but merely create heretical Churches, which continue to the present day. It would be beyond the scope of this work to give any account of Nestorianism ; suffice to say, that though relegated to the extreme East, it has had a long and varied history, and in point of missionary zeal can compare with any Christian communion, its conquests having extended to Persia, Central Asia, India, and China. The headquarters of the sect are now in the Turkish district of Hekkiari, on the borders of Persia.

A reaction against the heresy of Nestorius led his opponents into the contrary error. His theory destroyed the unity of Christ's person by separating the two natures. Eutyches, an archimandrite of Constantinople, in his desire to preserve this unity, confounded the two natures by teaching that the human nature was transformed or absorbed into the divine, and that, after the incarnation, Christ existed only in this divine nature. The partisans of this dogma were known as Monophysites ; and the heresy seems to have aroused more stir than any other, perhaps because no one could say whether he was a Monophysite or not until his definition of faith had been criticised by his enemies. Flavian, the Patriarch of Constantinople, held a Synod which condemned Eutyches. The latter demanded a General Council, which was summoned by the emperor at Ephesus, and at which Pope Leo was represented by delegates. This Council rehabilitated Eutyches, and deposed all his enemies from their Sees ; but its proceedings were violent and scandalous in the extreme. Flavian died of the blows he received ; and though the Emperor Theodosius confirmed the decisions of this Council, the Pope disavowed them, and proved the stronger. In a Synod held at Rome, he gave the Council of Ephesus the name of Council of Brigands, which has clung to it since, and insisted on the convocation of a new and valid Assembly of the Church. The cause of union was favoured by the death of the Emperor Theodosius at this juncture ; and his successor, Marcian, consented to submit the decisions of

Ephesus to another Council, but resisted the attempts of the Pope to have it summoned in Italy, and fixed the place of meeting at Chalcedon (the modern Cadikeui), opposite Constantinople, on the Asiatic shore. The Council was largely attended by Eastern bishops and by two delegates of the Pope, who, with the Patriarch of Constantinople, sat as presidents, though the business seems to have been chiefly directed by nineteen Imperial commissioners. The decrees of the Brigands' meeting were reversed, the bishops whom it had deposed were restored to their Sees, and the orthodox faith in one Christ "to be acknowledged in two natures without confusion, change, division, or separation," was solemnly proclaimed.

But the Monophysite doctrine was even less affected by anathemas than Nestorianism. It long survived in high places at Constantinople, and is even now professed by the Armenian, Coptic, Abyssinian, and Jacobite Syrian Churches. The last-named body derives its name from Jacob Baradai, bishop of Edessa (ob. 588), whose energy and genius gave a new life to the doctrines of Eutyches.

This state of things was most distasteful to the emperors. The Council of Chalcedon, instead of establishing unity, had given definite shape to discord. Catholics and Monophysites were everywhere contending, and not merely with spiritual or intellectual weapons. At last, in 482, the Emperor Zeno, with the assistance of his Patriarch Acacius, endeavoured to still the strife by the publication of an ordinance called the Henoticon—half creed and half law—in which he expressly stated that Christ was both God and man, but carefully avoided the use of the word "nature." This unhappy compromise not only pleased no one, but nearly led to a decisive rupture between the Eastern and Western Churches, and actually did produce a schism which lasted thirty years. The Pope Felix excommunicated Acacius, and the messengers, afraid to deliver the sentence publicly, pinned it on his back as he was officiating in his own cathedral. He at once retorted by excommunicating the Pope; and it was only in the reign of Justin (519) that unity was re-established and Rome triumphed.

A more serious attempt to reunite the Monophysites to the Catholic Church was made in the reign of the Emperor Justinian. It resulted in the holding of the sixth Œcumenical Council, and was further interesting as presenting a new phase in the relations between Constantinople and the Papacy. It will not have escaped the reader that the Pope was gradually arrogating to himself a special authority as a sort of court of appeal. He had insisted on summoning the Council of Chalcedon, his legates shared the presidency with the Patriarch of Constantinople, and he had successfully required the abolition of the Henoticon. But Justinian, whose great ideal in temporal matters was the reunion of the West to his Empire, was not the man to tolerate such pretensions in an Italian bishop. Pope Agapetus died in Constantinople, whither he had been sent by Theodahad, the Ostrogothic king, on a mission to the emperor. The Emperor and the Empress Theodora, who was a Monophysite, arranged with the deacon Vigilius, who had accompanied Agapetus, that he should be made Pope on condition of favouring union with the Monophysites. He was accordingly sent back to Rome, and Sylverius, who had meantime been elected Pope, was banished, and utilmately died in exile.

In 544 the Emperor published an edict condemning what were called the " three chapters " or articles. He had been led to suppose that the opposition of Monophysites to the Council of Chalcedon was based less on its statements respecting doctrine than on the approval which it seemed to bestow on Theodore of Mopsuestia, Theodoret, and Ibas who were suspected of Nestorianism. He hoped that by stigmatising the works of these authorities, without making any reflections on the Council of Chalcedon, he would put forward a compromise acceptable to many. The edict raised an uproar, particularly in the West, and Pope Vigilius seemed inclined to forget the terms on which he had been raised to his dignity. He was, however, speedily brought to book, and summoned to Constantinople, where he spent seven adventurous but ignominious years, during which he was excommunicated by a Synod which sat at Carthage, dragged from under the altar of a church where he had taken refuge, and proved to have made secret engagements with the Emperor. At last the fifth General Council met in 553, attended from the West only by five African bishops, for Vigilius could not be induced to be present. It acted as the Emperor wished, confirmed the four previous Councils, but condemned and declared contrary to the Council of Chalcedon, the "three chapters." The unhappy Vigilius shortly afterwards made a humiliating submission, saying that his opposition had been due to the influence of the devil. He was then allowed to leave Constantinople, but died before reaching Rome. Justinian caused Pelagius to be named his successor, and formally confirmed the election. The Imperial nominee accepted the decrees of the fifth Council, but by so doing, caused a schism in the West itself, for the Church of Aquileia remained in separation from Rome for a century and a half.

For about fifty years there was little controversy; but the experience of the Emperor Heraclius during his Persian wars led him to regret that the Eastern parts of his Empire were alienated from the Catholic Church, and, following the example of Zeno and Justinian, he endeavoured to invent a new compromise. His formula led to the Monothelete (one will) heresy, but was first stated in the form that there was but one energy in Christ, and it was hoped that, this once admitted, the dispute as to the natures might be forgotten. Sophronius, subsequently Patriarch of Jerusalem, opposed this doctrine, but the Pope Honorius, in reply to the Patriarch of Constantinople, who consulted him on the subject, seemed to approve of the idea that Christ had but one will. Sophronius wrote a pamphlet condemning these views as unorthodox, but Heraclius, who thought that he had at last found a successful compromise, approved by so high an authority as the Pope, published an edict, called the Ecthesis (638), in which he forbade any one to talk of energies, and laid down that "one will is to be confessed, inasmuch as the Saviour's manhood never produced any inclination contrary to His Godhead." This was accepted by the four Eastern Patriarchs, but Pope Honorius died, and John IV., who doubtless felt it was a dangerous precedent to let an emperor make edicts about doctrine, condemned the Ecthesis without delay.

Heraclius died in 641, but the dissension continued under his successor, Constans II. Moved by the protests of certain African bishops against the Monothelete heresy, the Pope wrote to the Patriarch, Paul of Constantinople, urging him to abjure his erroneous views. The Patriarch's reply was an animated defence of Monotheletism, and, on its receipt, the Pope excommunicated him. The Emperor replied in an edict called the *Type*, somewhat resembling the Ecthesis, but more peremptory, in which he ordered the question not to be discussed. This led to another duel between the Pope and Emperor, in which the latter evidently wished to imitate Justinian's vigorous handling of the relations between the Papacy and Constantinople. The Pope began by holding a Synod at the Lateran (649), in which he condemned the Type, and then wrote to the Emperor requiring him to condemn the Monothelete heresy. Constans, however, was prepared to assert his authority: the Exarch of Ravenna received orders to enforce the Type in Italy; the recalcitrant Pope was seized and shipped off to Constantinople (654), and, after much hard usage, was banished to Cherson.

A long struggle with the Saracens and the Arab siege of Constantinople left Constantine Pogonatus little leisure to deal with ecclesiastical affairs in the first part of his reign. When the danger had passed, he saw that his father's policy had not been a success. The controversy which the Type had contemptuously forbidden appeared to possess—perhaps because it was forbidden—a vital interest. Constantine, therefore, adopted a new policy. Like his father, he declined to meddle in the question of one or two wills, but he submitted the problem to the Church for decision by experts. In this frame of mind he wrote a letter to Pope Agatho, whom he civilly addressed as " Œcumenical Pope," and suggested the calling of a Council. The Pope gladly complied. The meeting assembled at Constantinople in 680, but was attended by three bishops from Rome, who brought a letter from Pope Agatho containing an exposition of the Catholic faith. The Council followed this document, condemned Monotheletism, and anathematised the memory of Pope Honorius.[1]

These General Councils suggest many interesting considerations, which can be only alluded to here. We see, on the one hand, that the Emperor, though recognised as the head of the Church, was made to clearly understand that he could not interfere in questions of doctrine—a line which even the Czars of Russia do not cross. On the other hand, the power of Rome grows stronger. In

---

[1] This condemnation of a Pope by a General Council is interesting as affecting the doctrine of Papal Infallibility, and was discussed at the time of the Vatican Council. The boldest apologists suggest that the acts of the Council were tampered with, and that Theodore should be read for Honorius. It has also been irreverently suggested that the Western mind of the Pope did not understand the problem propounded by the subtle East. Adopting this last view in a more respectful form, it may fairly be maintained that Honorius's error was one of negligence rather than of active commission, and that he never pronounced in favour of Monotheletism *ex cathedra* and as sovereign Pontiff.

spite of the cases of Vigilius and Martin, the Pope had acquired an immensely strong moral position by the time of the sixth Council. The Emperor requested him to summon the meeting; he prejudged the question under discussion in a Synod held at Rome, and sent, by his legates, a definition of what he held to be the Catholic doctrine, which was accepted by the Council. Thirdly, it must be noticed that the Councils implicitly affirm that Christian doctrine is a subject for faith and not for reason. Each heresy condemned was a well-meaning, though presumptuous, attempt to offer an explanation of the Godhead conceivable for the human mind. In every case the Church replied by formulating a mystery to be believed by faith, but, strictly speaking, inconceivable and incomprehensible for our finite intelligence.

During the eighth and the first half of the ninth century the Church was agitated by a new question—the propriety or impropriety of using images in Christian devotions. The crusade against sacred statues and pictures, initiated by the Isaurian and Amorian emperors, was called Iconoclasm, and its adherents Iconoclasts. The movement was essentially Asiatic. The emperors who began it belonged to the race of the hardy mountaineers of the Taurus, and it seems probable that they had come under the influence of the Paulicians (a sect of Manichæan origin), and perhaps of Mohammedanism. Though we know the Iconoclasts only by the accounts of their enemies, it is clear that the aversion to images was only one of many points in which they differed from the practice of the Byzantine Church. They further condemned the worship of the Virgin, the veneration of relics, the invocation of saints, and, above all, the practice of monasticism. There is a Mohammedan air about all these tenets; and it is very probable that Leo the Isaurian, observing the immense progress made by the new religion, and the abuses to which

Byzantine Christianity was prone, conceived the idea of purifying the worship of his Empire, and, at the same time, benefiting the State, by doing away with the increasing multitude of monks, whose useless lives seemed a real danger to society. It is also remarkable that the Iconoclast emperors were by no means Puritan fanatics; they were reproached with their frivolity and fondness for gorgeous ceremonies. Also, their power rested mainly on the army, which was strongly opposed to images—a very Mohammedan trait.

Leo began his crusade in 725. He destroyed many images, particularly the miraculous figure of the Saviour called ἀντιφωνήτης, closed the schools of theology, and deposed the Patriarch Germanus. The Pope, Gregory II., refused to recognise the Emperor's nominee as Patriarch, and strongly condemned Iconoclasm, which met with general opposition in Italy, and provoked serious disturbances. Leo then transferred Sicily, Southern Italy, and Illyricum from the ecclesiastical jurisdiction of Rome to that of Constantinople, and only recognised the Pope's power in the territory of the Exarchate of Ravenna. This important step was really the first formal distinction between the Eastern and Western Churches, and it was precisely over this point that the final separation occurred in 1054.

Constantine V., called by his enemies Copronymus, was a more violent Iconoclast than his father. He held a Synod in Constantinople which condemned the worship of images, and he instituted a persecution against their worshippers, and particularly against monks. Many of his victims are still revered as martyrs in the Orthodox Church. In his reign the Pope called in the aid of Pepin—the first move towards the creation of the Western Empire. The next Emperor, Leo IV., was an Iconoclast, though milder than his father, and was succeeded by his son, Constantine

VI. As the latter was but ten years old, his mother, the Dowager Empress Irene, ruled in his name. She was an Athenian princess, and therefore a fervent adherent of image-worship, for the geographical division of Asia representing Iconoclasts and Europe Iconodules is almost without exception. Constantine and Irene invited the Pope to summon an Œcumenical Council to decide the controversy; and the meeting duly assembled at Constantinople, but was broken up by the mutinous soldiery, who were still Iconoclastic. It then transferred its sittings to Nicæa, where, in 786, it pronounced in favour of the worship of images, though a careful distinction was drawn between veneration ($\tau\iota\mu\eta\tau\iota\kappa\grave{\eta}$ $\pi\rho\sigma\sigma\kappa\acute{\nu}\nu\eta\sigma\iota\varsigma$) and adoration ($\grave{\alpha}\lambda\eta\theta\iota\nu\grave{\eta}$ $\lambda\alpha\tau\rho\acute{\epsilon}\iota\alpha$), which is to be paid to God only. Rome and Constantinople were thus once more united religiously; but it was in the reign of Irene, as related elsewhere, that the Eastern and Western Empires were separated by the coronation of Charlemagne by the Pope—a step as important for ecclesiastical as for secular history.

The Iconoclastic movement, however, was not yet dead, and lasted another half-century. Nicephorus, an Asiatic by race, reversed the policy of Irene, and it was not until the European house of Macedonia came to the throne that image-worship was finally established. Leo the Armenian began his reign by attempting a curious compromise. He proposed to allow icons in churches, but to hang them so high that no one could kiss them. This, however, pleased nobody, and he found himself forced to become a thoroughgoing Iconoclast. Like Constantine V., he summoned a Synod, at which only the East was represented, and again condemned images and their worshippers. A little later the Emperor Theophilus (829–842), was a vehement Iconoclast. He was supported by the Patriarch, John the Grammarian, and his persecution of Iconodules was nearly as severe as that of Constantine V., except that he did not inflict the punishment of death for religious differences. It is instructive to notice that both the triumphs of image-worship took place in the reigns of women. On the death of Theophilus, his widow, Theodora, like Irene, became regent. She at once deposed the Iconoclastic Patriarch, proclaimed that all were free to worship images, and convoked a Synod which instituted the feast called "The Celebration of Orthodoxy" (still observed on the first Sunday of Lent), in which the re-establishment of Iconodulism is commemorated.

It may seem strange to have given so much space to the remote past of the Orthodox Church, but there is nothing disproportionate in the attention devoted to this period. It was the period of growth and formation. Of the two great movements we have briefly sketched, the first, the intellectual striving after definition, which brought about the Councils, created the accuracy of dogma—the orthodoxy of which the Church is so proud. The second, the Iconoclastic movement, ended in the establishment of a ceremonial and symbolism which too easily degenerate into superstition. The two together make up the Orthodox Church as she is at the present day. After the Iconoclastic controversy the development of the Church came to an end. The conversion of the Slavonic nations is certainly a brilliant achievement of missionary enterprise, but after about the ninth century the intellectual life and movement were dead and have never since revived. It is not enough to say that the East elaborated dogma and the West discipline. The quality of intellect which produced Monophysites and Monotheletes was quite capable of dealing with such subjects as Purgatory or the nature of the Eucharist. But when the Western Church was arguing out these and many other problems, the Eastern Church seems to have sunk into intellectual sloth, and to have been incapable of controversy, which, whatever ill may be said of it, is the surest sign that a religion interests those who profess it.

It must not be supposed that the controversies of the West led to innovations, and that the Eastern Church remained true to the primitive faith. She has simply no definite doctrines at all on a variety of points, because, from inertia, and perhaps we should add political troubles, she has never clearly posed or attempted to solve the questions which agitated the West. This attitude has some advantages. In all branches of the Eastern Church religious persecution is rare, and these large fluid views about many questions may seem to compare favourably with the rigid definitions of Roman Catholicism, and to approach the spirit of liberal and advanced Christianity. But this is not really true. The same priest who shows a becoming diffidence in laying down exactly what happens to the soul after death is in practice ready to excommunicate any one who makes the sign of the cross differently from himself. If we turn to any ecclesiastical history, we find that, till the end of the period of General Councils, Constantinople is the centre of the Christian world. Afterwards, the Eastern Church drops entirely out of sight, and is hardly mentioned in general works, so that the curious investigator has some pains in tracing her history in obscure and learned treatises.

A certain section of religious opinion often compares the Orthodox and Anglican Churches, and even makes efforts for their union. The element of truth in this view is obvious; both bodies are branches of the Catholic Church which protest against the claims of the Pope to supremacy. Nevertheless, the comparison is historically misleading. The Reformation, though also a political protest against Papal claims, was due to an intellectual movement, to an upheaval and revulsion, to the revolt of many intelligences in many countries against certain superstitions and abuses. The separation of the Orthodox and

Roman Churches had no such cause; it was based on no intellectual movement, it involved no important religious principle, except the quasi-political question of the position of the Pope. It was due simply to the fact that the East inevitably tended to separate from the West, and that no organisation, either political or ecclesiastical, could contain two such centres as old and new Rome. The distance between them naturally gave each a separate development which in time made each Church feel they were not really one body. But, on the other hand, it was only distance and want of contact which enabled them to remain united so long. But for the geographical separation of the countries, the schism must have happened in 800. After that period there was in the West a pope as religious, and an emperor as secular head of the Christian Church. In Constantinople there was an emperor as head of the same Christian Church, with a Patriarch subordinate to him. The Church containing these four incompatible personages was no real unity and could not but tend towards disintegration.

It must be remembered that at the period we have reached—about A.D. 850—no one had any idea of there being more than one Church in the sense of more than one religion. There were Churches of Constantinople, Rome, Alexandria, and Antioch, just as there are in England, Scotland, Ireland, and America Churches which are practically identical with the English Church; but there was nothing akin to the common modern idea of a Christianity divided into Roman Catholics, Greeks, Armenians, Protestants, Irvingites, and all the other religious denominations catalogued in " Whitaker." There existed only the Church—apt to split into factions over questions of ecclesiastical jurisdiction, but still essentially one—and heretics. The latter, in as far as they were not extravagant sectaries with pretensions to a secret special revelation, mostly in-

habited remote and inaccesible districts (such as Armenia
and Ethiopia) where they were not reminded of their difference from the rest of Christendom.

We have already sketched the relations between Constantinople and Rome up to the middle of the ninth century. The various Councils, the Henoticon of Zeno and
consequent schism, the treatment of Pope Vigilius by Justinian and of Pope Martin by Constans II., the Type, the
Ecthesis, the Anathema against Pope Honorius, the withdrawal of South Italy from the ecclesiastical jurisdiction of
the Pope, the Iconoclastic controversy and final triumph of
image-worship, are all important points in these relations,
which had reached a stage of tension that small personal
incidents might easily convert into a rupture.

The Emperor Theophilus was succeeded by his infant son,
Michael III., his widow, Theodora, and her brother, Bardas,
being co-regents.   The latter was in many ways an able
prince, but his immorality scandalised the pious and austere
Patriarch Ignatius (son of the Emperor Michael Rhangabe),
who refused him the communion on the Epiphany of 857.
Bardas on this deposed him from his See, and named in his
place Photius, one of the most interesting figures in Byzantine history.   He was at the time of his elevation to the
Patriarchal throne commander of the Imperial Guard and
private secretary of the Emperor, and, though a military
man, renowned for his vast erudition.   His subsequent
career proved him to be a master of subtle diplomacy, who
would have been a worthy occupant of the chair of St. Peter
had not fate made him its bitter adversary.   Though merely
a layman, he was at once consecrated deacon, priest, and
bishop.   There were precedents at Constantinople for this
cumulation of orders, but Photius doubtless felt that the
whole transaction lent itself to hostile criticism and would
receive it.   He therefore lost no time in informing the Pope
of his appointment and requesting his recognition.   The

Pope, suspecting no doubt that such loyal words from the pen of a Byzantine Patriarch must be prompted by some unusual circumstance, sent legates to inquire into the matter. Bardas and Photius made these officials believe that it was in the interests of the Papacy to recognise the latter in order to avoid a renewal of the Iconoclastic movement, and filled their purses with weightier arguments. A Grand Synod was held at Constantinople which, with the assent of the legates, confirmed the deposition of Ignatius and the appointment of Photius.

But by the time the legates returned to Rome, the Pope had already heard the other side of the question from Ignatius. He disavowed the action of his ambassadors, and in a Synod held at Rome (863) pronounced the deposition of Photius and his adherents, threatening them with excommunication if they did not withdraw. It would appear that the Emperor took part in the dispute, and addressed to the Pope a letter, which is now lost, although the answer of Nicolas is extant. In it he combats, in the most uncompromising language, the theory or practice of Constantinople which made the Emperor head of the Church, and made great capital out of an unfortunate phrase of Michael III., in which he seems to have called Latin a barbarous language. " Cease," said the angry Pontiff, " to call yourself Emperor of the Romans, since these Romans are barbarians in your eyes. It is ridiculous not to know the language of those whom you call your subjects." It was not, perhaps, very politic of the Pope to personally offend the Emperor, seeing that the emperors were not always firm supporters of the Patriarchs. In this case, however, another cause tended to unite Michael and Photius in a firm alliance against Rome. The kingdom of Bulgaria had been carved out of the territories of the Eastern Empire, and converted to Christianity by the labours of the Eastern monks, Cyril and Methodius. The Bulgarians, however, inquired of the Pope (as well as of Byzantium) what was the true Christian faith, and received from him the answer that the only true Patriarchates were those of Rome, Alexandria, and Antioch, and that the bishops of Constantinople and Jerusalem, though styled Patriarchs, had not the same authority, because their Sees had not been founded by Apostles. Nicolas followed up these disagreeable observations by a practical campaign against the Orthodox Church in Bulgaria so effective that he drove out the Greek monks and substituted for them Latin missionaries. The Emperor was furious, and ready to support Photius in any attack on the Pope, whose despotic temper had also alienated from him many of his own bishops. It was not, however, desirable to put forward the Bulgarian question as a pretext for the rupture. The personal and secular side of the controversy had already been somewhat too accentuated, and the Pope might find it easy to pose as the champion of pure and unpolitical religion assailed by an ambitious and usurping prelate and a grasping emperor. Photius, therefore, struck a deeper note, and boldly accused the Pope of heresy.

His chief weapon in this audacious attack was the Procession of the Holy Ghost. The Council of Constantinople, which completed the third article of the Nicene Creed, undoubtedly contained the phrase, " The Holy Ghost . . . . who proceedeth from the Father, who with the Father and the Son together is worshipped and glorified." What is known as the Filioque clause was first added in Spain in the fifth century. The Spanish Church had suffered much from Arianism, and it was no doubt felt that the doctrine of the Single Procession tended to establish a difference between the Father and the Son incompatible with true Catholicity. The matter was debated at the Council of Aix-la-Chapelle in 809, and though the Pope refused to dogmatise, the formula was gradually inserted into the Roman Creed.

Photius addressed an encyclical letter to the bishops of the East denouncing this heresy and other Latin errors, such as the celibacy of the clergy, the observance of fasts on Saturday, the use of milk during the first week in Lent, and the refusal to recognise the validity of confirmation conferred by priests. This letter was followed by a Council, which met at Constantinople in 867, and solemnly excommunicated the Pope. Unfortunately for Photius, in this same year, Basil the Macedonian assassinated Michael and seized the throne. He immediately deposed the Patriarch and reinstated Ignatius. Though this action was probably prompted by the personal opposition offered by Photius to the new emperor, it may also be explained by motives of policy. Basil I. was the first of those who hoped—and who have successively been disappointed in their expectations—that Eastern and Western Christianity could combine against the Moslim enemy. He made a short-lived alliance with the Emperor Louis II. against the Saracens, and was, therefore, naturally desirous of closing the breach between Constantinople and Rome. Overtures were made to the Pope, Adrian II., who insisted that the decisions of the Council of 867 must be formally reversed, and Photius with all his adherents excommunicated. The Emperor assented. The Pope sent legates to Constantinople, who held the eighth Œcumenical Council[1] (869–870) and anathematised Photius.

It is another proof of the genius of this remarkable man that this sentence by no means broke up his party. They continued faithful to him, and created a schism in the Patriarchal Church; while the hollowness of the *entente* with Rome, and the strength of the forces which dragged Greeks and Latins asunder, were apparent before the Council was over. An embassy from the Bulgarian Church, whose overtures to Rome have been already mentioned, arrived with a request for instruction in the true faith. The

---

[1] Not recognised by the Orthodox Church.

Oriental bishops were unanimous in insisting that Bulgaria belonged to the Eastern and not to the Western Church ; angry reflections were made on the interference of the Pope in other people's dioceses, and the Bulgarians were formally declared to be within the limits of the Patriarchate of Constantinople. The Papal legates protested, but, in striking contrast to the honours which had attended their reception, were unceremoniously embarked on a vessel which, oddly enough, was immediately attacked by pirates, who stole the Acts of the Council. Ignatius seemed likely to have as violent a controversy with the Pope as Photius, and John VIII., who had succeeded Adrian II., threatened him with excommunication. Photius was not slow to avail himself of his opportunities. Basil naturally desired to unite the Eastern Church, and the Pope, unable to find a satisfactory emperor in the West, was disposed to come to terms with Basil. The result of all this was that, when Ignatius died in 877, Photius again became Patriarch ; another Council was held at Constantinople (879–880); the Pope again sent legates, and again entirely failed to subdue the Church of Constantinople. The instructions given to the legates required that Photius should offer an apology for his previous conduct, and recognise that Bulgaria fell within the sphere of Rome. Instead of this, the Council declared all the proceedings against him null and void, again assigned Bulgaria to Constantinople, and maintained the exclusion of the Filioque clause. The Pope excommunicated him for the third time, but, secure under the protection of his old enemy, Basil, he maintained his position, without, however, making any further attack on Rome or bringing about a rupture between the Churches as he had done in 867. When Leo VI. succeeded Basil in 886, he banished Photius to a monastery, and named his own brother Patriarch.

It may seem strange that the Orthodox and Roman Churches should have continued in nominal union for more than a century and a half after this; but two explanations can readily be given. The first was the natural tendency already noticed to regard the Church as one. Controversy and struggle had been frequent, but had invariably ended in the expulsion from the Church of a small number, and the reaffirmation of the unity of the main body. No one recognised the possibility that the Church might split into two opposing halves. The second cause was that, during the years between Photius and Michael Cerularius many circumstances conspired to prevent the Popes and Patriarchs from attacking one another. The period was perhaps the most discreditable in the history of the Papacy; there was a succession of corrupt and scandalous Popes, many of whom were hardly ecclesiastics, and none of whom paid any attention to the questions of dogma and jurisdiction which had brought their predecessors into conflict with new Rome. During the same period the Patriarchs of Constantinople, though with one exception eminently respectable, were engrossed by personal struggles with the Byzantine emperors. In 906 Leo VI. contracted a fourth marriage, which was forbidden by the laws of the Church. He was, in consequence, excommunicated by the Patriarch Nicolas, whom he deposed, naming Euthemius in his place. As in the case of Photius, the deposed Patriarch had a large following. The matter was referred to Rome, and the Emperor's marriage sanctioned, though only as a special dispensation. Before his death the Emperor reinstated Nicolas, and Euthemius, now deposed, but supported, as his rival had been, by a strong party, divided the Church into two factions. In 933 Theophylact, son of the co-regent Romanus, though only sixteen years old, was enthroned as Patriarch, and the Pope, who was represented by legates at the assembly, sent a written permission allowing him and his successors to wear the pallium without reference to Rome. He filled the office of Patriarch twenty-four years, and by his debauchery and mundane tastes scandalised the Byzantine Church, which was unused to such a spectacle. Theophylact was succeeded by the austere Polyeuctes, who quarrelled with the Emperor Nicephorus on account of his marriage, and with the Emperor John Zimisces because he assassinated Nicephorus. These conflicts left him no time to quarrel with the Pope, but the anti-Roman feeling was growing. The Patriarch Sisinnius, at the end of the tenth century, renewed the attacks of Photius, and his successor Sergius omitted the name of the Pope from the Liturgy. The Emperor Basil II. and the Patriarch Eustathius (1019–1025) resumed friendly relations with John XIX., and unsuccessfully endeavoured to have the Church of Constantinople recognised as œcumenical in its own sphere (*in suo orbe*), in the same way as the Church of Rome was œcumenical for all Christianity. But the Pope would accept nothing but submission to his absolute supremacy.

The last blow which cleft asunder the already gaping fabric of the Universal Church—that glorious conception which, since the early ages of Christianity, has perhaps never really existed in fact, that splendid title which associated in a nominal unity such differences of rite, such divergences of sentiment, so many racial antipathies, so many discordant ambitions—this last blow was dealt by the monk Michael Cerularius, who was elected to the patriarchal chair of Constantinople in 1043.

Two causes led to the consummation of the schism at this particular epoch. The one was the presence of Latin churches and convents at Constantinople, which continually reminded the Byzantines that in language, rites, and religious discipline the Roman Church was different from their own. Seeing how lofty was the tone employed by the Pope in dealing with the Patriarch, we may suspect that his subordinates irritated both clergy and people by their arrogant pretensions. Cerularius was clearly supported by public feeling when he closed the Latin churches and convents. The second cause was that at this period the Normans invaded Apulia, and, as they acknowledged the supremacy of the Pope, the district thus became united to the Roman Church, from which, as we have seen, the Emperor Leo III. had detached it. Hereupon the Bulgarian archbishop of Ochrida, in concert with Cerularius, wrote a letter to John, Bishop of Trani, in which he called the Westerns half-Jews, half-Pagans, and stigmatised their use of unleavened bread, their omission of the Alleluia during Lent, the observance of fasts on Saturday during the same season, and the permission to eat the flesh of animals strangled. Nicetas Pectoratus, abbot of the convent of Studium, also published a dissertation in which he more particularly attacked the celibacy of the clergy.

The closing of the Latin churches, and these attacks on the Latin religion in Italy itself, could not but call forth a rejoinder from Rome. The Emperor Constantine Monomachus was, as the emperors always were, anxious to preserve religious unity, and Leo IX. sent legates to Constantinople in 1054 to see if peace could not be restored. Had the discussions been conducted with urbanity, the rupture might have perhaps been postponed, though not for long. As it was, the violent proceedings and language of the chief legate, Cardinal Humbert di Silva Candida, who poured upon the Greeks, and particularly on Nicetas, the whole vocabulary of theological invective, speedily brought matters to a crisis. On July 16, 1054, Humbert entered St. Sofia during divine service, and laid on the altar the decree of excommunication against the Patriarch and his adherents, after which he with some difficulty made his escape.

The event thus accomplished, though often obscured and misunderstood by being regarded as a trivial ecclesiastical dispute, ranks with the foundation of Constantinople

Q

and the coronation of Charlemagne as one of the turning-points in the relations of the West and East. Above all, it was for the East of cardinal and doleful import. In it found expression that dull antagonism, that deep-rooted want of sympathy between the two great geographical divisions of Christendom which prevented them from ever combining against the common aggressor, and which thus proved the main causes of the fall of the Byzantine Empire and the establishment of the Turk in Europe. Basil I. could not induce Louis II. to fight with him against the Saracens; the Crusades directed against the Moslim turned into attacks on Eastern Christendom; the Greek populace massacred the Latins in 1182; the Latins sacked and seized Constantinople in 1204; Western Europe declined to prevent the Turks taking Constantinople in 1453, just as they did not interfere to prevent the Armenian massacres of 1895–96. In these last two cases it is clear that, given the actual political and religious situation, nothing could have been done. Had there, however, been a real community of Christian feeling, such as undoubtedly unites together Mohammedans in different countries, neither one event nor the other would have been possible.

One interesting point about the schism under Cerularius is that, until it was a *fait accompli*, nothing was said about the Procession of the Holy Ghost. Even the position of the Pope was not much discussed. Cerularius appears to have been ready to allow him a general primacy, and to have called Constantinople the daughter of Rome; and there is no proof that he put forward any excessive claims on behalf of his own See. The points at issue were all trivial and external. It is a clear proof that the popular conscience of Eastern Europe must have felt that the Latins were essentially alien and hostile; otherwise, no religion could have divided on such ridiculous pretexts.

After the rupture Cerularius appears to have held a

Synod at Constantinople attended by the Patriarch of Antioch and the Metropolitans of Cyprus and Bulgaria, in which the Latin Church was condemned as heretical and the name of the Pope ordered to be omitted from the prayers of the Church. But our information about this Synod is scanty. It is clear that the animus of the Greeks against the Latins was even at this period much greater than that of the Latins against the Greeks. The Popes do not seem to have immediately perceived that the schism of 1054 was a more definite rupture than the many which had already occurred and been healed. During the later half of the eleventh century, Rome made many overtures for reunion, to which the Byzantine emperors lent a willing ear; as they seem at this period to have had hopes that, if the Churches could only be united, the Pope might recognise them as the temporal heads of Christendom. But the opposition of the Eastern clergy and people rendered all such efforts abortive.

The century and a half which followed the schism witnessed two movements, which, by bringing Greeks and Latins into more intimate contact, made plainer the jealousies and antipathies which divided the races and their religions. These movements, perhaps only two expressions of one tendency, were the development of Frankish commerce in the Levant, and the Crusades. The former led to the massacre of the Latins at Constantinople in 1182, the latter to the sack and capture of the same city by the Crusaders in 1204. In the course of the twelfth century, the commerce of the Empire passed almost entirely into the hands of the Venetians, the Genoese, and the people of Amalfi. They had their own quarters assigned to them in Constantinople, with their own churches and clergy, and were exempt from the heavy taxes with which the emperors crippled the industry of their own subjects. The animosity excited both among the clergy and people of Constantinople by the sight of privileged foreigners living in their city and prospering to their detriment, found at last expression in the slaughter already alluded to, which strikingly resembles the Armenian massacres of 1895–1896. The Latin quarter was sacked and burned, some 6000 people were killed, and the head of the Pope's legate, tied to the tail of a dog, was dragged through the city amid the strains of triumphal hymns.

Still more disastrous was the influence of the Crusades. In their original conception these expeditions were armies of united Christendom sent against the common Moslem foe. In 1095 the Emperor Alexius despatched an embassy to the Pope to beg for help against the Turks; during the first Crusade Pope Urban held a Council at Bari to examine the questions at issue between the Churches: the union of Christianity and the retreat of Mohammedanism seemed imminent. Exactly the opposite happened. The dissensions of the Churches were deepened and embittered, and the standard of the Prophet advanced triumphantly between its contending adversaries. Nor was this unnatural. The Holy Army, at the end of their long journey to the territories of the Empire, seemed to the Greeks not very different from the hordes of Turks or other barbarian nomads whom they knew too well. The hungry knights, who had acquired in their travels no Oriental languages, but a considerable talent for helping themselves, had continual misunderstandings with the natives, which won them a reputation for violence and rapacity. The Christians of the Levant, then as ever unable to resist any opportunity of making a profit, laid themselves open to accusations of treachery and dishonesty. These natural animosities were aggravated by definite ecclesiastical grievances. In the West the policy of the Papacy was distinctly hostile to Constantinople; the Pope meddled in the affairs both temporal and spiritual of Transylvania, Croatia, Servia, and Bulgaria. In the East the Crusaders established, not only Latin states but Latin Patriarchates, which made it more and more obvious that Eastern and Western Christianity were, for all practical purposes, different religions. The *odium theologicum* has never been more virulent or more general than in the Levant during the twelfth century; and it was apparently in the heat of this contest that was first coined the graceful expression of " infidel dog," now impartially applied by the Turk to Greek and Latin alike.

Finally, in 1204, the knights of the fourth Crusade, instead of attacking the Moslims, turned their arms against Constantinople, and, after sacking the city with every horror of war, set up a Latin empire, and named a Latin Patriarch to the See of St. Chrysostom. We have seen elsewhere the political consequences of this event, and it is easy to understand how it embittered, not only the clergy, but the populace of Byzantium against the Papacy. The antagonism, brought to a climax by this onslaught of Western upon Eastern Christianity, found subsequent expression in the saying of Notaras that he would rather see the Sultan's tiara in St. Sofia than a Cardinal's hat, and in the ultimate realisation of that wish.

It may be doubted how far the Pope was directly responsible for the attack on Constantinople. The best authorities absolve him of complicity in the enterprise before its execution. After its success, while maintaining an attitude of decorous and perhaps sincere regret at the internal struggles of Christianity, he proceeded to confirm the doings of the Crusaders for the profit and glory of the Church. In his letter of December 7, 1204, addressed to the Latin prelates at Constantinople, he charged them to place Latin priests " *in the churches abandoned by the Greeks,*" to provide for the celebration of public worship and the administration of the sacraments. In a subsequent letter he blamed the election of Morosini as Patriarch, because the electors had received no mandate from the Holy See; but added that, under the circumstances, in virtue of his pontifical authority, he confirmed their choice. The Latin Patriarchate lasted at Constantinople as long as the Empire, and was always conferred on Venetians. After the restoration of the Greek Empire the Pope continued to appoint titulars to the See, who still reside at Rome.

Regarded from an Eastern point of view nothing can be more scandalous than the history of the fourth Crusade, and, at the risk of being partial, it is well to be familiar with that point of view. Innocent III. proved himself a very fallible Pope when he expressed the opinion that the Latin conquest of Constantinople had united the two Churches. The Roman Church is still detested in the East with a feeling akin to, but stronger than, the "No Popery" sentiment in England, a feeling based in both cases on the political transactions in which that Church has played a prominent part. As might be expected, the Eastern Church, having got the worst in the struggle, is far more bitter than the Western. Rome considers the Orthodox Church as merely schismatic—that is, disobedient—whereas the Orthodox Church has often accused the Papacy of heresy. The overtures of the Popes to reunion, however much dictated by the lust of universal dominion, were still honest efforts to reunite the Church; the overtures of the Greeks were all obviously attempts to save the Empire from ruin by an ecclesiastical alliance which their religious feelings disapproved.

The period from the re-establishment of the Greek Empire to the capture of Constantinople by the Turks (1260–1453) is characterised by an almost uninterrupted series of these overtures. They were not inconsistent with the mortal hatred felt on the Bosphorus for Western Christianity. Gibbon remarked that " the friendly or hostile attitude of the Greek emperors towards the Pope and the Latins may be observed as the thermometer of their prosperity or distress." He might have added that the feelings of the populace of Constantinople form another thermometer, for the virulence of their hatred and outcry against the Latins varies directly as the magnitude of the concessions which policy forced the emperors to make to the Pope. Petrarch (Rer. Sen. L. 11, Ep. 1) thus speaks of the feelings of the Greeks for those fellow-Christians with whom they were so anxious to be united: "I am not sure which is worst (for Christianity), the loss of Jerusalem or such a possession of Byzantium. In the one Christ is not recognised; in the other He is insulted by such worship. The one (the Saracens) are enemies; the others, schismatics, worse than enemies. . . . There is no doubt that they consider us as dogs, and call us dogs whenever they can speak freely. If one of us enters their basilicas, they purify them with expiatory ceremonies as if they were defiled by blood or some horrible crime. This the Church of Rome has long known and endured. Considering how easily the scandal might be removed, I leave it to others to judge whether her attitude should be called lethargy or patience." [1]

Yet, in spite of this temper on both sides, unanswerable logic forced the Palæologi to see that the friendship of Rome was their only salvation from two dangers; and the strength of their conviction led them to shrink from no hypocrisy and duplicity, and to face dissension and indignation at home. The first and most obvious danger was the advance of the Turks. The second was the continual threatening of a new Crusade. The unhappy Greeks had

---

[1] "Nescio enim an pejus sit amisisse Hierusalem an ita Byzantium possidere. Ibi enim non agnoscitur Christus, hic læditur dum sic colitur. Illi hostes, hi schismatici pejores hostibus. . . . Constat quod nos canes judicant et si loquendi libertas affuerit canes vocant. Basilicas suas si quis ex nobis introierit quasi humano sanguine aut foedo facinore violatas reconciliant et expurgant. Et hæc quidem Romana ecclesia diu novit et passa est. Quod an dici torpor aut patientia mereatur cum tam facile dilui possit hoc dedecus judicandum linquo aliis."

already learned what they might expect from an enterprise directed nominally against the Moslim; they were now scared by the disagreeable doctrine, constantly more or less plainly advanced, that the first step towards turning the infidels out of Jerusalem was to turn the schismatics out of Constantinople. The fourteenth century witnessed a succession of Crusades and attempts at Crusade. The disturbed state of Europe, and the strifes of Popes with anti-Popes, and of both with Councils, precluded alike any effectual attack on the Moslims, and any serious attempt to re-establish the Latin Empire; but Pope Clement V. (1316) proclaimed that those who took part in a Crusade against Constantinople were entitled to the same indulgences as those who fought for Christianity in Palestine.[1] Such language might well alarm a stronger power than the Empire of the Palæologi, and we cannot be surprised at the sorry spectacle of emperor after emperor endeavouring to dispel the ever-recurring danger by promises which he knew he could not fulfil, and overtures in the name of his Church destined to be disowned at Constantinople if accepted at Rome.

Urban IV., who was elected Pope about the same time that Michael Palæologus restored the Greek Empire, had been Patriarch of Jerusalem, and Apostolic Legate in the Crusading army. He therefore took an interest in the affairs of the East, and not only used the most violent language against the Greek Emperor, but wrote to Louis IX. urging him to lead a Crusade (1262). Palæologus sent legates to the Pope, who returned an ungracious reply, laying on the Greeks the whole blame of the schism, and saying they deserved all the disasters which had befallen them. He also charged St. Thomas Aquinas to write a treatise confuting their errors. But for the moment the

---

[1] "Illam concedimus veniam peccatorum quam haberetis si transfretaretis in terram sanctam subsidium" (Raynald, 1306, 2).

danger of the Crusade passed by, and Palæologus consequently paid less attention to the Pope. When, however, in 1270, Louis IX. really started for the East, he felt that the crisis had come, and again despatched legates to Rome, who entered into serious negotiations, ending in the second Council of Lyons in 1274. At this meeting the union was proclaimed, and the Greeks approved the Filioque, though they treated the question as non-essential, and did not make the addition in their own Creed. " Hadst thou but seen, my son, the joy of that assembly," wrote the enthusiastic Pope to Palæologus, giving him a glowing description of the edifying scenes witnessed at Lyons. What the unfortunate Emperor really did see was the black looks of his own subjects. It was in vain that he openly explained that his only motive was the political necessity of having the Pope on his side. His own officials fell at his feet, and besought him not to endeavour to ward off a foreign war by creating a far more dangerous civil war at home. But the Emperor persisted in his policy. He deposed the Patriarch Joseph, and appointed in his stead Beccus, who shared the unionist views of the Court. On St. Peter's Day High Mass was celebrated in St. Sofia, to mark the union of the Churches. The Gospel was read in Latin and Greek, and the Pope prayed for. The popular indignation at these proceedings was so strong that it became the fashion not to speak of Greeks and Latins, but of Christians and Latins.

This was not a very satisfactory state of things, but worse was to follow. Two years later Pope Nicolas III. sent further demands to Michael. He insisted that the Filioque should not only be tacitly approved, but openly recited in the Creed, and, further, that a legate should proceed to Constantinople to publicly absolve the Byzantine clergy for their sins against the Holy See, and only then confirm them in their offices. The Emperor's position was indeed difficult. The Pope was on intimate terms with

Charles of Anjou, who desired the destruction of the Byzantine Power, and in Asia the Seljuks were uniting to attack the Empire. But even under these circumstances it must be admitted that the hypocrisy of Michael overstepped all bounds of decency. He summoned the clergy, and explained the position to them. He would not, he said, abandon a jot of the faith, or really insert the Filioque in the Creed, but he would give a soft answer to the legates, and send them back with vague promises to their master. This was done. The legates were overwhelmed with honours and promises; they were taken round the prisons to see the enemies of the union in chains, and were sent back to the Pope with an evasive answer. It took some time to go from Constantinople to Rome in those days, and months were important. In 1281 Nicolas was succeeded by Martin IV., also a friend of Charles, under whose influence he pronounced against Michael a frightful anathema, calling upon all princes to have nothing to do with him, and give him no help. No ingenuity could pretend that the union still existed, and the name of the Pope was again omitted from the diptychs. Next year Michael died— excommunicated by the Pope and refused Christian burial by his orthodox subjects.

His son, Andronicus II., was a slave to the most abject superstitions, and naturally unwilling to provoke the resentment of the ecclesiastics of Constantinople by any attempts at union. Disastrous as was his reign, he was relieved of one obstacle against which his father had to contend. The massacre of the French in Sicily in 1282, commonly called the "Sicilian Vespers," broke the power of Charles of Anjou, and relieved the Eastern Empire of one anxiety. It must be confessed that the internal discussions and dissensions of the Byzantine Church thus left to herself are not less ignominious than the hypocritical overtures of Michael. The Church of St. Sofia, defiled by the presence of Papal legates and the celebration of Latin rites, was solemnly washed and purified. The anti-unionists imprisoned by Michael were led in triumph from their prisons, and the following year a Synod was held at Blachernæ, at which the unionist clergy were denounced, and handed over to the populace, bound hand and foot. The Dowager Empress had to make a profession of orthodoxy, and undertake to never claim for the corpse of her husband a place in the Imperial tombs.

Much commotion was caused about this time by the quarrel between the Arsenists and Josephists. The former were the adherents of Arsenius, the uncompromising champion of orthodoxy who had excommunicated Michael Palæologus at the beginning of his reign; while the latter followed the comparatively mild Joseph, who, though removed from the Patriarchate by Michael to make way for Beccus, and restored by Andronicus, was held by the more rigid anti-Romanists to be tainted with the pollution of the union. The quarrel continued long after the death of both these worthies, and the Arsenists made themselves ridiculous by insisting with exaggerated emphasis on all the most degraded aspects of saint and relic worship. The difference was at last appeased at an assembly held at Adramyttium, under the presidency of the Emperor, at which the two parties agreed to submit to the judgment of God, and to lay on a burning brazier two scrolls containing their respective confessions of faith, the one which should remain unconsumed to be recognised as the truth. The result was almost miraculous, inasmuch as it proved the honesty with which the contest was conducted. To the general surprise both scrolls were burned, and the disputants, abandoning their pretensions, agreed to recognise the Patriarch.

A little later occurred the celebrated controversy of the uncreated light of Mount Thabor. Some monks of Mount

Athos, influenced perhaps by Indian or other Oriental ideas, imagined that by steadfastly contemplating their navels they could see a supernatural light streaming from that part of their person. For some strange reason this phenomenon was identified with the light manifested on Mount Thabor at the time of the Transfiguration, and asserted to be eternal and uncreated. This doctrine was ridiculed by the Calabrian monk Barlaam (employed by Andronicus III. as an ambassador to Rome), but was upheld by Palamas, Archbishop of Thessalonica, and by John Cantacuzene. The quarrel between the Palamites and Barlaamites, after distracting the Eastern Church, was at last settled by a Synod in a sense favourable to the former. This doctrine of the uncreated light of Mount Thabor is, I believe, the solitary intellectual effort of the Church of Constantinople in the realm of Christian dogma, after the epoch of the Œcumenical Councils.

This same monk Barlaam was sent by Andronicus III. on a mission to Rome in 1339. Brusa, Nicomedia, and Nicæa had then fallen before the victorious arms of the Turks, who thus left the Empire nothing but Chalcedon on the Asiatic shore. The only hope for Constantinople lay in a return to the policy of Michael Palæologus. Barlaam's proposals were ingenious. The schism was to be attributed to the devil, thus avoiding the delicate question of apportioning blame between East and West. The Orthodox Church, he said, was ready to hear and doubtless to accept any scheme of union laid before a General Council; but to make such a Council truly œcumenical the presence of the Patriarchs of Alexandria, Jerusalem, and Antioch was essential. But at the present moment the Sees of those prelates were in the hands of the infidels, and any discussion of the union must be preceded by a Crusade against the Turks. The Pope saw through these arguments with the perspicacity bred of conscious strength, and brought the question back to the main point, namely, that union with Rome must precede any material help from the West. But though the Papal reply to Andronicus was unsympathetic and hardly civil,[1] the question of reunion attracted at this period general attention. Treatises were written on the subject by Nilus Cabasilas, Archbishop of Thessalonica, and by the Dominican Humbert. The latter, though in many ways strongly anti-Greek, sensibly remarked that the difference of language was one of the greatest obstacles to union, and that nothing could be done unless prominent Greeks and Latins had opportunities of meeting freely and ascertaining one another's real sentiments.

During the minority of John V. Palæologus, the Empire was distracted by civil war in addition to its other dangers, and the usurper Cantacuzene made overtures for the assembling of a Council of reconciliation, which were favourably received by Clement VI., but before anything definite could be accomplished, the Pope died, and Cantacuzene was deposed and banished to a monastery.

John V. Palæologus went further in his advances to the Pope than any of his predecessors, and actually visited Rome in person. He was the son of Anne of Savoy, a Catholic princess who had abjured, but never ceased to love, the faith in which she was baptized, and who had imbued her son with ideas favourable to the Latins. Early training thus disposed the Emperor to turn towards the Western Church ; and the inclination was strengthened by the critical state of the Empire, now grown so desperate that it is a marvel how its fall was delayed for another hundred years. In 1355 he wrote a letter to the Pope entirely acknowledging his supremacy in return for a grant of material assistance ; and, when that assistance did not appear, paid a personal visit to Urban V. in 1369. The Pope had just returned

---

[1] It was addressed " to the Moderator of the Greeks, and the persons who style themselves the Patriarchs of the Eastern Church."

to Rome from Avignon, and welcomed the Emperor's visit as an occasion for restoring the prestige of the Papacy.   After making public submission to the authority of the Pope, John was treated with hospitality and honour, but found that, though he had humbled himself more than his predecessors, he was no more able than they to obtain from the stubborn Church of St. Peter either theological concessions or military aid.   An attempt to engage an English adventurer, called Hawkwood, for the defence of the Christian East fell through, and the Imperial visit to Europe came to a singularly ignominious termination, as John was detained some time at Venice from inability to pay his bills.   His submission to the Pope was purely personal, and seems to have had no effect on the relations of the Churches.

It was reserved for his grandson and namesake to make a last and more serious effort for union.   Manuel, the son of John V. Palæologus and the father of John VI., paid a visit to the courts of Europe in quest of assistance (1400–1402), but made no appeal to the Church, which was then divided by the schism between Popes and anti-Popes. Later in his reign he opened negotiations with the Papacy; and in his old age explained to his son, John VI., his ecclesiastical policy, which was, briefly, that union being really impossible, all serious attempts to establish it should be avoided, as only likely to make plain to the Turk the divisions of Christendom, but that feints of union and alliance with the Latins should be made whenever politic, not in the hope of producing any effect in the West, but merely to alarm the Turks.

John VI., however, desired a more active policy.   He had strong reason to require support against the Ottomans, and the Western Church was better disposed than usual to accept, and even to make overtures, inasmuch as she was herself divided by the quarrel between the Popes and the Councils first of Constance and then of Bâle.   These latter were indeed contending for one of the main principles of the Orthodox Church, namely, that in the last resort the appeal on all religious matters is not to the Pope, but to an Œcumenical Council, which is superior to a Pope; and the fact that the Greeks ultimately applied to the Pope and did not take the side of the Council, is but another proof of the disregard for religion which characterised all these attempts at union.

In 1435 Eugenius IV. sent to Constantinople as legate Nicholas de Cusa, who arranged for the holding of a Council in Italy to be attended by the Greek Church. The Council of Bâle in vain made rival overtures, the Pope sent a fleet to convey the mission, and in 1437 some 700 Greeks, including the Emperor, the Patriarch of Constantinople, delegates of the Patriarchs of Antioch, Alexandria, and Jerusalem, and the Metropolitan Isidore, representing the Russian Church, with a crowd of high ecclesiastical and lay dignitaries, disembarked at Venice and proceeded to Ferrara, where the proceedings of the Council opened (1438). Little progress was made here, and in 1439, when the Pope was, for various reasons, in a better position than he had been the year before, the Council was transferred to Florence. There were discussed the ceremonial of the Eucharist, the formula of consecration and the use of azymes, the nature of Purgatory and of the Beatific Vision, the Filioque clause, and the supremacy of the Pope. The Patriarch Joseph, who expired during the proceedings, recommended union and concession with his dying breath, and finally the Greeks yielded to the Latins on almost every point. Questions of ceremony were treated in a liberal spirit, but the supremacy of the Pope was recognised, and the Filioque clause admitted to be synonymous with the Greek formula that the Holy Ghost proceeds from the Father through the Son.

On July 6, 1439, the Act of Union was signed and

sanctioned by the Pope in the Bull Lætentur Cœli.   Only
Marc, the Bishop of Ephesus, refused to assent to the proceedings, and declined to accept a reconciliation purchased
at the price of such concessions.   But this uncompromising
prelate, whose last wish was that no Latin might pray for
his soul, expressed the real feelings of the Eastern Church.
The mission on their return found themselves regarded as
little better than traitors and apostates, who had sold their
faith to the Azymites for a not very obvious advantage.
After vain attempts to induce more influential bishops to
accept the dignity, Metrophanes, the Bishop of Cyzicus, was
elected Patriarch; but the only result of his efforts to
enforce the union was that the Patriarchate and the Church
of St. Sofia were disowned, and practically treated as schismatic by the rest of the Constantinopolitan Church.   In
1443 the Patriarchs of Alexandria, Antioch, and Jerusalem,
who had been represented at Florence only by deputies,
held a Synod, in which they denounced the union and abjured all communion with Rome.   The Russian Church,
with even greater severity, condemned and imprisoned
the Metropolitan Isidore.   In 1448 the Emperor John
himself was obliged to undo his own work and abandon
the union.

   Eugenius IV. honestly did his best to defend the
interests of what he regarded as the Eastern part of his
Church.   He could not rouse the great Powers of Europe
to a Crusade, but he at least sent Ladislas, King of Poland
and Hungary, against the Turks.   But it was too late:
Ladislas fell in the disastrous battle of Varna; in 1452
the Turks were at Roumeli Hissar on the Bosphorus.

   The reader who has followed the history of the previous overtures to Rome, will not be surprised to hear
that, under these circumstances, the union of the Eastern
and Western Churches again came to the front.   The
grotesque comedy was played for the last time, but in

its most extravagant form. The Greek nation presented an extraordinary combination of unprincipled duplicity, ready to sacrifice all religion for political interests, and wild fanaticism, ready to doom the State to instant destruction rather than admit the most trivial ceremonial changes, and believing that Constantinople would be saved from the Turks by the miraculous intervention of the heavenly host if she only resisted the shaven Latin priests and their offerings of unleavened bread. Constantine XI. first applied to Nicolas V. in 1451, and excused as best he could the manner in which the engagements made at Florence had been ignored in the East. He received a severe reply. All Christendom except the Greeks, said the Pope, knew of the union; only at Constantinople was it ignored. If the Greeks were ready to execute the decrees of Florence, the Church of Rome was ready to work for their defence; if not, the Pope would be obliged to act as seemed best for the salvation of the Greeks and his own honour.[1]

This letter and a much more disagreeable communication received from the Sultan Mohammed about the same time were sufficient to send another deputation hurrying from Constantinople to Rome, where they arrived about January 1453. The Pope again found himself unable to induce the Western Powers to undertake any sort of Crusade, but pledged himself to send what small material forces were at the immediate disposal of the Holy See, provided the Greek clergy and the Patriarch of Constantinople would abjure the schism, and formally acknowledge the Papal primacy. The Greeks assented, and Cardinal Isidore[2] was sent as Special Legate to receive their sub-

[1] "Si autem Unionis decretum cum populo suscipere recusaveris, compelles nos ad ea providenda quibus et saluti vestræ et honori nostro pariter consulatur."

[2] This personage was a Greek ecclesiastic, who had migrated to Russia, where he became Metropolitan of Moscow. He represented the Russian Church at the Council of Florence, and agreed to the union ; but, on returning, his action was disavowed and his person imprisoned. He succeeded, however, in escaping to Rome, where he was made a cardinal.

R

mission. On December 12, he celebrated a solemn Te
Deum in St. Sofia, assisted by the Patriarch, and the
Pope was again prayed for in that fane which has heard
so many rival prelates and prophets recommended to the
divine mercy.

This ceremony produced an explosion of fanaticism
unusual even in Constantinople. The mob shouted they
would rather be Turks than Latins; the priests who had
taken part in the unionist ceremonies were not allowed
to administer baptism or perform any religious rites; the
Church of St. Sofia was almost deserted, and the lamps
before the ikons were allowed to go out. Foremost among
those who denounced the union was Gregorius Scholarius
(known also by the monastic name of Gennadius), who
had attended the Council of Florence, but subsequently
recanted, resigned his offices, and retired to the monastery
of Pancrator. He refused to appear to the excited crowd
which, on December 12, surrounded his retreat and demanded his counsel, but caused a terrible placard to be
placed on the door of the monastery warning them that,
as a reward for abandoning their faith, they would lose
their city.

"Down with the Azymites!" cried the mob as they read
the tablet. "We need no Latins. God and the Madonna
saved us formerly from Persians and Arabs, and will save
us now from Mohammed."

On May 29, 1453, Mohammed took Constantinople.
The Greeks attributed the disaster to the Latins, and
particularly to the Pope; the Pope and his adherents
regarded it as the natural consequences of the schism.
In 1472 a Synod held at Constantinople formally denounced and abolished the union of the Constantinopolitan
and Roman Churches.

Before we treat of the position of the Orthodox Church
under her Mohammedan masters, it will be well to briefly

review the history of the Slavonic Churches of the Balkan Peninsula up to 1453.

The conversion of the Slav nations—the most glorious episode in the history of the Orthodox Church—was due to the initiative of the brothers Cyril (or Constantine)[1] and Methodius, natives of Salonica, who made it their life-task to disseminate Christianity by reducing the Slav languages to writing, and making translations of the Bible. Their labours were crowned with success (though at first they were confronted with the opposition of those who maintained that the Almighty could be properly addressed only in Greek, Hebrew, or Latin), and they converted to Christianity, not only the Slav populations of the Balkan Peninsula, but even the distant regions of Moravia and Bohemia. In Bulgaria, King Boris, who had been fighting with the Emperor, Michael III., was baptized. On the conclusion of peace, and after some opposition from a Pagan party among the nobility, Christianity was established as the State religion. The question of East and West—orthodoxy or Rome—which has never ceased to agitate the Bulgarian Church, and which was brought into notice so recently as 1896, in the case of another Boris, was at once raised. Placed geographically between Byzantium and Rome, the Churches of Bulgaria and Servia inclined now to one, now to the other, of their powerful neighbours, and at many periods of their history it is difficult to say to what communion they belonged. The time of Boris's conversion seems to show that it was due to Greek influence, but the prince was a man of wide views, and had no intention of blindly following the religion of Constantinople. He at once sent a mission to the Pope, to whom he propounded 106 questions on Christian life

---

[1] He became a monk, and in so doing, according to custom, changed his name. History knows him indifferently by his secular and religious designation.

and manners, some of them excessively curious, *e.g.* whether Christians might wear trousers.[1] Among these many naïve queries one was important: Was Bulgaria entitled to have a Patriarch? It must be remembered that at this period, and for many centuries afterwards, a Patriarch was regarded as the necessary complement of an emperor, and every ambitious Slav who called himself Czar felt it indispensable to have a spiritual counterpart. An older Christian than Boris might have known that the Pope of Rome was not to be got round so easily. In reply to his 106 questions, the promising convert received a great deal of good advice, and a bishop.

The subsequent struggle over the Bulgarian Church was carried on at Constantinople, as I have related in describing the quarrel of Photius with Rome. The Patriarchs of Constantinople considered Bulgaria as forming part of the diocese of Prima Justiniana, and were always reluctant to admit its ecclesiastical independence. Simeon, however, the son of Boris, who established the first Bulgarian Empire, took the title of Czar (Cæsar), and installed a Patriarch at Preslav, his capital. The patriarchal See was subsequently transferred to Sofia, Monastir, Vodena, and Presba, and finally to Ochrida. The Roumanian Church appears to have been connected with this Patriarchate. When, shortly afterwards (1018), the ferocious Basil Bulgaroctonos destroyed the Bulgarian Empire, he reduced the Patriarchate of Ochrida to the rank of a simple archbishopric, which rapidly fell into the hands of Greek prelates, who completely hellenised it. Hence, when the second Bulgarian Empire (1186–1398) was founded, a new national Patriarchate was established at Trnovo. A few years later the Czar Kaloyan made overtures to the Pope, and found his

---

[1] This is a curious instance of how costumes, or the significance attached to them, may change. The Bulgarians, like many Asiatics, wore baggy trousers, whereas the Greeks wore flowing robes. Boris thought the latter might be essential to Christianity.

religious inclinations towards Rome remarkably confirmed by the Latin conquest of Constantinople. Unlike the Greeks, who, in their hour of extremest need, could never bring themselves to yield to the demands of Rome, Kaloyan perceived that unqualified submission was the only practical policy. As a reward, Innocent III. sent Cardinal Leo to Trnovo with a royal crown, and a pallium for the Archbishop Basil as Primate of Bulgaria. On November 7, 1204, Leo consecrated Basil, as well as two Metropolitans, for Velbuzhd and Preslav, and bishops for Viddin, Nish, Uscub, and Branchievo, and on the following day crowned Kaloyan. Innocent undoubtedly intended to consecrate by these ceremonies a king and a primate, not an emperor and a patriarch, though in his letter he stated with politic inaccuracy that primates and patriarchs were much the same thing. The astute Bulgarian availed himself of this Papal statement that the two names were synonymous. In his letter of thanks he signed himself Czar, and expressed his gratitude for the consecration of the *Patriarch*.

In 1237, when the Latin Empire at Constantinople was weaker, Asen II. abolished the union with Rome, and re-established the national Patriarchate of Trnovo, with the consent, or at least without the opposition, of the Greeks. The Pope excommunicated him, and called upon Bela, King of Hungary, and upon the Latin Emperor, Baldwin II., to undertake a Crusade against Bulgaria. But the political circumstances of the moment were not favourable to such an enterprise, and no harm came to Asen from the Pope's threats. On the other hand, the Church of Constantinople soon regretted the recognition of the Bulgarian Patriarchate made in the hour of need, and refused to treat the Bishop of Trnovo as the head of an independent Church. In 1355 the Patriarch Callixtus of Constantinople endeavoured to insist on the mention of his name in the Bulgarian Liturgy as a sign of the recognition of his authority, but the request was not acceded to. The fall of Trnovo in 1393 involved the destruction of the national Church, and placed the ecclesiastical administration of the country in Greek hands.

Like Bulgaria, Servia was converted to Christianity by Cyril and Methodius, who baptized the King Radoslav about the middle of the ninth century. The early history of the country, both secular and ecclesiastical, is inextricably mixed up with that of Bulgaria, and, even when it becomes separable, follows the same lines—alternate dependence on Rome and Byzantium in troublous times, and the creation of an independent Patriarchate whenever circumstances permitted. About 1050, Michael Voislavich, actuated probably by fear of the Normans, recognised the authority of the Pope, and received from Gregory VII. the title of king and a consecrated banner. It is not clear how long this union lasted, but it had certainly ceased to exist in the reign of Stephen Nemanya, about the middle of the next century. The youngest son of Stephen Nemanya, St. Sava, was a monk of Mount Athos, who became one of the greatest legendary and religious heroes of his country, where his name is still revered and his exploits repeated in the tales and songs of the people. He was evidently a person of extreme prudence, who knew how to make the best of other people's disputes. He induced Theodore Lascaris and the Patriarch Germanus, whom he visited at Nicæa, to declare the Servian Church autocephalous; but the authority of the Pope was recognised by the mission of a legate, who crowned Sava's brother Stephen as king (Kral) of Servia, Dioclea, Terbunia, and Dalmatia in 1217. In 1222, however, Sava crowned his brother again with a diadem sent from Nicæa, and anointed him with the rites of the Orthodox Church.

It will be observed that there is a close analogy between these proceedings and the policy of Kalojan and Asen during the same period. Only, whereas the Bulgarian Church made submission to Rome when the Latin Empire was strong, and declared herself independent when that Empire was too weak to object, the Servian Church contrived to be simultaneously recognised by both parties, though she subsequently threw in her lot with the East. St. Sava's See was Uzhitsa, but the residence of the primate was transferred, at the beginning of the fourteenth century, to Ipek, which long continued to be the ecclesiastical centre of the country. In 1346, when the Servian kingdom attained its greatest extent and glory, Stephen Dushan styled himself Emperor of the Servians and Greeks, and consequently required a Patriarch. A Synod of Servian and Bulgarian clergy raised the Archbishop of Ipek to this dignity, and the newly-elected prelate placed the Imperial crown on Dushan's head at Üsküb. Henceforth the Servian Church was long recognised as autocephalous, and did not fall with the conquest of the kingdom by the Turks or become Hellenised until a comparatively late period. But what occurred at Constantinople was repeated on a small scale in Servia. The Turkish conquest was to a great extent due to the religious dissensions of the country, and to the fear that, if they accepted the assistance which the Hungarians were ready to offer, they might fall into the hands of the Pope.

An important place in the religious history of the Balkan Slavs is occupied by the heretics known as Bogomils, a Manichæan sect of Asiatic origin. It is remarkable that most of the heresies which agitated the Byzantine Church—Monophysitism, Iconoclasm, and Bogomilism—were Asiatic, and had certain features in common. The Bogomils appear to have been an offshoot of the Paulicians, a sect of Armenian dualists, whose teaching early found a congenial soil among the Danubian Slavs. About 750 the Emperor Constantine Copronymus, who, as an Iconoclast, was perhaps not hostile to Paulician doctrines, transplanted a large body of these heretics to Thrace, where their religion spread rapidly, and was constantly reinforced by new colonies sent from Asia, the largest transplantation taking place in the tenth century under the Emperor John Zimisces. In spite of persecution by Rome and Byzantium alike, the sect continued in full vigour up to the time of the Turkish conquest, particularly in Bosnia, where it seems to have been almost the national religion.

The tenets of the Bogomils, like those of the Iconoclasts, are known almost exclusively from the statements of their enemies. The best accounts are given by Presbyter Cosmas, a Bulgarian priest, who wrote some ecclesiastical treatises in the epoch of Czar Samuel, and by Euthymius Zygabenus (in his "Panoplia"), a commissioner appointed by the Emperor Alexius Comnenus to examine the heresiarch, Basil. It would appear that there were two sects—one simple Dualists; the other believing that God had two sons, of whom the elder, Satanael, created a very unsuccessful world, which the younger, Christ, was sent to reform. They all agreed, however, in condemning the worship of images or saints and mariolatry; they objected to the sign of the Cross, and probably disbelieved in the Crucifixion; they apparently observed ceremonies analogous to baptism and the Eucharist, but did not believe that the sacramental elements underwent any change. Holding that matter was evil, they were naturally inclined to asceticism, and objected to marriage and the use of wine and meat. They were hence, like many similar sects, divided into two classes—the simple believers who followed the way of the world, and the adepts who led "the celestial life." The latter practised severe fasting and abstinence; they slept in the open air, took no thought for the morrow, lived on alms, and continually mumbled prayers as they walked. They appear to have attached great importance to prayer, but are said to have objected to the use of any formula except the Paternoster, which they repeated five times a day and five times each night. It is also remarkable that they held it lawful to conform externally to other religions. It is pretty clear from these characteristics that the Bogomils were one of the many sects which arose from a mixture of Dualistic and other pre-Christian religions with Christian and, later, with Moslim ideas. The doctrines of the Yezidis, Druses, Sabeans, Kizilbashes, and of many dervishes have probably been formed by similar processes; and perhaps the strange sects still found in Russia—the Philippowtsy, the Dukhobortsy, the Skoptsy, and many others— are closely allied to the Bogomils. The latter, however, have a twofold historical importance not possessed by any of their congeners. Firstly, their doctrines spread westward and produced the Albigenses, Cathari, and other precursors of modern Protestantism; secondly, they created a religious quarrel in the Slavonic states, which not only facilitated the Turkish conquest, but also prepared the way for the acceptance of Mohammedanism by large bodies of Slavs, especially in Bulgaria and Bosnia.

In treating the Bogomil heresy, one must qualify the praise usually bestowed on the Orthodox Church that she never persecuted. On the contrary, the Bogomils were put to death by thousands for their religious belief. Alexis Comnenus burned the heresiarch, Basil, in the Hippodrome, and Manuel, in 1143, again made the stake the punishment of this heresy. This persecution took a curious form in the bands of brigand monks who ranged over Macedonia and Greece in the twelfth century, waging war against Pagans and heretics. In the reigns of Alexis I. and II. constant complaints were made of these bands, who, a strange mixture of fanatics and marauders, overran the country, and, under pretence of suppressing heresy, defied the authority of the Church, and behaved much as the modern Bashi-Bozuks.

Let us now turn to the history of the Byzantine and Balkan Churches after the Turkish conquest of Constantinople.

Strange as it may seem, the immediate result of the Mussulman domination was beneficial to the Church, in as far as her prosperity can be separated from that of the whole Christian population. The Turks were well aware of the Greek plans for union with Rome and the formation of a Christian alliance against Islam, and the conqueror saw plainly that the bigotry of the Orthodox Church was the chief obstacle to any such union. In the hour of extremest danger fanatics had cried,"Better Turks than Latins!". Whatever the value of Latin help might have been (and the Turks, who regarded the Pope as a sort of magician who bore mysterious sway over the West, greatly exaggerated it), Orthodoxy had deliberately rejected that help and proclaimed far and wide that the fall of Constantinople was the result of the impious overtures made to Rome. Mohammed was delighted to encourage this temper and to teach the Byzantine Church to regard him as her benefactor and protector against the Pope. In pursuance of this policy he named to the Patriarchate, which internal dissension had left vacant for two years, Gennadius, the fanatical monk whose ominous scrolls had so excited the populace during the last attempt at union, gave him the rank of a Pasha of three horse-tails, and solemnly invested him with his own hands, in imitation of the ceremony performed by the Christian emperors.

But, as a Moslim, he was ready to give much that his orthodox predecessors had kept for themselves. The Emperor had always been head of the Church, and, in virtue of his sacrosanct character, had interfered in and controlled the course of ecclesiastical policy. A Mohammedan sovereign had no such ambitions. While reserving a full right to hang or otherwise correct any troublesome priest, Mohammed put the whole " Greek religion," as he phrased it, under the control of the Patriarch, who thus acquired an almost Papal authority, which he had never enjoyed in

Christian times. Further, the peculiarities of Mohamme-danism tended to exalt the position of the Patriarch. Islam has never clearly distinguished between the Church and the State, between religion and law, between temporalities and spiritualities. By tolerating the Christian religion the Con-queror implied that Christians were allowed to preserve, not only their religion in the strict sense of the word, but all their observances, usages, and customs, provided they clearly understood that they were, collectively and individually, the inferiors of Moslims, and paid tribute in humble gratitude for the privilege of being allowed to exist. The Patriarch was the head, not only of the Church, but of this tributary community, the representative of the Greek nation, the recognised intermediary between them and the Ottoman Government, a chief empowered to settle all disputes and other business matters arising between Christians, provided no Moslim was concerned. All questions respecting mar-riage and inheritance were referred to the ecclesiastical tribunals, and as the Greeks were unwilling to go before Turkish courts, and the Turks cared little how Christians settled matters among themselves, the authority and juris-diction of the Patriarch gradually extended to all civil cases. He was allowed to levy tithes and dues from his flock and to keep Zapties in his service. In fact, the pressure of the Turkish yoke was felt almost exclusively by the rural popu-lation, among whom must be counted the parochial clergy. The upper classes, lay as well as clerical, and the monks, who formed at this time so large an element, suffered but little. The higher clergy found themselves possessed of a power and influence which were new to them, while the peculiar inaptitude of the Turks for commerce and money-making enabled the laity, especially in the capital, to amass enormous fortunes. Subsequently, the Phanariots took a large share in the administration of the Ottoman Empire as middlemen, and their exactions and oppression became a byword; but in the years which immediately followed the conquest it was distinctly the Church which was favoured by the Turks as a matter of deliberate policy, and which prospered at the expense of the community. The clergy in return did not hesitate to exhort the people to obedience, and tacitly acquiesced in the levy of tribute children required by the Ottoman Government to be educated as Janissaries in the Mohammedan faith.

Such a position was false and unnatural. A Christian Church could win no enduring prosperity by aiding a Moslim ruler to oppress Christians. The first few Patriarchs seem to have felt their disgrace, for one resigned and one tried to commit suicide; but the demoralisation and decay of all principle implied by this unholy alliance with the Sultan reacted, as the politic Mohammed had doubtless foreseen, on the Church herself, and bred universal corruption and consequent weakness. The apologists of the Orthodox Church have often piously thanked God that she showed little of that worldliness and statecraft with which the Roman Church has been reproached. This is true enough if it means that she never had the power or greatness necessary to commit Imperial sins; but the history of the Patriarchs of Constantinople under Turkish rule is not pleasant reading, and presents a melancholy record of corruption and crime of little interest and no grandeur.

Gennadius only held office for five years, and in 1458 resigned, and retired to a monastery near Serres. The disorder and corruption of the clergy, the incessant intrigues and dissensions, of which the Patriarchate was the centre, rendered his position intolerable. Besides, he was soon taught that if the Turks were ready to exalt the Greek clergy at the expense of the Greek nation, they were quite determined to keep the Church in order, and make it plain that whatever privileges she enjoyed were favours which might be withdrawn as easily as they had been given.

Mohammed founded the school of the Phanar; but he also turned the Patriarch out of his cathedral, the Church of the Twelve Apostles, on the site of which a mosque was erected, and forced him to live on the shore of the Golden Horn. Joasaph, the successor of Gennadius, made desperate by the intrigues and squabbles of his Synod and subordinates, tried to commit suicide by throwing himself into a well, but was fortunately rescued, and " the Greeks," as Finlay says, " were spared the scandal of hearing that their Patriarch had voluntarily plunged into the pains of hell to escape the torment of ruling the Orthodox Church on earth." He was, however, banished by the Sultan for refusing to recognise an illegal marriage between a Vizier and a Christian girl, and was succeeded by Marcus, in whose primacy first appeared the terrible evil of simony and open sale of the patriarchal chair, which for some time formed so marked a feature of the Constantinopolitan Church.

After the conquest of Trebizond in 1461, many noble families migrated from that town to Constantinople, and naturally aspired to the Patriarchate, as the most important office open to them, thus producing another element of discord among the unhappy Greeks, who were now rent by the factions of Trapezuntines and Constantinopolitans. The former determined to oust Marcus; and, after vainly bringing various charges against him, offered to pay to the Ottoman treasury an annual tribute of 1000 ducats if their own candidate, a monk named, appropriately enough, Simeon, were elected. It is said that the Sultan smiled when this arrangement was submitted to him for the Imperial sanction, which it promptly received. The next year, however, Dionysius, Metropolitan of Philippopolis, offered an annual tribute of 2000 ducats, and Simeon went the way of Marcus, but must have been consoled by the peculiarly ignominious fate of his antagonist. Dionysius was accused of having carried compliance so far as to submit to the initiatory ceremonies of Islam, and actually had to convince a sceptical Synod, by ocular demonstration, that the charge was unfounded. He then resigned, after fulminating anathemas against those who had insulted him. His successor, Rafael, was a Servian, who purchased the Patriarchal dignity for an annual tribute of 2000 ducats, as well as an entrance present of 500 more. The Greek historians describe him as a confirmed drunkard, who often appeared in church in a state of disgraceful intoxication; but perhaps some allowance must be made for *anti-Slavonic* bias.

After this the price of the Patriarchate increased by leaps and bounds. For a short time the official valuation was 3000 ducats a year, but when the great principle of *bakhshish* had once been admitted it was not easy to limit it. Viziers, eunuchs, favourites, and women all demanded their share. In 1583, an ignorant monk, whose brother was a rich merchant, paid 12,000 ducats to various parties to be elected in the place of Jeremias II. The Patriarch of Alexandria and other Greeks in vain protested that they could not elect this incompetent man. They gained nothing, except that they had to pay 3000 ducats themselves to escape punishment for daring to oppose the Sultan's *congé d'élire*. Arrangements were soon made for the deposition of the monk, and Metrophanes of Philippopolis bought the See for 24,000 ducats. There was, however, a strong party for the re-election of Jeremias, who, finding that the Porte refused to accept his candidature, offered 40,000 ducats if his brother Nicephorus could be elected. Metrophanes, by unheard-of efforts, collected a like sum and laid it at the Sultan's feet. "The man is worthy of his office," said his Majesty; "let him alone." In 1620 the Grand Vizier demanded from Timotheus 100,000 ducats, on the ground that he had named 300 Metropolitans during his ten years' tenure of office. Cyrillus Lucaris, the successor of Timotheus, was deposed by the Jesuits and their party for 40,000 ducats, and reinstated for 180,000 more.

Naturally, these enormous sums did not come from the pockets of the Patriarch. As the Turks treated him, so he treated his own subordinates. The tribute of the Patriarchate was paid from the money received for consecrating bishops; the bishop paid this money from the sums he received for consecrating priests; who in their turn found the wherewithal by insisting on payment from their flocks for the performance of the simplest religious rite. The visitations of Metropolitans were dreaded almost as much as those of Pashas, and the whole fabric of the Church seemed converted into a vast mechanism for extorting money from the unhappy Christians for the most shameful purposes. The feeling with which the higher clergy regarded one another is illustrated by the regulation according to which the Patriarchal seal was split into four parts, each kept by a Metropolitan, the Patriarch alone possessing a key necessary to unite the four together, so that the presence of five persons was required to authenticate any document.

The Church of Constantinople was at its greatest degradation in the sixteenth and seventeenth centuries. The Turks soon learned that Christianity was not likely to combine against them, and that the Pope was little more than an Italian prince, who had his quarrels with Venice and other neighbouring states like anybody else. The union, which they had once feared because the last princes of Byzantium had seemed to regard it as an infallible means of saving the Empire, inspired them with no further anxiety. They had, therefore, no further reason to conciliate the Church of Constantinople, which they had at first regarded as a source of danger, and treated it and all its belongings with that contemptuous scorn which is so prominent an element in the Osmanli character, and which was not unnaturally excited by the spectacle of grovelling ecclesiastics outbidding one another with the bribes they offered to their Moslim masters. Selim I. and Ibrahim both formed projects of exterminating all the Christians in the Empire, and were with difficulty dissuaded by their Muftis, who refused to declare that such a massacre was sanctioned by Moslim law. The same Selim, and, later, Murad III., threatened to convert all the churches of the capital into mosques, and were only prevented by the deputations, headed by the Patriarch, who enforced their appeals to the privileges granted by the conqueror by enormous presents. It became the custom for the Turks to subject the clergy to open insult and abuse; the Grand Vizier did not scruple to call the newly-elected Patriarch, Dionysius, a dog before all the Divan; Patriarchs were deposed and changed as often as possible in order to secure more frequent bribes, and at least three were hanged. The troubles of the Orthodox Church were further increased by the hostility of the Latins, and particularly of the Jesuits, who, under the protection of the French, rapidly increased in power, and usually sided with the Turks against the Oriental Christians.

It is hardly surprising to find that this dark period was characterised by the number of conversions to Islam. This phenomenon is easily explained by the miserable condition of the rayahs, the enormous taxes, the powerlessness of the Church to defend, and the constant spectacle of a privileged class, which could be entered by the repetition of a formula. The wonder is that Christianity survived at all under such circumstances; and the Turks themselves felt the movement was dangerous, because if it was allowed to go too far there would not be enough tributaries to make life easy to the Moslims. In a similar spirit the Kurds have, in recent times, more than once deprecated excessive massacres of Armenians, on the ground that if too many of the latter were killed they themselves might be forced to till the ground and work. Hence, in 1691, the Grand Vizier tried to amend the condition of the rayahs, with a view to making them content with their lot.

I must not forget to notice the Patriarch Cyril Lucaris, for his career, melancholy and ineffectual as it was, affords at least an example of a man who rose above the intrigues and corruption of his time, and devoted himself to interests worthy of a Christian bishop. A Candiote by birth, he was educated in Germany, where he came under Protestant influences. The German reformers had already made overtures to the Orthodox Church. Melanchthon sent a letter to the Patriarch Joasaph in 1558, and a Lutheran embassy, headed by the Tübingen divines, Jacob Andreæ and Martin Crusius, visited the Patriarch Jeremias in 1576–1581. These steps led to no result, but Lucaris, when he returned to the East imbued with Calvinistic doctrines, made serious efforts to draw his co-religionists nearer to the Western reformers. He was made Patriarch of Alexandria in 1602, and of Constantinople in 1621, and was constantly engaged in correspondence and negotiation with the English as well as the Lutheran Church. He exchanged letters with Archbishop Laud and presented Charles I. with the " Codex Alexandrinus." In 1629 he published a " Confession of Faith," of Calvinistic tendency, in which he admitted that the Church was not infallible, and that the Scriptures, without the interpretation of the Fathers, were the origin and standard of orthodoxy. He met with bitter opposition, not only from the Greeks, but from the Jesuits, who, in 1638, incited the Porte to close the printing-press opened under his patronage by the monk Metaxa. He was five times deposed and restored to the Patriarchate until, in 1638, he was thrown into the prison of the Seven Towers and probably murdered. The Orthodox Church hastened to disavow the most distinguished of her sons. In 1639 Cyrillus Contari, the successor of Lucaris, held a Synod in Constantinople, in which both the confession and its author were anathematised (τῷ τοιούτῳ παγκακίϛτῳ αἱρετικῷ ἀνάθεμα). A second condemnation was pronounced by the Synod of Jassy in 1642, and, thirty years later, Dositheus, Patriarch of Jerusalem, in a Synod held at that city, published a rival confession, still accepted by the orthodox, in which he reasserted that the Church is infallible, and her authority equal to that of Scripture.[1]

The eighteenth century is marked by the rise of the power of the Phanariots, or Greek aristocracy of the Phanar, who had a practical monopoly of the two important offices of Dragoman of the Porte and of the Fleet, as well as of the Hospodarships of Moldavia and Wallachia. Their object was to hellenise the Christian races of the Ottoman Empire, which meant that those unfortunate populations had to submit to a double yoke—Turkish and Greek. In Roumania the whole administration was in Greek hands, but in Bulgaria, Macedonia, and Servia, the Turkish functionaries remained, and the Phanariot influence was confined to ecclesiastical and educational matters.

In some ways the Church lost authority during the eighteenth century. The Patriarch was no longer the sole head of the nation, and civil business naturally came to be more and more transacted through the Dragomans of the Porte and Fleet. But, on the whole, the clergy gained more than they lost. The sufferers were the peasantry, particularly the Slavs of the Balkans.

The old Slavonic autocephalous Churches of Ipek and Ochrida were both destroyed by the Phanariots, with the double object of extending Greek influence and filling the

---

[1] He said that the Church is ὡσαύτως τῇ θείᾳ γραφῇ ἀδιάπτωτος καὶ ἀένναον κῦρος ἔχουσα, and that the episcopate is radically distinct from the other orders of the clergy and infallible, because God is present with His Church through the bishops, and does not allow them to fall into heresy (τό πνεῦμα οὔκ ἐᾷ αἱρέσει ὑποπεσεῖν τὸν ἐπίσκοπον). This doctrine is not very logically defined, as no clear distinction is drawn between the episcopate and individual bishops, like Cyril Lucaris, who obviously can err.

exhausted treasury of the Constantinople Patriarchate with additional tithes and revenues. Ipek retained its independence after the Turkish conquest, but received a heavy blow in 1679, when the Emperor Leopold, fearing that the bishop of the Servians might come to terms with the Turks and establish a power independent of Austria, invited the Patriarch Arsenius to emigrate from Ipek into his dominions. Arsenius migrated with 37,000 families to Carlovitz, and much of old Servia was occupied by Albanians. The Patriarchate of Ipek was finally abolished in 1766 by the Patriarch Samuel of Constantinople, who was equally successful the next year in destroying the Bulgarian Church of Ochrida. This See, as we have seen, had long been hellenised, but it was still nominally autocephalous. In 1737 John Ypsilanti tried to persuade the Porte that Ochrida was a centre of Austrian intrigue and ought to be directly subordinated to Constantinople; but the Porte thought this proposition was an intrigue and executed Ypsilanti. In 1767, however, Arsenius, the Bulgarian bishop of Ochrida, was obliged to retire, and was exiled to Mount Athos, where he shortly had the satisfaction of being joined by the Patriarch Samuel, for the Porte was fond of reminding successful Greeks that they, too, were Giaours and really no better than Slavs or Roumanians.

From an ecclesiastical and religious point of view little can be said in praise of the Phanariots' rule, for it accentuated all the worst abuses and corruptions of the Greek Church. The Phanariot clergy in Bulgaria, Eastern Roumelia, and Macedonia were little more than a body of rapacious and extortionate tax-gatherers sent to fleece the Slavonic populations for the Patriarch of Constantinople. They exacted payment for the performance of all religious functions under various names. The tax paid for the maintenance of the Patriarch was called βοήθεια; for the consecration of priests, ἐμβρατάκια; for saying prayers, παρρησία; for prayers for the dead, ψυχομερίδια; for consecrating a church, ἁγίασμα; and many more. Monasteries were let to the highest bidder, who turned out the monks or not as he chose. The Slavonic clergy had no education, influence, or chance of promotion; they were often kept by their Greek superiors as domestic servants, and beaten in church during divine service if they happened to anger their masters. The morals of these latter were in harmony with their corruption and tyranny. The road to their favour generally lay through the mistresses whom they openly kept, and their demands were a terror to the village maidens or to those interested in the latter's chastity. The dissemination of the Greek language and culture over the Balkan Peninsula was, perhaps, a laudable object, but we cannot help regretting the barbarous and wanton destruction of Slavonic manuscripts and monuments by which it was accompanied. In some places the people ceased even to know the Cyrillic alphabet, and, as late as 1825, the Metropolitan Ilarion is said to have publicly burned all the Slavonic books in the old library of the Trnovo Patriarchate.

One small Slavonic Church, however, that of Montenegro, resisted Hellenism and the Phanar as successfully as the Government withstood the Turks. When the last of the house of Crnoievic left Montenegro, the Government was entrusted to the Bishop Babylas; and from 1516 till 1851 the country was ruled by Vladikas, or prince-bishops. They were at first elective, but after 1696 the office became hereditary. Babylas established a printing-press at Obod, where a number of devotional books were printed; but it was destroyed a century later, and the little principality was too much occupied in defending itself against the Turks to pay much attention to literature or theology.

There is little to be chronicled about the Church of Constantinople in the eighteenth century. In 1722, a Council was held in the Phanar in order to end the schism between Orthodox and Melchites, which had divided the Church of Antioch since 1560. An encyclical letter, drawn up by this Council, enumerated and anathematised the errors of Rome, including the Pope's damnable habit of having a cross embroidered on his shoes.

The eighteenth century was characterised by the predominant influence of the Greeks under Turkish rule; the nineteenth century by the revolt attempted or successful against that rule of the Christian subjects of the Porte. With the increasing weakness of the Ottoman Empire such a movement was inevitable, and it was only natural that the prominent and privileged position of the Greeks should have ripened their aspirations before those of the down-trodden and almost hopeless Slavs. But it was equally natural that the Phanariot aristocracy and the higher clergy should be opposed to such revolutionary movements. They both of them owed their position entirely to the Ottoman Government; and such literary apostles of the liberation movement as Eugenius Bulgares and Coraes recognised this alliance between the Turk and Orthodoxy in their polemics against Orthodox bigotry, and their efforts to secularise education and to regenerate the Greek language, which, in its written form, was a pedantic ecclesiastical jargon hardly intelligible to the people. But no hostile and satirical critic could have better defined the position of the Greek Church than did the Patriarch Anthimus of Jerusalem in a work directed against the doctrines of Eugenius. He explained that, when the last Emperor of Constantinople embraced the errors of the West, the mercy of the Almighty sent the Ottomans to protect the Greeks against heresy, and thus shut them off from the influences of Catholicism, Lutheranism, Calvinism, and the other diabolical artifices by which Satan had enslaved Europe.

The insurrection began first in Wallachia and Moldavia

(March 1821) and Gregory, the Patriarch of Constantinople, and his colleague of Jerusalem, at once signed a Bull anathematising the leaders of the insurgents. "Gratitude," began the Patriarchal letter, "is the first of all virtues, and only the most abandoned of mankind requites good with ingratitude." In the name of these elevated principles the rebels were adjured to lay down their arms and not revolt against their benefactor, the Sublime Ottoman Porte. This document was sent to the Metropolitan of Wallachia for publication, but it is not surprising to hear that when it was read in the church at Bucharest the tumult was so great that it was impossible to proceed. The Patriarch's anathemas recoiled on his own head. His brother, the Bishop of Tripolitza in the Peloponnesus, placed himself at the head of the insurgents, and Gregory was hanged in the Phanar with six other bishops on Easter Sunday. His body was given to the Jews, who were ordered to cut it into bits and throw it to the street dogs. They preferred, however, to sell it to the Christians for 100,000 piastres, and it was solemnly interred at Odessa two months afterwards. In Constantinople many churches were destroyed, and several bishops were executed in various parts of the Empire. Eugenius, somewhat irregularly appointed Patriarch by the Sultan, published a new encyclical, in which he again exhorted his flock not to forget all the benefits of the Ottoman Government, and called on them, in the name of the Holy Ghost, to submit "to our most clement sovereign." But the inhabitants of Greece proper, who were less under the immediate influence of that gentle rule, replied by a manifesto, signed by twenty-eight bishops and nearly one thousand priests, proclaiming the freedom of Hellas. The insurgents applied in vain for help and sympathy to the Pope, Pius VII., and Anthimus, the successor of Eugenius, sent them another exhortation to obedience in 1822; and in 1828 the Patriarch Agathangelus made a last appeal to all Greeks in whom "every spark of piety and good sense was not extinct" to submit to the "world-renowned clemency of the Ottoman Government." Capodistrias, the head of the provisional government in Greece, received an embassy from the Patriarch the same year, but replied that he could not listen to any proposals for submission. He asked, however, for his Holiness's blessing, and promised to recognise him as the head of the Church. This, however, was not done. In 1833, when the little Greek kingdom had been established, a Synod met at Nauplia to regulate its ecclesiastical affairs, declared (1) that the Hellenic Church was autocephalous, and that no foreign authority had any power over it; (2) That the supreme ecclesiastical power should be a Holy Synod to be appointed by the king, after the example of the Russian Church. This naturally widened the breach already made with the Patriarchate, and it was not till 1850 that the latter, acting to a great extent under the influence of Russia, recognised the Hellenic Church as independent.

The history of the modern Servian and Roumanian Churches is somewhat similar to that of the Hellenic Church. I have related how the Patriarchate of Ipek was suppressed in 1766. After that period Servia (an expression, it must be remembered, which denotes very different areas at different dates) became merely an ecclesiastical province of Constantinople. But in 1830 the Sultan issued a Hatt-i-Sherif allowing the Servians to elect a Patriarch with the confirmation of Byzantium, and in 1838 the seat of ecclesiastical government was fixed at Belgrade. The head of the Servian Church is styled merely Metropolitan, but has the authority of a Patriarch, and, since Servia became independent, his Church has been recognised as autocephalous.

The Roumanian Church also is autocephalous under a Metropolitan. This country, which until 1812 included Bessarabia, was subjected to an even stronger Hellenic influence than Servia or Bulgaria, as not only the ecclesiastical, but the civil government was administered by Greeks. Its comparative security and prosperity led to the establishment in it of a great number of philanthropic and educational institutions as well as numerous monasteries, all of them liberally endowed, and many possessing enormous estates. The most important part of the income of the Patriarchate of Constantinople was derived from ecclesiastical property in Roumania. Until 1861 the Church was administered by two Metropolitans residing at Belgrade and Jassy respectively; but when the union of the Principalities under Couza was proclaimed in December 1861, the Church was declared autocephalous, and placed under the supremacy of a Metropolitan residing at Bucharest with an Archbishop at Jassy. The relations with the Patriarchate were much embittered by the fact that the Government sequestrated all the ecclesiastical property mentioned above, which was regarded at Constantinople as being Greek. But the Roumanian Church is now recognised by Constantinople and the other Patriarchates as autocephalous.

The recent history of the Bulgarian Church is more complicated, and politically of considerable importance. It therefore merits a more detailed examination.

Bulgaria awoke to a dim consciousness of her existence as a nation towards the end of the eighteenth century. The first revolt was naturally against the Phanariot bondage, for until the removal of the Greek ecclesiastical despotism it was hardly possible for the Bulgarians to combine against the Turks.

The pioneers of the Bulgarian religious movement were the Archimandrite Neophit Bozveli and Ilarion Mikhailovsky, who demanded the establishment of a national hierarchy. Neophit founded a Bulgarian Church in Constantinople, and, though the hostility and persecution of the Greeks, who secured his banishment to Mount Athos, prevented him from accomplishing more during his life, the agitation which he started continued after his death and attracted the attention even of the Ottoman Government. In 1851 the Porte ordered the Patriarchate to name a Bulgarian bishop, but though Ilarion was duly consecrated, the order was nullified by his appointment to a See *in partibus* (Macariopolis). At this period Odessa was the centre of Bulgarian nationalist activity; a Committee was established there, and great results were expected with the assistance of the Russian Government. The Crimean war dashed these hopes to the ground; but the Russian occupation of the Danubian provinces had at least the effect of familiarising the Russians with the Southern Slavs, and for the next few years we find them ready to assist the Bulgarians in building churches and schools both in the present Principality and in Macedonia. In 1856 the Powers prevailed upon the Porte to publish a Hatt-i-Humayun promising not only full religious toleration but also various reforms, and in particular that the various taxes paid by Christians to their bishops and the Patriarchs should be replaced by a regular salary given to those officials—stipulations which were perhaps more distasteful to the Greeks than to the Turks. In 1857 the inhabitants of Widdin petitioned the Ottoman Government for the grant of a regular salary to their Metropolitan, and many similar requests followed from other towns, but all were refused by the Patriarch Cyril. The next year the Porte summoned an assembly (ἐθνοσυνέλευσις) to discuss the question of religious reforms. It was attended by twenty-eight delegates from the provinces, but by various devices the Greek party reduced the Bulgarian representatives to four, three of whom made a protest and retired, so that only the deputy of Trnovo remained to support the Bulgarian cause. It is not surprising that his efforts were in vain, and that the assembly, which was closed in 1860, affirmed that the Church could take no account of distinctions of race and nationality in the selection of bishops, and even went so far as to deny the existence of the Bulgarians as a separate people.

This refusal produced the outburst which had long been prepared. As Ilarion, the titular Bishop of Macariopolis, was saying Mass on Whitsunday 1860 in the Bulgarian church at Constantinople, the congregation clamoured that he should omit the Patriarch's name from the intercessory prayer, an omission which we have already noticed as the outward sign of schism in the earlier quarrels between Rome and Byzantium. After a decent protest he complied; the example was followed all over Bulgaria, and the agitation became so considerable that the Grand Vizier visited the province in person and arrested or dismissed a number of bishops against whom there were serious complaints. The Patriarch Cyril resigned, and Joachim was appointed in his stead. He at once excommunicated Ilarion, and having thus satisfied ecclesiastical etiquette, asked the Bulgarians what they wanted. They replied by naming seven points, which included ecclesiastical autonomy and a national hierarchy under an elective archbishop, in return for which they were ready to recognise the authority of the Patriarch and pay him a fixed yearly sum. The Patriarch refused their proposal, and offered instead fifteen promises, which included the appointment of Bulgarian or at least Bulgarian-speaking bishops to all Bulgarian districts. But these promises did not inspire confidence, and were rejected. The Patriarch was able to represent the Bulgarians as intractable, and induced the Porte to banish Ilarion and other prelates to Asia Minor.

We have seen that from her birth the Bulgarian Church wavered between the East and the West, and it is not surprising to find that the struggle with the Constantinople Patriarchate was accompanied by a movement in favour of union with Rome. A deputation proceeded thither in 1861, and Joseph Sokolski, said to have been an ex-brigand, was consecrated Bishop of the Bulgarian Uniat Church. But the movement was not successful. Sokolski was mysteriously spirited off to a Russian monastery, and few Uniats now remain except in the district of Philippopolis.

Meanwhile the dispute about the various points and promises continued, and was complicated by a new proposal of eight points, submitted to the Porte by delegates from the Bulgarian dioceses, and including a Synod of six Greek and six Bulgarian bishops, a mixed Council with six Bulgarian lay delegates, and a Metropolitan to reside in Constantinople. Troubles in Servia and the bombardment of Belgrade led the Porte to think it prudent to humour the Bulgarians. A Commission of Greeks and Bulgarians was summoned to consider the eight points, the bitterly anti-Bulgarian Patriarch Joachim was deposed, and his successor Sophronios was recommended by the Porte to find a conciliatory solution of the difficulty. But in vain; the Greeks rejected all the eight points, and declared the expressions " *Bulgarian* Church " or " *Bulgarian* bishop " to be uncanonical and opposed to the doctrine of the Universal Church. As some compensation, the Porte allowed the banished Bulgarian bishops to return to Ortakeui.

This was in 1864. Great excitement ensued in Bulgaria and Macedonia. The Porte made considerable changes, described as reforms, in the provincial administration, and established the modern system of vilayets in the place of the old pashaliks. Bulgaria was called the vilayet of the Danube, and administered by Midhat Pasha. In 1869 the Grand Vizier laid before the Patriarch another project of ecclesiastical organisation, which, it was thought, would satisfy both Greeks and Bulgarians, but the former refused it. Then, on February 28, 1870, the Sultan issued a firman constituting the Bulgarian Church. The sphere of this Church was not merely the modern Principality of Bulgaria, which did not then exist, but that area plus the vilayets of Adrianople, Salonica, Kossovo, and Monastir. The head of the Church so created was styled the Bulgarian Exarch. He was to reside at Constantinople,[1] and had the right to name bishops in Macedonia as far south as Florina, though, as a matter of fact, none were appointed for several years.

Great Britain, France, and Russia all used their influence to induce the Sultan to issue this firman. We have always favoured Bulgarian aspirations; the French seem to have thought it possible that the Bulgarian Church might unite with Rome and strengthen Catholic interests in the East; and the Russians were actuated by Panslavic ideas, which were then beginning to become popular. But, quite apart from external pressure, the Turkish Government had good reasons for their action. It was a practical exemplification of the maxim *divide et impera*. They had previously regarded all Eastern Christians as being much the same, and had lumped them together under the designation of Rûm. The very name of Bulgarian had almost dropped out of usage. But now it appeared that there were different kinds of Christians who quarrelled with one another. It was clearly politic to accentuate the differences and perpetuate the possibilities of quarrel. Experience has proved the justice of these calculations. Nothing has strengthened the Sultan's hold on Macedonia so much as the dissensions between the Exarchate and the Patriarchal Church.

It will be seen that the principle on which this Bulgarian Church rested is essentially different from that which underlies the Churches of Greece, Roumania, and Servia. In the

---

[1] At present the Bulgarian Church within the limits of the Principality is governed by a Synod which sits at Sofia, but the Exarch, who still resides at Constantinople, is head of the whole body both in Bulgaria and Turkey.

case of these latter the lay and ecclesiastical administrations of the country have been taken out of the sphere of the Sultan and the Patriarch of Constantinople respectively. But when the new Bulgarian Church was founded there was no Bulgaria, and now its boundaries are not co-extensive with those of the Principality. It is established in districts where the Patriarch of Constantinople had representatives before its creation, and it is for all practical purposes a hostile and proselytising sect, claiming all persons belonging to a certain race. The Patriarchate appealed to the un-doubted principle of the Orthodox Church that there can be only one bishop in one diocese, and stigmatised by the name of Phyletism the doctrine that persons of a particular race or language are entitled to a separate ecclesiastical administration. No doubt the contention of the Patriarch is supported by all the history and teaching of orthodoxy, but, on the other hand, the Phanar had only its own policy to thank for the birth of a rival Church. That policy had long ceased to have anything universal or œcumenical about it—it was simply Greek ; it did not rise impartially above distinctions of race and language, but by its attempts to Hellenise all ecclesiastical institutions and to destroy all non-Hellenic elements, it drove the latter into rebellion.

In 1872 the Patriarch held a local Synod at Constantinople, which, in August of that year, pronounced the Bulgarian Church schismatic. The Churches of Antioch, Alexandria, and Athens confirmed the sentence of excommunication. The Church of Jerusalem did so less definitely, because they made a great deal of money out of Bulgarian pilgrims. The Russian Church, followed by those of Servia and Roumania, maintained an equivocal attitude. On the one hand, Russia has never officially acknowledged the Bulgarian Church for fear of offending the Œcumenical Patriarch, and Bulgarian prelates have never been allowed to officiate publicly in Russian churches. On the other hand, the Russian Synod has always refused to officially recognise the Patriarch's anathema, and Russian ecclesiastics have secretly supplied the Bulgarians with holy oil. Finally, the Emperor of Russia became godfather to Prince Boris when he was received into the Bulgarian Church. In these questions the Russians are actuated by two ideals or sentiments, Panslavism and Panorthodoxy. The former is really linguistic, and aims at extending Russian sympathy and support to such races as the Bulgarians and Servians who speak languages almost intelligible to Russians. But Panorthodoxy, if I may use the word, tends to regard Russia as the head, not only of the Slav races, but of all orthodox nations. One manifestation of this tendency is the interest taken by Russia in the Abyssinians and the Nestorians on the ground that they are Orthodox, which, of course, they really are not. Now, the only prelate who could have any pretensions to represent the United Orthodox Church, is the Œcumenical Patriarch. As we have seen, his position is not so great as his title implies, but it is recognised that he enjoys a certain pre-eminence, and Russian Metropolitans kiss his hand when they come to Constantinople. From this point of view Russia must naturally wish to prevent a vigorous Slavonic Church from being in direct opposition to the Patriarchate.

It may perhaps be well to give a list of the Orthodox Churches in a tabular form. They are twelve or thirteen in number, according as we reckon the Bulgarian Church or not :—

1. The Patriarchate of Constantinople, with eighty-two Metropolitans.

2. The Patriarchate of Alexandria, with only one Metropolitan.

3. The Patriarchate of Antioch, with fourteen Metropolitans.

4. The Patriarchate of Jerusalem, with one Metropolitan, five Archbishops, and five Bishops.

5. The Church of Cyprus, with one Archbishop and five Bishops.

6. The Church of Mount Sinai, with one Archbishop.

7. The Hellenic Church, or Church of the Kingdom of Greece.

8. The Church of the Kingdom of Servia.

9. The Church of the Kingdom of Roumania.

10. The Church of Montenegro.

11. The Patriarchate of Carlovitz (south of the Danube not far from Peterwardein), consisting of a Patriarch and ten Bishops, who have jurisdiction over the Orthodox Church in the Austrian dominions.

12. The Russian Church.

13. The Bulgarian Church.

The Russian Church is incontestably the most important of the Orthodox Churches of the present day, but its history has not been very eventful. It was in its origin an offshoot of Constantinople, and for nearly 600 years remained nominally in the jurisdiction of the Œcumenical Patriarch, though its geographical position secured for it practical independence. The Metropolitan resided first at Kieff, then at Vladimir, and after 1320 at Moscow. In 1582 the Patriarch Jeremias appointed Job, the forty-sixth Metropolitan, to be Patriarch of Vladimir, Moscow, and all Russia. Ivan the Terrible, overwhelmed with remorse for the murder of his son, had made many costly offerings to the See of Constantinople in order to secure absolution, and Jeremias, much in need of funds to pay the Sublime Porte, was happy to confer favours on the lavish penitent. Though he rejected the Czar's invitation to fix his residence in Russia and make her the centre of the Church, he gladly visited Moscow, performed the ceremony of institution, and caused the Russian Patriarchate to be recognised by a general Synod held at Constantinople.

This Patriarchate continued to exist until the time of

Peter the Great, and the most notable name connected with it is that of Nikon. This energetic and ambitious prelate, who occupied the Patriarchal throne in the middle of the seventeenth century, provoked by his reforms the great schism (or *raskol*) from which spring the various sects of Old Believers, who still form no inconsiderable portion of the population of Russia. The changes which occasioned this disruption relate to absurdly trivial points, such as the text and orthography of the liturgy and other sacred books, which had been mangled by generations of ignorant copyists, the shape of the Cross, and the number of fingers (two or three) to be used in making that sacred sign. Naturally, a quarrel respecting such details of ceremonial was only the outward expression of more seriously divergent tendencies. In the time of Nikon the Russian Empire, still almost in its childhood, was the battlefield of a struggle between Polish and Russian ideas and institutions. The Poles represented Roman Catholicism and aristocracy, whereas the Russian people have always had in their composition a strong vein of anti-aristocratic and anti-sacerdotal sentiment. In spite of the period of serfdom through which he has passed the Russian Muzhik is not servile; he thinks of God and the Czar in one category, and of the rest of the world as more or less equal in another. However superstitious he may be, he does not allow his priests to assume the position of directors or masters, and is very ready to exercise the right of private judgment. Nikon evidently wished to introduce into the Russian Church the aristocratic and hierarchical principles of the West. He was wealthy, and surrounded himself with ecclesiastical pomp, and apparently aimed at securing for the See of Moscow a supremacy analogous to that of Rome. In some ways his efforts were successful. The State aided him in his reforms, and endeavoured to coerce, though it could not suppress, the Old Believers with the secular arm. But his arrogance and ambition alarmed the Czar, who had no desire to see established in Russia an ecclesiastical power which might impair his autocracy, and Nikon was deposed and banished. His fall was only a preliminary step towards the abolition of the Russian Patriarchate, which was completed by Peter the Great at the beginning of the eighteenth century. Peter not only suppressed the Patriarchate, but effectually prevented the Russian Church from becoming a rival to the secular power by giving her no primate or personal head distinct from the emperor.

The ecclesiastical government was, and still is, vested in the Holy Synod, consisting of five or six bishops and of lay officials representing the sovereign. The Russian hierarchy contains three Sees, which are considered to be of the first class: Kieff, Old Novogorod and St. Petersburg (united in the Metropolitan residing at the latter), and Moscow, but none of these prelates have authority out of their own dioceses. But the Holy Synod is held to possess collectively authority equal to that of a Patriarch, and, as representing the Church, ranks after the Patriarchates of Constantinople, Alexandria, Antioch, and Jerusalem. This peculiar constitution has produced in Russia an almost Mohammedan confusion of Church and State, or at least of religion and politics. The ancient Georgian Church, which had been a dependency of Antioch and Constantinople successively, was, in 1801, incorporated in the Russian Church. Its Metropolitan, who bears the title of Georgian Exarch, has a seat in the Holy Synod.

The ecclesiastical merits of the Orthodox Church are obvious; she is clearly closer, not, perhaps, to Christ, but to the Christianity of 400 A.D., than either Rome or Canterbury. But if we consider her practical influence, it is hard to form a very favourable opinion. The noblest and most dignified communion is, no doubt, that of Russia, which has always combined Christianity and patriotism, and consequently been able to lead the whole nation. In many instances individual Greek priests or monasteries have fought against the Moslims in the same spirit, but, as a whole, the Church of Constantinople divorced Christianity and patriotism, and was content to make the best of the Turks.

But in Russia and the Levant alike the power of the Church seems to be ceremonial rather than moral. " By their fruits ye shall know them," and the fruits of the Orthodox Church lack spirituality. She has quickened neither the moral sense nor the intelligence of her followers, and their undoubting faith in dogma, and punctilious observance of ritual, will not be thought great qualities by those who do not consider the dogma and ritual in themselves important.

This moderate success in the practical sphere is largely due to the character of the priesthood. Few distinguished men are to be found even in the higher grades of the hierarchy. All the lower clergy are simple peasants— husbands of uncomely peasant women and fathers of many urchins—in no way distinguished from their neighbours except by trade. One man is a cobbler, and knows how to make boots and shoes; another is a priest, and knows how to read the Mass. The peasant of the Balkans regards the two trades as on the same footing. He has no doubt that it is as necessary to be prayed for as to wear boots. But the ceremonies performed by the priest are for him simply practical operations with a view to his comfort in another world, and not intended to ennoble his life down here. Though the contest between Christianity and Islam is the most important feature of the East, though Turkish institutions give such great prominence to ecclesiastical matters, the Orthodox Church has failed to use her opportunities; she has neither spread light nor infused energy.

CHAPTER VII

MANY travellers arrive at Constantinople under the impression that it is inhabited by Turks, or by Turks and Greeks. After a while they begin to realise the astonishing complexity of the population, talk glibly about Kurds and Albanians, and flatter themselves that they can at once detect an Armenian by his nose, or a Greek by his facial angle. But in most sciences progress obliges us to reject or qualify those crisp and distinct definitions which attract and convince a beginner, and ethnology is no exception to the rule. A few years' observation in Turkey shows that it is impossible to draw hard and fast lines between the different races. One is assured that people who are apparently Greeks are really Vlachs, or hears that a Greek village has become Bulgarian, and perhaps by a second transformation Servian. It will, therefore, be well to understand clearly at the outset what is meant by the word race [1] as applied to the inhabitants of Turkey.

Human beings may be classified according to several principles, and, consequently, most names applied to large bodies of men have several meanings. One principle is politico-geographical; the words Russian, German, and Italian designate inhabitants of Russia, Germany, and Italy, and subjects of the sovereigns of those countries. But, except for political purposes, such a principle is easily

---

[1] It may be said that the application of the word race to Greeks, Bulgarians, Albanians, &c., is not scientific. But there is no other convenient word. Nationality or community are misleading from their political associations.

seen to be misleading.   Large areas nearly always contain
more than one race : Tartars are not Russians, though
they live in Russia; and there is an obvious difference
between Englishmen and British subjects.   Small areas, on
the other hand, do not as a rule contain the whole of a race.
There are clearly many Greeks outside Greece, and many
Finns outside Finland.

Another method of classification is by physical characteristics, and it is commonly assumed that these, more
or less, coincide with national distinctions.   People often
talk of a German or Russian type, and think that the two
races can be distinguished by their build and features, as if
they were two kinds of animals.   But the external differences between Europeans of different nations depend mainly
on expression, manner, and costume, and not on any
physical characteristics which can be defined and registered.   Every purely physical system of classification cuts
across all the usual national and linguistic divisions, and
unites in one group people who, according to other criteria,
have nothing to do with one another.   Anthropologists
usually classify the human race by the shape of the skull.
The only objection to this system (provided it is certain
that time and climate do not change the shape of skulls)
is that it tells us so little.   If we know something of the
language or religion of a people, we can probably find out
something of its history; or if, as is the case of the
Basques, the comparison with other languages gives no
result, it is clear that we have to do with an isolated and
ancient race.   But physical characteristics have in Europe
no connection with either language or culture; neither the
Celtic-speaking peoples nor those who introduced the
Hallstadt culture can be identified with any physical type;
and statements about a dolichocephalic Mediterranean race
amount to little more than an assertion that the inhabitants
of the shores of that ocean have long heads.   From a

urely zoological point of view this does not tell us very much. The idea that the northern and southern shores of the Mediterranean were originally peopled by one race is interesting, but it derives its chief support, and all its interest, from other than craniological considerations.

However, my object here is not to discuss the foundations of anthropology, but to make it clear that the races of Turkey must not be regarded as so many physical types. For instance, the Southern Serbs and Albanians have the same physical characteristics, but they differ in language and customs, and are, in one sense of the word, different races. All existing races are mixed, for the different kinds of mankind are merely varieties and not species. When the mixture takes place between widely separate varieties, especially if they differ in colour, such as negroes and Englishmen, we recognise the fact and call the results half-breeds; but we generally ignore it when it takes place between white varieties. It would be amazing if the people who are now called Greeks were of the same physical type as what are styled Ancient Greeks, which generally means the inhabitants of Athens and Sparta. The Greeks have spread all round the Ægean and Black Seas, and come into contact with the inhabitants of the littoral. The Macedonian Empire must have had a large non-Hellenic substratum. Constantinople and all continental Greece were for centuries ruled and occupied by the Romans, and during many subsequent centuries invaded and colonised by Slavs. The Crusades and the Latin conquest brought a large influx of western Europeans, commonly called Franks; and, in later times, extensive Albanian settlements were made in Greek districts. Clearly, the modern Greek must be of very mixed blood.

Another curious case affecting the question of physical types is afforded by the Hungarians. They are some of the best-looking people of modern Europe; whereas all contemporary records are agreed as to the extreme hideousness of the Huns, who must have had pronounced Mongolian features. Therefore, either the Hungarians are not descended from the Huns, in which case we have a transference of name and language, or else the physical appearance of the race has completely changed. It must be remembered that, in many cases, where no great barriers exist, environment tends to assimilate physical types without admixture of blood. This is seen even in such extreme cases as the American negroes who speak English, and enjoy the same rights as white men, nominally in the Southern, and really in the Northern States. In full-blooded Southern negroes the peculiarities of negro physiognomy are not developed as strongly as in negroes born and bred in Africa; and full-blooded negroes in the North, though retaining the black skin and woolly hair, have often lips and noses which are almost European. Among European races, where there are no such peculiarities of colour and hair, environment may obliterate physical distinctions more completely. It is easy to find Greeks, Albanians, Bulgarians, and Vlachs who could not be taken for anything else, but many districts tend to produce types characteristic of a particular area. In Southern Albania, Greeks, Albanians, and Vlachs look very much alike, and a Southern Albanian and a Greek resemble one another more than do a Southern and a Northern Albanian. Similarly, in Central Macedonia, at such a town as Monastir, there is a family likeness among the Christian inhabitants whether they call themselves Greeks, Vlachs, or Slavs. On the other hand, some local peculiarity in costume will often create an impression that its wearers are a distinct type. For instance, around Koritza the men wear a sort of blue frock, which makes them look quite different from the surrounding population, although they are, like their neighbours, a mixture of Greeks, Vlachs, and Albanians.

A third and very important method of classifying mankind is based upon their languages. There are, of course, many and obvious exceptions to its accuracy: the negroes in America speak English, the Jews of Salonica and Constantinople Spanish, and the Bulgarians a Slavonic tongue. But, making all allowances for such cases, similarity of language always implies contact at some period, and probably union in some kind of state or national organisation. If we knew nothing of the history of the Jews or negroes, and had to draw conclusions from Judæo-Spanish and Negro-English, we might safely infer (it is to be feared we should really infer much more) that the speakers were people who had a close connection with the English or Spaniards, but were separated from them by some barrier, local or other, which imparted to their language a very un-English or un-Spanish character. And this, though vague, would be quite correct as far as it goes. Possibly no inspection of Bulgarian would suggest that the Bulgarians are anything but Slavs (though modern Bulgarian shows remarkable peculiarities); but even in this case language is not really misleading. The original Bulgarians, no doubt, were quite different from the Slavs, but their later history connects them with the Slavs far more closely than with any Hunnish or Turkish tribe; and it must be confessed that we get a better idea of them by thinking of them as Slavs than by thinking of them as a sort of Huns or Finns. The great danger of linguistic classification is not that it brings together the wrong nations, for it always brings together people who have something important in common, but that it is liable to create imaginary races corresponding to linguistic generalisations. The resemblances between Greek and Sanskrit make it certain that the inhabitants of Northern India and Greece must at some time have been in contact with one another, or each in contact with a third body of men speaking a similar language. But we have no right to conclude that the present speakers of Aryan languages are descended from a race called Aryans (or of any other name) any more than we have to conclude that the speakers of Romance languages are descended from the Romans.

Languages in Turkey form, on the whole, the best criterion of race in the popular sense—that is to say, when we talk of Greeks or Bulgarians we mean people who speak Greek or Bulgarian. But some qualifications must be made. Mohammedans, particularly of the upper classes, who migrate from their homes in the provinces, generally drop their original languages, and, in the second generation, speak Turkish only. This is the case with many Albanians in Constantinople and elsewhere. Of such, it would be more correct to say that they *were* Albanians than that they *are* Albanians. Many districts, too, are bilingual; but it may always be assumed that Greek or Turkish is an acquired language, and that the second one gives the speaker's real race. A Greek does not learn Vlach or Albanian, but Vlachs and Albanians find it advantageous to learn Greek, which in a certain sphere is cosmopolitan. Of the Slavonic dialects of Macedonia I shall speak later. They are very fluctuating, and as a rule the establishment of the Servian or Bulgarian school is sufficient to decide whether a village will speak Servian or Bulgarian.

Lastly, mankind may be classified by their manners and customs, the most important of which is religion. Classification by religion is not very scientific, but it is the Turkish principle, and therefore requires attention here. The Turk divides the population of the Ottoman Empire into Millets, or religious communities. They are Islam, or Mohammedans, of whatever lineage and language: Rûm, or Greek, including all members of the Orthodox Church who recognise the Patriarch of Constantinople; Bulgar, or Bulgarians, those who recognise the spiritual authority of the Bulgarian Exarch; Katolik, or Catholics; Ermeni, or Gregorian Armenians; Musevi, or Jews; Prodesdan, or Protestants.[1] This system leads to the strangest results. It divides the Armenians into two—for a Catholic Armenian is, in Turkish estimation, not an Armenian, and not to be killed, or, at least, not at the same time as his Gregorian brother—and it combines many races under the comprehensive names of Islam and Rûm. Popular language follows the same method. A Bulgarian means a member of the Bulgarian Church, and if a Bulgarian-speaking village recognises the Patriarch of Constantinople and not the Exarch, its inhabitants are as often as not called Greeks. Of late years there has been much dispute as to whether certain parts of Macedonia are Servian or Bulgarian, and many villages which were formerly reckoned as Bulgarian have declared themselves Servian. But the Servians in Turkey have no independent Church, and recognise the Patriarchate. Hence Servians, as opposed to Bulgarians, are called Greeks.

Another strange consequence of this system is that race—or whatever we call the quality indicated by such words as Greek, Servian, and Bulgarian—is regarded, not as something natural and immutable, but as a matter of conviction, which can be changed as easily as religion. In the last century the population of the Balkan Peninsula was considered to be Greek; no educated Christian would have given himself any other name. Now the inhabitants of the part which is still Turkish territory recognise that they have affinities with the surrounding states of Greece, Servia, Bulgaria, and Roumania, but are not always sure with which. The politics of Macedonia are well described by the word " Propaganda," which is in common use in the country, and has passed into its various dialects. All the non-Turkish races have a " national idea," or, to be

---

[1] The Servians and Vlachs are not recognised as Millets.

more exact, a certain number of energetic politicians try to force the idea into the heads of their fellows. As meetings and all the ordinary forms of political agitation are forbidden under the government of the Sublime Porte, this Propaganda has only two directions open to it— linguistic and ecclesiastical. Each race is desirous to have its language taught in its schools and used in its churches, if possible, under the superintendence of its own bishops; and hence, although the clergy are too ignorant and unorganised to exert over their flocks an influence like that wielded by Roman Catholic priests in other countries, ecclesiastical matters excite universal interest.

The Propaganda are, so to speak, missionary enter-prises which, by means of schools and churches, try to convert people to the Bulgarian or Servian faith. Had the celebrated Captain in the Comic Opera, who "in spite of all temptations to belong to other nations" remained an Englishman, lived in Macedonia, there would have been nothing comic in his assertion. It exactly represents the attitude of many Macedonians. Many others do yield to temptations, which often take a very material form. In order to understand the Macedonian question, and, in particular, Macedonian statistics, this peculiar system of altering race-names must be borne in mind. A victory, a defeat, some real or imagined change in the attitude of Austria or Russia, will be sufficient to make hundreds, perhaps thousands of people, pass from one party to another. In one sense, a race in Macedonia is merely a political party, but it may perhaps be better defined as a body of people, with a common language and customs, and generally[1] with a common religion. It may be ob-jected that though people can suddenly change their

---

[1] The Albanians form an exception. I think even the Porte recognises that an Arnaut is an Arnaut, whether he calls himself Catholic, Orthodox, or Moslim.

religion, they cannot so change their language. The explanation is twofold. Either, as in the case of the Slavs, they speak an uncultivated dialect of their own, but can understand Servian and Bulgarian almost equally well, or else they are bilingual. But many Slavs, though a decreasing number, the so-called Βουλγαροφῶνοι, belong to the Patriarchal Church, but speak only a Slav language. In this case it seems unreasonable to call them Greeks, though whatever strength they have goes to support the Greek cause.

The Turks call the Greeks who inhabit Ottoman territory Rûm, the kingdom of Greece and its inhabitants being distinguished as Yunanistan and Yunan. These latter words are derived from Ἰωνία, and Rûm is a corruption of Ρωμαῖος. In the early centuries of the Byzantine Empire the name Ἕλλην was associated with paganism. The Greek-speaking provincials were called Ἑλλαδικοί, and the population of the capital Ρωμαῖοι, or Romans. This name became the general designation of the Byzantine Empire and its inhabitants, so that even the Seljuk Sultanate of Konia styled itself Rûm, because it was conquered from that Empire. At the present day popular Greek, as opposed to classical or learned Greek (Ἑλληνικά), is still called Ρωμαϊκά; but a Greek both in the kingdom of Greece and in Turkey describes himself as Ἕλλην or Ἑλληνᾶς.

The Greeks are widely distributed through the Ottoman Empire. They form the majority of the population in the coast towns of the Ægean and Marmora, and much the same may be said of the Turkish shores of the Black Sea. Even in those Euxine ports which belong to Russia and Roumania, they form à characteristic and powerful element. In the interior of Asia Minor they are most abundant in the vilayets of Trebizond and Aidin and the district called Karamania, in which latter they use the Turkish language, but write it in Greek letters. The population of the Archipelago, including Crete and Cyprus, is almost wholly Greek, the Cretan Mussulmans being Mohammedan Greeks, and not Turks. The islanders form in many ways a distinct type. They have been exempt from the invasions or influence of Slavs, Vlachs, and Albanians,[1] but have received a considerable admixture of Frankish, and particularly of Venetian, blood. This, and the pursuit of such active occupations as navigation and fishing, have created a finer physique than is common on the mainland, and also developed mental activity and energy. Many eminent Greeks, whether Corsairs, Ottoman functionaries, or patriots, were islanders. The typical Greek is, however, a dweller in towns. In European Turkey the only large masses of Greek peasantry are found in the three-pronged peninsula north of the Gulf of Salonica, and in the region behind Constantinople, which is, however, sparsely populated. In the kingdom of Greece a large part of the rural population was clearly in its origin Albanian or Vlach. This urban character of the Greeks is, like so many other peculiarities, not of recent date, but goes back to Byzantine times. In the seventh and eighth centuries the invasions of barbarians, and the utter neglect shown by the Government for the provinces, drove all the wealthiest and most intelligent elements of the population into the towns. Doubtless these elements were various in their origin, but they soon became characterised by linguistic and religious homogeneity and a common aptitude for commercial and intellectual rather than for military pursuits. After the Ottoman conquest the Greeks were not a local population, but a superior class of Christians, forming a counterpart to the Turks. South-Eastern Europe was ruled by the Turks; but until this century its religion, education, com-

---

[1] The Albanians got as far as Hydra and Spezzia, which are, however, actically parts of the Morea.

merce, and finance were in the hands of Greeks. The early conquests and colonies of the Slavs had no effect on this pre-eminence. The empires of Simeon and Dushan did not spread Bulgarian or Servian civilisation; they simply imitated Byzantium. On the whole, the Greeks have shown extraordinary tenacity in preserving their language and religion. There are exceptions, of course, such as the Cretan Moslims; but, at least on the continent of Europe, there is no body of Greeks like the Beys of Bosnia, the Bulgarian Pomaks, or the Mohammedan Albanians. The servility of the Phanariots did not take the form of adopting the Turkish language or the Mohammedan religion; on the contrary, they were the uncompromising apostles of Hellenism. It is clear that one reason for the fall of the Byzantine Empire was that the Byzantines took far more interest in their Church than in their government, and their descendants were animated by the same spirit. The impulse towards political independence in 1823 did not come from Constantinople or Salonica.

After the conquest Mohammed II. strengthened the Greek element in Constantinople, but weakened it in the provinces. As many of the nobility as could fled to the Christian states of Europe, and wars and misfortune had so reduced the population of the capital that a third of the space enclosed by the walls was uninhabited. To fill this void, Mohammed forced 15,000 Greeks from the provinces to settle in Stamboul, and reorganised the Greek Millet, or nation, under the Patriarch[1] as head. After the conquest of Trebizond he removed two-thirds of the inhabitants, and sent the upper classes to Stamboul, thinking it dangerous to allow any powerful body of Greeks to exist except under his immediate personal supervision. The rural

[1] Some details respecting the history of the Patriarchate, which is for some time the history of the Greeks, are given in the chapter on the Orthodox Church.

districts were kept quiet by the levy of tribute children for the Janissaries. The more potential patriots they produced, the more actual oppressors they raised up for themselves, and their own strength fought against them. But the capital was exempt from conscription, and for some time the Greeks enjoyed there comparative freedom and prosperity. The Patriarch, as head of the Greek Millet, had the rank of Vezir, and superintended the administration of justice in cases affecting Christians only. All matters concerning marriage, divorce, and inheritance, as well as minor offences, were dealt with by his tribunal. He was surrounded by a number of lay officers with high-sounding titles, recalling the old Byzantine court, such as Grand Logothete, Grand Treasurer, Chartophylax, and many others. Under his presidency the Synod busied itself, not only with ecclesiastical affairs, but also with the management of schools and hospitals and the administration of the revenues of the Millet. The rule of Mohammed was also advantageous to Greek commerce; for the abolition of the privileges accorded to foreigners by the Byzantine emperors, and the indifference of the Turks to mercantile pursuits, left the Christian subjects of the Porte in a favourable position. All Christians were, however, subjected to the Harach, or capitation tax, which Mohammedans did not have to pay.

This favourable condition of the Greeks did not last long. The greater part of the sixteenth and seventeenth centuries was for them a period of obscurity and oppression, as may be seen from the almost total cessation of literature. Several causes contributed to this result. The concessions of Mohammed II. were partly prompted by fear. When his successors knew the Greeks better, familiarity bred contempt. The ferocious Selim I. contemplated a general massacre of Christians, and was deterred, not by the danger of the project, but by the honesty of his Mufti, who declined to give it the sanction of a *fetva*. Another enemy appeared in the Jesuits and other Catholic orders, who began to settle in Turkey and received the protection of France. The old feud between the Churches broke out again, and the Catholics did all they could to injure the educational and ecclesiastical projects of the Greeks. But perhaps the chief cause of this abasement was to be found in the Greeks themselves. The shameless venality and corruption of priests and laymen alike justified the contempt of the Turks, and prevented any sort of union or national feeling. Still, even in this period the Greeks were the chief Christian race. Little as we hear of them, we hear less of the Servians and Bulgarians.

In the later half of the seventeenth century things began to improve. The tribute of children for the Janissaries ceased to be taken, and the strength of the rural provinces was no longer drained. The young Pallikars, who had previously become the Sultan's soldier slaves, now grew up in their own homes, and, being Christians, could not fight under the banner of Islam. They found their occupation, either as Klephts or Armatoles.[1] The former of these words, generally translated brigand, was applied to open rebels against the Ottoman Government; the latter to a force of Christian gendarmes, allowed to bear arms, and charged with the duty of preserving order and keeping the Klephts in check. The origin of both classes is obscure. Brigandage was prevalent in Byzantine times, as it is likely to be in every country where the communications are bad, the population adventurous, and the Government weak. It would be natural if the peaceful inhabitants had protected themselves by forming a local gendarmerie, but there seems to be no evidence for the existence of the institution before the Turkish conquest. Both Klephts and Armatoles come

---

[1] Κλέφτης, a thief; Ἀρματωλός, a man-at-arms. By a curious error, committed even by Greeks, this last word is often written Ἀμαρτωλός, a sinner.

into greater prominence with the abolition of the conscription. They were especially numerous in the northern parts of Thessaly and the mountains of Pindus, Olympus, and Pelion. The Turks are said to have created fourteen Armatol-liks. or police districts, and as there were few Ottoman officials in the country, and the Προεστώς, or head of the local Greek municipality, had control over the armed gendarmerie, the Christian population enjoyed comparative independence. In judging the Klephts, we must remember that the profession of brigand has always met with indulgence and sympathy in the East. Such as still exist in European Turkey are mostly Moslims, whose exploits are followed with a friendly interest as long as they only attack Christians. With advancing years they retire, obtain a full pardon, and are much respected. It is also significant that at the present day Armenian revolutionaries are officially called brigands (*eshkiya*) by the Porte. We may therefore believe that the Klephts had a political character, and aimed at throwing off the Turkish yoke.

> Μάνα, σοῦ λεώ δὲν μπορῶ, τοὺς Τούρκους νὰ δουλεύω.
> Θὰ πάρω τό τουφέκι μου νὰ πάω νὰ γίνω Κλέφτης.

" Mother, I tell you I cannot serve the Turks. I will take my gun and go and become a Klepht." But the young gentleman and his companions probably somewhat confused a love of adventure with efforts after political independence. At any rate, as long as the Turks left the Armatoles to deal with the Klephts, there was no serious revolutionary movement. The War of Independence was preceded by a series of measures dictated by fear of the Armatoles, which made them openly combine with the Klephts.

The Klephts passed the winter, when an outdoor life was impossible, in hiding, often on the Ionian Islands; but in summer they took to their haunts in the wooded mountains. During the day they concealed themselves in gorges or caverns called λημέρια,[1] and at night they issued forth to kill Agas and Albanians, or, for want of better booty, to levy contributions from monasteries.

Ἐξηντ Ἀγάδαις σκώτωσα καὶ ἔκαψα τά χώριά τους
Κ᾽ ὅσους 'σ τὸν τόπον ἄφεσα καὶ Τούρκους καὶ Ἀρβανίταις
Εἶναι πολλὸι, πουλάκι μου, κὰι μετρημὸν δὲν ἔχουν.

" Sixty Agas I slew and burnt their villages, and as for the Turks and Albanians that I left (dead) on the field, they are many, my bird, and cannot be numbered," says the brigand's head to the eagle in the ballad. They certainly habitually and deliberately robbed and killed Turks and Albanians merely because they were Turks and Albanians, but in spite of such acts they appear to have maintained a higher level of chivalry than the other side. Their exploits were marked by blood-thirsty daring, but not by the atrocious cruelty and wanton outrages which stain the memory of most Pashas whose names have been preserved. The ballads which tell of the doings of the Klephts are one of the most precious heirlooms of the Greek people, and outweigh all the pompous prose and stilted tragedies composed in modern Greek in virtue of their natural language and genuine feeling. One of the most celebrated and beautiful is the dying speech of Demos, translated into German by Goethe ; but most of the pieces preserved in Fauriel's Collection (*Chants Populaires de la Grèce Moderne*) repay perusal.

The condition of the Christian provinces was also[2] ameliorated by the revised and juster system of taxation introduced by the Grand-Vizier Kyöprülü-Zade-Mustafa. He argued that excessive oppression of the Christians was like killing the goose that laid the golden eggs. The maxim *ex nihilo nihil fit* hardly applies to Turkish finance, for they

---

[1] Ὅλη ἡμέρα, a place where one stays all day.
[2] It may seem odd to treat the rise of the Klephts as an amelioration, but the power of killing Turks is regarded by the Eastern Christian as the most precious, as it is the rarest, privilege.

do seem to take money out of empty pockets. But clearly more taxes can be taken out of full ones.

Still more striking was the improved position of the Greeks in the capital which begins with this period. The quarter called Phanar, on the Golden Horn, had become the residence, not only of the Patriarch, but of a Greek aristocracy. They were not the descendants of the old Byzantine nobles, who all either emigrated or were slain, but of the more prominent families, half clerics and half merchants, who grew up round the Patriarchate. Also they contained a strong Italian element; for side by side with such names as Mavrocordato, Ypsilanti, and Karadja, we also find Rosetti, Morousi, and Giuliani. The churches and buildings of the Phanar are still remarkably unpretentious, and recall the time when the residents thought it wise to have no external sign of wealth and prosperity though the interior of their houses was marked by profuse luxury. As the military power of the Turks declined, they began to feel the need of diplomacy and of treating and negotiating with other nations, which, in their original arrogance, they had always refused to do. They did not, however, on that account show the slightest disposition to learn European languages or adopt European ways, but merely employed a large number of interpreters and go-betweens. At first Jews and renegades were chiefly used; but about the middle of the seventeenth century it seems to have occurred to the Porte that the Phanariots would be admirable instruments for the purpose. Years of oppression and insult had reduced them to a satisfactory state of servility; they had no military instincts, and they were very clever. To the subtlety bred of theological disputes they added the shrewdness of merchants, and were rarely prevented by any scruples from getting the best of either an argument or a bargain. At first they held very humble posts as clerks and translators, but in 1669 the Grand Vizir Kyöprülü Ahmed created for his secretary Panayoti,[1] who had rendered him great services in Crete, the office of Divan Terjumani, or Dragoman of the Porte. Panayoti was succeeded by another distinguished Chiot, Alexander Mavrocordato, who signed the Treaty of Carlovitz as Turkish plenipotentiary. With such occupants the post of Dragoman of the Porte became that of a Minister rather than of a mere interpreter, and the foreign affairs of Turkey, at least as far as concerned details, were in the hands of the Greeks. Mavrocordato was styled the depositary of secrets, Mahrem-i-esrar, or, in Greek, ἐξ ἀπορρήτων, which corresponds to the Latin *e secretis*. The Dragoman of the Porte proved so satisfactory that the Turks proceeded to appoint a second official with the title of Dragoman of the Fleet, or Tersane Terjumani. He was the secretary of the Capitan Pasha, or Lord High Admiral, who, in addition to his purely naval functions, was Governor of the Archipelago. The Dragoman of the Fleet became his intermediary in all dealings with the inhabitants and authorities of the islands, and gradually acquired almost absolute authority between the shores of the Ægean. It became the custom for him to buy of the Capitan Pasha all the offices in the latter's gift and then to resell them at a profit.

The Greek element and Greek influence had long been strong in Wallachia and Moldavia, but after 1716 the Porte, distrusting the national party in those principalities, reduced to a system the practice which it had hitherto occasionally followed of giving them foreign governors. From that date until the Greek War of Independence, Phanariots, chiefly of the families of Mavrocordato, Ghica, Soutzo, and Ypsilanti, were regularly appointed as Hospodars of the two provinces, and maintained quasi-royal state at Bucharest and Jassy. They brought with them a train of officials, priests,

---

[1] He was a Chiot, and called τό πράσινο ἄλογο or ὁ πράσινος ποντικός, because, according to the proverb, sensible men are as rare in Chios as green horses or green mice.

and creditors, and altogether overwhelmed the Roumanian element.

Though the Phanariots never held the same political position in the Slavonic parts of the Balkan Peninsula as on the northern bank of the Danube, they managed to secure in them a preponderating influence by means of their Church. They destroyed the ancient and independent Sees of Ipek and Ochrida, and made the whole ecclesiastical organisation of Macedonia, Servia, and Bulgaria dependent on the Patriarchate of Constantinople. Their bishops made tax-collecting tours like Turkish pashas, and the dues which they extorted were remitted to the Phanar, and expended on Hellenic objects. Monasteries and their estates passed into Greek hands. Greek literature and Greek schools formed the only available means of education, and educated Serbs and Bulgarians called themselves Greeks.

Thus in the middle of the eighteenth century Christian Turkey was in the hands of the Greeks. But there was another side to the picture. The governors and bishops who dealt so freely with Roumanians and Slavs had to be careful how they punished a Turkish brigand, and might be deposed or executed if they offended one of the Sultan's eunuchs. The ballad of Kyritsos Michalis,[1] a rich Greek of Achelos, on the Black Sea, gives a vivid picture of this state of insecurity, and its want of detail and explanation of the disaster it records are more forcible than any elaborate description could be :—

"There was a certain Greek called Kyritsos Michalis. He had immense wealth and great power, and he sat quietly at home, and his mind was easy. They read a letter before the Divan, saying that he troubled the country and was seeking after war. When the Sultan heard it, he was very angry. He sent for the Kapuji Pasha, and hastily addressed him. ' Haste to Achelos, to the house of Michalis;

[1] Fauriel, vol. i. p. 211 ff.

there see that thou hang him before his door; and see that thou take his little son, and take care that thou lose not a pin of all his possessions.' He weighed anchor at midnight; he went to Achelos. He flew like a bird; he went like an arrow. When Michal Bey saw him, he rose to meet him. 'Hail, my master, sit down and eat.' 'I have not come to eat nor yet to drink, but to perform the bidding and the will of the Sultan.' He cast the rope about his neck, and straightway took him before his door and hanged him. And he found his little son, and took him too, and put him into the galley with all his father's wealth."

The Phanariots have fared ill at the hands of historians. They are detested by all whose sympathies lie with Slavs or Roumanians, and not overmuch loved by Philhellenes. Their administration was no doubt bad. They were tyrannical by order of their masters, and tyrannical on their own account, in order to show their independence when they dared. They maintained their position so long because they were in sympathy with no section of the provincial population. As soon as the Turks suspected them of any inclination towards Hellenic patriotism (in which cause they were very lukewarm), the whole system came to an end. The great vice of their rule was its venality. Hospodars, dragomans, and patriarchs alike bought their offices for enormous sums, which ultimately came out of the pockets of the unfortunate peasantry in the various districts. The Porte changed them all as often as possible, in order to increase the number of sales, but left them a free hand in the matter of filling their own pockets. The Hospodars kept up an extraordinary pomp and luxury in their capitals; but contemporary travellers speak of the poverty and depopulation of Roumanian villages in terms which remind one of those used of Armenia at the present day. Yet justice is not always done to the activity of the Phanariots. They revived and diffused the culture which led to the awakening of the Christian races of South-Eastern Europe. It was not an unworthy, though it appears to be an unpractical, idea to unite those races under one Church and one language; and for such a purpose Greek was the only possible language. It is regrettable that they should have destroyed Slavonic books, but it does not appear that they drove out Slavonic or Roumanian culture. They introduced Greek culture in the place of no culture at all, and thereby aroused native genius, and ultimately excited it to rivalry. The transition from the period of the Phanariots to that inaugurated by the Greek Revolution of 1821 was due to three causes, for some of which they were clearly responsible : the spread of education, the rise of commerce, and the distressed condition of the Greek provinces.

The books of the Phanariots belong to that large class of literature which adds nothing new to the art or science of the human race, but is still of great importance to those who write and read it, because they have access to nothing better. The end of the sixteenth and beginning of the seventeenth centuries were marked by the cessation of Greek literature in Constantinople. Greek writers indeed there were, but they were mostly either Cretans, like Cornaros and Scleros, or else resided abroad like Allatios, who wrote his " Hellad " in Italy. But with the middle of the seventeenth century a new era opens. The atmosphere of the Phanar was not congenial to poetry or romance, but theology flourished in it, as well as the safer forms of science and history. The first two Dragomans of the Porte were both literary characters. Panayeti translated the Catechism of the Orthodox Church into the popular language, and Alexander Mavrocordato wrote " Moral Essays," a " History of the Jews," and a " Treatise on the Circulation of the Blood." Later, there was a considerable importation of French books, many of which were translated into Greek. The Greek spirit found its fullest development in the border lands of Turkey, which were just out of the reach of the Sultan's arm. Greek colleges, theatres, and newspapers sprang up at Vienna, Odessa, Bucharest, Jassy, and Corfu, and there were Greek colonies and printing-presses in Vienna, Moscow, and Leipzig. Even in Turkey itself there were large educational establishments—for instance, at Kuru Cheshme on the Bosphorus and Cydonia[1] (Aivali) on the coast of Asia north of Smyrna. This latter place is an example of the privileges granted to the Greeks in the times when the Turks were not afraid of them. In 1740 the zeal of the monk Œconomus and the wealth of the banker, Saros Petraki, obtained from the Sultan firmans ordering all Turks to leave Aivali, and establishing there an independent Greek municipality. The place was christened Cydonia, and for half a century was a sort of Oriental Boston, famed for its fine streets, public gardens, University, libraries, and municipal buildings, for the wealth, culture, and refinement of its inhabitants. It is now called Aivali once more. On the outbreak of the Greek Revolution the Turks burnt the town, and the cultured inhabitants either fled or were killed.

Of the Greek writers, two had a definite political importance, Rhigas (1753–1798) and Coraes (1748–1833). Like contemporary Armenian patriots they both of them lived abroad. Rhigas was the author of some popular and spirited national songs, of which the best known begins, " Ὣς πότε, Παλληκάρια, νά ζῶμεν 'σ τά στενά ; " " How long, heroes, shall we live in the mountain passes ? " He also laid the foundations of the society from which was developed the celebrated Hetaireia, and he entered into negotiations with Pasvan Oglu of Widdin,[2] who seemed inclined to play a part similar to that subsequently acted by Ali of Janina. But Rhigas was betrayed by a comrade to the Austrian police,

---

[1] Or Kydonies.　　　　　[1] See page 75.

handed over by the Austrian Government to the Turks, and executed at Belgrade. Coraes lived chiefly at Paris, and published several political works, including the energetic appeal to revolt known as the Σάλπισμα πολεμιστήριον. He also edited the "Hellenic Library" of ancient Greek authors, and began a Greek-French Lexicon.

The commercial ability and activity which distinguished the Greeks at all periods received a special encouragement and development after the Treaty of Kainardji, concluded between Russia and Turkey in 1774. An article of this Treaty allowed the appointment in all seaports of consular officers who, together with their assistants, dependents, and servants, enjoyed certain privileges and immunity from Ottoman jurisdiction. Not only were these officials generally Greeks, but the Porte allowed the Ambassadors to distribute a certain number of *berats*, or letters conferring these privileges and immunities, on any one they chose, even on persons without official position. Finally Selim III., seeing how eagerly these *berats* were sought, thought it prudent to grant them himself in return for considerable fees. Thus arose a class of privileged merchants, known as Beratlis, who were exempt from the dangers and difficulties which generally attend the acquisition and preservation of wealth in Oriental countries. Armenians and Jews reaped the advantages of this system as well as Greeks, but did not become so prominent, because they had not the same maritime aptitudes as the latter. The carrying trade of the Levant was soon almost entirely monopolised by vessels owned and manned by Greeks, and the commerce of the Ægean, Adriatic, and Black Seas was in their hands. Seafaring Greeks entered the mercantile marine instead of the navy, and thus weakened the Ottoman fleet, and at the same time strengthened the Greek nation. Wealthy Greek commercial houses grew up, not only at Salonica and Smyrna, but at Odessa and Taganrog, at Trieste and Venice, and even in London and Moscow. The effect of this rise of Greek communities outside Turkey was very important. The priests and functionaries of the Phanar knew that they only ruled through the Turks and found no difficulty in believing that, as they were the Vice-Regents of the Sultan, so the Sultan was the Vice-Regent of God. But the Greeks in Italy, Russia, and the more distant parts of Europe did not depend on the Turks. The French Revolution familiarised them with the idea of revolt; they were all of them ready to aid the cause of freedom with their money, and quite a respectable number ventured to return to the lion's den. The patriotic society of Rhigas, which had apparently collapsed with his death, was revived in 1814 at Vienna under the title of Φιλομοῦσοι. Its nominal objects were educational and literary, but it was the parent, or at least the affectionate brother, of a more celebrated political association called φιλικὴ Ἐταιρεία, Ἐταιρεία τῶν φιλικῶν, or more briefly the Hetaireia.

The Hetaireia was founded in 1815 by four obscure Greek merchants of Moscow, three of them natives of the Morea, and was somewhat like the Carbonari of Italy. Its members adopted mysterious language and ceremonies, resembling those of Freemasons, and described themselves as the agents of an unknown power called the Ἀρχή, which at the appointed hour would deliver Greece from the. Ottoman yoke. That it was suited to the needs of the time is shown by the fact that in 1820 the number of its members was estimated at 200,000. Even now the words " Society " or " Committee " fill the Porte with unreasoning terror, and Fellows of the Royal Society would doubtless be arrested if they were rash enough to describe themselves as such in Constantinople.

Thirdly, the War of Independence was brought about by the bad state of the Greek provinces. If the Turk caresses with one hand he slaps with the other, and the favour shown to the Phanariots found its natural counterpart in the curtailment of the liberty enjoyed by the rural population. The pleasant family arrangement of Armatoles and Klephts, who understood one another very well in spite of skirmishes, was modified by the appointment of the Dervendji Pasha, charged with the supervision of the roads and passes leading from Macedonia and Epirus into Thessaly and Acarnania. After the middle of the eighteenth century this office was generally conferred on Albanian chieftains, who with their followers devoted themselves to the congenial task of harrying and oppressing the Greeks, with the result that the distinction between Klephts and Armatoles became obliterated, and both were in arms against the Turks.

Farther south other causes produced distress and discontent at the end of the eighteenth century. The fortunes of the Morea had been more varying than those of any other province of the Ottoman Empire on the European continent. Mohammed II. subdued the greater part of it, but some towns were left in the possession of Venice. In 1540 these were given up, and the Turks were in sole possession until 1684, when the Venetians, taking advantage of the weakness and embarrassments of their opponents, reconquered the Morea, which remained in their hands thirty years, until it was taken back by the Turks in 1714, and recognised as Ottoman territory by the Peace of Passarowitz in 1718. The Greeks did not relish the Venetian rule, which merely means that by giving them security of life and property it left them leisure to complain of minor grievances,[1] but we can hardly doubt that this contact with Western Europe was a stimulating influence which prevented the Morea from falling into the same sloth as the more northern regions.

---

[1] Similarly, before the Armenian Massacres of 1895, the Russian Armenians professed to prefer the government of Turkey to that of Russia, on the ground that "the Turk takes the body, but the Russian takes the soul."

All through the eighteenth century there was a certain connection between Greece and Russia. From the time of Peter the Great the Russians began to interfere in Ottoman affairs, chiefly in Wallachia and Moldavia as being nearest, but also in Mount Athos and Southern Greece. In the reign of the Empress Anna, Marshal Munich attempted to raise a revolt in the Morea, and though it came to nothing, Russian pilgrims and adventurers continued to tell the Greeks they must look to the Czar for assistance, and many Greeks entered the Russian service. One of these, a certain Papadopoulo or Papas Oglu,[1] interested Orlow, the favourite of Catherine, in a project of revolt and the foundation of an independent Greece. The plan seems to have had the direct approval of the Russian Government. In April 1770 a Russian fleet appeared at Vitylo, and the whole of the Peloponnesus rose in insurrection. The result was disastrous for the Greeks. It is true that the Russians defeated the Turks, but they transferred their operations to a more northern sphere, and the outcome of the whole business was that they annexed the Crimea, and left the Morea to its fate. The Greeks complained that they were betrayed; the Russians accused them of cowardice, and said they would not fight for their own freedom. Both reproaches had some truth in them. Most Oriental Christians (in spite of repeated experiences to the contrary) expect the Powers to do everything for them, and the Russians are not the only people who have begun by interfering on behalf of oppressed Christians, and ended by somewhat irrelevantly taking a piece of Turkish territory.

About 50,000 Greeks were massacred. Albanian troops poured in from the North, and after the war was over

---

[1] Papadopoulo and Papas Oglu are Greek and Turkish respectively for "priest's son." The individual in question is also called Papazolis, which must be a Grecised form of Papas Oglu.

were allowed to remain in the country, which they pillaged
and ravaged so thoroughly that in a short time the
Christians had hardly any villages or property left. The
Albanians then began to attack the Mussulman population,
and Greece seemed at the mercy of a gang of bandits. It was
nine years before the Porte was able to reassert its authority,
but in 1779 the Capitan Pasha succeeded in routing the
Albanians near Tripolitza and exterminated them. Nevertheless when war broke out again with Russia in 1787, the
Porte again sent bands of Albanians into the Morea. It
may be imagined what suffering all this anarchy entailed on
the unfortunate Greeks, and what desires of revolt it must
have inspired. A little later the creation of the United
Republic of the Seven Ionian Islands, inspired hopes as
well, for it showed that a sort of independence was not
impossible.[1] In the North, also, things tended to increase
both the strength and the discontent of the Greeks. As
mentioned, after about 1740, the Porte charged Albanian
Pashas with the maintenance of order in the mountains.
Greek local independence and prosperity suffered severely
for a time, but the combination of Klephts and Armatoles
against the soldiers of the Dervendji Pasha, formed an
opposition of considerable military force.

At the end of the eighteenth century appeared the
celebrated Ali Pasha of Janina. He was no friend of the
Greeks, and they endured much at his hands; but his real
object throughout his long life was to create for himself
an independent principality, and for this purpose he was

---

[1] The history of the Seven Ionian Islands (Corfu, Paxo, Zante, Ithaca,
Cephalonia, Santa Maura, and Cerigo), is even more complicated than that of
the Morea. From the fifteenth century till 1797 they belonged to Venice, and
in the latter year were ceded to France, but in 1799 were made into a Re-
public guaranteed by Russia and Turkey. France acquired them again in
1807, but from 1809 to 1814 they were gradually taken by England. In 1815
they were formed into "the United States of the Ionian Islands under the
protectorate of Great Britain," and in 1863 incorporated, with our consent,
in the kingdom of Greece.

anxious to weaken Ottoman influence in his neighbourhood by every means he dared employ. As his Albanians had no desire to be anything but soldiers or bandits, this policy caused the Greeks to come to the front as landowners and officials, and, though Ali dealt severely with the Greek armed bands, his natural love of tortuous diplomacy caused him to often intrigue with them even in the earlier part of his career. When the Sultan declared him a rebel in 1820, he summoned a meeting of Greeks, and invited them to join with him in fighting the Turks. He would have much complicated the cause of Hellenic independence had he lived, but he died in 1822 after doing the Greeks more good than he ever intended.

The first outbreak of the insurrection was eminently unsuccessful. The Hetaireia chose as their head Alexander Ypsilanti, the son of a Hospodar and a Russian officer, who proceeded to raise the standard of revolt in the Danubian principalities in February 1821, with the complicity of Michael Soutzo, Hospodar of Moldavia. But he met with little sympathy from the Roumanians; a national insurrection in Wallachia merely embarrassed him; he was disowned by the Russians, and crushed by the Turks in June of the same year.

Meanwhile the movement which had failed in the North began with greater vigour in the South. It appears that the Dragoman of the Porte, John Callimachi, warned Halet Effendi,[1] the favourite of the Sultan, of the insurrection which was preparing in Roumania, accusing in particular the Hospodar of Moldavia. This latter was a creature of Halet's, who flew into a passion, and most unreasonably banished Callimachi. When it was impossible to deny the fact of the insurrection, Halet accused all

---

[1] He was officially only Nishanji, or Keeper of the Privy Seal, but he enjoyed enormous influence, and made and unmade Grand-Viziers as he chose. A few years ago Izzet Bey had a somewhat similar position.

manner of Greeks of complicity so as to attract less attention to the part played by Soutzo, and by himself in
screening him. A series of massacres and executions commenced; prominent Greeks were put to death without
regard to their innocence or guilt; a *jihad* was proclaimed,
and the fanatical populace burnt many Greek quarters.
Simultaneously an insurrection broke out in the Morea.
It was not apparently caused by events at Constantinople,
but it was certainly embittered by them, and there commenced a wholesale vendetta in which a massacre on one
side was answered by a massacre on the other. The first
rising in the Morea occurred at the end of March. On
Easter Day (April 22) the Patriarch of Constantinople was
hanged at the gate of his church. Many bishops and notable
persons were executed on the same day, and the fury
of the Moslim populace found expression in slaughter and
outrages all over Thrace and Macedonia. The insurgents
in the Morea replied by almost exterminating the Turkish
population, and the massacre of Moslims at Vrachori, Tripolitza, Athens, St Spiridion, and elsewhere showed that
the Greeks had the same temper which prompted the
massacre of Chios and many other atrocities on the
Turkish side. I draw attention to this, not from a desire
to prove that Turks and Greeks are all much of a muchness, but because it is important to realise that the Turks
really have cause to fear Christians. Otherwise such events
as the recent Armenian massacres would be inexplicable.

At first, this southern insurrection was entirely successful. The courage of the Greeks was maintained by the
accession to their ranks of numerous Philhellenes, and their
pockets were filled by two European loans. But in 1824,
the Sultan gave a new turn to the fortunes of war by
ordering his vassal Mehemet Ali of Egypt to invade the
Morea, and the latter despatched his son Ibrahim Pasha
to execute the task. The Greeks were unprepared. Dis-

sension and fighting had broken out among their leaders; their fortifications had fallen out of repair, and the European loans had been mysteriously squandered. Ibrahim took Navarino and Tripolitza, and then commenced a systematic massacre with the apparent object of exterminating the Greek population. The capture of Athens and the siege of Missolonghi in 1826 produced a deep impression in Europe. Popular feeling in Russia called for an intervention in favour of Orthodox Christianity, and the new Czar, Nicholas I., was more disposed to act than his predecessor. Russia, France, and England agreed that Ibrahim's devastation of the Morea should be stopped, and Greece made autonomous. A combined squadron made a demonstration at Navarino with the object of bringing Ibrahim to reason. They did not intend to engage him, but the obstinate Pasha fired on an English boat, and in the battle which ensued his fleet was annihilated. In 1830 Greece was recognised as independent.

As I am treating of the populations of Turkey rather than of European politics I will now leave the kingdom of Greece and retire behind the Ottoman frontier. The Turkish Empire gets so little praise that it is worth while to pause a moment and reflect what a curious exhibition of strength it afforded at this juncture. It was almost simultaneously threatened by Ali Pasha, and by risings in Roumania and Greece. It not only mastered them all, but in the midst of the crisis deliberately exterminated its own Janissaries, a proceeding which would have in itself convulsed any ordinary state. It is true that Greece was detached, but that was the result of the action of Europe, without which probably no Greeks would have been left. Nor did the Ottoman Empire emerge from the struggle changed and chastened as might have been expected. Though it destroyed at one blow its army of Janissaries and its civil service of Phanariots, it cannot

be said thereby to have altered its character. Without
Janissaries, and without Phanariots, it is still, in the last
decade of the nineteenth century, very much what it was
in the first.

The detachment of Greece was, however, followed by
an attempt to content the Greeks within the empire. It
is true that they were no longer allowed to hold high
office. There were no more Greek dragomans and hospodars, and the Phanariots fled, as the old Byzantine
nobility had fled after the conquest of Mohammed. A few
went to Greece, but the larger number settled in England,
France, Austria, or Russia, where they founded important
commercial houses. Most persons in Constantinople who
now bear Phanariot names are foreign subjects with the
nationality of the country where their grandparents settled.
But this exodus of the Phanariots, though it destroyed the
pre-eminence of Greek commerce in the Levant, did not
affect the mass of the population, who had derived little
material benefit from their régime. As at the end of the
seventeenth century the Kyöprülüs had thought it politic
to favour the Christians, so Sultans Mahmud and Abd-ul-
Mejid, assisted by such Ministers as Reshid, Ali and Ahmed
Vefik Pashas, who saw the danger arising from Russia
in the North and in the South from the kingdom of Greece
and the quasi-independent Mehemet Ali, did their best to
satisfy the Greek rayahs. They must clearly have succeeded to a certain extent, although most of their so-called
reforms prove illusory when examined, for the exodus into
the kingdom of Greece was smaller than might have been
expected; and on subsequent occasions when war has broken
out between Greece and Turkey there has been no revolt
within the Ottoman dominions, nor have we heard of Greek
atrocities or massacres of Greeks in the Balkan Peninsula.

But, though there is little to chronicle respecting the
Greek rayahs in the last three quarters of a century, the

period has been eventful, but not advantageous for the Μεγάλη ἰδέα, the great idea, as it is called—the idea, that is, that Hellenic influence should be supreme in South-Eastern Europe. The Greeks are, perhaps, still the most intelligent and best educated of the Sultan's subjects, but they are no longer in any way predominant among the Christians. The Bulgarians have a Church and Millet of their own, and the Servians and Vlachs, though less definitely recognised by the Turks, have separated themselves from the Greeks and do not co-operate in the Hellenic cause. Thus, the Greeks, instead of representing Christianity and education for all Eastern Europe, have come to be one of many political parties, and not even the strongest of them.

The most important incidents for Hellenism in this century were the Greek War of Independence and the Firman of 1870 constituting the Bulgarian Exarchate, which may be said to have halved the number and influence of the Greeks in European Turkey. Between these events come two other measures affecting the well-being of the Orthodox community, which until 1870 is not distinguished from the Greeks. They are the Hatt-i-Sherif of Gulhane (1839) and the Hatt-i-Humayun of 1856. The only claim which these acts have on our attention is, that it is important to realise that they were of hardly any importance. When one reads definite imperial rescripts abolishing certain institutions and establishing others in their place, one is apt to believe that a new order of things was really introduced. But the definite language of these decrees had no counterpart in facts. At most, the change was only made for a few years.

The Hatt-i-Sherif of Gulhane abolished the farming of taxes, created a Council of State, a Penal Code, and a State Bank, and informed the inhabitants of the Ottoman Empire that the institutions which it established secured the life, honour, and property of all the Sultan's subjects, without

distinction of religion.   As a matter of fact the condition
of the Christians remained just the same after this Hatt as
it was before ; but it is curious to notice that the opposition
to the abolition of tax-farming came chiefly from the
Christian Sarrafs, or money-changers, of Constantinople.
Two years later the old system was avowedly restored.   The
second Charter of Reforms, the Hatt-i-Humayun of 1856,
was mainly the work of the Powers who fought with
Turkey during the Crimean War, and who felt that, as they
had prevented Russia from assuming a protectorate over
Ottoman Christians, they must do something to protect
them themselves.   In the period before the Crimean war
Russia had helped the Turkish Greeks mainly by the ready
grant of Russian nationality to those who paid a brief visit
to Russian territory.   This effective but highly irregular
form of protection was hotly contested by the Porte, but
continued more or less until the conclusion of the war
discredited Russian influence and brought about a change
of feeling.   The allied Powers were anxious not to disinte-
grate the Turkish administration, but to ameliorate the
Central Government, and their efforts in this direction
called forth a plentiful crop of reforms.   In 1855 a law
was made admitting Christians to the army, and the result
brings into relief the peculiar characteristics of Turkey.
Nothing could be more plausible than this law.   It is one
of the first conditions for the unity and homogeneity of a
State that all classes of the population should have the
same right of bearing arms and defending their country.
Yet the measure was never executed, simply because all
sections of Ottoman subjects objected to it.   The Moslims
said that their lives would be in danger if the Christians
were armed ; and the Christians said that they could not
fight under the standard of the Prophet or against other
Christians.

Next year followed the Hatt-i-Humayun of 1856.   It

reaffirmed in a stronger form the principal provisions of Gülhane; it abolished tax-farming and bribery; it again proclaimed perfect toleration and the absolute equality of all religions; and enumerated a whole catalogue of reforms, administrative, financial, ecclesiastical, and judicial. Many of these, however, came into collision with Greek interests, notably the provisions which assigned fixed stipends to the clergy instead of allowing them to take what dues they could from their flocks. It is said that when the Archbishop of Ismidt, after hearing the imperial rescript read, saw it replaced in its silken envelope, he ejaculated, " Pray God that it may stay there." No supernatural intervention was necessary to produce that result. The Hatt-i-Humayun was communicated to the Powers, who solemnly stated, in the Treaty of Paris, that they recognised " the high value of this communication," but no one else paid any attention to most of its provisions. In one point, however, it did not prove a dead letter, but led to further changes. The Porte, observing perhaps that there existed in the different religious communities a certain antagonism between the lay and ecclesiastical elements—to which latter, Turkish regulations gave such an exaggerated prominence—proceeded to reorganise them in a manner which strengthened lay influence. In 1862, the Greek Millet, which still included the Slavs, was given a constitution, consisting of a Synod of twelve bishops, a National Council of twelve laymen, and a General Assembly. This arrangement led subsequently to considerable friction between the conservative and liberal elements. At present the reduced Greek Millet is administered by a Synod and a mixed National Council of twelve members, eight of whom are laymen.

As pointed out above, a race in Turkey depends chiefly on community of language and religion. I have spoken elsewhere at length of the Orthodox Church, and it remains that I should say something of the Greek language. Of the great tongues of the world it is perhaps the most remarkable. It is widely spoken, for it is the chief medium of commercial communication all over the Levant, including the Black Sea and the Eastern shores of the Adriatic, and it is even more widely studied. Young Englishmen still devote many years to an attempt to master its complexities, and the votaries of science, who scoff at a classical education, enshrine their thoughts in a remarkable dialect which seems to presuppose an acquaintance with the vocabulary (though not always with the structure) of Greek. The position held by Greek in European literature and education is unique. It cannot be compared to that of Latin, for the diffusion of Latin is due, not to Cicero or Virgil, but to the fact that it was the language of the Church and the bar. But the admiration and study of Greek in the West seem to be due almost entirely to the brilliancy or importance of a small portion of its literature, which has affected the culture of all Europe and also had a remarkable effect on the modern developments of the language.

It is often said that ancient and modern Greek are practically the same, and that, allowing for the difference of the subjects treated of, there is little difference between the language of Plutarch or St. Paul and the language of a modern newspaper. As a bare statement of facts this is no doubt true, but it is apt to mislead unless we realise how artificial the language of the newspaper is. Finlay observes that Arabic and Greek seem to be less changeable than other languages, and the observation is very just with the same limitation as to the character of this immutability. If Arabic were written in an alphabet which represented the popular pronunciation, and in a style which represented the popular grammar and vocabulary, it would be seen that the languages spoken in Morocco, Egypt, Syria, and Zanzibar are as different as any four Romance languages from one another. But the Arabic alphabet obliterates differences of pronunciation. Colloquial words and forms are excluded by preconceived literary ideas, and the less cultivated a dialect is the more classical does written composition affect to be. Spoken Moorish is hardly intelligible to an Eastern Arab, but written Moorish is almost Koranic in its purity.

The fact is that language is at the mercy of literature all the world over. Danish, Swedish, Icelandic, and perhaps even Norwegian, are considered as separate languages because they have each of them a fairly old literature which has cherished and developed their peculiarities. Little Russian is hardly recognised as a language at all, because it has not much literature, and every effort is made to tone down its peculiarities and merge it in ordinary Russian. Similarly, the real spoken modern Greek is as different from the Greek of Plutarch as the Arabic of Tangier from the Arabic of Mohammed, or as Italian from Latin, but it has never had a *vates sacer*, or received the approval of literature. It is said that Dante debated whether he should write his great poem in Italian or Latin, and that by choosing the former alternative he conferred on the spoken language a dignity and authority which it did not before possess. If this change had never been made, if people used Italian for conversation or popular songs, but thought it too homely for serious subjects, and took to mediæval Latin whenever they had occasion to write a leading article or a tragedy, the Italians of the present day would be like the Greeks.

This condition of the Greek language is no doubt also largely due to the fact that since Byzantine times it has been subject to Oriental influences. Classical Greek took, or rather inaugurated, the modern view of literature, namely, that it should use the grammar and more or less the vocabulary of ordinary life. Plato and Aristophanes write the same language, just as modern French comedians and philoso-

phers write the same language.   But this view, though it
seems to us obvious, is really rare out of Europe.   The
Oriental regards literature as something sacred or official ;
he does not read novels, comedies, satires, or any works
which are obliged to have recourse to ordinary language ;
he listens to popular stories and popular songs, but does not
write them down ; he expects a written chronicle or poem
to be full of hard words and decorously obscure.   The
Byzantine Greeks had something of this habit of mind ;
their literature was not popular and contemporary in the
same sense as the plays of Aristophanes or the speeches of
Demosthenes.   It was ecclesiastical and learned, and though
they might treat of the present they had their eye on the
past.   The Byzantine Churchmen wrote like the Fathers (on
the same principle that the Mollah writes like the Followers
of the Prophet), and the Byzantine historians wrote like
Plutarch.   Such an artificial language seemed less unnatural,
because, even in ancient Greece, particular dialects had
been appropriated to particular styles of composition.   In
Turkish times this tendency towards archaism became even
more accentuated.   Phanariot literature reflecting the influence of the Greek Church and the Ottoman Court could
hardly be original or free from pedantry.   The country
population, and especially the Klephts, were far from
pedantic ; they had vigorous, emotional, eventful lives, but
they were not literary.   Printing books was out of the
question, if any one had been disposed to write them, and it
is only from popular songs that we know that artistic feeling
and style were not entirely dead.   Hence there were, at the
beginning of this century, two languages—one simple and
natural, following a development which was healthy and
normal, even if it showed traces of wounds and scars ; the
other artificial, archaic, and retrograde.

It is to be observed that the difference between these
two languages is not merely one of style like that existing

between spoken and written Turkish. The most elaborate
Stambouli jargon, however overloaded it may be with Persian
and Arabic words, employs the grammatical forms of common
speech. But written and spoken Greek—which may for
convenience be distinguished as Hellenic and Romaic—differ
in their grammar, in the articles, pronouns, and inflections,
and any description of Romaic as " corrupt " and Hellenic
as " correct " overlooks the fact that the former is the result
of natural processes similar to those which have developed
the Romance languages. Thus, the use of ς to form the
nominative plural is extended (ὥρα, plural ὥραις or ὥρες) ; a
form resembling the stem takes the place of the classical
nominative (ἡ γυναῖκα for ἡ γύνη—cf. fiore, in Italian, for flos) ;
the dative vanishes ; the personal pronouns have new and
mostly shorter forms, ἐμεῖς, μᾶς, σέις, σᾶς, &c. ; who is ποιός,
which ποῦ, that (conj.) πῶς, The verb has lost the infinitive
and uncompounded future, and exhibits a number of new
forms, such as ἔκαψα (= ἔκαυσα), λεῖς or λές (= λέγεις),
φαντάστηκα (= ἐφαντάσθην), πές (= εἰπέ). Most common
objects are known by unclassical names. Just as French
employs maison, cheval, and feu, and not derivatives from
domus, equus, and ignis, so Romaic employs σπίτι, ἄλογο,
and φωτιά ; water is νερό, bread ψωμί, and wine κρασί.

This Romaic language does not commend itself to the
educated modern Greek ; and it is only with great diffidence
that a foreigner can express a contrary judgment, for native
opinion as to what sounds well or ill, what is possible or impossible in a language, is necessarily final. But why do the
modern Greeks so despise Romaic, and apply to their
Hellenic resuscitations words implying some moral superiority ? Hellenic vocables and constructions are constantly
recommended to a foreigner on the ground that they are
" higher " or " better." Why is it lower or worse to write
δός του το than donne-le-lui ? Was the brigand, who said of
the sixty Agas ἔκαψα τά χωριά τους (Fauriel i., No. vii.),

grammatically inferior to his French translator, who says, " J'ai brulé leurs villages? " Illorum villages would not be an improvement. But modern Greek writers (at least in Constantinople) are of a different opinion. They revel in the dative case, and forms like ὑμᾶς, ὑμῶν, ὑμῖν; and for " I can stay at home," they write δύναμαι νὰ μείνω κατ᾽ οἶκον, whereas no one would ever say anything but ᾽σ τό σπίτι. A foreigner can hardly criticise, but one cannot help feeling that this is much as if an Italian thought he could add dignity to his language by the use of words like nobiscum, or by saying he would remain ad domum. Nor is it plain why the vocabulary of Romaic should be thought vulgar. It is not, as often said, a jumble of Greek, Italian, Turkish, and Slavonic. Considering the close relations which have existed between the Greeks and Slavs, the Slavonic words are surprisingly few, and the Turkish and Italian elements, if we deduct words referring to Turkish customs and nautical terms, are probably not so considerable as the French element in German. There is no harm in borrowed words unless their proportion to the native vocabulary is excessive. Why then does the modern Greek try to persuade the inquiring foreigner that he calls an umbrella ἀλεξίβροχον, when he really calls it ᾽Ομπρέλα? The English are not ashamed of " umbrella," though it is not of British origin. It is, indeed, a very beautiful word; and had fate ordained (as might well have been the case) that it should mean " a little shady bower " it would have been considered a remarkable instance of a poetical idea finding expression in harmonious sound. I cannot even see that there is any objection to calling a gun τουφέκι. The Klephts called it so, and they shot much better than the modern purists. To insist in using no words but those of Greek origin is surely as unreasonable as it would be for Englishmen to refuse to talk of " lieutenants" or " khaki," and invent Anglo-Saxon equivalents.

The Romaic language is certainly somewhat chaotic; it offers many alternative forms, and no one has ever decided which shall be adopted. But if it has to be rejected *in toto*, if the Greek people, instead of systematising and developing their living language, feel that they can make nothing of it, and must have recourse to a lifeless language, it is a very remarkable phenomenon. One is tempted to think it can only mean that growth, vigour, and creative power have come to an end, and that the modern Greeks' only claim to attention is that they are supposed to be the descendants of the ancient Hellenes. I should feel some delicacy in putting forward this distressing idea if I thought it true, but I do not. The people who fought in the War of Independence did not live in the past, and their language was not pedantic.

$$\text{'}A\pi\text{' } \tau\grave{a} \; \kappa\acute{o}\kappa\kappa a\lambda a \; \beta\gamma a\lambda\mu\acute{e}\nu\eta$$
$$T\hat{\omega}\nu \; \text{'}E\lambda\lambda\acute{\eta}\nu\omega\nu \; \tau\grave{a} \; i\epsilon\rho\acute{a}$$
$$K a\grave{i} \; \sigma\grave{a}\nu \; \pi\rho\hat{\omega}\tau\text{' } \; \grave{a}\nu\delta\rho\epsilon\iota\omega\mu\acute{e}\nu\eta$$
$$X a\hat{i}\rho\text{' } \hat{\omega} \; \chi a\hat{i}\rho\text{'}, \; \text{'}E\lambda\epsilon\upsilon\theta\epsilon\rho\iota\acute{a}$$

is not precisely classical Greek, but it is good enough for poetry and politics. One thing is certain, namely, that none of these artificial literary languages, whether Turkish, Arabic, or Greek, produce anything of literary value.

It must be confessed that, though at the beginning of this century the Greeks showed more energy than any other Christian race, those who now remain in Turkey (except the islanders) are not remarkable for physical vigour or military capacity. This is, no doubt, partly due to the fact that the people who revolted against Mahmud were largely Hellenised Vlachs and Albanians, who, under the modern system, would not be regarded as Greeks. Now-a-days the robust agricultural population is rarely Hellenic in its sympathies, for, as already mentioned, there are comparatively few parts where it is really Greek. In the south, below the Slavonic region, the Greek element is strong; but in Thessaly, as well as on the Turkish side, much mixed with Albanians, Vlachs, and Turks. The middle and north of Macedonia is mainly Slav, except in the Albanian districts, and the only considerable masses of Greek population are in the parts known to the Ancients as Chalcidice and Thrace. There are few Greek country gentlemen, but there are Greeks in every seaport as surely as there are fish in the sea; and in the most remote and un-Hellenic towns there are pretty sure to be Greek bankers or traders. The Greek peasantry, though not particularly good agriculturists, are infinitely more intelligent and enterprising than any other in Turkey. They are not *adscripti glebæ* like the Slavs, who, if left alone, die where they were born, nor are they occupied in tribal quarrels like the Albanians. Every Greek is endowed with a surprising energy and versatility, and a readiness to adopt any career which fate may open to him. The son of a farmer aspires, not to succeed his father, but to go to Smyrna, Salonica, and Constantinople, and make his way in the world. Three professions are specially congenial to them—the law, medicine, and banking. The Sultan employs a Greek as his chief physician, and even in Asia Minor the provincial lawyers are mostly Greeks.

Thus the Greeks represent to a large extent the intelligence of Turkey. They are no longer recognised as the upper layer of the Christian population, nor are they largely employed by the Porte. A contemporary list of nearly six hundred Ottoman officials contains only about thirty Greek names, and the bearers mostly fill subordinate positions. The Greeks are inclined to politics, public speaking, and the press, all of which are hateful to the Ottoman Government, and they, therefore, are not regarded with favour; but in all the learned professions their intelligence and ambition secure them pre-eminence, and in the most trying circumstances they manage to lead a busy life. In a convenient corner at Therapia, there sat for many years (and perhaps sits still) the head and body of what would have been a very proper man, but for the accident that he had been born without any legs. He did not whine or mumble as many beggars do, but saluted the passers-by with a graceful bow, and received with the dignity of a courteous tax-collector the alms which his persuasive tongue never failed to elicit. In this way he was said to have become exceedingly rich, and to support eleven blind sisters who lived in Mitylene. Every evening an attendant removed him to his home, and when, on the approach of winter, the Ambassadors left Therapia, he left too, took a first-class ticket to Mitylene, and spent the cold season in the bosom of his family.

The term Levantine is for most purposes synonymous with urban Greek. It is true that many Levantines are Catholics and Franks, but clearly the characteristics which mark the Christian communities of such towns in the Levant as Constantinople, Smyrna, and Salonica are derived from the Greek element. Levantine life generally strikes a stranger as a curious mixture of Paris and the East. The better families copy European fashions and speak French extensively; but one feels that, according to Oriental custom, their existence is really divided into the departments of Selamlik and Harem, which means the difference, not only between the men's and the women's part of the house, but between formal and domestic life. A European when received by a well-to-do Greek family notices few signs of Oriental manners. Perhaps jam and water may be handed him on a tray, and cause him some perplexity as to how to dispose of them; perhaps the host may be fingering a rosary, not to count his prayers, but as a mere pastime to occupy his fingers. But the frock-coats of the men and dresses of the ladies are probably of the most correct style, and Eastern influence is not more marked than it would be

in an English house at Pera. One is, however, obscurely
conscious that the whole business is a ceremony and a show;
and the impression is confirmed by those rare peeps into
domestic mysteries which fall to a foreigner's lot—passing
visions of inner rooms where there are more divans than
chairs, men in slippers and dressing-gowns, and numerous
elderly, black-robed female relatives who attend to the
household duties, and do not appear in society. In Smyrna
these family scenes sometimes present a very singular aspect
in consequence of the employment of the *tandour*, a kind of
stove under a quilt. The ladies of the family sit round the
stove and draw the quilt up to their chins, which makes
them look as if they were all in bed together.

One ancient art the modern Greek has certainly lost,
namely, architecture. This is largely due to Turkish influence. The Turks, retaining many of the migratory habits
of nomads, did not encourage the building of large or substantial houses, and prudence restrained the Greeks' natural
love for artistic display externally. With the exception of
some quite modern residences, Greek houses are generally
crooked, rickety tenements, mostly of wood, with steep, shaky
staircases and many windows. It requires the summer sun
and air to make them even picturesque; for a brief period
the bright-coloured walls and irregular outlines, overgrown
with vines or other leafy creepers, have a romantic charm;
but in winter the mud in the streets, and the cold and damp
within, combated but not conquered by a pan of burning
ashes called *mangal*, form a sad picture of inartistic dis-
comfort. Of all methods of warming the *mangal* is the
least satisfactory. You cannot add fuel and make it burn
up; it is simply a pile of hot ashes, which is bound to grow
colder and colder as you try to warm yourself.

Like most of the intelligent and money-making races of
the world, the Greeks are very conspicuous. Russian towns
where there are Jews seem to be inhabited exclusively by

Jews; and the same may be said of Turkish towns where
there are Greeks. Turks and Russians sit at home when
nothing calls them out; Jews and Greeks stand about in
the streets watching to see what will turn up. The Greek
women spend most of their time in sitting at the window,
and a house is valued in proportion to the facilities which it
offers for this amusement. On feast days, however, they
issue forth in their best clothes, and solemnly promenade
up and down some street which fashion has set apart for
this purpose. In each town the Greek community is kept
together by various scholastic and charitable institutions,
and often possesses a *syllogos*, or literary and philosophical
society, where the more educated members meet together.
The various districts usually have for centre a parish church,
to which are attached, besides the necessary priests, lay
officials, generally three in number, called *ephors* (ἔφοροι),
who are a sort of churchwardens, but more important, inasmuch as they are concerned with the proper registration of
the parish and the payment of taxes. The belief in the
power of ceremonies is great, and the threat of excommunication much feared. It is a common practice, when anything
is missed in a house, to take all the servants before a priest,
and make them swear to their innocence, and it is said that
the guilty will sometimes confess sooner than swear falsely.
The ceremonies of the Orthodox Church in Turkey are less
splendid and striking than in Russia, doubtless in order not
to excite Moslim fanaticism. The midnight mass on Easter
Eve is comparatively rarely performed; and instead of the
gilt crowns which form such a picturesque feature in a
Russian marriage, garlands of flowers are placed on the heads
of the bride and bridegroom. Funerals are celebrated with
great pomp, and the top of the coffin is open, displaying the
face of the corpse. It is often said that this custom originated in the fact that the Turks once discovered that a
quantity of arms had been smuggled in closed coffins, and

ordered that coffins should be open for the future; but I doubt
if this explanation is true, for in Russia it is the custom in
country districts to carry the corpse to burial with the face
exposed, though, for sanitary reasons, it is forbidden in towns.
It is a strange and ghastly custom of the Greeks to exhume
the dead after three years, and if decomposition is complete,
to place the bones in a mortuary chapel.   If the body is not
entirely decomposed, it is thought a very evil omen for the
fortunes of the soul in the next world, and the words, " May
the earth not eat you," are considered a horrible curse.

It would be unfair to regard the Greeks as mere Levantines, for there are other and more poetical aspects of the
race.   The coasts and islands of the Archipelago have a
poetry and beauty of their own, which is certainly not
Turkish.   We associate the Turk with the rich shady gardens round Broussa, with its many-coloured minarets, its
mosques with unnumbered lamps and plashing fountains.
We associate the Armenian with the bare plateaux of Asia,
the castellated rocks, the half-burnt church, and the dark
underground houses, partly human dwellings and partly
stables.   But when we think of the strangely exhilarating
and clear atmosphere which bathes the coasts and islands
of the Ægean; of the rocky promontories which take such
startling tints from the setting sun, or shine in the moon-
light with a distinctness unknown in other lands; of the oak
groves of Olympus, untrodden by Turkish foot; of the Vale
of Tempe, where the Peneus rushes under overhanging poplars
and vine-clad rocks—we feel that these landscapes have a
common charm, and that the charm is Hellenic.   Perhaps
the most characteristic and attractive of Greek lands are the
districts on the south-eastern frontier, which runs so as to
leave Tempe to the kingdom of Greece and Olympus to
Turkey.   On the southern bank of the Peneus, about 800 feet
above the river, is the large village of Ambelakia, surrounded
by the vineyards which give it its name, and commanding

a magnificent prospect of Mount Olympus, or Elymbos, as it is now called. In the village are many large houses with lower storeys of stone and superstructures of wood. They date from the end of the last century, when Ambelakia was a considerable commercial centre, and had direct mercantile relations with Europe, in consequence of a special kind of dyed thread manufactured by the inhabitants. Some curious traces of this connection with the West still remain, among others the existence in most of the older houses of libraries of eighteenth-century French literature. The wooden walls of the upper storeys are ornamented with pictures of Stamboul, and still more imaginative representations of Paris. In so large and wealthy a village, it is inevitable that some of the unpoetical modernisms introduced by progress and prosperity should be visible, but the elevation and inaccessibility of the place (it can only be approached by a bridle-path) have preserved many old features. At the foot of the mountain, before commencing the winding ascent, I was entertained with a lunch of lamb cooked in the Klepht style—that is, roasted whole in a trench dug in the earth for the purpose; and on feast days national costumes and national dances may still be witnessed.

One of the most interesting of Greek lands, which deserves some mention here, both on account of its intrinsic importance and of its close connection with the politics of South-Eastern Europe, is Crete. The history of this island differs from that of most of the Levant, in that it was held by the Saracens from 823 to 961, and subsequently, for more than four and a half centuries (from the fourth Crusade to 1669), remained under Venetian rule. It was hence subjected to a stronger and more continuous Frankish influence than any other part of the Ottoman Empire. The population has naturally a considerable admixture of Italian and probably of Arab blood, but is not blended with Slavs, Albanians, or Turks; for though the Turks have sent many officials and troops to Crete, they have never attempted to colonise the country. The Cretan Moslims are merely converts to Islam, of the same race and language as the Christian population. It seems as if fate had ordained that dissension and disunion should reign in every part of the Ottoman Empire. On the continent of Europe the Christians quarrel with one another because they are of different races; in Crete a homogeneous race plunges about once in every ten years into internecine war because its members are divided between two religions. It is a land of insurrections. Both in 1770 and 1821 the Cretans rose in sympathy with the Greek cause; and on the latter occasion the trouble which they occasioned to the Porte was so serious that Mahmud ordered his Viceroy, Mehemet Ali of Egypt, to occupy the island. This Egyptian occupation lasted from 1824 to 1841, when the Porte resumed direct administration. The failure of the Ottoman Government to practically enforce in Crete the provisions of the Hatt-i-Humayun of 1856 led to a rising in 1857–1858. This movement was followed by others in 1866–1868, 1877, 1889, and 1896. The history of them all is the same. Each terminated in some kind of firman or ordinance issued by the Sultan under the pressure of the Powers, and assuring to the island some form of constitutional government, and some financial or other privileges. In each case the firman was never really executed, and as each successive Constitution proved illusory, the discontent broke out again. The most celebrated of these Constitutions was that known as the Halepa Part of 1878, which established a sort of Parliamentary government and a General Assembly. But the struggles between the political parties thus created, the tendency of the Turks to foment such dissensions, and the sympathetic attitude of the kingdom of Greece, brought about another outbreak in 1889, after which the numbers and powers of the Assembly were somewhat curtailed.

I visited Crete in the spring of 1895, when the last insurrection had not yet broken out, and the maintenance of peace and order seemed possible and even easy. The ports of the island recall the coast of the Adriatic rather than of the Ægean, and the lion of St. Mark may be seen carved on old buildings. The population are bold and stalwart, and one feels at once that the literary and financial atmosphere which surrounds the continental Greeks has no place here. Popular opinion, however, agrees with St. Paul in considering that Epimenides' unflattering criticism of his countrymen is true; and the Cretans are not in the least ashamed of it, holding, like many old families, that antiquity imparts dignity to any peculiarity. The interior of Crete possessed in 1895 no carriage roads at all, the only communication being narrow bridle-paths kept in not over good repair. A wider road was considered dangerous, because the Turks might have been able to drag cannon over it. Every village seemed a collection of forts. The houses are built of solid, almost cyclopean, masonry, and their massive walls often show signs of having withstood fire and bullets. As there are no hotels, the traveller has generally to depend on the hospitality of monasteries, which is always freely given. The Cretan monk has little in common with the gentle, contemplative, but incurably lazy denizens of Mount Athos. Once when riding up to the monastery of Arcadi by a road overhung with cherry-trees in full blossom, I met a company of unusually fine-looking labourers dressed in high boots and leather aprons, who, bill-hook in hand, were occupied in hedging and ditching. Their chief advanced, handling his bill-hook in a somewhat martial manner, and having made sure that I was not a Turk, invited me to the monastery. He proved to be an Archimandrite, but even in their robes neither he nor his subordinates entirely lost their air of yeomen. This monastery is celebrated for the siege which it underwent in 1867 at the hands of the Turks, who managed to drag cannon up to the surrounding hills. According to the tradition, the Hegumen Gabriel rather than yield blew up the powder magazine of the convent, killing all the Christians who had taken refuge in it as well as two hundred Turks.

The population of Crete is said to be two-thirds Christian and one-third Moslim, but the general character of the island is certainly non-Mohammedan. According to statistics there are 150 mosques against 3000 Greek churches and 50 large monasteries, and, as in Bosnia and other countries where the Moslims are of European race, the precepts of the Prophet meet with scant observance. Wine is freely drunk by the adherents of both religions, the bottle in common use being a double-magnum. The perpetual quarrel between Christians and Mohammedans, which forms the chief feature of Cretan politics, is not due to fanaticism, but is really a sort of vendetta, somewhat similar to the Albanian blood-feuds, and is accepted by all Christians as part of the natural order of things when it does not assume too serious proportions. In ordinary peaceful times perhaps half-a-dozen were killed on either side every year; but clearly a strong hand and an adequate police force were required to prevent this national habit from developing into civil war. Had such simple requisites for the maintenance of order been forthcoming, Crete would probably have been happy under any government, Turkish, Greek, or other. But they have never been forthcoming. The Porte have always persisted in regarding every little disorder as a rising of Christians, and in employing troops to crush it. The result has always been doubly unfortunate. The troops irritated the population, and created that disaffection which they were intended to suppress; and the civil authorities were weakened, because the administration of the island was periodically taken out of their hands, and entrusted to a military governor. Also the finances were in confusion; there was no money to pay the very inefficient police force which existed, and all the evils which arise from this peculiarly Turkish habit of employing unpaid soldiers and gendarmerie became rampant.

At the end of 1895, the Mussulmans in Crete, as in other parts of the Ottoman Empire, became somewhat excited, and on the Christian side there was formed the body called Epitropi.[1] This band could have been easily suppressed at first, and was of no importance; but gradually it became more definitely political, and the Christians, seeing that all the moderate proposals made by the Assembly for a better gendarmerie and financial reform received no attention, became more and more disaffected. Serious disorders in the summer of 1896 brought about the intervention of Europe, and on 27th August of that year an international arrangement made at Constantinople, which was satisfactory to the Christians of Crete, received the sanction of the Sultan. It had exactly the same fate as the five or six similar schemes of reform which had preceded it. It was never put into execution, and the massacre of Armenians at Constantinople distracted the attention of the Powers. As has often happened, the Porte baffled the attempts of those who wished to interfere in its affairs by the multitude of the problems it offered them. Crete was neglected, and went on from bad to worse, until serious fighting and slaughter occurred in January 1897. The sympathy of Greece became uncontrollable, and in the middle of February Colonel Vassos landed Greek troops in Crete. The Powers interfered, and the island was occupied by international forces, which could, however, do nothing except in the coast towns. The excitement of the Greeks became more and more intense. In defiance of all reason and the

[1] Ἐπιτροπη.

advice of Europe, they insisted on provoking Turkey to war, and whatever little prudence the Government wished to exercise was neutralised by the bands of the patriotic society called Ethnike Hetaireia. As a result of the disastrous war which ensued, Greece agreed to evacuate Crete and place her interests in the hands of the Powers, who proceeded to negotiate the terms of peace on her behalf with Turkey. Their labours terminated in a Treaty (November 1897) which included a strategical rectification of the northern frontier of Thessaly to the advantage of Turkey, and the payment of an indemnity by Greece.

Meanwhile Crete, the cause of all the trouble, had been somewhat forgotten. It was nominally governed by the admirals of the Powers, representing the "Concert of Europe." The results of this famous Concert were somewhat negative, and afforded abundant material to scoffers and caricaturists, who were a little apt to forget that any machinery, however clumsy, which restrains the great nations of Europe from going to war on issues which are not vital must be of immense value to humanity. Early in 1898 Germany and Austria withdrew from the Concert as far as Crete was concerned, but the other four Powers continued their joint action. In September a bloody outbreak at Candia hastened the solution of the question. By the middle of November the Turkish troops were forced to evacuate the island, and though the suzerainty of the Sultan was expressly recognised, a National Government was installed, and Prince George of Greece named as High Commissioner on behalf of the Powers, though a few months before the Porte had scouted the idea of entrusting the administration of the island to him.

Nothing throws a more illustrative light on the modern Ottoman Empire than these events in Crete, and the Turco-Greek war. Firstly, all the trouble in Crete was unnecessary and might have been easily avoided. Under any ordinary administration the island would have given Europe no more trouble than Corsica. It was not needful to make a new Constitution or introduce elaborate reforms, but merely to put into practice any one of the numerous statutes, instruments, and firmans defining the government of the island—merely, in fact, to have a proper police force and regular finances. One would have imagined that, when all Asiatic Turkey was convulsed with the quarrel between Moslims and Armenians, the Porte would have thought it peculiarly desirable to keep the rest of the Empire quiet. There was no possible advantage in allowing disorders to occur in Crete, and there was imminent danger of losing the island or seeing it become practically autonomous like Samos. Yet the Ottoman Government acted against all their own interests, and not once only, but at every stage of the question stubbornly refused to take any of the simple steps required to ensure peace and contentment. Haunted by the idea of a Christian rising, they alarmed the Cretan Mussulmans, and their whole policy tended, not to unite and pacify the population, but to divide it into two hostile camps. In Crete the maxim, *divide et impera*, has not proved successful. Secondly, the attitude of the Greeks, both in the kingdom of Greece and on Ottoman soil, was very remarkable. The former could not expect to fight the Ottoman Empire with any prospect of success; in such a conflict they could only be saved from annihilation by the interference of Europe; and all experience taught them the same lesson—not to put their trust in such interference. Nevertheless, they flew at the Turks, as if the bird of Athene should fly at an eagle. A nation which can be carried away by an idea and is at the mercy of its imagination, is not to be despised. Of such stuff are heroic peoples made. But when the Turkish legions inundated Thessaly, the Greeks appeared to be inspired, not by the spirit of

Leonidas or Tyrtæus, but by that of the prudent poet who sang that—

"He who fights and runs away,
Will live to fight another day."

They have been severely criticised; but the judgment of events, from which there is no appeal, declares that their calculations were not entirely wrong. The kingdom of Greece has not been annihilated, and Crete is practically detached from the Ottoman Empire under the rule of a Greek prince.

If, as we have so often heard from so many different sources, all Macedonia groans under the Turkish yoke, it is strange that the Christian inhabitants of that province did not rise to assist the Greeks. Had Hellenes and Slavs combined against the Turks, the latter would have been in a very difficult position. But no such combination took place. The animosity of the Christian populations against one another proved, as it always has proved, stronger than their common animosity against the Turks. After the war the Christian Vlachs of Thessaly petitioned the Powers that their district might be made a Turkish province. Even the Greek communities of the Ottoman Empire made no sign of sympathy. The enormous Greek populations of Salonica and Constantinople remained perfectly quiet; and when Hellenic troops landed on the coast of Macedonia, north of Salonica, in order to cut the railway communication with Constantinople, the peasants bade them retire. "We will welcome you when you come as conquerors," they said, "but we do not wish to pay after you have been defeated for the damage you have done."

The attitude of the Powers is also remarkable, and shows the highest development of the principle that the affairs of the Ottoman Empire are of international concern. They behaved like the managers of a prize-fight. They held the

stakes—Crete—*en dépôt,* and laid down rules for the game—
for instance, that the aggressor would not be allowed to
obtain any advantage from the conflict, whatever the result
might be.   The Turks entered the ring somewhat with the
air of a champion whose conduct in the past is not above
criticism, and who is anxious to wipe out any ugly stories
by ostentatious fair-play and scrupulous obedience to the
ruling of the umpires.   The Turkish soldiers were ordered
not to molest or pillage the Greek villages in Thessaly, and
wherever the inhabitants remained this order was executed
to the letter.   But the places abandoned by the Greeks were
burned and pillaged.

CHAPTER VIII

THE BULGARIANS AND SERBS

NOWADAYS most people would admit that, excluding the Albanians, the population of Eastern Europe south of the Danube and Drave and north of the latitude of Salonica is mainly Slavonic. I include in this name the Bulgarians, for though not originally Slavs they have been completely Slavised, and all the ties arising from language, religion, and politics connect them with the Slavs and not with Turkey or even Hungary. Such a general description of the inhabitants of an extensive area is, of course, subject to many qualifications. Not only is there a large Greek population in such districts as Seres and Drama, north of Salonica, and in the country between Adrianople and Constantinople, but there are considerable Greek *enclaves* among the Bulgarian population, *e.g.* at Dimotiko on the Maritsa and near Philippopoli, as well as many scattered settlements of Vlachs and Turks. Every ethnographic map of the Balkan Peninsula gives a different view of the arrangement of the populations, varying according to the date, and often according to the political opinions of the author, and a traveller may often find that the statements of the latest authorities have ceased to be correct. I myself imagined there could be no doubt that the northern littoral of the Ægean is Greek, but a few years ago the Greek Archbishop of Gümürjina complained to me that his flock were all turning Bulgarian and speaking that language.

The history of the last fifty years in South-Eastern Europe is to a great extent the history of the disentanglement of the Slavonic races from Turks and Greeks, and to this is now succeeding the disentanglement of the Slavonic races from one another. In the early part of this century all Christians in Ottoman Europe were called Greeks, as we have seen in the last chapter, and as late as 1878 the accurate and talented authoress of " The People of Turkey,"[1] no doubt faithfully reflecting local opinion, considers that the inhabitants of Veria, Doiran, Vodena, and Strumnitsa are Greek rather than Slavonic. Ten years later, the progress made by Bulgarian schools and the Bulgarian Church persuaded most people who were interested in the question without being prejudiced that the whole of the Ottoman part of the Balkan Peninsula west of Prishtina, and of Ochrida, was for practical purposes Bulgarian. This view had hardly time to become a commonplace before politicians put forward another idea, not without the support of scientific men, namely, that the districts in question are indeed Slav, but Servian and not Bulgarian. Those who knew Macedonia were astonished to hear that Servian Consuls were appointed at Vodena and Seres to protect the interests of the Servian communities in those parts. Associations in Sofia and Belgrade did all that arguments and subscription lists could do to prove that the whole of Macedonia belonged to the nation which they represented; and the result of the Turco-Greek war of 1897 discredited still further the already weak Hellenic cause, and disposed those Slavs, who were officially called Greeks, because they belonged to the Patriarchal Church of Constantinople, to call themselves Servians.

In a previous chapter I have traced the history of the Slav settlements and kingdoms south of the Danube. We saw there how these regions were invaded from the north-west by Slavonic tribes, apparently closely akin to

[1] By a Consul's daughter and wife.

those who occupied the centre of Europe, and from the north-east by the Bulgarians, a race probably allied to the Finns, but who soon lost their original language and customs, and became completely Slavised. They were more energetic in temper, and less fragmentary in their political ideas than the pure Slavs, and twice became the dominant power in the Balkan Peninsula: firstly, during the Empire of Simeon in the tenth century; and secondly, during the Vlacho-Bulgarian or Asenid Empire, which was contemporary with the Latin domination in Constantinople, and which was broken up by the increasing strength of Servia. The Servian people had been from their first appearance split up into independent tribes, and experienced much difficulty in attaining any political union; but in the middle of the fourteenth century, under Stephen Dushan, they burst forth in a brief blaze of glory, and conquered nearly all South-Eastern Europe, except Constantinople itself. But all these States, whether Bulgarian or Servian, were, though considerable, ephemeral, and both Bulgaria and Servia succumbed to the Turks, more on account of their own inherent weakness and disintegration, than on account of the energy of the Ottoman armies. It is remarkable how long the earlier Sultans temporised with them, how often they recognised their provisional independence, and contracted marriages with Slavonic princesses. One is tempted to compare the conduct of the Turks to a cat playing with a mouse, but a juster simile would probably be a near-sighted man stumbling along in an unknown country and suspecting obstacles where there is really a level road. They feared, not unnaturally, that Christendom would unite against them, in which case their position would have been perilous; but that union never took place, and as far as we can tell they might safely have advanced with greater boldness than they displayed.

Before the conquests of Mohammed II. the Turks had already established their capital at Adrianople, and hence the district where their influence was strongest, and where independence was most completely obliterated, was the country north-west of Constantinople—that is, Bulgaria. The disappearance and resurrection of Bulgaria are probably without parallel in history. For more than three hundred years the national life was suspended. We know that education, religion, and culture were in the hands of Greek ecclesiastics, and that there were bands called Haidud and Momcheta, who corresponded to the Klephts and Armatoles of Northern Greece. Beyond that there is hardly anything to record. In 1834 Kinglake proceeded from Belgrade to Constantinople, and must have passed straight across Bulgaria. Yet, in the well-known description of his travels, "Eothen," he makes no allusion to that country or its inhabitants. Even forty years ago the name Bulgarian was almost unknown, and every educated person coming from that country called himself a Greek as a matter of course.

In 1762, Paysi, a monk of Mount Athos, wrote a work called "The History of Bulgaria," and somewhat later Venelin, a Russian who had travelled in the Balkan Peninsula, published his "Old and New Bulgaria." To such a pass had Bulgaria come, that we must reckon as important events in the national history obscure works which recognised her existence! Venelin's book brought about the foundation in 1835 of a school at Gabrovo, where a certain Aprilov taught in Bulgarian, and disseminated the novel idea that education was not necessarily an exclusively Greek product. This educational movement was the real precursor and cause of the national awakening; for, though political combinations often appeared likely to enfranchise Bulgaria, they always failed to do so, doubtless because the country seemed to be an integral part of the Ottoman Empire, and not detachable like Greece or the Danubian Principalities. We hear that at Tilsit Napoleon contemplated a partition of Turkey by which Bulgaria was assigned to Russia, and that Russia occupied the country in 1810 and 1827. But no immediate consequences ensued from these occupations.

The first practical step in the direction of Bulgarian independence had nothing romantic or heroic about it, being merely an ecclesiastical quarrel. Revolt from the Phanariot clergy was a necessary preliminary to revolt from the Turks, and a long struggle (which I have sketched in Chapter V.) culminated in the recognition by the Sultan of a Bulgarian Church, independent of the Phanar. By a Firman, dated February 28, 1870, the head of this Church, who received the title of Exarch, was allowed to appoint bishops and subordinate clergy in any district of the Empire as far south as Florina, in which there might be a majority of Bulgarians, and those who joined this Church were constituted a Millet, or community, enjoying the same privileges as the Greeks and Armenians. That is to say, the Bulgarians were allowed to manage their own ecclesiastical and educational institutions, and to a certain extent to settle legal disputes among themselves. This measure was not in any way restricted to the modern Principality of Bulgaria, which did not then exist, but embraced all Bulgarians in the Ottoman Empire who might choose to avail themselves of it.

The Sublime Porte had been glad enough to encourage the Bulgarians in their quarrel with the Greeks, and thus divide its Christian subjects; but it had no desire to create a strong organisation of Slavs within its territory, and therefore, with characteristic dilatoriness, executed the Firman only in a partial manner. The Exarch was indeed appointed, but no bishops were named in Macedonia. Still the Bulgarians were now clearly distinguished from the Greeks. They knew themselves, and were known to Europe, as the inhabitants of certain territories with certain national ideals. Such a condition could not remain stationary. The blood of the people had been stirred, and wanted something more than priests and schools. An insurrection, which broke out first in Herzegovina in 1874, gradually involved all the Slavonic peoples of Turkey. In 1875 the phrase "Bulgarian atrocities" gained a terrible notoriety in Europe. The massacres so designated were provoked by the plots of a revolutionary committee somewhat similar to the Greek Hetaireia, the members of which matured their plans in Odessa, Bucharest, and other border-lands of Turkey, and occasionally visited Bulgaria for the purpose of inciting to insurrection. No doubt the Bulgarians perpetrated many outrages on individual Turks, but the wholesale cruelty with which the local Ottoman authorities suppressed the movement was out of all proportion to the provocation, and defeated its own object. According to the story, when the Turkish High Commissioner surveyed the ruins and corpses of Batak, he said to the officer who was responsible for the destruction, "How much did the Russians pay you for this piece of work?" The Russo-Turkish war did not, however, follow immediately. A domestic crisis occurred in Constantinople. First Sultan Abd-ul-Aziz, and then a few months later his successor, Murad, were deposed. Servia and Montenegro declared war on the Porte, but, though they were defeated, Europe interfered, and, recognising that the condition of several Turkish provinces was a European scandal which called for reform, summoned a Conference of the Powers at Constantinople. But the Ottoman Government absolutely refused to execute the recommendations of the Conference, and Russia declared war. The first outcome of this conflict was the Treaty of San Stefano, made directly between the Porte and Russia, which provided for the creation of what may be conveniently termed Greater Bulgaria, which took in a large part of Macedonia, and extended to the coast of the Ægean. But this Treaty was revised in 1878 at the Congress of Berlin. The Macedonian and Ægean provinces were left under direct Turkish rule, with a promise of the introduction of reforms. North of the Balkans was constituted an autonomous Principality under the suzerainty of the Sultan called Bulgaria, and south of them a province called Eastern Roumelia, which was granted "administrative autonomy," but was a direct dependency of the Ottoman Government. But this complicated arrangement was brought to an end in 1885, when Prince Alexander cut the Gordian knot and proclaimed himself "Prince of the Two Bulgarias of the North and South."

Recent as is their independence, the Bulgarians have certainly done their best to make up for the mute inglorious period through which they previously passed. Probably no country of the same size ever attracted so much attention and did so many startling things in twenty years. Bulgaria has usually maintained a position in the first page or even the first column of telegrams of the *Times* (a truly British test of importance), while virtuous States, like Switzerland and Denmark, have languished in obscure paragraphs. These twenty years are filled with a long catalogue of stirring events of a mediæval flavour, contrasting strangely with the respectable nineteenth-century Constitution and liberal institutions which Europe presented to the young Principality. It would hardly be convenient to examine in detail this interesting series of elections, ejections, wars, unions, ruptures, executions, assassinations, and reconciliations. They are too recent for impartial judgment, but it is clear that much of the peculiar character of this period was due to the eminent statesman Stambulov, who for many years disposed of the destinies of his country. For all the world the Russian Empire is a phenomenon of importance, but for the little Christian States of the Balkans the attitude they shall adopt towards it is more than the half of politics. On the one hand that Empire is the most powerful of protectors; on the other she has in past history sometimes shown a disposition to incorporate rather than protect. Stambulov's policy was shaped by the fear of some such danger. At all hazards he was determined that Russia should not exert excessive influence in his country, and he did not even shrink from bringing about a suspension of relations with his overwhelmingly powerful neighbour. For years Russia and Bulgaria did not know one another, to use the language of social life, and the Czar, though he did not interfere in the government of the country, refused to recognise the existence of the Prince. Perhaps it was essential in the infancy of Bulgaria to take such strong measures to preserve her independence, but the time has now come when every impartial person must admit that the estrangement so created was unnatural and could not endure. The mass of the Bulgarian people could never forget what they owed to Russia, and however much we may deplore Stambulov's tragic end, we must admit that his policy could not have been continued indefinitely, and that the country is more tranquil now that normal relations are restored.

It must not be supposed from what I have said of the exuberant political activity of Bulgaria that the country has not made solid progress in other directions. On the contrary, the Bulgarians are the most industrious and laborious of the populations of South-Eastern Europe. In agriculture, manufactures, commerce, education, literature,[1] and military matters alike, they have made enormous strides. It is only necessary to go westward from Turkey and cross the frontier to see what twenty years of autonomy have done. In that brief space one seems to advance, not twenty, but two hundred years. No one who knows Bulgaria would have

---

[1] The novels of Vazov have real literary merit, and are probably superior to anything published in modern Greek or Servian.

any doubts as to her brilliant future did not the political quarrels of the present ominously resemble those of the past. One is tempted to believe that wherever there are , three Bulgarians, two will combine against the third, and the third call in foreign assistance.

But the Principality of Bulgaria is not co-extensive with the Bulgarian race, and is practically not part of Turkey, though technically it is under the suzerainty of the Sultan. It is rather to the other division of the Bulgarians, those who are still under the immediate government of the Sublime Ottoman Porte, that I here invite attention.

The Firman of 1870 and the Treaty of San Stefano had made the unity of the Bulgarian-speaking race a familiar idea, but the arrangements sanctioned by the Treaty of Berlin were not entirely favourable to the inhabitants of Macedonia. They had no share in the politics of the Principality; and though they were nominally a community like the Greek and Armenian rayahs, they were really less well represented, for they had no mixed or lay National Council, and their only corporate organisation was ecclesiastical. But in the fifteen years which followed the Treaty of Berlin they quietly and unostentatiously made the best use of the institutions and opportunities at their disposal. Bulgarian churches and schools were opened in all the Slavonic districts, including the town of Salonica; and the Turkish authorities, always jealous of the Greeks, and rendered exceptionally suspicious by the events of 1886, favoured the Bulgarians as long as they did not become too strong. They were allowed to have bishops in Ochrida and Üsküb; in 1894 two more were appointed in Veles and Nevrokop, and in 1898 three more, at Monastir, Dibre, and Strumitza. The Church of the Exarchate was really occupied in *creating* Bulgarians. It offered to the Slavonic population services and schools, conducted in a language which they understood, and showed a genuine interest in their education. It is perhaps somewhat surprising that the Bulgarians did not join their National Church *en masse*, but two causes made it less popular than might have been expected among the ignorant and thrifty peasantry. Firstly, its language was the Bulgarian of Sofia and not the local dialect; and though it was understood by the Macedonians much better than Greek, those who had not been educated in the new schools were often puzzled by it. Secondly, the Exarchate followed the same plan as the Patriarchal Church of taking fees for the performance of religious ceremonies, and it seems that the dues which it exacted were higher than those required by its rival. Also, the Greek priests were unwearied in their denunciations of the Exarchate; they argued that it was the creation of a Mohammedan power, that its baptisms and marriages were not really valid, that the dead whom it buried turned to vampires. Such arguments had a certain weight, particularly among the women, and partly account for the fact that a large number of Bulgarians continued their allegiance to the Patriarch of Constantinople.

I visited Macedonia first in the autumn of 1894, arriving by the Vranja-Üsküb railway. Bulgaria and Servia are not the most civilised countries in the world, but when one passes through them to Turkey, one feels that the line which divides Europe into two categories is the Ottoman frontier. There is something awe-inspiring about any frontier; at an unseen arbitrary line men and manners suddenly change, and the traveller is subjected to the tortures of the custom-house, and perhaps of the quarantine. But the Turkish frontier is peculiarly terrible, and I never cross it without a spasm of alarm. How many people have I seen there overtaken by mysterious visitations of fate— some turned back, some sent on under arrest, some requested to wait a few days, inquiring spirits deprived of their guide-books and dictionaries (on the ground that such literature is seditious), and sportsmen robbed of the guns with which they had thought to shoot big game. Nor is the appearance of Turkish territory reassuring. Whether one goes through Adrianople to Constantinople, or through Üsküb to Salonica, the sides of the railway look desolate and lifeless; hills overgrown with dwarf oak alternate with plains whose bareness is half covered with scrubby grass. There are few signs of cultivation, and fewer of human habitations. Oriental railways have a way of only skirting the edge of cities, and stations are sometimes several miles from the places whose names they bear. The deserted appearance of the land is intensified by the Turkish habit of constructing towns (such as Kumanovo and Chatalja) in depressions of the undulating plains, where they are invisible at a short distance.

Üsküb, the first considerable town on the railway, is admitted by all authorities to be a place of very mixed pepulation. The vilayet of Kossovo, of which it is the chief city, may be described as a prolongation of Bulgaria, Servia, and Albania; and all these elements are represented in the capital, while in the country round are a goodly sprinkling of Turkish country gentlemen. Servian influence has been active here almost as long as Bulgarian, and it is one of the few places where the enemies of the Servian party have to admit that it is substantially represented and has not been artificially created. There are few real Greeks in the town, and those mostly bankers or substantial tradesmen; but, as I have mentioned, some confusion arises from Servians being styled Greeks because they take the side of the Patriarchal Church against the Bulgarians. In 1894 the Turks were inclined to discourage the latter element, because it had grown too strong. After the privileges granted to Bulgarians in the spring their bishop at Üsküb grew bold and tried to open new schools and churches, but the Vali summoned him and said, " O Bulgarian, sit upon the eggs you have, and do not burst your belly by trying to lay more."

I found Bulgarian influence even stronger at Veles, also called Kyöprülü (or Bridgetown), a picturesque city built on the sides of a valley, through which flows the Vardar. The Christians, who form two-thirds of the inhabitants, are almost entirely Bulgarians, though much of the wealth of the town is in the hands of the minute Greek colony. I stayed in the house of one of its members, and, out of deference to his feelings, called on the Greek bishop. The episcopal residence was old, battered, and dirty, as was also its occupant, who had practically no flock to tend, and looked the incarnation of a decaying cause. What a contrast to this was the Bulgarian bishop, who had only been appointed that spring! He was surrounded with all the pomp of cavasses, dragomans, and secretaries. He himself was a vigorous middle-aged man, who had been educated in Russia, and looked a worthy representative of the Church militant.

Leaving the railway at Gratzko, a few stations south of Veles, I proceeded by road to Ochrida, through Monastir, across the centre of Slavonic Macedonia. Railways are generally supposed to stimulate and develop industry, but in Turkey, though they may have this effect on the larger centres, they have the special property of destroying roads in their vicinity and hence producing greater stagnation in remote districts. Formerly the road between Gratzko and Monastir was a great highway for traffic and one of the finest *chaussées* in the country, but after the construction of the Salonica-Monastir railway it only served local needs and was allowed to fall into disrepair, and has in many places become almost impassable. The landscapes of Central Macedonia, though more picturesque than the scenery at the sides of the railway, are almost equally monotonous, and the same description will serve for half-a-dozen localities— a wide, dreary plain surrounded by wooded mountains and showing little trace of life except a few peasants struggling to till the soil with very primitive instruments. On the lowest slopes of the mountains straggle a few Bulgarian and Turkish hamlets, the latter easily distinguishable by their minarets. High up are one or two apparently inaccessible Vlach villages, and in some kind of gorge opening into the plain lies almost invariably the principal town of the district.

Though the Bulgarians have become completely Slavised and can with difficulty be distinguished as a body from the Servians, yet the faces of the Macedonian peasantry have a look which is not European, and recalls the Finns of the Volga or the hordes of the Steppes. Lives of sullen obstinate labour and minds occupied ceaselessly with petty questions of household thrift, unillumined by any ideal or romance, have rendered the features of men and women alike flat, rigid, and stony. The Turkish peasant shares this capacity for continuous animal toil and indifference to distractions; but the conviction that he is naturally the superior of all Christians gives him the dignity which arises from a privileged position, whereas the Bulgarians after centuries of ignominy have only just succeeded in asserting their independent existence as Christians. Yet that *labor improbus* which specially characterises the race might no doubt produce as remarkable results in Macedonia as in Bulgaria.

Leaving Gratzko early in the morning, I arrived about 10 A.M. at a lonely and dilapidated inn, which had evidently seen better days in the times when there was no railway. The landlord was a Greek, inn-keeping being one of the characteristic Hellenic professions, and spoke a curious form of literary French. On my inquiring where he had picked up this dialect, he replied that he had spent nine years in prison at Rhodes, and had beguiled the tedium of his sentence with study. This frank confession emboldened me to ask into what particular misfortunes he had fallen. He said with some hesitation that he had been suspected of acting in collusion with a band of brigands who had formerly flourished in the neighbourhood. Trusting that prison discipline and liberal studies had made him see the error of his ways, I hurried on somewhat rapidly to Monastir, for the mountain passes of Macedonia are very lonely, and it is better to meditate on stories of brigandage in comfortable towns than on foggy hilltops.

Monastir is one of the strongholds of Greek influence. Perhaps the percentage of real Greeks is not much greater than in Üsküb and Veles, but in 1894 the Bulgarians had no bishop, and had not been able to unite and organise themselves as in those towns. Both the Servians and Roumanians are energetic in prosecuting their respective Propagandas, but there is still a large colony of Greek-speaking Vlachs, who are hardly distinguishable from true Greeks except by their descent. Many of them are very rich and enterprising, and have business in Cairo or even in Manchester. About half of the town population is Mohammedan, for in Europe at any rate the Turks prefer to keep together, and, except in a few special districts, show little disposition to spread over the country. The awakening of the Christian population is generally accompanied by a movement from the villages into the towns. This was very marked in Monastir. The influence of the Greeks and the weakness of the Bulgarians naturally made the Ottoman authorities indulgent to the latter, and the outskirts of the town were full of little wooden houses occupied by peasants, who thought they could better their condition by leaving the villages and taking to the humbler forms of trade. Thus, as in the case of the railways, the progress of the Christians often reacts unfavourably on the country districts. They collect in towns, engage in politics, and being more or less under the observation of the foreign

Consuls, are spared many troubles. But the villages become depopulated, isolated, and neglected, and more and more at the mercy of tax-gatherers, brigands, and other birds of prey.

The financial administration of Monastir was a byword, or rather a pleasant jest, for the criticisms passed on the feats performed by the local budget-makers contained no indignation, and the narrators seemed moved by a certain sympathetic admiration as they described how Commission after Commission of Inquiry had come to curse, and gone back with pockets full of money and reports full of blessings. On the present occasion it was officially stated that the roads were in a bad state owing to the recent heavy rain, and it was curious to see how experienced persons spoke of the chances of getting through. On the one hand it was highly probable that the roads were in a disgraceful condition, but on the other was it not equally probable that the local authorities were proposing to spend money on roads which needed no repairs? They would take two-thirds of the money and the contractors would receive one-third for doing nothing. As far as Ochrida at any rate the road was fairly good, with the exception of a large hole in the side of a precipice down which the post had fallen the day before. After narrowly escaping the same fate, I descended the mountains to the shores of the lake. Here the Zapties who accompanied me began to tell alarming stories of the exploits of a brigand called Karabajak ("black legs") who infests that part of the country. This was of course done with a view of proving that they were affording necessary and effective protection and deserved commensurate *bakhshish*; but it appeared that the individual in question had really killed two soldiers a few days previously and disappeared owing to a fog. He was also said to be a pirate and to attack boats on the lake.

The recollection of Ochrida makes me retract much

that I have said about Macedonian scenery.   Probably few
except travellers have heard of the Lakes of Ochrida and
Presba, yet they are some of the most beautiful in Europe.
One would not wish to see Macedonia overrun with tourists
or converted into an Oriental Switzerland, but as long as
people rush to India, Egypt, and America, and remain ignorant of such excellent things as these lakes, the waters of
Vodena, the forests of Mount Olympus, the apples of Kal-
kandelen, and the fish of Ochrida, Europe must be admitted
to have a great reserve of pleasure and beauty which is
seldom drawn upon.   No sportsman, as far as I am aware,
has tried his hand at the huge lake trout of Ochrida.   I am
not a sportsman myself, and cannot conceive why anybody
should try to catch a big fish with a rod when he can pay
a fisherman to catch him with a net.   The latter method is
in vogue at Ochrida, but if any one tries the former, he
would probably taste to the full all the peculiar pleasures
which it affords, and by whatever mode the fish are captured they are certainly most excellent eating.   Not less
remarkable than the fish which throng the depths of the
lake are the boats which move slowly over its surface.
They are of a strange and primitive construction, and certainly could not escape from Karabajak should he attempt
a piratical expedition, for they move at the rate of about
two miles an hour.   Indeed they are platforms rather than
boats, for they are flat-bottomed, and logs of wood project
at the sides to make them steadier.   In the forepart are
three rowers, who stand on steps one above the other, but
all on the same side.   The result of their labour is naturally
to make the boat turn round in a circle, and movement in
a straight line is rendered possible only by the counteracting
force of an old man who sits in the stern and steers with an
oar.   It is one of the most perfect contrivances for wasting
labour and obtaining a minimum of result from a maximum
of exertion ever invented.

Ochrida itself is situated at the northern end of the lake, where white cliffs frequented by noisy waterfowl rise straight from the waves. The town is in two parts, the lower or Mohammedan and the upper or Christian. The inhabitants of the latter are almost exclusively Bulgarian, for though Ochrida forms the western outpost of the race— Albania beginning immediately beyond—it is in some ways its focus. Here was the capital of Samuel, here are the remains of his castle and cathedral, and here is still an active Bulgarian bishop doing his best to revive the glories of the ancient Metropolitan See. Just before my visit the work of Bulgarian education had been peculiarly active, and the Ottoman authorities co-operated with the Greek arch-bishop in trying to suppress it. A rule was suddenly made that Bulgarian schools must be registered in the name, not of the community, but of a special person. This does not sound very terrible, but in the East one must distrust in-novations and look below the surface. Had the rule been allowed to stand steps would no doubt have been taken to gradually remove the persons in whose names the schools were entered, and then to prove that the schools were non-existent. These machinations were, however, defeated, and the schools are now registered in the name of the bishop as an official, not of the particular bishop for the time being. There were but two Christians on the Town Council, though the Mohammedans are only a third of the whole population, and there were many complaints of heavy taxation, grapes and fish—the chief local products—having to pay more than twenty per cent. of their value.

As not infrequently happens in Turkey, I was enter-tained by a Bulgarian gentleman who spoke excellent English. This is the result of the education given at Robert College on the Bosphorus, which is much frequented by Bulgarians, many of whom after leaving rise to pro-minent positions. Among the higher officials at Sofia

English is spoken more commonly than French. European
manners penetrate more slowly, and though the outward
sign of education is the wearing of a frock-coat at all
times and seasons, the peasantry, at least in Macedonia,
show no signs of changing their dress or customs. Dress
in the East is a matter determined by rank or race, and
is not affected by such trifles as climate or temperature.
Some people think it proper to go about almost naked,
others bury themselves under a mountain of clothes; but
all would scorn the idea of putting on an overcoat because
it was cold, or leaving off a fur-lined robe because the
thermometer was at 90° in the shade. Bulgarians belong
to the class of heavy dressers; men and women alike
swathe their persons in as many layers of thick padded
garments, sheepskins, and furs as it is physically possible
to get into. On festival days the women put on a gala
costume, the lowest visible stratum of which is generally
a white linen gown, with elaborate woollen embroidery on
the skirt and sleeves. Over this come various sleeveless
garments cut so as to show the aforesaid embroidery, and
finally a thick quilted jacket and voluminous sash. On
the head is worn a cap, from which hang behind long
strings of gold braid. Such a costume does not seem
convenient for dancing; but on feast days the Bulgarian
maidens so attired will spend the whole of a hot summer
afternoon in pounding through the *hora*, a monotonous
and interminable dance, which apparently consists in forming a circle, and moving round and round to the sound
of the bagpipes. These latter are the national instrument,
and are thought by the Turks to be specially characteristic
of Bulgarians, as the following story will show. The servants who wait at the Porte on the Grand Vizier are still
mutes, though not, as formerly, persons specially mutilated,
but children born deaf and dumb. They use a language
of signs, and have some special gesture to describe the

representative of each nation. When they want to indicate the Bulgarian Agent they imitate a man playing on a bagpipe.

Another Bulgarian pastime is the recitation of popular songs. These are not quite so elaborate as the national epics of the Servians, but are often of considerable length. When at Ochrida I heard a schoolboy recite a poem which occupied an hour and a quarter. In spite of its dimensions, the plot was remarkably simple, and, I fear, very probable. The Pasha of Sofia summoned before him a Bulgarian hero to whom he was under obligations, and said that, to his great regret, he was obliged to execute him immediately. The hero wanted to know why. The Pasha replied that he did not know, but that he had received orders from Constantinople. Executed the hero was, but after much more arguing than ordinary Pashas would stand. These poems are written in short verses of eight or six syllables, sometimes with rough, irregular rhymes. Many of them deal with the exploits of the Haiduds or Bulgarian Klephts, but others are love songs. The Bulgarian peasant regards his daughters primarily as workwomen, and is unwilling to part with them. Hence girls are married much later than is the general custom in the East, and the opposition of parents to their love affairs forms the theme of many poems.

The salient characteristic of the Bulgarians is, as I have already mentioned, their industry. Macedonia is far from standing on the same economic level as the Principality, nevertheless if one goes northwards from the Albanian to the Slavonic districts, say from Koritza to Monastir, one cannot help noticing the change which marks the frontier of the Bulgarian race. The fortress-like castles built in the hillsides disappear, and with them disappear the fine manners and lavish hospitality with which the Albanians treat a stranger when they have made up their minds not to kill him. In their stead we find villages of unpicturesque houses, surrounded by fields of maize, and gardens rich in such unromantic vegetables as the pumpkin. The chief man of a Bulgarian village is generally known as the Chorbaji, or "soup-maker," and is often a person of considerable wealth. With the exception of a certain amount of pasture land belonging to the village as a community, the land belongs to individuals who can dispose of it by will or otherwise, the communal system of tenure which prevails in some Slavonic countries being unknown. Estates, or Chiftliks, belonging to country gentlemen, or Beys, are common. As a rule, the Bey does not pay wages to his workpeople, but supplies the peasants who dwell on his estates with seeds and agricultural implements, and after the Government have taken the tithe in kind, divides the remainder of the product equally between the villagers and himself. The former have thus almost the same incentive to industry as if they owned the lands.

The country between Seres and Philippopoli is inhabited by people called Pomaks, who are commonly described as Mohammedan Bulgarians. This district is really as unknown as if it were in the centre of Africa, and I can add nothing to our knowledge of it from personal observation. The best information appears to agree in holding that the inhabitants speak a Slavonic language, and are nominal but very lax Mohammedans who have adopted Islam as a protection, but hardly observe its precepts unless they are among Turks. They are said to be exceedingly wild and ignorant, but whether they are merely ordinary Bulgarians who have changed their religion and been cut off from the national life, or whether there is any reason to think that they are descendants of the Pechenegs or Kumans I do not know. The problem is complicated by the fact that in this district there are also settlements of real Turks.

The Pavlikans form another small but curious section of the Bulgarian population. They are apparently the descendants of the ancient Asiatic heretics called Paulicians,[1] colonies of whom were established in Thrace by more than one Byzantine emperor, notably by John Zimesces. But if so they show no traces to-day of their Asiatic origin, and are all Catholics. In the time of the Emperor Alexius they were subjected to severe persecution, partly religious and partly political, for they were said to be on good terms with the Pechenegs and to incite them to invade the Empire. It is probable that this persecution made them detest the Orthodox Church, and that at some unknown epoch when they abandoned their own religion they accepted Rome out of enmity to Byzantium. At present they are found chiefly in and around Philippopoli, but also near Sistovo. It is persistently asserted by their Orthodox neighbours, though it may be only a popular calumny, that they eat carrion.

The Servians have long asserted that Üsküb and the north-western districts of Turkey are inhabited by Servians, but about the year 1896 circumstances led them to put forward more extensive claims and to take a greater interest in Macedonia. The summer of 1895 was marked by the assassination of Stambulov and a strong Macedonian agitation in Bulgaria. There is always a large Macedonian element both there and in Servia, for the more intelligent classes tend to leave Ottoman territory whenever they can. Unlike the Greek, the Slav has in Turkey no career before him. As long as he is a rayah he does not become an official, financier, or merchant, but he expands and flourishes under a Christian government. The Macedonian immigrants in Bulgaria are bolder, cleverer, and more ambitious than the natives of the Principality, and could not be easily controlled by the Government, if it wished to do so. Macedonia is also the question of international politics which is of greatest importance for Bulgaria, and the immigrants find no lack of sympathy and encouragement. In these circum-

[1] *Vide* Chapter VI. p. 263.

stances it is easy to understand that the Macedonian society, though nominally a mere private enterprise, became possessed, not only of great influence, but of material power. Unlike such earlier associations as the Hetaireia it did not observe any secrecy, but adopted the most modern procedure of mass meetings and public ventilation of grievances. Side by side with this more Oriental methods were employed, based on the unhappy theory, responsible for so much bloodshed, that the best way of attracting the attention of the Christian Powers is to provoke the Turks to commit atrocities. Several bands of the well-known type—half-robbers, half-patriots—crossed into Turkey, and one of them burnt the Moslim village of Dospat. They entirely failed to produce the uproar which they desired; but they did attract the attention of Servia and of other more important Powers to the fact that Slavonic Macedonia was becoming a sort of *Bulgaria irredenta*. There followed the reconciliation of Russia and Bulgaria, the official recognition of Prince Ferdinand, and the reception into the Orthodox Church of the infant heir-apparent. There was talk about reforms in Macedonia, and numerous propositions and promises. There was also talk of a reconciliation between the Patriarchal Church and the Exarchate. This put the Bulgarians in a difficult position. No professing Christian could do otherwise than deplore the existence of the schism, and the moment the Patriarch was disposed to heal it Christian feeling and ecclesiastical logic demanded a friendly reception of his overtures. On the other hand, the separation of the Churches was the mainstay of Bulgarian influence in Turkey, and their union would have meant its collapse. Naturally, therefore, the Bulgarians preferred to remain under the Patriarchal ban.

The Servian cause profited by all this. The Porte was delighted to find that it could foment a Servo-Bulgarian quarrel, just as it had fomented a Greco-Bulgarian quarrel a quarter of a century before. When the Servians, alarmed at Bulgarian pretensions in Macedonia, demanded that their interests should also be respected, they obtained a ready hearing. They did not get what they wanted—the petitioners of the Sublime Porte rarely do. But they were used as pieces in the game and humoured for the moment. Servian Consulates were established at such places as Seres, where the name of Servian was almost unknown, and a general permission was granted to open Servian schools in the vilayets of Monastir and Salonica. The Servians petitioned to be made a Millet like the Greeks and Bulgarians. This request was not granted, but the Porte utilised it to prove that the Bulgarian suggestions for Macedonian reforms were "not in harmony with the needs of the local population." Foreign Powers also suspected Bulgaria of wishing to " precipitate events" in Macedonia and approved of her influence being counterbalanced, and the Œcumenical Patriarch reasoned in much the same way. After much hesitation (for Bulgarian and Servian prelates were equally distasteful to the Phanar) a Servian *locum tenens* was appointed to the See of Üsküb. As soon as the Servian Propaganda had made some way in its new sphere the Porte increased the quantity of inflammable matter by appointing three new Bulgarian bishops of Dibre, Monastir, and Strumnitsa (January 1898). The result of all this was that there was established in Eastern Macedonia, not perhaps a strong Servian party, but at least an energetic faction ready to declaim and riot on the least provocation, and maintaining that the Servian race extends from Belgrade to the Ægean.

Before attempting to decide whether certain districts of Turkey are Servian or Bulgarian it will be well to inquire what is meant by those words. It is easy to select people who bear the two national names and are clearly distinct from one another in physique, language, and customs; but there is also a large population which is not so obviously differentiated. We can hardly be wrong in considering that the original Bulgarian type is preserved in the somewhat Mongolian figure and features which are common in the eastern part of the Balkans, and are found as far west as Ochrida—heavy frames with broad, flat, stolid faces, small eyes, and straight, black hair. As the Servian type may be taken the tall, broad-headed men who are found in South Servia, Bosnia, and Montenegro. But these two types by no means coincide with the people who call themselves Servians and Bulgarians. The Bulgarian type is found all over Northern Servia as far as Belgrade; and the Albanians, though so clearly separated from the surrounding Slavs in language and customs, are physically undistinguishable from them. The tall, broad-headed men form an anthropological but not a political or linguistic unit. Neither does history, though often invoked by politicians at Sofia and Belgrade, enable us to say whether Macedonia should be called Bulgarian or Servian. Both countries have at different epochs possessed almost the whole of the Balkan Peninsula; but instead of talking of the Empires of Simeon, Asen, and Dushan, it would be better to speak of their *reigns*, for each of these larger States was created by the enterprise of a single monarch and collapsed with his death, without permanently influencing the conquered populations. The Bulgarians have no more claim to all the countries conquered by Simeon than the French to the countries conquered by Napoleon, and the fact that Dushan was crowned at Üsküb has about the same importance as that William I. was proclaimed Emperor of Germany at Versailles.

The evidence of language may justly be held to be more important. It would appear that in the ninth century one Slavonic language was spoken from the Ægean to the Adriatic, since the preaching of Saints Cyril and Methodius and their translation of the Bible were intelligible to the whole Balkan Peninsula. This language, which is commonly called old Bulgarian, though we are hardly warranted in assuming that it was peculiar to the Bulgarians, is a pure Slavonic tongue, highly inflectional and clearly related to what is generally known as Church Slavonic, the ecclesiastical language of the Orthodox Slavs, which, though dead, is still to a large extent intelligible to the peasantry in Russia and elsewhere. Modern Bulgarian is very different from this old Bulgarian, and owing to the black darkness which falls on Bulgarian history after the time of the Asenids, we know nothing of its origin or development. In its present form it is characterised by a number of peculiarities which distinguish it from all other Slavonic languages.[1]

The most remarkable of them is the total loss of nominal inflection and of the infinitive, which suggests the explanation, confirmed by history, that Bulgarian is a Slavonic language mangled by a non-Slavonic race. But this view presents difficulties of detail. What was the distorting influence? It can hardly have been the original tongue of the un-Slavised Bulgarians, for though we know

---

[1] It possesses a definite article which is suffixed to substantives and adjectives—e.g. vălk, a wolf; vălkat, the wolf; vălcite, the wolves. This is a less distinctive phenomenon than is generally supposed. It exists in the adjectival declension of Servian and Russian. The former has a definite and indefinite declension of the adjective, the difference between which can often, but not always, be expressed by our articles "a" and "the"—mlad čovjek, a young man; mladi čovjek, the young man. A suffix with much the same meaning as our article is found in such different languages as Armenian, Persian (indefinite), Roumanian, Danish, and Albanian. Bulgarian has also lost all case inflections, except in the pronouns. The nominative and accusative are identical, and the genitive and dative are indicated by the preposition na. Sestra, sister, is, according to the grammar of other Slavonic languages, a nominative; but the Bulgarian says, az imam edna sestra, I have a sister, and kniga-ta na sestra-ta, the book of the sister. In the verb the infinitive has entirely disappeared, and, as in modern Greek, can only be expressed by a somewhat clumsy periphrasis, az moga da čakam, I can wait (lit. I am able that I should wait). Phonetically, Bulgarian is characterised by the frequent occurrence of a dull sound similar to the u in but, and generally rendered by ă.

nothing of it, all the probabilities are in favour of its having been an agglutinative language, similar to Turkish, Finnish, and Hungarian, with no article and many cases. Also it had probably no distinction of gender, whereas the modern Bulgarian faithfully preserves the triple genders of Slavonic. Nor will the imitation of modern Greek, which might well have occurred in Phanariot times, explain all the phenomena. Modern Greek has no infinitive, but it has not lost the accusative, much less the genitive cases. Perhaps the peculiarities of Bulgarian may be attributed to Vlach or Roumanian influence. We know that in the tenth century there was a close connection between the north and south banks of the Danube; the Empire of Asen is generally styled Vlacho-Bulgarian, and at the present day there are large settlements of Vlachs not only in Macedonia but in the Principality of Bulgaria. The Roumanian language has a highly-developed suffixed article; but apart from the inflection of this suffixed article, it has almost entirely lost its case forms, and though the Latin infinitive (*facere*) still exists, it alternates with a periphrastic form (*a face*).[1]

For practical purposes literary Bulgarian has a great resemblance to Russian—so much so that a person well acquainted with the latter language can generally read the leading articles in a Bulgarian newspaper. But this similarity is superficial; it is the result of imitation not of common origin, and lies more in vocabulary than grammar. Bulgarian literature, as well as Bulgarian freedom, began under Russian auspices, and the whole terminology of politics and the abstract sciences was borrowed *in toto*. As these borrowed expressions are formed from Slavonic roots their

---

[1] But it must be admitted that the inflected Roumanian article keeps up a semblance of nominal inflection which Bulgarian has lost. Compare *caselor* and the Bulgarian *na kashti-te*, both meaning "of the houses." The latter is clearly a greater advance towards our analytical mode of expression. Exactly similar to the Roumanian forms are dialectical Bulgarian forms, in which the article is declined : *ot gyaula-ta-go*, *Giaulu-tu-mu* (Ofeicoff, *La Macédoine*, p. 290).

foreign origin is not obvious, and it is easy to imagine that they are native products. But the simpler a Bulgarian sentence is, the less apparent is the resemblance to Russian. Probably no Russian would understand such a phrase as *Az go običam po mnogo ot sebe si* (I love him more than myself), though every word of it is Slavonic. Also the verbal forms of Bulgarian resemble Servian rather than Russian.

Servian is a pure Slavonic language little affected by extraneous influences except that it has borrowed a number of Turkish words. It includes Bosnian, Montenegrin, and Croatian,[1] which only differ in slight dialectic peculiarities, and in the country south of the Drav and western Danube it is incontestably one of the most important forms of European speech. In contrast to Bulgarian it is highly inflectional, possessing seven cases, and a double adjectival declension. As in most Slavonic languages the tenses are somewhat scanty, and the uncompounded forms do little more than distinguish past and present time; but an infinitive is in use as well as several participial forms.[2]

[1] Croatian looks different from Servian because it is written in a modification of the Latin alphabet invented by Louis Gaj in 1831, whereas Servians use a variety of the Cyrillic alphabet invented by Vuk Karajich at the beginning of this century. This alphabet rejects the hard and soft signs of Bulgarian and Russian, and represents the *y* sound by the Roman letter *j* which does not harmonise very well with the Cyrillic characters. There are special signs for *ly* and *ny*. There is some reason to think that Saints Cyril and Methodius invented, not the alphabet which bears their names and which on this hypothesis is a later simplication, but the older Glagolithic or Glagolitsa still used for ecclesiastical books in some parts of Dalmatia.

[2] The phonetic system offers many peculiarities: *l* is often suppressed or vocalised—*e.g. vuk*, wolf, for *vulk ; Beograd* for *Belgrad*, the national capital. I have noticed, however, that the difference in pronunciation between such words as the Servian *Znao* and the Russian *Znal* is less than the orthography suggests. The so-called hard *l* is certainly very different from our consonant. There is a system of so-called accents, which is, I believe, unique in Europe and approaches the tones found in the monosyllabic languages of South-Eastern Asia. Servian grammarians distinguish four accents, found on the first syllable of the four following words: *riba, vòda, žêdja, víno*. I must confess that, after studying Servian for two months with a native, I could never distinguish these accents. The language has not a marked tonic

Literary Servian and Bulgarian are thus clearly distinguished, yet it is not always easy to say which of them is spoken in a particular district of Macedonia. One of the most remarkable features of the Slavonic languages is their close resemblance to one another,[1] and the comparative absence of dialectic variation; there is no linguistic area in Europe which can be compared in size to that occupied by Russian. This characteristic is probably connected with another, namely, that the Slavonic-speaking nations are mostly dwellers on plains, which facilitate intercourse and uniformity. We should therefore expect to find much greater variety in the mountainous districts of the Balkan Peninsula, and this is, as a matter of fact, the case. The identity of the language of Montenegro with that of Servia is easily explained, for the Black Mountain was the refuge of the Servian aristocracy after the Turkish conquest; but with this exception most of the mountain regions present linguistic peculiarities, which sometimes recall Bulgarian or Servian, but sometimes differ from both.[2] It is no doubt true that the Slav inhabitants of Old Servia speak Servian, and those of the districts im-

accent like English, Russian, and modern Greek. People sometimes ask whether one should say *Serájěvo* or *Serajévo, Herzegóvina* or *Herzegovína.* One should say neither. The accent is distributed over the whole word, and is perhaps strongest on the first syllable. Further, Servian has an aversion to nasals and a preference for the vowel *a*, and it possesses a multiplicity of palatals represented by *č, ć, dj,* and *dž.*

[1] This resemblance seems to me to be emphasised by the fact that they are all written in reasonable phonetic alphabets. If the Romance languages adopted the same system their close relationship would be more apparent.

[2] They possess nasalised vowels and many forms of the suffixed definite article, the Bulgarian forms (*t, ta, to, te*), being supplemented by similar forms with the initial consonants *s, n,* and *v.* Not only the third person plural but the third person singular sometimes ends in *t*, which is an undoubtedly primitive trait. In Russian and Macedonian we find such forms as *znajet,* he knows; *znajut,* they know; in Bulgarian, *znae* and *znajat ;* but in Servian the *t* is lost in both numbers, *zna* and *znaju.* If the more or less sporadic appearance of case forms recalls Servian rather than Bulgarian, still the preservation of *l* (*pisal* and *välk,* not *pisao* and *vuk*), the formation of the future by prefixing *shte, če,* or *ke,* the periphrastic infinitive with *da,* and the genlrae phonology show analogies with the latter language.

mediately south of Bulgaria and Eastern Roumelia, Bulgarian. But of the dialects of Central Macedonia one can only say that, if any one of them had received a separate literary development, it might have become a separate language. A Macedonian at the present day can more or less under-stand either Servian or Bulgarian, but Servians and Bulgarians can understand one another—when they choose.

Another argument which is often invoked by the Servians is the existence in Macedonia of certain customs alleged to be distinctively Servian and not Bulgarian. The most remarkable of these is the Slava, or festival of the family saint.[1] It is the practice in the Orthodox Church for each individual to be named after a saint, who is re-garded as his or her patron, and the festival of this patron (or name-day) is kept with more ceremony than a birthday. But in Servia each family has a patron saint, supposed to have been selected at the time of its conversion to Christi-anity, whose feast-day is celebrated by a banquet at which bread is broken ceremonially and religious toasts are drunk. But though the Slava is of more importance in Servia than elsewhere, it also exists in Bulgaria and Roumania, and is said to be observed even in the neighbourhood of Sofia.

The result of this investigation, then, is that it is not easy to distinguish Servians and Bulgarians beyond the boun-daries of their respective countries. We have in reality three categories: pure Slavs, Slavised Bulgarians (the original un-Slavised Bulgarians having long ago disappeared), and pure Slavs who have been influenced by Slavised Bulgarians. All three categories have been subjected to a strong and often continuous Greek influence, to say nothing of the Turks and the inconspicuous but ubiquitous Vlachs, who are probably responsible for many peculiarities. Among people who have thus acted and reacted on one another, it

---

[1] Villages and other communities also celebrate Slavas in honour of patron saints.

is rash to make sharp divisions, or to say that certain customs or linguistic peculiarities distinguish a certain race, and perhaps it is not safe to go beyond the following : The Slavonic population of the villayet of Kossovo, north-west of Üsküb, is homogeneous with that on the other side of the Servian, Montenegrin, and Bosnian frontiers, the mountaineers of South Servia being very unlike the tradesmen and farmers of the north. The Slavonic population east of the Struma, and much of that between the Struma and Vardar, is mixed, but homogeneous with the population of Bulgaria, which is also mixed. It would appear that the original dividing line of language and customs between Servia and Bulgaria passed near Nish, and that before 1876 the people of that town, which is now thoroughly Servian, called themselves Bulgarians. Of the remaining Macedonian Slavs, an impartial observer can only say that they are intermediate between the Serbs and Bulgarians; but I think that traces of Mongolian—that is, Bulgarian —physiognomy can be seen as far west as Ochrida.

The practical conclusion is that neither Greeks, Servians, nor Bulgarians have a right to claim Central Macedonia, The fact that they all do so shows how weak each claim must be.

A natural incapacity to combine in large political units, and a tendency to break up into small groups, have obscured the numerical importance of the Serbs, so that few people realise the extent of the area inhabited by a Servian-speaking population. It comprises not only the kingdom of Servia, Old Servia with the Sanjak of Novi Bazar, Montenegro, Bosnia, and Herzegovina, but also the Austrian provinces of Dalmatia, Istria, Slavonia, and the southern part of the Banat or country north of the Danube between Belgrade and Orsova. There is an enmity between the Servians and Croatians, and some authorities consider that the latter were not originally Slavs. But at the present day their language is indubitably Servian, though they use the Roman and not the Cyrillic alphabet.

The population of Northern Servia, which is naturally that most seen by travellers, is not a good or characteristic specimen of the race. After the loss of the national independence, all the most distinguished and valiant Serbs retreated to the mountainous districts of Bosnia and Montenegro or became Mohammedans, with the result that the plains or northern portion of the present kingdom of Servia contain the descendants of the least vigorous and enterprising portion of the nation. Servia deserves better than Bulgaria the title of the Peasant State which has been applied to the latter, for the Chorbajis formed a sort of upper class between the peasants and the Turks, whereas in Servia the most absolute social equality prevails. Poverty is almost unknown, and nearly everybody is comfortably off. Some of the well-to-do peasants are considerable landed proprietors, and possess incomes of £1000; but as a rule they make no attempt to imitate European ways or abandon their simple, homely, but rather slipshod life. The only outward sign of wealth which they exhibit is a brougham, in which they proceed to town on market-days. One characteristic of this part of Servia which strikes a traveller coming from Turkey or even from Bulgaria is the extent of cultivation. There is no waste land. Every inch is private property, and used for the cultivation of corn and maize, for pasturage, gardens, and orchards, in the latter of which grow the plum-trees that produce the national drink of slivovitz, or plum-brandy. But equally striking are the simplicity of the methods of cultivation, and the amount of weeds, not humble tares, but enormous thistles and creeping plants, which strangle the crops, run riot in the gardens, and invade the highroads. In this, as in other matters. the Servian has no eye for neatness or finish. Unlike the Bulgarian, he is not naturally laborious, and as soon as he has performed the simple operations necessary to secure the existence (but not the perfection) of his maize, his plums, and his pigs, he sits down in the village wine-shop, not so much to get drunk as to engage in endless and resultless political discussion. This universal comfort has, of course, its good side; it is better than being fleeced by Janissaries, but it does not conduce to progress in any direction. The absence of large fortunes makes it difficult to execute any works requiring capital or enterprise. Mines cannot be worked; roads are few, because the expense of constructing and maintaining them falls on the villages through which they pass, and which are too self-centred and self-satisfied to make any sacrifices; and no form of trade seems to flourish except the export of raw products. The Servian breeds pigs, but he cannot export ham.

Far more interesting and picturesque are the mountaineers, who are found, not only on both sides of the Turkish frontier, but also about the valley of the Drina, which separates Servia from Bosnia. In these districts upland pastures coloured by alpine plants alternate with forests of gigantic pines, and the river-courses flow through deep gorges, of which a well-known example may be seen from the train after leaving Nish for the East. In the west of Servia, about a day from Uzhitsa, I have passed through another ravine, which was even narrower and deeper, in so much that it was almost dark except at mid-day. It appeared to have no name, for the immediate vicinity was uninhabited, and the peasants were quite ignorant of the country ten or fifteen miles from their homes. They have a martial air, and resemble the Montenegrins in their dress and habits, but have in some ways better preserved the original Slav customs, as they still retain the old system of Zadruga, or communal village based upon the family. In its most ancient form, which now survives in only a very few localities, the Zadruga consists not merely of one family but of one house, a vast, shapeless building, to which a new room is added whenever a male of the family marries. In most cases, however, the plan of a communal house has been abandoned, and the Zadruga is composed of a number of huts close together, each occupied by a married couple. The property of the Zadruga is held in common, and the entire community, often as many as sixty or seventy persons, is ruled by the oldest man, whose authority is despotic, and without whose permission no member can emigrate or marry. As a rule, this patriarch is the eldest of several brothers, and on his death his authority passes to the one next in age ; but should his widow survive him, she is treated with great respect, and no important step is taken without consulting her. Marriages are a constant source of dispute in Zadrugas ; for even more than among the Bulgarians women are regarded as workers, and as a woman passes into her husband's Zadruga, each family is anxious to marry its sons but to retain its daughters as long as possible. The result of this system is that elopement is the ordinary preliminary to wedlock.

Even in large villages and small towns in Southern and Western Servia the remains of the Zadruga system may be observed, each quarter being usually inhabited by a particular family, from which it takes its name. But except in these districts the communal system exists no longer. The Servian Government guarantees to every taxpayer two and a half hectares of land, which cannot be seized for debt. This regulation is said to have in some ways an unfortunate effect, as the peasant is unable to borrow money in order to improve his estate. He cannot mortgage his land, and has usually nothing else on which to raise a loan.

Owing to the rarity of towns and large settlements in Southern Servia, the inhabitants are accustomed to meet periodically at some central point where a temporary village of booths is constructed, and a fair held for the sale of cattle and other produce. Oxen are roasted whole, and when the day's business is over a banquet follows with national songs and dances. It is on such occasions that one hears recited the popular epics, which are sung in a monotonous chant to the accompaniment of a single-stringed guitar, but with such genuine feeling and expression that the whole effect is not unpleasing. As in most Oriental countries the professional minstrels are often blind men, but in the remote districts the peasants are proud of their powers of recitation.

All the races of Turkey—Greeks, Slavs, Roumanians, and Albanians alike—are fond of narrative ballads, which are indeed the characteristic literary product of the Balkan lands. They are generally anonymous pieces, composed in short lines of from eight to ten syllables (though Greek affects longer metres), and recounting either love stories or some incident in the unending struggle of the Christians against the Turks. Among the other races these poems are of moderate length, and often very short, but among the Serbs they have grown to the proportions of a national epic, which may almost be compared to the Kalevala. The date of their composition is unknown, but they were collected and arranged by Karajich about fifty years ago, and published by him. The historical ballads are written in a ten-syllabled metre, with occasional variations, and fall into three chief cycles, those which describe the glories of Dushan's reign, those which lament the battle of Kossovo, and those which recount the exploits of Marko Kralyevich and his wondrous steed Sharats. As I have elsewhere pointed out, this personage is less important for history than for romance, but he has secured a place in popular imagination and popular poetry which has been denied to worthier heroes. High praise must be given to the simplicity, vividness, and deep feeling of these ballads. Modern Servian literature is perhaps not so good as Bulgarian, but the emotional and poetic, if somewhat undisciplined, character of the Slav finds adequate expression in the less formal styles of composition.

During the sixteenth and seventeenth centuries quite a school of Servian writers—particularly poets—flourished at Ragusa, and wrote many epics and dramas which show signs of Italian models. In the inland districts, however, literature decayed, and, as in the case of Greek, an artificial language founded on the ecclesiastical Slavonic was used for the few books which were published. The eminent writer and patriot Vuk Karajich (1787–1864) was successful in producing a linguistic revolution, and in making his countrymen adopt the spoken language for literary purposes. He reformed the orthography, rescued the popular songs from oblivion, translated the New Testament into the popular language, and, in a word, destroyed the Oriental idea that literature is not meant to be understood.

During one of my journeys I was the guest of the Archimandrite of a large monastery near the Drina. The Church seems less influential in Servia than in the rest of the Balkans, for its services are little frequented; and the power of the clergy has been diminished by a law forbidding them to become deputies, on the ground that they are servants of the Crown and eligible for pension. Nor are the monasteries, as religious institutions, in a flourishing condition. Eastern monasticism has never developed the virtues of practical charity or literary culture which adorn the orders of the Roman Church. Its followers are either, as on Mount Athos, absorbed in the practice of a selfish and somewhat superstitious piety, or, as is commonly the case in the interior, take to the healthier pursuits of country gentlemen. My host on the present occasion was of the latter sort. His monastery was large, but there was only one other monk, who acted as his chaplain and occasionally read prayers. In the chapel was preserved a sword with which one of his predecessors had slain many Turks. Ecclesiastical architecture and frescoes in this distriet are curious as being Italian rather than Byzantine in character, and it is clear that Roman influence must have been dominant here in the fourteenth and fifteenth centuries. Patriotic historians have even conjectured that the Renaissance originated in Servia, and spread to Italy. The Archimandrite occupied himself with the management of his estate, which was considerable in extent and apparently well managed. In the morning he did accounts, in the afternoon he rode over the property and inspected crops and trees, and in the evening he dispensed a copious hospitality to his guests. He was however, I heard, unpopular in the neighbourhood, and involved in perpetual quarrels with the peasantry, because he refused to allow them to cut wood in certain forests where they claimed that custom gave them the right. These secularised monasteries are not uncommon in Macedonia. A notable instance is that of St. Naum at the southern end of the lake of Ochrida, which is used as a meeting-place of merchants and tradesmen, and for the holding of fairs. One of the most important of Servian monasteries is that of Chilendar ("thousand lions") on Mount Athos, built by Stephen Nemanya, and inhabited by Slavonic monks. Of late years it has been a bone of contention between the Servians and Bulgarians, the former contending, contrary to the analogy of other institutions, that since it was founded by a Servian sovereign it must belong to the Servian Government.

West and south-west of Servia lie Bosnia and the Herzegovina,[1] which are theoretically Turkish provinces "administered" by Austria under the Treaty of Berlin. The population consists of Mohammedan Beys, being Servians who adopted Islam to acquire or preserve a privileged

[1] "The Duchy," from the German *Herzog*.

position, and a Christian peasantry, almost exclusively Orthodox in Bosnia, but partly Catholic in the Herzegovina. Sometimes a family divided itself between Christianity and Islam so as to have friends on the right side whatever happened. In such cases the members of the family recognise each other as relatives, but generally use different names for the two branches conveying the same meaning in Slavonic and Turkish respectively—*e.g.* Raikovich and Jenetich (Rai and Jennet meaning " paradise "), Sokolich and Shahinagich (Sokol and Shahin both meaning " falcon ").[1] As in the case of most European races who have embraced Mohammedanism, the acceptance of the new faith seems to have been only superficial, and it is said that pictures representing vines and drinking scenes may be found even in Bosnian mosques.

The Austrians have done their best to conciliate the Mohammedans and Catholics, and though they met with a desperate resistance when they took over the provinces, they have been on the whole very successful. The Orthodox population express less satisfaction, but it may be doubted if their complaints represent any serious undercurrent of revolutionary feeling. Panslavist agitation is much talked of in the Austrian Empire, but it is rather a means of extorting concessions from the Government than a serious project of disruption. The Bosnians, Bohemians, and Poles would probably be very unwilling to be really detached and made independent unprotected States. The dissatisfaction of the Bosnian Christians is no doubt due to

---

[1] It is often curious to observe the genesis of family names among the Southern Slavs. Most of them are very recent. Thus in one case the grandfather kept a tavern, and was known by the Turks simply as Sharabji, "the wine man." The son thought that the rising fortunes of the house required a family name, and by adding a Slavonic affix to the Turkish designation became Sharabjieff or Šarabdžiev. The grandson, who lived in days when Turkish words were considered barbaric and unpatriotic, substituted for Sharabji the Bulgarian equivalent Vinar, and became Vinarov. In many parts of Bulgaria a man and his wife still use different family names.

the fact that Christian communities who have been under the sway of the Sultan, as soon as they have forgotten the material insecurity which prevailed under that rule, regret the easy-going tolerance of the Turk. The Porte does not like being reformed, but at least it does not try to reform other people, and as we have seen allows the laity as well as the clergy a considerable measure of autonomy in matters relating to schools, parochial discipline, and quasi-religious institutions. A European Government is obliged to exercise more supervision, which, among other results, causes the State to interfere with the disposal of sums which were formerly administered by irresponsible persons somewhat to their own advantage, and it is not unnatural that this diversion of public funds from private pockets should be regarded as an encroachment on religious liberty.

The Mohammedan population do not regret Turkey. A large number of those who emigrated after the first occupation subsequently returned, saying that they found things worse on the other side of the frontier; and when, in the spring of 1897, Mollahs and other fanatics attempted to enlist Bosnians to fight for Turkey against Greece, only about a hundred responded to the appeal. This is remarkable, for there is a continual exodus of Moslims both from Bulgaria and the Caucasus into Turkey. The difference no doubt depends upon race. It is difficult to disentangle the various European races, but there is clearly a great gulf fixed between Europeans and Asiatics in the broad and popular sense of the words. It is in vain that you offer the Asiatic liberty, security, and good government. He will accept and even thank, remembering the proverb, "Kiss the hands that you cannot cut off"; but he would in his heart prefer to be fleeced and tyrannised over by some Sultan, Khedive, or Amir, and, if he gets the chance, will remove to some country "where the Mussulmans still are men." But the Mussulman Bosnians have quite different feelings. They embraced Islam out of policy, their ideas are not essentially different from those of other Servians, and they are quite capable of appreciating the material prosperity of their country under the Austrian rule.

But though no impartial critic can deny that Serajevo and Mostar offer a brilliant contrast to such towns as Monastir and Üsküb, it must be admitted that the problem so successfully solved by Austria is not the real crux of the Eastern question. She administers a country inhabited by Christian and Moslim Serbs, but what European Power or what European method could deal satisfactorily with a country inhabited by Turks, Albanians, Greeks, Vlachs, Bulgarians, and Servians, all ready to cut one another's throats? The Turks are at their worst when governing a single Christian race, as the Bulgarians twenty-five years ago or the Armenians to-day, but they display great ability and a very fair sense of justice in managing five or six aspiring nationalities. However irksome the regulations of the Porte may be, it is the only Government which gives its Christian subjects full liberty to fight their quarrels out— and that is the only form of independence which they really appreciate.

Neither can it be denied that the Ottoman Government is capable on occasion of showing great patience and moderation. In 1895, when Northern Macedonia was invaded by Bulgarian bands who desired to provoke a disturbance, it is well authenticated that the Turkish troops who were sent to repel them were instructed not to harm a single Christian of the country; and that in places where the inhabitants were afraid to go out into the fields for fear of meeting either the bands or the Ottoman soldiers, the latter cut their corn for them lest it should spoil by standing too long, and presented the full amount to the head-men of the villages.

Conterminous with the Herzegovina is the little independent Principality of Montenegro, divided from Servia by the Sanjak of Novi Bazar, which is jointly occupied by Austria and Turkey. The approach to Montenegro by the Bocche di Cattaro is one of the most remarkable sights in Europe. Above that strange landlocked harbour towers a mountain mass, on the sides of which is seen, as if engraved, a zigzag path leading straight up into the clouds. Sturdy horses drag the traveller up this steep and narrow way beyond the clouds to the heights of the Black Mountain,[1] whose frontiers do not come down to the sea at this point. The boundary is passed unnoticed, for alone among European States Montenegro has no custom-house, at any rate not here. The land beyond the clouds is composed of blocks of stone — grey, hard, repellent, intolerant of the scanty vegetable life which tries to squeeze itself out between them. On dry days one is blinded by the flying dust, on wet ones the clouds seem to dissolve in a sheet of water and to inundate the mountain tops. The inhabitants of this strange country are the very opposite of the Servians. Instead of being all peasants they are all chiefs and princes, and have that air of well-built, well-mannered aristocracy which is so rare in the plains. A series of brilliant marriages attests that the royal houses of Europe consider the blood of the Princes of Montenegro as good as their own. All this part of the Adriatic coast, whether it is called Montenegro or Albania, is really independent. The geography of the country has always prevented any effective conquest by the Turks; in both Montenegro and Albania "a small army is defeated and a large one starves." But the Albanians, though practically independent, have never been united by any religious or political idea. They have served the Porte and to a large extent become Mohammedans. The Montenegrins, on the other hand, united by the double bonds of Orthodox Christianity and feudalism, have

---

[1] Montenegro is the Venetian translation of Crna Gora, "black mountain."

been loyal to one another, and have opposed to the Turks a continuous and successful resistance.

Montenegro is heard of first as the residence of the princely family of Balsha, and in early times had to struggle against Turkey, Venice, and Servia, all of which were anxious to annex it.   After the fall of Servia, Bosnia, and Herzegovina, it received a notable addition of population from the Slav nobility, who preferred to take refuge in the mountains to becoming Moslims.   Such a population had natural aptitudes for keeping the Turks at bay, but they were also apt to quarrel with one another, and the relative freedom of Montenegro from such disputes is to be explained by the singular form of polity adopted.   From 1389–1516 the country was ruled by a dynasty known as the Black Princes, but after the latter date the Government was exercised by a Vladika, or Prince Bishop, whose holy office raised him somewhat above political jealousies, just as his celibacy protected him from the family feuds which had been the bane of most Slav dynasties.   At first the office of Vladika was elective, but from 1696–1851, it was hereditary in the family of Petrovich, the nephew succeeding to the uncle.   In 1851 Danilo II. assumed the power as a mere civil ruler, abandoning the ecclesiastical part of the office.   He was assassinated in 1860, and succeeded by the present prince, Nicholas.

CHAPTER IX

THE ALBANIANS AND VLACHS

SOME maps mark the port of San Giovanni di Medua on the Eastern coast of the Adriatic and some do not. When the traveller is dropped there by the Lloyd's steamer, he wonders which are right. Certainly the locality is the landing-place for Scutari in Albania, it figures on Lloyd's time-tables, and is the terminus of a projected railway. On the other hand there is little to distinguish it from the rest of the coast; a rotten pier, some sheds, an inn, and ten Turkish soldiers constitute its claims to be called a town. Having realised that it would not be wise to stop long at Medua, you are confronted with the problem of how to leave it. The railway has really terminated in somebody's pocket, and has never been heard of on the spot. You cannot drive—because, firstly, there are no carriages, and, secondly, there is no road. It is therefore necessary to hire some lean and sullen nags, and a native with a sense of direction, and plunge into the country hoping to some time reach the town and lake of Scutari.

Turkey is not remarkable for luxuriantly fertile landscapes, but Northern Albania is more desolate, uncultivated, and uninviting than any other district. With the exception of a passing view of Lesh or Allesio, one sees nothing between the sea and Scutari which can be called a town, and hardly any villages. The few khans on the way are mere shelters and can hardly be dignified by the style of inns, for not even a crust of bread can be found in them. Shortly before Scutari is a wooden bridge over a river,

2 B

where the traveller has to dismount and negotiate with the Turkish custom-house. This establishment is marvellously polite to the armed natives who swagger across the bridge bristling with rifles and daggers and smoking contraband tobacco, but asserts its authority by ransacking the baggage of harmless tourists. On entering the town we pass by the Konak and barracks. They are spacious buildings with ample grounds, which enable the Vali and troops to take their exercise judiciously in the official precincts without obtruding their presence on the inhabitants of the town. The Albanian part of Scutari is dirty and melancholy. Most of the larger houses are built within courtyards, and the streets are bordered by blank walls. I happened, how- ever, to see the town first on a Monday, when it presents a more animated appearance, for it is on this day that Albanians—at least Christian Albanians—marry. The gloomy high-walled alleys are enlivened by processions of red-robed matrons leading veiled brides who are expected to feign reluctance, close their eyes, and only follow the road to the altar when led and pushed by their nearest relatives. The priests who perform the ceremony bear the unreverend title of Don, and have long moustaches, for in Albania no man is considered respectable without these appendages, and when practical interests are at stake the Church of Rome does not go in for hair-splitting. It is a strange place, inhabited by strange people, without character and yet full of character. They are so devoid of both originality and unity that it is in vain to seek for anything in politics, art, religion, literature, or customs to which the name Albanian can be properly applied as denoting something common to the Albanian race. Yet they certainly have an individuality, which refuses to be controlled and forces both the Sultan and the Pope to modify their systems to suit its idiosyncrasies.

The Albanians are generally and, in all probability,

correctly identified with the ancient Illyrians; but the ᵛ
justice of the identification depends mainly on the fact
that it commits us to very little.[1] The Illyrians were simply
the inhabitants of Illyria, or Illyricum, a district on the
east of the Adriatic and north of Epirus, but not clearly
defined, and embracing different areas at different periods.
Nothing is really known about them except that they were
brave and intractable, hard to subdue, and slow to adopt
Greek and Roman civilisation.   In these qualities they certainly seem the prototypes of the modern Albanians; but
in order to make the relationship between the two clear
we must inquire what is meant by an Albanian.   The
eastern coast of the Adriatic has been repeatedly invaded
and colonised by Slavs, but it presents two phenomena
which appear to be pre-Slavonic — a race with marked
physical characteristics, and the Albanian language.   The
men belonging to this race are comparatively blonde, and
some of the tallest and broadest - headed people in the
world.   They form one of the most distinct ethnic types
of Europe, and are called by Deniker the Dinaric race.   It
is true that the majority of the persons who belong to this
group at the present day—the Dalmatians, Croatians, Montenegrins, Bosnians, and many Servians — speak Slavonic,
and regard themselves as Slavs; but the physical peculiarities mentioned can hardly have been imported by the
Slavs, for they do not characterise them in other parts
of Europe.   We must therefore suppose that these tall,
broad-headed men represent an older substratum;[2] and

---

[1] The identification of the Albanians with the Pelasgi has less to recommend it.   If we admit that we know nothing about the Pelasgi (which
appears to be the case), the identification does not advance us, and if we
connect the Pelasgi with any particular district or style of architecture, then
there is no evidence for identifying the Albanians with them.

[2] Mr. Tozer, in his "Highlands of Turkey" (vol. i. p. 293), says, however, of
the Mirdites: "They are a wiry, active people, but small in stature; indeed
they appeared to us quite pigmies after seeing the Montenegrins." I cannot
confirm this from my own observation.

since we know that Slavonic languages were introduced into the country, and since Albanian is a non-Slavonic language, of whose introduction we have no record, it is permissible to conjecture that it was the language, or rather is the descendant of the language, spoken by this older population. Its principal features are compatible with the system of Aryan European languages, and some of them show marked resemblances of detail to Greek. Yet Albanian as a whole is so odd and capricious, that one wonders if it is not a mosaic like Hindustani.[1] The area in which it is spoken has apparently increased in historic times. It is only in the country of the Mirdites, south of the river Drin and west of Dibre, that all the names of localities are Albanian. In the other districts inhabited by Albanians they are mainly Slav. It seems probable that the constant incursions of Slavs from the North during the sixth and succeeding centuries of our era confined the older population to a narrow mountainous district from which they did not emerge before the thirteenth century. It is also remarkable that the legends of several tribes trace their origin to an illicit union of an Albanian with a Slavonic girl.

At present the Albanians inhabit the Turkish vilayets of Scutari (or Shkodra) and Janina, as well as the adjoining portions of Kossovo and Monastir. They are also found on Greek territory in the western parts of Thessaly, in Hydra, and Spezzia, and appear to have once occupied the whole country almost as far as Athens, to say nothing of their invasions of the Morea. There are also about 80,000 of them in South Italy and Sicily, descendants of the refugees who fled after the Turkish conquest.

The name Albanian appears in Greek as Ἀρβανίτης or Ἀλβανίτης, and in Turkish as Arnaut, but is hardly used

---

[1] See Note I. on the Albanian language, p. 419.

by natives. It is said, however, that the words Arbœri and Arbœreç are applied to the country of the Liaps south of Avlona and to its inhabitants, and are also used in Italy and Hydra. The national designation is Shkyipetar,[1] sometimes written Skipetar, an orthography which, though simpler, somewhat obscures the pronunciation. It appears to be derived from a word signifying an eagle, a name which a race of mountaineers might well give themselves. Two other names are in common use, namely, Gheg (Gegœ, Gegari) and Tosk (Toskœ, Toskœs, Toskœri), the former of which is applied to the Northern Albanians, and the latter to the Southerners. These names, though in common use and very convenient, are not thought quite complimentary, and may be compared to such a designation as Yankee applied to New Englanders. The two sections differ from one another so considerably as to almost form separate nationalities, and may be most conveniently treated separately.

The Ghegs are mountaineers inhabiting the vilayet of Scutari and the Sanjaks of Ipek, Prisrend, and Prishtina in Kossovo, as well as Dibre and Elbasan in Monastir. Their southern limit is the river Shkumb. They are divided into a number of tribes or clans such as the Hotti, Clementi, Castrati, Grudi, and many others. Some of them, for instance the Clementi and Castrati, are nomadic, spending the summer in the mountains and descending in the winter to the shores of the Adriatic. The important tribe of Mirdites, who inhabit a mountainous district to the south of the Drin, are in many ways a more considerable division than the others. All these tribes are engaged in perpetual quarrels and vendettas, which appear to be due to a naturally warlike disposition and an absence of occupation. It is certainly wrong

[1] Çkyipœtar, Albanian ; Çkyipœri, Albania ; Kouvendon Çkyip, to speak Albanian.

to ascribe them, as is often done, to religious animosity, for the Albanians are not at all fanatical. The mistake is, however, excusable, for the occasional riots at Scutari, which naturally attract the attention of Europe, do happen to take the form of a quarrel between the townsmen, who are mostly Moslims, and the surrounding tribes, among whom the Christians are in the majority. But the quarrel is essentially town *versus* country, and the incidents of shooting at a cross or placing a pig's head in a mosque are merely time-honoured ceremonies for declaring war. The Mirdites, who are all Catholics, are the solitary example of a tribe belonging entirely to one religion, all the others containing both Christians and Mohammedans.

The whole of Albania may be said to be only nominally subject to Turkey. In the vilayet of Scutari the subjection is hardly nominal. There is a Turkish Governor, a few troops, and a custom-house, but otherwise Turkish law and institutions are not recognised. There is no conscription, though the natives, who are always ready to fight, are often employed as volunteers. No taxes are paid except the tithe, and that only occasionally, and more as a friendly act than a debt which can be claimed of right. Above all, no Albanian can be tried for capital offences by Turkish law, but must be handed over to his tribe to be judged according to its peculiar customs. It is said that the Albanians have so great a contempt and loathing for theft (which must be carefully distinguished from the noble act of killing a man and taking his money), that they allow it to be dealt with by the Turks. But cases of such procedure are rare.

The Vali is assisted by a Tribal Council, composed of delegates from the chief tribes, who meet at Scutari, and are consulted by him. No measure has any chance of being executed without their consent. Each tribe has its separate internal organisation, which varies considerably in different cases. The chief is often called Baryaktar (from the Turkish Bairakdar, "standard-bearer"), and with the assistance of a Council of elders manages the ordinary affairs of the tribe, administers justice, and executes sentence, the commonest form of punishment being to confiscate the cattle of the offending party. There is also a General Assembly, to which every house sends a delegate. It meets regularly twice a year in spring and autumn, but must also be specially summoned to consider questions of general importance, such as the commencement or conclusion of a tribal vendetta.

In the vilayet of Scutari, where the inhabitants are not irritated by any attempt to bring them under Ottoman law, things are better than in those districts of Kossovo and Monastir which are inhabited by Ghegs. In these provinces the Porte is loth to admit that the Albanians are entitled to exceptional treatment, and consequently endeavours to subject them to the general regulations respecting military service and the payment of taxes. The result is chronic discontent and disobedience, with occasional outbreaks, which are carefully hushed up, but may be detected by the transference of officials and the withdrawal of troops. On one occasion two Mutesarrifs and a Kaimmakam were driven out of their districts by the inhabitants, and sought refuge in a neighbouring provincial capital. The Turkish papers, which possess extraordinary powers of euphemism for the description of disagreeable incidents, said that they were staying with the Vali on a friendly visit while awaiting promotion. They shortly received it, and did not go back to Albania.

The same independence appears in matters of religion. The Albanians have a natural aversion to obedience in the spiritual as well as in the temporal domain. At the time of the Turkish conquest they were nominally Christians, though, from the number of Pagan customs which still survive in their weddings, funerals, and other ceremonies, it may be surmised that their conversion was only super- ficial. Subsequently they distinguished themselves by em- bracing Islam more readily than any other European race. This change of faith took place principally at two epochs, firstly, immediately after the conquest, and secondly, in the seventeenth century, when there occurred a wholesale apos- tasy due to the fact that there was a good career open to European Mussulmans at the period. But even in the present century tribes and villages have changed their religion for very trivial causes. According to the story, part of one Christian tribe became Mohammedan because their priest, who served several villages and visited them first, insisted on saying Mass at an unreasonably early hour. On the whole, the Northerners have been more faithful to Christianity than the Southerners, doubtless because they were allowed to carry arms. At the present day the Christians among the Ghegs belong to the Roman, and among the Tosks to the Orthodox Church, but in the northern division many Eastern practices are said to be still observed, such as the Communion of the laity in two kinds. The Roman Catholic Church in Albania is under the pro- tection of Austria, and not of France as in other parts of Turkey.

The outward signs of Islam are few; mosques are rare, wine is openly drunk, and professing Moslims swear by the Virgin. Arms make the man, and priests of all religions are held in small repute, as may be gathered from the following popular story. When Mohammed went up into heaven he saw an angel standing with a large drum. In answer to his questions he was told that whenever any minister of religion, whether Mollah, Priest, or Rabbi, did an unselfish act, the angel struck his instrument in order that all the celestial host might rejoice over the gratifying

news. "Most interesting," said the Prophet, "I should like
to wait and see him strike the drum." "Certainly, if you
wish it," replied the courteous guide, "but it's only fair to
tell you that he has been standing there since the creation
of Adam, and has not struck it yet." The majority of
Moslim Albanians belong to the Bektashi dervishes, who, in
spite of the fact that they were officially connected with the
Turkish Government through the Janissaries, are one of the
most unorthodox Mohammedan sects, and are said to teach
in secret, not only pantheism, but also the doctrine that
no moral precepts are binding on the elect.

Trade, manufactures, agriculture, art, and literature are
alike neglected in Albania. There is a certain consumption
of cheap Austrian goods, and the Austrian Lloyd's steamers
touch along the coast; but the ports consist, like Medua,
of a few offices on a desolate shore, and are not connected
with the interior by any serviceable roads. Manufactures
are nil; the women of each household make the clothes
and linen required by the family; the village carpenter and
itinerant gipsy blacksmiths supply most other needs. The
country is bare and uncultivated, except for a few fields and
gardens round each village. The native costumes universally
worn, even by the richer classes, are certainly picturesque,
but otherwise the artistic sense seems lower than among the
Turks—houses, churches, and mosques being alike of a hard,
ungainly simplicity. The villages are small, and the dwellings, with high walls and no windows except in the top
storey, resemble fortresses, which indeed they are.

Native literature is almost non-existent. Translations
of parts of the Bible and a few religious books have been
published, and Albanian newspapers are printed in Italy and
Brussels, but hardly ever reach Albania. An effort has been
made of late years, in connection with Protestant missionary
enterprise, to establish an Albanian school and printing-press
at Koritsa, but owing to the united hostility of Turks and

Greeks, both of whom blandly assert that the Albanian language does not exist, it has not had the success it deserves. It is said that a Greek Archbishop, in one of those phrases which one would wish to have turned otherwise, denounced the printing-press for disseminating " the New Testament and other works contrary to the teaching of the Holy and Orthodox Church."

Many Albanians who can read and write foreign languages do not understand their own when they see it printed. This is perhaps not astonishing, for no one has ever decided in what alphabet Albanian ought to be written, and at least four systems are in vogue.[1] This is partly the fault of the Turks, who object to the language being printed or taught in schools, although it is the universal medium of conversation; but it must be admitted that this suspicion and intolerance of the Ottoman Government are of recent date, whereas the sterility of Albanian authors has been chronic in all ages. Even the popular songs and stories are strangely meagre and devoid of national colour. There is nothing to be compared to the national epics of Servia; the exploits of Scanderbeg are unsung among his forgetful countrymen. It would appear from the collections published that the popular stories are mostly versions of well-known Indo-European fables, and contain little that is characteristic of the country or the people; while the songs seem to have been composed chiefly under Moslim influence, and are modelled upon Persian and Turkish verses. But the bul-

---

[1] One employs the Greek alphabet pure and simple; another, used in Kristoforides' translation of the Bible, uses both Greek and Roman letters, with many diacritical marks—e.g. ǵaštę-δitę, sixty. Books published at Bucharest are printed in a fanciful and unsightly variation of the Latin alphabet, also with some Greek characters. Finally, more than one attempt has been made to write Albanian in Latin letters. I here follow the system of M. Dozon (*Manuel de la langue Chkipe*), whose grammar I have used. It is more suited to French than English readers, but I have thought it best not to alter it. In it æ=u in *but*, ç=sh, tch=ch, dh and th are the Greek δ and θ, and the other vowels are pronounced as in French.

bul's notes seem out of tune on the Acroceraunian mountains, and in any case the soul of the people is little disposed to find expression in speech or song.

It is in fact no exaggeration to say that the only occupation of Ghegs in their own country is fighting with one another. They emigrate with facility, for the ties which attach them to their families and dwelling-places are but weak; and those who seek their fortune in other parts of Turkey easily gain a living by their intelligence which, though it finds small room for display in their native mountains, is really very great. The upper classes become officials; the lower have a special predilection for the trades of mason and cavass. But in the vilayet of Scutari itself, few follow any calling but that of shepherds.

Two states of social relations are recognised, the one called Bessa, " peace," or rather " truce," and the other Gyak, or " blood-feud." The sanctity attaching to the former has gained the Albanians a reputation for trustworthiness which they do not deserve, for they are a treacherous people; and their rigid code of honour is due, not to any acute sense of chivalry, but to the fact that a nation which spends so much time in quarrelling is obliged, by the instinct of self-preservation, to strictly define the occasions when killing is not permitted—a close time, so to speak—for otherwise existence would become impossible. Thus you may not kill a man in his own house, nor any one with whom you eat salt (the invariable prelude to an Albanian repast in order to make sure that the guests will not kill one another or the host), nor a man who is escorting a woman, though there is no objection to one woman killing another or a man if she can. Nearly all the tribes have historic vendettas which are rarely extinguished, and new feuds continually arise over the most trivial incidents. When whole clans take part in a feud, it is generally arranged that fighting shall be restricted to a particular time near evening. The shepherds pasture their flocks during the day, knowing that they will not be touched by the enemy, and towards sunset the fray begins. If it is necessary to go to town for market or other reasons, a suspension of hostilities is arranged for a few days, and then the feud begins again.

As some counterpoise to all this fighting and killing may be mentioned the custom of fraternal friendships, by which two young men vow to assist and defend one another through their whole life. These unions are regarded as peculiarly sacred and as creating relationships so intimate that the children of the two parties may not marry. It is said that among the Mirdites the two friends first receive the communion together and then drink wine in which is mixed a small quantity of the blood of each. There is a story that two such friends once fell in love with the same Turkish woman. They discovered their rival ambitions and agreed to end the difficulty by simultaneously plunging their daggers in the lady's heart. Their action has popular approval, but the Turkish woman must have had her own views, if she had time to form any, about Christian brotherhood.

The Mirdites are much more numerous than the other tribes, being, according to some authorities, more than 30,000 in number. They form a small independent State, the capital of which is Oroshi, the residence of the princely family. This family is said to be descended from a warrior called Džon Marku, who lived some two hundred years ago, but in recent times it has been chiefly associated with the names of Prenk and Doda. The first of these is said to be merely the Albanian equivalent of Peter, but it is tempting to connect it with Princeps, and it appears to have become in practice a royal designation. Most of the Ghegs wear a peculiar kind of red baggy trousers embroidered with black braid, but the Mirdites are distinguished by dressing chiefly in white. Their costume consists of a long white woollen coat, tied round the waist with a red girdle, and white trousers fastened tightly round the ankles. They wear white felt caps and shave their heads, except at the back where the hair is allowed to grow long. They are all Catholics and their peculiar marriage customs involve them in continual quarrels with their Mohammedan neighbours. Every man who aspires to win popular respect endeavours to carry off a Moslim damsel. The lady is probably willing enough herself, but the proceeding generally involves an exchange of shots with her male relatives. Mirdite women mostly marry Christians of other tribes. As long as they are unmarried they are kept in great seclusion and may not speak to or be spoken to by any man out of their immediate family circle. Should any one so far forget himself as to pay a compliment to a Mirdite belle either he or she must be shot—a rule which affable strangers will do well to remember.

The Southern Albanians differ from the Northerners in many important respects. Their generic name is Tosk, which has often been conjectured to be the same as Tuscan, though no one has ever explained what the connection may be. The natives of the country round Janina and Prevesa are known as Chams, and those of the district round Premeti as Liaps. They can be at once distinguished by their costume, the *fustanella*, a voluminous white petticoat reaching to the knees and similar to that worn by a ballet-dancer. This dress certainly looks somewhat strange when worn by stout and stalwart men, but its effeminate appearance is somewhat lessened by the custom which prescribes that it must always be soiled and dusty, "clean petticoat" being a term of reproach implying sloth and cowardice. The *fustanella*, though never worn by the Ghegs, is not peculiar to the Tosks, being in general use in Greece, even in the Morea, and also among the rural Turks in the Valley of the Vistritza.

The Tosks are nominally subject to the ordinary Ottoman regulations for conscription and taxation, and, unlike the Ghegs, have no tribes, but a system of territorial magnates called Beys, who were formerly the recognised and are still the practical rulers of their districts, except in the vicinity of large towns. As a rule a Bey who is the head of his family is not in the Government service, but some near relation holds the office of Kaimmakam or Mudir and keeps up communications with the authorities. The higher administrative posts are filled by Turks, but some of the principal natives have received the title of Pasha from the Sultan. The Tosks are milder and more civilised than the Ghegs. They have fewer blood-feuds, and these are mostly of a private character between individuals or families and do not involve whole tribes and districts. The Chams and Liaps have, however, a bad reputation, and are said to have done a good deal of pillaging during and after the last Turco-Greek war.

Southern Albania, though wild enough according to our standards, is far more fertile than the North. The bare, inhospitable mountains, that seem made of cast-iron, are replaced by ranges covered with oak forests, and many of the Beys have extensive estates where agriculture is practised on a large scale. Their houses, though not coming up to European ideas of a nobleman's country-seat, are veritable palaces compared with the simple dwellings of Gheg chieftains, and the hospitality which they dispense is princely.

I once visited a prominent Bey in Southern Albania. A mile or two from his house I was met by a party of horsemen bearing salutations and a roast goose, the latter as a sort of snack, for Albanian etiquette requires that a guest should be treated as if he had the appetite of Gargantua. The house was a veritable castle, built in the style of a Turkish *konak*, but larger and more solid, and filled with a bustling crowd of retainers in the *fustanella*, not one of whom ran any danger of incurring the reproach " clean petticoat." My host was a man about fifty, who wore a somewhat modified form of the national costume, and was accompanied by his son, dressed rather incongruously in a frock-coat. Conversation respecting his lands and cattle was varied with frequent offers of *raki* and *hors d'œuvres*, and at last an enormous dinner was served. This proved a somewhat embarrassing ceremony. I had to sit down alone; the retainers stood round the room or ran about bearing dishes. The Bey, with a towel thrown over his arm, insisted on waiting on me despite all protest, and plied me with monstrous mountains of viands, which he sometimes put into my mouth with his fingers, until this solitary banquet seemed to partake of the character of a surgical operation. My distended feelings were somewhat relieved by the arrival of the Bey's father. It appears that in this part of Albania a man of middle age generally performs the functions of head of the family, and the seniors only appear on occasions of ceremony and preserve their reputation for wisdom by never doing anything but give good advice. The deep respect of the Bey for his parent caused him to desist from stuffing me, and he stood motionless with his hands clasped over his stomach, an attitude which I might have adopted with much more propriety. The father was dressed in a Turkish uniform, and was styled Pasha, which title the Porte had given him in the hope of "conciliating local suscepti-bilities," a piece of diplomacy attended by very moderate suc-cess. The Pasha talked much and well. Albanians, despite their many peculiarities, are distinctly Europeans, and not Asiatics. Those of them who have held high office have an insight into politics, of which they can make no practical use in their own country, but which is theoretically far more advanced than any Turkish views.

Whenever I have been in Albania it has always been the marrying season. It would appear that all marriages are crammed into a few weeks, with which my visits have coincided, and that except during these periods Albanians are exempt from those temptations which beset the ordinary European male at all times. Etiquette requires bridegrooms to pay a visit to the principal persons of the neighbourhood, and on this evening three arrived. It is not thought right that they should say anything on such occasions, and after sitting speechless, with heads bowed down under the weight of imminent matrimony, they departed as they had come with silent salutations.

Next morning one felt something was going to happen. There was an air of preparation and mystery throughout the household; doors were shut and guarded as if to screen some solemn spectacle from the profane gaze. Finally, I was told that the grandfather of the Bey had come to see me, and desired my presence. The apparition of the father had been somewhat of a surprise, but the existence of this older generation was almost supernatural. I was bidden to an inner room, where there sat on a divan the oldest and largest man I have ever seen. The mystery which had attended his entry was explained; doubtless some strange mechanical appliance was necessary to get him through the door, for he certainly could not have walked through it. His turban was as a coachman's umbrella, and his white moustaches like a mammoth's tusks. He was dressed in cloth of gold and silk sashes, and profusely ornamented with revolvers and yataghans. His face and eyes seemed to be made of horn, and incapable of expressing any feeling but dignity and the embers of ferocity. Before him stood in a humble line, with folded hands, three generations of descendants and a row of dependents, and I was requested to seat myself by this living mountain. Conversation with the patriarch was not sparkling or frivolous; it consisted of deliberate compliments divided by two minutes of deep reflection. Only for a moment did he show any human interest; it was when he inquired, with a passing flash in his horny eyes, whether it was true that in a certain place the Turkish tax-collectors had been repulsed with considerable loss.

The whole of the Tosk country has been strongly influenced by Greece, or rather it would be difficult to say whether Epirus is Greek or North-Western Greece Albanian. Though the southern dialect of Albanian is used for conversation, Greek is universally understood, and since the time of Ali Pasha of Janina, who made it the official language, is almost exclusively employed in written communications. On the rare occasions when Albanian is written, Greek characters are generally employed. Such of the Tosks as are Christians belong to the Orthodox and not to the Catholic Church, but the great majority are Mohammedans; for in most places those who wished to retain their ancient faith after the Turkish conquest found it impossible to compete with their apostate brethren, and followed their example in order to obtain such privileges as the right to bear arms. A characteristic instance is the story of the Karamurtads, or inhabitants of thirty-six villages near Pogoniani, which was related to me by a Bey. Till about a hundred years ago these people were Christians, but finding themselves unable to repel the continual attacks of the neighbouring Moslim population of Leskoviki, they met in a church, solemnly swore that they would fast until Easter, and invoked all the saints to work within that period some miracle which would better their miserable lot. If this reasonable request were not granted they would all turn Mohammedan. Easter Day came, but no sign from saint or angel, and the whole population embraced Islam. Soon afterwards they obtained the arms which they required, and had the satisfaction of massacring their old opponents of Leskoviki and taking possession of their lands.

It is not surprising to find there is no history of Albania, for there is no union between the North and the South, or between the different northern tribes and the different southern Beys. Only two names emerge from the confusion of justly unrecorded tribal quarrels, and claim somewhat doubtfully a place in European history—those of Scander-beg and Ali Pasha of Janina. I have related elsewhere [1] the career of the former in outline. He was apparently a brave man and a capable general, but he did not succeed in uniting his nation or in creating any sort of State which could maintain an opposition to the Turks. After his death, though the Northern Albanians continually and successfully resisted the practical assertion of Ottoman rule, they also continually embraced Islam, and furnished the Turks with officials and soldiers. In the South the connection between the Turks and the Albanians was more intimate during the eighteenth century. They were the enemies of the Greeks, and the Porte, fearing the Greek Klephts and Armatoles, appointed Albanians to the offices of Dervendji Pasha, or superintendent of the mountain passes, who was charged with the supervision of Epirus, Acarnania, Northern Thessaly, and Southern Macedonia.

Ali Pasha came from the stock of these Southern Albanians,[2] and illustrated in his career most of their pecu-liarities. They desired to be the lords of the Greeks and independent of the Turks. But the two ambitions were incompatible, and neither the Albanian people nor Ali gained any more solid advantage than the pleasures incidental to a life of successful adventure. Ali was the son of the Bey of Tepeleni, a small town situated to the north of Janina. His father died when he was very young, and, if the legends are true (which is by no means certain), he was educated by his mother Khamko, a lady of great family, and equally remarkable for her pride, vigour, and ferocity. Sword in hand, she led her retainers into battle, and protected her

[1] Page 48.
[2] He sometimes claimed to be a Turk of an Asiatic family, but it appears that this was not true, and merely a way of flattering the Ottomans.

son's possessions, which were attacked by the people of Gardiki, the hereditary enemies of the family. On one occasion, however, she and her daughter were captured by her foes and subjected to great indignity, on which the two women swore they would never rest until they had slain every man in Gardiki. Ali's first appearances in the field were not creditable, and it is said that his angry mother gave him a distaff, saying he could use it better than a sword. Ultimately, says the story, he discovered a secret treasure, raised with it an army of mercenaries and routed his foes. As soon as he entered his ancestral possessions in triumph, he murdered his brother, and then imprisoned his mother on the charge of having committed the crime. She died shortly afterwards. But though Ali can hardly be described as a dutiful son, he remembered and executed her sterner wishes. Many years later he sacked Gardiki, and put the whole male population to death, in revenge for the insults which their fathers had offered to his mother and sister forty years before.

Once securely established in his family estate, Ali devoted himself to the achievement of his design of becoming an independent prince. He won the good graces of the Porte by helping to subdue the Pasha of Scutari, who was in rebellion, and was made assistant to the Dervendji Pasha. In this post he at first combined with the Klephts against the Ottoman authorities, but was soon deposed by the latter. Seeing that he had made a false move, and that it was of capital importance to conciliate the Porte, he won his way back to favour by heavy bribes and efficient military assistance. He was made Pasha of Trikala, in Thessaly, and added to it the Pashalik of Janina, which he is said to have seized by means of a forged firman. That such a proceeding was possible, and that the Porte ultimately sanctioned it, throws a remarkable light on the provincial government of the period. His position now enabled him to handle *la haute politique ;* and at the beginning of the nineteenth century he showed considerable skill in negotiating alliances alternately with Napoleon and the English, by which he obtained Preveza and Parga.　His conquest of Suli is more celebrated.　The Suliots have somehow acquired in popular estimation the reputation of being Greeks.　As a matter of fact they were a tribe of Christian Albanians forming a small independent State somewhat analogous to that of the Mirdites in the North.　They inhabited a wild cluster of mountains near Arta, intersected by black precipitous gorges, through one of which flows Acheron, the River of Hell.　Ali desired to incorporate this little community in his dominions, and, after a prolonged, determined, and bloody war, succeeded in doing so.　The conquest of Suli was due mainly to the treachery of a portion of its inhabitants, but the fall was attended by romantic and heroic incidents.　Women took part in the fighting, and threw themselves from precipices rather than be taken captive; and a priest named Samuel, who had inflamed the religious fanaticism of the Suliots, blew up himself and his adherents by setting light to a powder magazine.

The surviving Suliots fled to the Ionian Islands, but seventeen years later, in 1820, when Ali had been declared a rebel, the Turks brought them back as likely to be the worst enemies of the formidable Pasha.　But the Suliots and Turks could not get on together or fight side by side; there was less difference between them and the old tyrant than might have been supposed, and they ultimately made common cause with him and the Greeks.　They formed themselves into an organised military community, and cut a prominent figure on the Greek side in the contest against the Turks.

By the acquisition of Preveza, Parga, and Suli, Ali had created for himself a Principality of considerable size and practically independent.　Within it he maintained good order by a somewhat strict system of discipline, constructed roads and encouraged trade, but his abominable and ostentatious cruelty (we are told that one way of flattering him was to remind him of the elaborate tortures which he had inflicted) detracts considerably from any praise which we may award to his administration. His attitude towards the Greeks varied at different periods of his career. As long as he was building up his power he entertained the most friendly relations with them, but when he felt himself secure he endeavoured to exterminate the Armatoles by a process of gradual and systematic assassination. Fate, however, caused him to enter again into alliance with them and appear in his last days as the champion of Greek independence and the enemy of the Turks.

His success and audacity had long attracted the unfriendly attention of the Porte, and in 1820 Sultan Mahmud resolved to crush him. He was deposed from his office, and ordered to hand his Pashalik over to the nominee of the Sultan. Having no hope left with the Turks, Ali openly espoused the cause of the Greeks. He summoned an assembly of Greeks and Albanians, and addressed to them a discourse in which he represented himself as the champion of liberty and religious toleration against the Porte, and promised a Constitution to the Christians. His words did not inspire confidence or produce any immediate practical result, and, had he lived longer, the weakness of the ties that connected him with the Greeks would no doubt have become apparent. But his example showed that it was possible to carve an independent Principality out of the dominions of the Porte and to oppose an armed resistance to the Sultan, and thus produced a profound effect on the temper of the Greeks.

When Ali refused to resign his position at the Sultan's order, an army was sent against him, under the command of Hurshid Pasha, who succeeded in forcing him to take refuge with a few followers in the citadel of Janina, where he was closely besieged, but having established himself and his treasures on the top of a powder magazine, threatened to blow the citadel up if he were attacked. Hurshid replied that if Ali did not surrender he would come himself and apply the match, thus destroying the romance but leaving all the inconvenience of an explosive death. At last Ali agreed to retire under safe conduct to a small island on the Lake of Janina and there to await the return of a messenger sent to Constantinople to bring the Sultan's orders. But no new orders were necessary. On that island he was killed, for though one of the most perfidious people in the world, he seems to have forgotten that the Turks might beat him at his own game. According to the story still current at Janina the Turkish troops killed him by firing through the floor of the room in which he slept. According to another version more widely spread he was visited by his friend Mohàmmed Pasha, Governor of the Morea, who, as they were parting with profound bows on the termination of an exceptionally amiable interview, suddenly drew a yataghan and drove it into his heart. At any rate, in February 1822, his head, with those of his three sons and his grandson, was despatched to Constantinople and exhibited in the outer court of the Sarai, as seen and described by the Rev. R. Walsh, chaplain of the British Embassy.[1]

Ali no doubt aided the cause of Hellenic independence, but his memory and that of those like him has left a lurid trace in popular speech. Most Eastern nations commonly employ some such phrase as "God is not without mercy," which means, "Cheer up; things may take a turn for the better." One Greek equivalent for this is, "Don't despair. God is not an Albanian." ('Ο θεὸς δὲν εἶναι Αρβανίτης).

The chief abiding consequence of Ali Pasha's career was that it inspired the Porte with a distrust of the Albanians.

[1] Narrative of a Journey from Constantinople to England.

After the Greek War of Independence four powerful chiefs—Mustafa, the last hereditary Pasha of Scutari, Veli Bey of Janina, Silehdar Poda, and Arslan Bey—agreed to forget their private differences and to make common cause against the Turks. Reshid Pasha, the Grand Vizier, determined to crush this movement, and commenced by an act of which one can only say that it was worthy of Ali Pasha himself. He proclaimed a general amnesty and invited all the Albanian Beys to a peaceful conference and a grand banquet to be held at Monastir. About five hundred appeared headed by Veli and Arslan, and were received with every attention. When they repaired in gala costumes to the parade ground, where the banquet was to be held, they were suddenly surrounded by Ottoman troops and killed to a man. Though Arslan succeeded in breaking through the Turkish lines, he was pursued and slain a few miles outside the town. After this massacre it only remained to crush Silehdar in the South and Mustafa Pasha in the North. The former, who had made himself master of Janina, was easily disposed of, and all Epirus was brought into subjection. Mustafa Pasha was less easy to deal with, and was conquered only thanks to the inveterate hostility of the Christian races to the Albanians. After being severely defeated in Perlepe, he was besieged in Scutari and compelled to surrender. After this the Porte abolished the hereditary Pashalik and appointed Turkish Pashas to the office.

Since this period there are few political events to be recorded of the Albanian people. About the year 1880 was formed what was called the Albanian League, an association of chiefs which was supposed to aim at the union and independence of Albania. I have often heard it said that originally this league was not anti-Turkish, but was in its earlier stages encouraged by the Ottoman authorities, in order to impress the Powers as a national protest against the cession of Dulcigno to Montenegro. Subsequently, however, the Turks became alarmed, broke up the league, and banished some of its most prominent members, including the Mirdite chief, Pip Prink Doda.

At the present day the Porte seems to be nervous and apprehensive about the condition of Albania, but unwilling to take any decided action. In one sense the Albanians are no doubt disaffected; they dislike the Turks, and resent any interference with their own customs, which are mostly incompatible with a decent administration, even in the Turkish sense. But in estimating the practical dangers which may arise from such a temper we must remember the national incapacity for union. Albania presents nothing but oppositions—North against South, tribe against tribe, Bey against Bey. Even family ties seem to be somewhat weak, for since European influence has diminished the African slave-trade, Albanians have taken to selling their female children to supply the want of negroes. Had they ever been ready to combine against the Turks, there seems to be no reason why they should not have preserved the same kind of independence as Montenegro; but from the first some of the tribes and clans endeavoured to secure an advantage over the others by siding with the invaders. Indeed, their present quasi-independent position is less the result of their own valour than of Turkish policy. In many ways they are in Europe what the Kurds are in Asia. Both are wild and lawless tribes who inflict much damage on decent Turks and Christians alike. Both might be easily brought to reason by the exhibition of a little firmness. But as it becomes clearer and clearer that the Ottoman Empire is a battle ground between Islam and Christianity, and that the Christian races will detach themselves whenever they can, the authorities become more and more unwilling to take any action against Moslims. The Porte shows an extreme delicacy and timidity in dealing with Albanians, Kurds, and Arabs, feeling apparently that any quarrel with their subjects would be a scandal and endanger the sacred character of the Sultan as the head of all Islam, which has been put forward so prominently of late years. The least symptom of Moslim discontent paralyses the Central Government. It is not perhaps wonderful that brigandage should be tolerated when Christians are the principal sufferers; but it is somewhat remarkable that the Turks should allow their officials to be expelled and their troops prevented from making roads by a disorderly population, who might easily be kept in order by a firm hand.

Politically, Albania is hardly a danger for Turkey, for Albanian patriotism is not a home product. Papers and books on the national movement are written at Bucharest, Brussels, and various Italian towns, but they are not read at Scutari or Janina. The stock grievance of this literature is that the Turks will not allow Albanian to be taught in the schools, and endeavour to ignore the existence of the language; but, though the complaint is well founded, I doubt if the mass of the people have much feeling on the subject. The Albanians are always ready to fight for any cause or no cause. They might be a source of great weakness to the Turks in time of disaster, though even this must be qualified by the consideration that many of them have always been willing to fight on the Turkish side; but they show no sign of combining and detaching themselves from the Turkish Empire as an independent State like Greece, Roumania, Servia, and Bulgaria.

Scattered over Macedonia is found yet another race of great interest and some importance—the Vlachs or Wallachs. They remind one of those ingenious pictures in which an animal or a human face is concealed so as not to be obvious on first inspection, though when once seen it appears to be the principal feature of the drawing. In the same way, one may live and travel in the Balkan lands without seeing or hearing anything of the Vlachs, until one's eyes are opened. Then one runs the risk of going to the opposite extreme, and thinking, like Roumanian patriots, that most of the inhabitants of Macedonia are Vlachs in disguise. There are many reasons for this curiously inconspicuous character of the Vlachs. They still retain the old habit which Servians and Bulgarians have outgrown of calling themselves Greeks. They have no political organisation or Church of their own ; and though they have their own language, they are nearly all bilingual, and do not obtrude their peculiar tongue on strangers. Their villages are nearly always placed in the highest and least visible spots, the favourite position (naturally somewhat rare) being a hole on the top of a hill. This custom no doubt originated in the time of the barbarian invasions, when the plains were overrun with Slavs, Bulgars, and Avars, but it has been maintained on account of its obvious advantage as a means of eluding the Turkish tax-collector. Snow or mud renders such villages inaccessible in winter, and in summer they are almost uninhabited, at least, by men. Every Vlach has a natural love of wandering about in the open air in charge of animals. Many are shepherds ; but perhaps the most characteristic of their trades is that of Kiraji, or an owner of horses and mules, who either lets them out to travellers or wanders through the country himself as a travelling merchant or peddler on a large scale. In the summer months one can hardly travel anywhere between the Danube and the Pindus without meeting long strings of pack-horses winding up the mountain passes or plodding across the dusty plain, conducted by roughly-dressed, handsome men, whose bright eyes and unusually intelligent faces make one wonder why they do not play a more conspicuous part in the Eastern world. But it seems as if they had little desire to do so.

The headquarters of the Vlachs are in the Pindus range,

which traverses Northern Greece and Southern Macedonia. The town of Metsovo, on the road between Trikkala and Janina, whose streets are staircases cut in the rock, and the houses limpets that adhere to the mountain sides, is in some sense a national capital. More sporadic settlements occur to the North, notably round Berat and Koritsa in Turkey, and in Bulgaria, on the upper waters of the Ister, and north of Vratza. People called Roumanians or Wallachians also inhabit the Danubian Principalities, and form a considerable part of the population of Northern Servia, east of the Morava, of Transylvania, Bukowina, and Bessarabia. It is said that there are also Vlachs in Dalmatia and Istria. These various populations do not form a political, nor, as far as I can judge, a physical unit. But they do form a linguistic unit, and most of them practise certain birth and marriage ceremonies (*e.g.* the anointing of the door-posts by a bride) which seem to be derived from a common Roman origin. The languages spoken by the Vlachs of Macedonia and by the Roumanians north of the Danube are not quite identical, but both are dialects of one form of a Romance or modern Latin language. Those who are accustomed to the Western descendants of Latin —Italian, French, Spanish, &c.—find this Eastern tongue odd and barbaric, but its derivation from Latin is as clear as its strange appearance.[1] Roumanian- and Macedonian-Vlach agree in phonetic peculiarities, which produce such forms as *opt*, *noapte* (*nopte*) for *octo* and *nox*, *popor* for *populus*, *limba* for *lingua*, in the general system of declension and conjugation, and in such remarkable uses as the preposition *a* (instead of *de*) to represent *of*, and numerical expressions like *patru spredece* (*quattuor supra decem*) for fourteen. The differences between them lie mainly in the vocabulary. In addition to the common

---

[1] It is often more strikingly like Latin than any Western language : *e.g. mult*, much ; *suntu*, they are.

Latin element, Roumanian contains a quantity of Slav words which do not appear in Vlach, and Vlach contains a quantity of Greek words which are unknown in Roumanian.[1] Also there are some minor differences in the conjugation, particularly in the compound tenses, and Vlach has some phonetic peculiarities, the most remarkable of which is the change of *f* into *h* before *i*: e.g. *hilliu*, son; *hievra*, fever, *hiu*, *hii*, *himo*, *hiba*, forms derived from the Latin *fio*, which appear in Roumanian as *fiu*, *fi*, *fimu*, *fia*.[2] But the substantial identity of the languages is indisputable, and the problem before us is to explain how the same dialect or variation of Latin is found in the plains of the Danube, in the Carpathians, and in the mountains of Macedonia and Thessaly. There appears to be absolutely no record of any invasions or immigrations from Roumania southwards which would explain the presence of the Southern Vlachs. Had any of the numerous hordes who poured into Macedonia and Thessaly spoken Latin we should certainly have heard of it, and it is therefore necessary to suppose that the Latin element was previous to the Slavs. In the fifth and sixth centuries Latin was no doubt the language of the people in the Balkan Peninsula and in the provinces north of the Danube. Greek, it is true, was establishing more and more firmly its position as the language of government, trade, literature, and religion, but it was essentially a coast language, and was not spoken by the inland peasantry. There is not, I believe, any direct evidence as to the extent to which Latin was spoken north of the Danube from A.D. 400–600, but as for the south, an oft-quoted anec-

---

[1] Thus, in a Vlach fable with a Roumanian translation (Obedenaru: *Texte Macedo-Romane*. Bucure, 1891), occur the words: *arisesce* ($= \dot{a}\rho\acute{e}\sigma\kappa\epsilon\iota$), pleases; *ora* ($= \ddot{\omega}\rho a$), time; *alihia* ($= \dot{a}\lambda\acute{\eta}\theta\epsilon\iota a$), truth; *tora* ($= \tau\hat{\omega}\rho a$), now; *apofasişi* ($= \dot{a}\pi\acute{o}\varphi a\sigma\iota s$), resolved; *etia* ($= a\iota\tau\acute{\iota}a$), cause, which are all otherwise rendered in the Danubian version of the same fable, where, however, occur the Slav words: *tovaraş*, companion; *glasu*, voice; *vreme*, time; *rob*, slave; *pricina*, cause, which appear to be unknown in Vlach.

[2] *Vide* Note II. on the Vlach language, p. 421.

dote[1] represents one Macedonian muleteer saying to another, in A.D. 587 : *Torna, torna, fratre,* " Turn, turn, brother." The people who spoke this Latin language belonged no doubt to different stocks.   Both north and south of the Danube, the Roman legionaries and the Roman colonists must have left a good deal of Italian blood behind them, and the Greek influence cannot have been exclusively intellectual, but in all cases the main constituent of the race must have been the aboriginal local population.   It is therefore probably correct to identify the Vlachs of Thessaly, Macedonia, and Bulgaria with the ancient Thracians, in the same way as the Albanians are identified with the Illyrians, but in neither case does the identification add much to our knowledge.   This Latin-speaking population was, during several centuries, invaded and harassed by hordes, of whom the Slavs were, at any rate linguistically, the most important.   North of the Danube Latin held its own as the dominant language, though it accepted a large percentage of Slavonic words into its vocabulary.   Probably the Italian element in the population was stronger there, and perhaps the continued presence of Bulgarians who had not lost their original speech, and of such tribes as Avars, Kumans, and Pechenegs weakened the influence of Slavonic. South of the Danube Slavonic drove all other popular forms of speech out of the plains; but Albanian and Latin held their own in the mountains, whither those who spoke them retired, impelled no doubt, not only by the necessity of finding natural fortifications, but by an instinctive liking for high places.   The largest mountain settlement of these Latin speakers was in the Pindus and Agrapha mountains, which explains the considerable Greek element in their language.

[1] During the campaign of Comentiolus against the Avars in 587, the baggage fell from a mule.   The muleteers behind, not wishing to be stopped while the animal was reloaded, called out to the man who was leading it, " Turn back, brother."   The words were misunderstood as an exhortation to retreat before an advancing enemy, and a panic ensued.

The name Vlach or Wallach seems to be the same as Wloch, the Polish word for Italian, and to have been originally applied by the Slavs to people of Latin speech, just as they called people of Germanic speech Nemtsi. The Vlachs style themselves Armâni,[1] a variation of Români or Romans. They are sometimes called Kutzo-Vlachs (Lame Vlachs) or Tzintzars. The latter name appears to be due to an attempt to imitate their language, in which the sound of *ts* is very frequent. There are also found in Thessaly, particularly in the district of Sofiades, near Trikkala, people called Karaguns (" black furs "), who have the appearance and dress of Vlachs, and follow the same trades, but speak Greek. One also hears of Albano-Vlachs, which apparently means Vlachs who live among Albanians and speak their language, but I am not sure that it denotes any definite tribe or body of people.

The Vlachs have even less history than the Albanians. In critically estimating the value of statements made about them, one must remember that the old chroniclers and, to a certain extent, modern authorities have a tendency to use the name, not in a national or linguistic sense, but as signifying simply " shepherd." Whatever political importance they may have had seems to have been greatest in the eleventh and twelfth centuries. Thessaly was then known as Great Wallachia (Μεγάλη Βλαχεία), and the Jewish traveller, Benjamin of Tudela, who passed through the district about A.D. 1160, describes the prosperity and magnificence of the Vlach towns. The founders of the Vlacho-Bulgarian Empire[2] were apparently Vlachs, and, if the revolt which led to the establishment of that Empire was caused by an attempt of the Byzantine Court to impose extra taxes on cattle, we may very well believe that the

[1] *â* in Roumanian is pronounced almost like the Russian and Polish *y* in such words as *mylo*, soap.
[2] *Vide* p. 33.

first impulse came from Vlach herdsmen. But if so, they contributed nothing but the first impetus; the Empire of the Asenids shows no traces of Vlach influence in its institutions or language, and the Latin conquerors of Constantinople do not seem to have had any sympathy for this Latin-speaking population of the East or to have been even conscious of its existence. After this period we hear no more of the Vlachs as a political power until very recent years. They did not even fight among themselves like the Albanians, but tended their beasts, made money, and called themselves Greeks.

When Macedonia became the battlefield of nationalist Propagandas, when Greeks were proved to be really Bulgarians, Bulgarians really Servians, and everybody something different from the name he bore, it was only natural that the Vlach element should be brought into prominence, and a theory started that most people in Macedonia were, with or without knowing it, really Vlachs, and this theory naturally found favour in Roumania. Vlach schools were established in Monastir and elsewhere, and an agitation was commenced for the appointment of a Vlach bishop, under the leadership of a certain Apostol Margaritti, who laboured hard and with fair success to weaken Greek influence and win the favour of the Turks. The weakness of this Propaganda was on the ecclesiastical side. The Orthodox Church had always been unwilling to admit that the spoken language of a district ought to be its ecclesiastical language; that because a province was peopled by Bulgarians it ought to have a Bulgarian bishop and a Bulgarian liturgy. But the case of the Vlachs was worse. It was impossible to find a single Episcopal See in which the majority were Vlach-speaking, and a Vlach bishop could be provided with a flock only by uniting the folds scattered through various dioceses. Neither the Patriarch nor the Exarch, who were both sounded, felt able to sanction such an arrangement, or to consecrate such a bishop. The strength of the movement came from the Porte itself. When Greece and the Slavonic States on the borders of Turkey proved that the population across the frontier was Greek or Slav, the Turks did not much like the science of ethnography, and thought it was only a disguised form of annexation. But when the Roumanians proved that the Pindus was inhabited by Roumanians, this seemed a harmless scientific theory, none the worse for being unpalatable to Greeks and Slavs. Roumania could never become conterminous with the Pindus or hope to add it to her territory. Accordingly, a recognition that the inhabitants of that mountain, and of other regions, were neither Greeks nor Slavs was a very convenient answer to many arguments based on the needs of the majority of the Christian population. Besides, the Vlachs and Turks got on together admirably. When the tax-collector called, the inhabitants of the villages were never at home, and this simple arrangement was accepted by both parties. For some reason or other—perhaps a natural disinclination to martyrdom in any cause—the Vlachs have never aroused the love of "atrocities" latent in the breast of the Turkish soldier. After the Greco-Turkish war the Vlachs of Thessaly petitioned the Powers that they might be placed under the Ottoman, and not under the Greek Government. This petition was perhaps not quite unsolicited, but it was also not quite insincere, for the Vlachs are certainly a proof that Christians who have no political aims or ambitions can be happy and quiet under Turkish rule.

In spite of all the pains that have been spent on Vlach educational movements, Vlach literature is even more scanty than Albanian. There are, however, a number of popular songs and fairy stories which show considerable force and descriptive power. The supernatural personages in these legends are generally called fairies (*dini*, from the

Turkish *Jin*); but the incidents often recall those of classical mythology, a resemblance which may be due to Greek influence quite as much as to the Roman origin of the Vlach language.   Thus, in the story of Perpilliṭa, we find the three Fates (*Mire*, that is, Μοῖραι); a hunter who, as a punishment for watching fairies bathe, is turned into a stag and nearly killed by his own dogs, reminds us of Actæon; and a flying horse,[1] of Pegasus.   A lady is rescued from a demon on condition that her lover does not look back at her, and, in fables, the human race learns wisdom, for the Vlach hero did not commit the fault of Orpheus, and was properly married by the rites of the Orthodox Church.

Remarkable in another way is the ballad of the "Bridge of Arta."[2]   The king of the country summoned three Vlach brothers, who were masons, and bade them build a bridge across the river, on condition that, if they could not complete it in seven years, their lives should be forfeited.   Six years did they toil, but every night the river destroyed the work of the day.   In the seventh year a bird told the eldest brother to bury the wife of the youngest alive in the foundations.   He accordingly privately told her to bring dinner to them at the bridge, and then suggested to his brothers that they should bury one of their wives according to the bird's advice, and choose the one who should happen to bring them dinner.   There is something treacherous in the whole story, for when the woman comes with the dinner, and inquires why her husband is crying, he says he has dropped his ring in a pit, and asks her to descend and recover it.   As soon as she has entered the pit the brothers wall her up, in spite of her prayer that an opening may be left sufficient to let her suckle her child.

[1] The horse is called Ballia.   This is perhaps from the Slavonic *Bel*, white, but one cannot help thinking of Xanthos and Balios, the horses of Achilles.

[2] The ballad also exists in an Albanian version, in which the bridge is called the Bridge of Scutari.

It does not look as if the Vlachs would ever be an important political factor in the East, except in as far as they tend to support the Ottoman Empire. They have shown an admirable fidelity to the Orthodox faith, and have never, I believe, become Mohammedans or even Catholics. But beyond this they show little zeal; it is their friends rather than themselves who desire to create a Vlach Millet and a Vlach Church; and though, in a way, they are proud of their race, that unobtrusiveness which is their most marked quality prevents them from making any display of a national movement. Yet they must not be considered as simply shepherds and peasants. Many of them are bankers and men of substance in whom the inherent love of wandering takes the form of business journeys to other countries; and the towns which they inhabit, though deserted for so much of the year, are generally much better built than those of the Slavs and Greeks. A similar liking for massive, unbreakable objects is shown in the dress of the women, who delight in wearing heavy tiaras and ornaments of coarse silver. Perhaps with the Roman language they acquired a taste for solid architecture, which is singularly absent in the Levant. The Turk, who regards all buildings as temporary shelters, never troubles how they are constructed; and his Christian subjects, who have better traditions, are afraid to erect anything sufficiently imposing to attract attention. But the Vlachs have a genius for well-built stone houses, provided with comfortable, quasi-European furniture; and I have even known one with whom I stayed go so far as to replace a broken window pane, not with brown paper, but with a new piece of glass—a proceeding, I believe, unique in the Levant.

NOTES TO CHAPTER IX.

I. Note on the Albanian Language.

The Albanian language is so little known and so curious that it merits some description. It does not, indeed, offer to the philologist so piquant a problem as Basque, for it is clearly an Aryan tongue, but it is one of the least studied languages of Europe, and its exact affinities are not easy to determine. It is full of words borrowed from Italian, Slavonic, and Greek, and often much curtailed and corrupted in the borrowing. *Çpi*, a house, is apparently the Latin *hospitium*, which appears as σπίτι in Greek ; *koengœ*, a song, is *canzone ; pralhœ*, a story, *parola ; lyigœ*, law, and *zakon*, custom, are clearly taken from Italian and Slavonic. But since the original substratum of the language is Aryan, it is often not easy to say whether a particular word is borrowed or is merely the Albanian equivalent of the forms met with in other tongues.

Such words as *ñoh*, to know, and *çoh*, to see, seem to be original. But is *vit*, a year, a corruption of ἔτος or an independent formation ? What is the relation of *lyoumœ*, a river, to *flumen ;* of *ouyk*, a wolf, to *vuk* and λύκος ; of *çkrouan*, to write, to *scribere ;* of *keky*, bad, to κακός ; of *dhe*, earth, to γῆ and δᾶ? Are the Albanian forms loan-words or coincidences ?

The grammar of Albanian is simple but irregular. The forms are not numerous or hard to construct, but it is often impossible to say what method of declension or conjugation a particular word requires. Especially frequent is the practice of using more than one root to form the tenses of one verb like our own *go, went ;* so in Albanian the present tense is *vin* and the aorist *erdha*. It looks as if these forms had been borrowed from the Italian *venire*, and the modern Greek εἶρτα (= ἦλθον) respectively. It is perhaps not fanciful to think that this sterile but lawless language reflects the character of the people.

The nouns are declined in two ways according as they are considered as definite or indefinite. In the indefinite declension, the cases are somewhat imperfectly distinguished ; in the definite, there are as many as four distinct cases. This definite declension does not, however, entirely supersede the definite article, for there is also a prefixed article, used mostly with adjectives, and a conjunctive article, which emphasises the genitive relation, e.g. *briri i lyopœsœ*, the cow's horn (literally, horn-the the cow-the-of). The verb possesses five simple and six compound tenses, the latter being formed with the aid of the auxiliaries *yam*, I am, and *kam*, I have.

For the information of the curious reader, I subjoin an extract from an Albanian translation of the Bible (Gen. iii. 1–5) with a literal translation, which will give an idea of the genius of the language.

Edhe	gyarpœri	içte	mœ	i	ourte sœ	gyithœ	çtœzœt'
And	serpent-the	was	most	the	cunning	all	beasts-of-the

e	fouçœsœ	kyœ	bœri	Zoti	Perœndia.	Edhe	gyarpœri
of-the	field-of-the	which	created	Lord-the	God.	And	serpent-the

i	tha	grouasœ	A		me	tœ	vœrtetœ	tha
to-her	said	woman-to-the	Interrogative particle	In	the	true	said

Perœndia	mos	hani	nga	ç' dô	drou	i	kopœçtit?	Edhe
God	not	eat-you	from	any	tree	of-the	garden-of-the?	And

grouaya	i	tha	gyarpœrit	Nga	pœmet	e	drouñvet
woman-the	to-him	said	serpent-to-the	from	fruits-from-the	of the	trees-of-the

kopeçtit	munt	tœ	hame.	Po nga	pœma	e	drourit
garden-of-the	it-is-possible	that	eat-we.	But from	fruit-the	of-the	tree-of-the

kyœ	œçte	nde	mest	tœ	kopœçtit	Perœndia	tha mos hani
which	is	in	middle	of-the	garden-of-the	God	said not eat-ye

nga	ay	kyœ	tœ	mos	vdisni.	Edhe	gyarpœri	i	tha
from	it	in order	that	not	die-ye.	And	serpent-the	to-her	said

grouasœ.	Me tœ	vertetœ	noukœ	dotœ	vdisni.	Po	Perœndia
woman-to-the.	In the	true	not	shall	die-you.	But	God

e	di	se	atœ	ditœ	kyœ	tœ	hani	nga	ay	dot'	ou	hapene
it knows	that	the	day	that	may	eat-you	from	it	will	be	opened

youve	sutœ	edhe	dot'	ine	posi	Perœndirra	touke	ñohourœ	tœ
your	eyes	and	will	be-you	as	Gods	in	knowing	the

miren'	e	tœ	kekyenœ.
good	and	the	evil.

Gyarpœri is perhaps the same root as *serpens*. The last *r* is not radical, and *gy* in Albanian sometimes represents *s* in other languages, e.g. *gyaçtœ*, six. Perhaps *gyak*, blood, is *sa-n-guis*.

Zot, Lord, or master, is possibly akin to Greek words meaning living or vigorous.

Ç' dô, any, literally, "what (you) like." *Cf.* Latin *quivis, quilibet.*

Kopeçtœ, garden, is perhaps related to κῆπος, and *drou*, a tree, to δρῦς.

Vdisni.—It has been conjectured that this word is akin to
φθείρω.

Dot' ou hapene.—The passive of the aorist and optative is
formed by prefixing *ou* to the active.

Youve, your.—It is one of the eccentricities of Albanian that
(according to one system of orthography) the second personal pronoun of the plural is *you*.

II. NOTE ON THE VLACH LANGUAGE.

The following is an example of the popular Macedonian dialect,
taken from a fairy story (Dr. M. G. Obedenaru. Texte Macedo-
Romāne publicate după manuscrissele originale de Prof. Bianu.
Bucuresci, 1891). A fairy, who has married a king, explains to him
her apparently strange conduct in destroying his commissariat :—

Tora nică un mistirvhiu m̃i arĕmâne ni-spus fŭră
Now still a mystery for-me remains not-explained without

sĕ chiĕră chirò. Voĭŭ sĕ ḍîc co itia a versari-lliĕĭ a
losing time. I wish to say that the-cause of the-throwing-away of

zairei-lliĕĭ ieste aesta care va sĕ 'ṭi spun de aŭaçe 'năinte.
the-grain is that which [I] will you explain from here before.

Mai-mar-lu cap a osti-lliĕĭ 'şi avea sburită cu ehṭirĭ-lli
Most-great-the chief of the-army had an understanding with the-enemies

a tĕĭ, açelli ci vorŭ sĕ 'ṭi llie amirarillia. Şi aşịçe
your, those who wish that from-you they-take the-kingdom. And so

ehṭirĭ-lli îllĭ tăxiră multa tutipotă tea sĕ 'şi faca açea
the-enemies to him promised much money that-he-might-do that

çị lĕ didea de mână a lor.
which to-them gave hand to them.

That is—"Now there still remains a mystery which I must
explain to you without loss of time. I mean that the reason why
I destroyed the grain is the following : The Commander-in-Chief of
your army had an understanding with your enemies who wish to
take your kingdom. And so your enemies promised him much
money that he might do what suited them."

Tora, mistirvhiu, chiro, itia, and *ehṭiri* are from the Greek Τῶρα,
Μυστήριον, καιρός, αἰτία, and ἐχθροί. *Taxiră* is possibly derived
from τάσσω, which, however, means to order or appoint rather than
to promise. *Zaireill*iĕĭ and *amirărillia* are derived from the Turkish
zahire and *emir*, which were originally Arabic words. *Spun* and

spus come from the Latin *expono* and *expositus*, and *chiera* from *perdere*. For this change of consonants, which seems peculiar to the Macedonian dialect, *cf. chietra* (πέτρα), *chielle* (*pellis*), *şerchi* (*serpens*), and also *cicior*, foot, which appears in Roumanian as *picior*. It is the converse of *fapt* and *nopt*, from *factus* and *nox*.

Tutipota, all powerfulness, as an expression for wealth, ought to be characteristic of the speakers. A literal rendering of some of the expressions is more intelligible in French : *Voĭŭ sĕ dic* is *je veux dire ; de aŭaçe 'nainte, d'ici en avant*, straight away ; *işi avea sburita, s'était entendu*. The extract illustrates another peculiarity of both the Danubian and Macedonian Vlach—their plethora of affixed articles and of pronouns, representing what the Latin grammar calls the *Dativus commodi vel incommodi*. Albanian shares this peculiarity to some extent.

The Roumanian (Danubian) version of the above extract is given as follows :—

" Acuma, ânca un lucru ascunsŭ îmĭ rĕmâne ne-spus. Voĭŭ sĕ dic cŏ pricina aruncări merindi-lor ieste asta care o sĕ'ţi o spuĭ d 'acilea 'nainte. Căpitanu al mai mare peste oste se vorbisse cu vrăjmăşi tĕĭ ăia care vorŭ sĕ'ţi ie impĕrătia. Şi aşea vrăjmaşi îĭ făgăduiră multă avere ca sĕ facă ce le venea lor maĭ bine la mână."

In this version the Greek and Turkish words disappear, and we find the Slavonic words *pricina*, cause ; and *vrajmaş*, enemy. But Slavonic words are not wanting in Macedonian Vlach.

CHAPTER X

THE ARMENIANS

"'Tis the most distressful country that ever has been seen."

SOME races seem doomed to failure as corporate bodies; they cannot succeed in forming national political organisations strong enough to hold their own against the adverse circumstances by which they are surrounded. A familiar example of this is afforded by the Poles: they appear to possess all the lighter and more attractive virtues, bravery, wit, and charm; yet any one can see that the restoration of the Polish kingdom is an impossibility, and that the partition of Poland, though it may awaken sympathy and inspire indignation, was due, not only to cruel fate, but to certain faults in the national character, such as want of coherence and of capacity for united action.

The Armenians are another example of political failure. Like the Poles they are divided between three empires, Russia, Persia, and Turkey, but in other ways they offer more analogies with the Jews than with any European people. The Israelite and the Armenian both possess an extraordinary aptitude for finance and commerce, particularly such pursuits as banking in the higher, and money-changing in the lower walks of life; both have wandering instincts with the necessary adaptability to varying circumstances; both, in spite of outward conformity to ordinary social usages remain faithful to their somewhat peculiar forms of religion. But there is this difference between the two peoples that though one, and perhaps the most important, section of Armenians are cosmopolitan financiers who not only form a considerable proportion of the population of Constantinople, but also have such distant centres as Manchester in the west and Madras in the east, another section, who are chiefly agriculturists, still dwell in Armenia, little affected by external influences. Unfortunately, however, they do not constitute the whole or even the majority of the inhabitants of the districts comprised under that vague name, and this circumstance is the chief cause of their troubles.

It is hard to say what are the limits of Armenia, for it is not a recognised political division of the globe. The very name is rigidly forbidden in Turkey, and all maps marking any district as Armenistan are confiscated, nor would the Russian Government much relish such an appellation as applied to the southern part of Transcaucasia. Armenia simply means the districts inhabited by Armenians, but there is a certain tendency, not altogether logical, to restrict it to the Turkish provinces in Asia Minor where the Armenians are most numerous, and particularly to the vilayets of Erzerum, Van, Sivas, Harput, Bitlis, Diarbekir, and part of the vilayet of Aleppo. Nevertheless, the Armenian population is relatively densest in the Russian provinces of Kars and Erivan, where are situated Echmiadzin, the seat of the Catholicos, or head of the Armenian Church, and the ruins of Ani, one of the most ancient and remarkable of Armenian cities. Armenians also form a considerable element in the population, not only of the vilayets above enumerated, but of most inland districts of Asia Minor north of Aleppo, particularly in the provinces of Angora, Broussa, and Trebizonde. The last-named is remarkable as being the only maritime district where they muster in force. As a rule they avoid the sea as regularly as Greeks are attracted to it, and but few of them are found in the south-western corner of Asia Minor.

The name Armenia clashes to a certain extent with

another local designation—-Kurdistan—which is commonly applied to the vilayets of Erzerum, Bitlis, Van, and Diarbekir, and to an even more extended tract. It means simply the country inhabited by Kurds, just as Armenia means that inhabited by Armenians. In many parts of Asia Minor the population is mixed, and while the Turks prefer to call such districts Kurdistan, the friends of the Armenians style them Armenia. The expressions Greater and Lesser Armenia are sometimes applied to the Armenian districts respectively east and west of the Euphrates.

The Armenians, like several other nations, do not use the name by which they are known to foreigners, but call themselves Haik and their country Haiasdan. According to the national tradition they are descended from Haik, the grandson of Japhet, whose dynasty came to an end in 328 B.C. in consequence of the conquests of Alexander of Macedon. After his death Armenia was for a short time ruled by the Seleucids, but, as their power decayed, there arose in Asia Minor a number of states which combined Greek culture with indigenous elements. One of them was called Armenia, but, if the Armenian race was then distributed as at present, it must have extended into other kingdoms. An important influence at this period was the Parthian dynasty of the Arsacides, whose territorial limits were somewhat fluctuating, but who must have been the suzerains, if not the sovereigns, of a considerable Armenian population. Somewhat later the Romans appeared upon the scene. Dikran, or Tigranes, King of Armenia, opposed them in alliance with his father-in-law, Mithridates, King of Pontus, who had recourse to the characteristic Oriental method of a systematic massacre of Romans throughout his dominions. Tigranes, as well as Mithridates, had to pay for these doings, and was conquered by Lucullus and Pompey some fifty years before the birth of Christ.

There ensued a period of nominal Roman supremacy and

real anarchy during which various native rulers achieved occasional independence by playing off the Romans on the west against the Persians on the east, but it is clear that there was no fixed national Government. In the first half of the third century after Christ the power of Persia greatly increased under the Sassanid dynasty. Shapur, or Sapor I., of that line defeated the Roman Emperor Valerian and conquered Armenia, but it was recovered for the empire by Diocletian, who established Tiridates as king. The reign of this sovereign marks an important epoch in the history of the country. He began by persecuting Christianity, and imprisoned his cousin, St. Gregory the Illuminator, for fourteen years in a dry well. At the end of that period he accepted in a literal sense the proverb respecting the position of truth and embraced the new religion.

A large part of Armenia was given back to Persia by the Emperor Jovian in 363, and about 440 Theodosius II. made an arrangement by which he retained the western part for the Romans but ceded the eastern part, or Persarmenia, which became a Persian province, and was administered by governors appointed by the Persian Court, and sometimes of Armenian, sometimes of Persian origin.

The conquest of Persia by the followers of Mohammed did not do much to emancipate Armenia, for from the seventh century onwards it was the scene of incessant disputes between the Byzantine Empire, various Mohammedan rulers, and native princes. These latter had no pretensions to be kings of any united kingdom which could be called Armenia, but from time to time dynasties arose which commanded the allegiance of certain districts. Such were the Pagratids (or Bagratids) who ruled in Northern and Central Armenia from 743 to 1079, and the Ardzrunian dynasty of Vasburagan, who came to an end about the same time. The last native dynasty was that of Rhupen or Reuben, in the Taurus (1080 till 1393), who formed alliances with the

Crusaders, and also with the Mongols, but were unable to withstand the advancing tide of triumphant Islam. The last king of this dynasty—Ghevont or Leo—died in exile at Paris in 1393. After this date almost the only thing to be related of the history of Armenia, until quite recent times, is that Shah Abbas laid the country waste in 1604, and transported 40,000 persons to Julfa in Persia.

Though few rays of light pierce the darkness which surrounds the Armenians from this period until the present century, it is easy to imagine the evils of their position. Much of the territory which they inhabited lay between Turkey and Persia, and formed the battleground of occasional conflicts between those Powers. Oriental frontiers are generally vague, unless they have been "rectified" by European commissions, and it is one of the maxims of Oriental statecraft that it is a good thing to keep the border districts desolate and depopulated, in order that when your enemies invade your territory they may not find much in the way of supplies, and may have some difficulty in advancing. The Armenians suffered severely from the application of this principle. Devoid of all national government, they were raided alternately by Turks and Persians, and harried continuously by local Mussulman chiefs. The government exercised by Turkey and Persia alike meant little but the exaction of tribute and taxes, with occasional sanguinary reminders that it was the business of Christians to keep quiet. But no doubt their remoteness, and even the very badness of the government, produced certain countervailing advantages. There was no attempt at interference in matters of detail; no Phanariots imposed upon them an alien Church or language; and though condemned to political extinction, they never lost their national consciousness, as did the Bulgarians after the Turkish Conquest, but preserved their religion, speech, customs, and idiosyncrasies as stubbornly as the Jews.

Peculiarly admirable is their fidelity to Christianity, for few races have produced more martyrs in ancient as well as in modern times, or come in contact with more persecutors.

The Armenian Church is not, strictly speaking, orthodox or in communion with the Churches of Russia and Constantinople. It was not represented at the Council of Chalcedon, and never signified its adherence to the doctrines there promulgated. It has been contended that this abstention was involuntary, and due to the remote position of the Armenian bishoprics and the unsettled state of the country, but some of the formulæ of the Armenian Church seem tainted with that form of monophysite heresy styled Aphthartodocetism—the heresy, that is, of believing that the mortal body of Christ was incorruptible. It is perhaps more important to notice that the Armenian liturgy and ceremonial have been developed separately from those of the Greek Church, and have an individual character of their own. Externally they are strikingly Oriental, and somewhat quaint according to Western, even Greek, ideas. During the Mass the assistants rattle a strange instrument somewhat resembling the Egyptian sistrum, and composed of a cross set with jangling rings. The altar is not concealed behind a screen, but during the more solemn portions of the service a curtain is drawn round it, which may suggest to irreverent minds that the priest is going to bed. As in the Greek Church, ecclesiastics are divided into the ordinary clergy who marry, and monks who do not. The higher clergy, invariably chosen from the monastic order, are called Vartabeds. The head of the Church is styled Catholicos (in Armenian, *Katoghikos*), and resides at Echmiadzin, in Russia. The same title is borne by prelates resident at Aghtamar (an island in the lake of Van) and at Sis, in Cilicia. This hierarchical arrangement has nothing to do with the Armenian Patriarch of Constantinople, who, according to strict ecclesiastical ideas, is merely a bishop, neither greater nor less than others. Owing, however, to the Turkish system of classifying and organising the subject races of the Ottoman Empire according to their religions, the Patriarch became the official head and representative of the Armenian community in Turkey, and practically, though not theoretically, a more important person than the Catholicos of Echmiadzin. On the whole, the Armenian clergy, though not more educated, are superior to the Greek. They do not attempt to make money out of their flocks, and they have never espoused the side of the Porte against their fellow-Christians. Armenian patriotism and the Armenian Church have always been identified.

Physically the Armenians are a short, solidly built, thick-necked, large-nosed race of men, with features of the type often called Jewish. It may be observed that this physiognomy is not really characteristic of the Israelites, but is simply Oriental. It is equally common among the Georgians, Persians, and Afghans, whence some ingenious persons have surmised that the latter are the lost tribes. The ethnology of Asia Minor, and above all that of the districts near Caucasia, is even more complicated than that of the Balkan Peninsula, and historical data are wanting as to the rise or immigration of many of the tribes now found there. We are therefore, as in many other countries, dependent mainly on linguistic criteria, according to which the Armenian language is a branch of the Aryan or Indo-European family, though the relationship is sometimes obscured by its extraordinary system of phonetics.

Readers of "The Romany Rye" will perhaps remember that when the author tried to teach Belle Armenian, that lady said it sounded more like the language of horses than of human beings. It not only possesses an unrivalled collection of difficult and not very euphonious sounds, both guttural and sibilant, but seems to revel in piling them one on the top of the other, and in beginning words with at least three consonants. The following are specimens of its vocabulary [1]: *Jshmarid*, true; *grnal*, to be able; *pzhishg*, a doctor; *prrngthsnel*, to kindle; *ashharh*, world. Of course no human tongue can really pronounce these awful combinations without interpolating a dull vowel sound similar to the Hebrew *sheva;* but even with this assistance the majority of Armenian words sound, to our ears at any rate, singularly inharmonious. *Asdgh*, star; *tusdr*, daughter; *achkh*, eyes, represent well-known European roots, but in no other language do they appear in so unlovely a form, and few will think it pretty to call a girl *aghchig*, or one's parents *dsnoghkh.* The grammar of Armenian, unlike its pronunciation, is simple. The noun has four or five cases,[2] some of which, however, require to be helped out with prepositions, and the verb [3] four tenses (besides infinitives, imperatives, and participles). The conjugation is, however, somewhat irregular, and occasionally displays a capriciousness which reminds one of Greek. The pronouns and numerals have some resemblance to those of other Aryan languages.[4]

The above remarks apply to the ancient or classical Armenian, in which are composed the most considerable literary works of the language. Modern Armenian, which

[1] *J, sh, ch, ts, ds* are pronounced as in English ; *zh*=*j* in French ; *th, kh,* as in soft hat and black hat; the former also appears in the combinations *ths* and *thsh* represented by single letters in the Armenian alphabet ; *gh* is a deep guttural, *rr* (one letter in Armenian) a strong *r*, and *ḥ* is the German *ch.*

[2] *e.g., Mart*=a man. Singular : nominative, *mart ;* genitive and dative, *marto ;* accusative, *z mart ;* ablative, *i marto ;* instrumental, *martov.* Plural: nominative, *martkh ;* genitive and dative, *martoths ;* accusative, *z marts ;* ablative, *i martoths ;* instrumental, *martovkh.*

[3] The present tense of the verb *yel* (to be) is : Singular—1, *yem ;* 2, *yes ;* 3, *ê.* Plural—1, *yemkh ;* 2, *êkh ;* 3, *yen.* The verb *unil* (to have) is similarly conjugated—*unim, unis, uni ; unimkh, unikh, unin.*

[4] The pronouns are as follows : First person, *yes, mekh ;* second person, *tu, tukh ;* third person, *inkhn, inkhiankh.* The numerals are : 1, *mi (meg) ;* 2, *yergu ;* 3, *yerekh ;* 4, *chworkh ;* 5, *hink ;* 6, *veths ;* 7, *yevthn ;* 8, *uth ;* 9, *inen ;* 10, *dasn.*

is used for conversation, and possesses a small literature of novels and periodicals, differs somewhat from the older form of speech. It is full of foreign words, and has simplified the inflections. It has also developed a suffixed definite article. It exists in several dialects, of which the most cultivated and most important are those of Constantinople and Tiflis. It is also the custom of the Armenians in Turkey to write Turkish in their own alphabet, and Turkish newspapers so printed are published at Constantinople.

This alphabet, like the Cyrillic, owes its existence to missionary zeal. At the beginning of the fifth century the Bishop Mesrob, in his desire to spread the knowledge of the Holy Scriptures, is said to have invented letters for both the Georgian and Armenian languages. The older uncial forms of these two alphabets are very similar, and both show traces of being borrowed from the Devanagari characters of India. There is also a remarkable superficial resemblance between the capital letters of Armenian and of Ethiopic. The more modern cursive alphabet differs considerably from the older form, and, though it represents very exactly the sounds of the language, the differences between many of the letters which it comprises are so slight that, unless it is exceptionally well printed, reading becomes a severe labour for the eyes. Ancient Armenian literature is copious, but somewhat devoid of general interest, as it consists almost entirely of historical and ecclesiastical works, among the latter an ancient translation of the Bible. The chief historian is Moses of Khorene. All these works are distinguished by learning and solidity rather than by spontaneity or beauty, and though some of the hymns found in the service books show originality and power, the language has produced little poetry, and the popular songs fall short of the standard reached by Greeks and Slavs. It would seem that the race has little artistic feeling. The ruins of Ani are certainly fine, but in modern times it is difficult to point to anything distinctively Armenian in architecture or ornamentation. This sterility is no doubt largely to be attributed to the Turkish yoke, but, as the Armenians, though a downtrodden race, have been always stubbornly conservative of many peculiarities, it is fair to assume that the artistic instinct was not strongly developed in the national character—not so strongly, for instance, as the religious and money-making instincts. As a rule an Armenian (or a Jew) will suffer martyrdom rather than change his religion, or lose a lira.

If we sum up the characteristics of the Armenians, they would seem to be somewhat as follows: Firstly, they are a race with little political aptitude or genius for kingdom-building. This want of capacity was not due to the Turkish Conquest. Even before that event they had proved unable to hold their own; they were divided by continual dissensions, and became alternately the vassals of Parthians and Romans, Persians and Greeks. This was partly the result of their geographical position, but after all they had no one but themselves to thank for that position. They seem to have had a natural aversion to the coast—otherwise they might have occupied Constantinople and the mountains of the Caucasus. A nation holding those two fortresses would indeed have been strong. Secondly, the Armenians do not belong to the Orthodox Church. The differences which divide them from that communion may be absurdly trivial, but their consequences are real and important. The average Greek or Slav does not regard the Armenian as a brother Christian. At the time of the Bulgarian "atrocities" the Russian peasantry were shocked at the idea of Pravoslavnys[1] being slaughtered, but the Armenian massacres of 1895–96 did not arouse any popular indignation in Russia. They were regarded as shocking, just as a

[1] Orthodox Christians.

massacre of Catholics in China might be shocking, but they did not seem to come nearer home—neither did the Œcumenical Patriarch, or any other acknowledged authority of the Orthodox Church, display any practical indignation at these outrages.

Thirdly, the Armenians are a people of great commercial and financial talents, supple and flexible as those must be who wish to make others part with their money: stubborn to heroism in preserving certain characteristics, but wanting withal in the more attractive qualities, in artistic sense, kindliness, and some (though not all) forms of courage.

The fate of the Armenians has largely depended on their association with the Kurds. These Kurds are an Iranian people, speaking an uncultivated dialect akin to Persian. They are divided into sedentary and nomadic tribes, both of which, but more especially the latter, are lawless and practically independent. They are governed by their own chiefs, or Agas, and pay scant attention to Turkish officials. In some districts, for instance the Dersim, their recognition of the Sultan's Government is hardly nominal. Of late years an effort has been made by the Ottoman Government to create among them a military organisation analogous to that of the Cossacks in Russia, or rather to that which the Cossacks once possessed. The troops so formed are styled Hamidie, and on paper are very numerous. But in reality little has been done, except to distribute arms and uniforms among the wild tribes. They cannot be induced to submit to military discipline; the regiments which figure in the Ottoman army list can rarely be persuaded to appear on parade; the officers sent to command them often reside comfortably in the nearest town, and are careful not to interfere much with their troops: and the chief practical result is that deeds of violence increase, because their perpetrators are regarded as Ottoman soldiers not amenable to the jurisdiction of the tribunals. The Kurds are nominal but very lax Moslims. Their religious observances seem to contain many Christian as well as older heathen elements, but they have an intense respect and veneration for certain Sheikhs of their own, who are generally fanatical without being orthodox Mohammedans. It is not easy to disentangle the relations of Kurds and Armenians, for few travellers have had the necessary knowledge to enable them to make trustworthy reports about the interior of Asia Minor, and our information is inadequate except as concerns the larger towns. In many cases the Kurds appear as simple brigands and, even when judged by a robber's standard, needlessly cruel and barbarous. But it also seems certain that in several districts at least there is a feudal connection between them and the Armenians. The latter recognise a certain Kurdish chief (or tribe) as their overlord, and pay tribute. In return the chief and his clan protect them against other Kurds. One disadvantage of this system is that Armenians are regarded by Kurds as their property, and therefore if one Kurd has a grudge against another he is as likely to kill his Armenians as to carry off his cattle. Kurds are not found in the more western vilayets inhabited by Armenians, such as Angora, but in the eastern provinces the population may generally be reckoned as one-third Turkish, one-third Kurdish, and one-third Armenian. These wild tribes are really a bane to respectable Moslims and Christians alike; but of late years the growing distrust of Christians has forced the Kurds and Turks into a somewhat unnatural alliance, just as in Europe the Porte is always ready to condone the misdeeds of Albanians in order to keep up the fiction that the Moslim subjects of the Sultan are a solid and united body.

There are two mountainous districts in Anatolia, which form, as it were, islands of compact Armenian population in a sea of surging nationalities. They are Zeitun, in the province of Aleppo, among the Taurus mountains, and Sassun, to the west of Lake Van. Both have been the scene of considerable disturbances, probably because the inhabitants were of a more robust and vigorous physique than other Armenians, and further differed from them in being armed and enjoying practical autonomy. ✓

Before turning to the history of the Armenians in the present century I should advert to the distinction between Gregorian [1] and Catholic Armenians, who are considered by the Porte as different millets or communities. The Gregorians are the adherents of the Armenian Church founded by St. Gregory, and constitute the great majority of the Armenian people. The Catholics are numerically a very small body, and live chiefly in Constantinople and the more western towns, such as Angora. They are not found at all among the rural population, but in cities their wealth and prosperity render them an important element. Their origin seems to date from the time of the Crusades, when many Latin churches were founded in the Levant, but they first became important at the end of the last century, when a considerable number of converts were made to the Roman Church. One of these was the monk Mekhitar, who subsequently fled to the Morea and to Venice, where was founded the convent on the island of Saint Lazaro, which for some time formed the residence of Byron and which still may be visited. The name Mekhitarist is generally restricted to the Armenian Catholics in Italy, but the Church in Constantinople increased and prospered under the protection of the French, who regarded it with special favour. In 1856 there arose a dispute, generally connected with the name of the Catholic Patriarch Hasun, which threatened to divide the community, the majority of whom objected to the policy of the Patriarch, which they considered too subservient to Rome and anti-national. In the Bull known as Reversurus, the Pope asserted his right to interfere in

---

[1] There are also a certain number of Armenian Protestants.

the affairs of the Armenian Catholic Church, particularly in the election of bishops and in finance. The Hasunists supported the Papal pretensions, but their opponents refused to admit them and deposed Hasun. The difference was at last arranged, largely owing to the mediation of France. Hasun was made a cardinal, and Monsignor Azarian was accepted as his successor by both sides. Many Catholics, however, joined the Gregorian Church.

In the seventeenth and eighteenth centuries the Armenians were active chiefly in the sphere of commerce, and carried on a regular and important traffic along the great trade routes of Asia Minor, particularly those connecting Trebizonde, Erzerum, Tabriz, and Isfahan. But in the time of Peter the Great and Catharine II. they already began to have aspirations towards independence. They made appeals to those sovereigns, and received promises from them in return, but no material change in the position of Armenia occurred until the Treaty of Turkmenchai in 1829, when the Russians took the eastern part of Transcaucasia, as far south as the River Aras, and thus incorporated a large Armenian population and the ecclesiastical centre of Echmiadzin. In 1836 was published an ordinance, or Polozhenie, regulating the condition of the Armenian community, and more especially defining the hierarchical position of the Catholicos as head of the Gregorian Church. But this interest in Armenian affairs was accompanied by a desire or tendency to assimilate. It was pointed out that the difference between the Armenian and Orthodox Churches was so small that the spirit of Christian brotherhood naturally suggested their union. This was true enough, but it offended the national and patriotic ideas of the Armenians. They valued the peculiarities of their Church, not from any fanatical conviction of their truth, but because those peculiarities were essentially Armenian and characteristic of the nation. The patriotic writers

Hachadur Abovian, author of *La Plaie de l'Arménie,* and Nalbendian, gave expression to Armenian discontent against both the Sultan and the Czar. Meanwhile, another centre of national sentiment arose in Paris, where an Armenian college had been founded. The young Armenians who were educated there, and who imbibed the liberal ideas of which France supplies so many successive crops, made their influence felt, chiefly in the constitution of the Armenian community of Constantinople. Previous to 1847, the management of that community was in the hands of the Gregorian Patriarch and of certain notables, who did not, however, meet in any sort of council. In 1847, the prevalent desire for a more definite and regular form of national government led to the creation of two councils, to assist the Patriarch, one ecclesiastical and the other lay. Both, however, were elected by the notables, and in no sense constituted a popular representation of the nation. They, therefore, in no way satisfied the aspirations of the "Jeune Arménie," or liberal and educated party, who continued to work and agitate for a more popular and democratic form of government, until their efforts culminated in what was called the Armenian Constitution of 1860. It reorganised the millet and provided for the appointment of all officials by election, for universal suffrage, and for popular education. It also contained a good many general statements as to the duties of individuals towards the nation (*i.e.* the Armenian people), and of the nation towards individuals. The Porte confirmed this instrument three years later. Its title of Constitution and the use in it of the word "nation" are somewhat misleading. It did not really accord any autonomy to the Armenians in the sense of adjusting their relations towards the Sultan, who retained his absolute power over one and all of them, but merely authorised certain changes in their relations to one another. It is somewhat surprising that the Ottoman

Government should have raised no objections to the text submitted to them ; but they, no doubt, attached little importance to the whole affair.   The Armenians had hitherto managed their churches, schools, and hospitals in one way ; they were now allowed to do so in another.   Their methods of electing bishops and councillors affected the Ottoman Empire no more than the method of electing London school boards affects Greater Britain.   The Turks had no suspicions, for at this time they and the Armenians got on excellently together.   For the latter Russia was the enemy.   She had acquired a large accession of Armenian population, but had shown a desire not to protect and develop but to obliterate.   She afforded, indeed, security for life and property, but she hampered with many restrictions the Armenian Church, Armenian schools, and the Armenian language.   The Turks, on the contrary, were perfectly tolerant and liberal as to all such matters.   They did not care how the Armenians prayed, taught, and talked, and in many ways found them the most useful and loyal of their Christian subjects.   There were several reasons for this.   The Armenians were thorough Orientals, and much more in touch with Turkish ideas and habits than Greeks or Slavs.   The richer ones entirely understood and sympathised with Turkish methods of transacting business ; the poorer were extensively employed in Moslim houses in certain branches of domestic service.   The eyes of the Greeks were always turned to Hellas, and every one, as soon as he made his fortune, was anxious to become a Hellenic subject.   But there was no Armenia.   With the exception of those who settled abroad for commercial purposes, the Armenians were quite content to live among the Turks, and spend their money in Turkey.   They spoke Turkish, often even among themselves, and though their accent and phraseology were not always those of the Osmanli, the language was practically a second mother tongue to them.

Kurds and Zapties, perhaps, rendered life a little too eventful, but on the whole the money-changers gained more than brigands and tax-gatherers took, and the balance of wealth remained with the Christians. The Turks treated them with good-humoured confidence, and the phrase, *millet-i-sadika*, "the loyal community," was regularly applied to them. The Moslims did not, of course, consider them as equals; they regarded them much as the kinder class of proprietors in the Southern States regarded their slaves— as people to whom they might trust their business, money, and even their children, but who were almost as far removed from them as a pet dog.

During the Russo-Turkish war the Armenians showed little enthusiasm for the Russians, but some of those near the Russian frontier, notably the inhabitants of Bayezid, were, nevertheless, massacred by the Turks, and the Treaty of San Stefano, which concluded the war, contained the following article (No. 16): "As the evacuation by the Russian troops of the territory which they occupy in Armenia and which is to be restored to Turkey might give rise to conflicts and complications detrimental to the maintenance of good relations between the two countries, the Sublime Porte engages to carry into effect, without further delay, the improvements and reforms demanded by local requirements in the provinces inhabited by the Armenians, and to guarantee their security against the Kurds and Circassians."

This treaty was superseded by the Treaty of Berlin (signed July 13, 1878), which restored to Turkey the districts of Alashgird and Bayezid, and contained the following article (61): "The Sublime Porte undertakes to carry out, without further delay, the improvements and reforms demanded by local requirements in the provinces inhabited by Armenians, and to guarantee their security against Circassians and Kurds. It will periodically make known the steps taken to this effect to the Powers, who will superintend their application."

On June 4, 1878—that is, between the Treaties of San Stefano and Berlin—a bilateral Convention was signed between Great Britain and Turkey to the following effect :—

" If Batoum, Ardahan, Kars, or any of them shall be retained by Russia, and if any attempt shall be made at any future time by Russia to take possession of any further territories of his Imperial Majesty the Sultan in Asia, as fixed by the definitive Treaty of Peace, England engages to join his Imperial Majesty the Sultan in defending them by force of arms.   In return his Imperial Majesty the Sultan promises to England to introduce necessary reforms, to be agreed upon later between the two Powers, into the government and for the protection of the Christians and other subjects of the Porte in these territories.   And in order to enable England to make necessary provision for executing her engagement, his Imperial Majesty the Sultan further consents to assign the island of Cyprus to be occupied and administered by England."

In one way neither Article 61 of the Berlin Treaty nor the Cyprus Convention produced much effect.   Great Britain, indeed, appointed a number of military Consuls to various posts in the Armenian districts, who made tours and reports, but no attempt was made to introduce the promised " reforms and improvements."   But in another way these instruments had a great effect, for they familiarised the Armenian people with the idea that they were entitled to the grant of special privileges from the Porte ; and this idea was easily exaggerated into another—the possibility of founding an Armenian kingdom, or at least an Armenian autonomous province.   The common people undoubtedly looked to Great Britain for the realisation of these ideas, regardless of the fact that that Power was obviously anxious to continue on friendly terms with Turkey, and not to weaken the Ottoman Empire.

The period which followed the Russo-Turkish war witnessed another remarkable phenomenon—the development of Nihilism in Russia. It was a period of secret societies, revolutionary papers, plots to assassinate princes, and hopelessly unpractical patriotic movements, the essence of which was the desire to do something striking, and so attract sympathy or inspire fear, without regard to consequences or any clear ideas of reconstruction. This spirit inspired many of the inhabitants of the Caucasus, and naturally spread to the Armenians of Tiflis and Transcaucasia. At first it was directed chiefly against the Russians, and by a natural interaction the discontent of the Armenians increased the severity of the Czar's government, and that severity in its turn increased the discontent. In 1882 the *Mshak*, an Armenian political paper published at Tiflis, was suppressed. Two years later the Government insisted on the election of the Catholicos Makar in opposition to the will of the people, and a large number of schools were closed. Finding that the Russian police were too well informed and too vigorous for the comfortable existence of secret societies in Tiflis, the Armenian patriots migrated westwards, and made Paris, London, and Geneva their headquarters. In 1887 was founded in Paris the celebrated secret society called the Hintchak, and from 1888 to 1892 an Armenian doctor called Nazarbek published at Geneva several revolutionary papers and reviews, one of which was also called *Hintchak* and another *Aptak*.

It was inevitable that all this movement should affect the Armenians of Turkey, and equally inevitable that by so doing it should destroy the few merits of the Ottoman administration—its easy tolerance, and its readiness to let Christians prosper financially and commercially at the expense of Moslims. Every Turk, from the Sultan to the private soldier, has a frantic terror of secret societies and plots, not altogether unnatural, if we remember the part played by the Hetaireia and the Bulgarian committees. As in the case of Greece and Bulgaria, the Armenian patriots were somewhat chary of appearing in Turkey, but they sent emissaries to work upon the feelings of the people and distribute revolutionary literature. The change produced in Ottoman feeling was enormous. The Turks had formerly regarded the Armenians as the best kind of Giaour —harmless, serviceable, comfortable infidels, whom one could not expect to meet in heaven but who were very · useful here below. But it now appeared that this was not the case. The *millet-i-sadika*, the loyal people, no longer deserved that title: they were as seditious as Greeks and Bulgarians; they had secret committees and revolutionary printing-presses; they were probably arming and conspiring to massacre good Moslims. Subsequent events can only be understood if we realise that the fears of the Turks, however unfounded we may think them, were wide-spread and quite genuine.

Another element in the new situation created between 1880 and 1890 was formed by the Protestant missionaries. They were mostly Americans by nationality, but their connection with the Evangelical Alliance of London brought them into contact with the British authorities. I should be sorry to say one word which could be construed as reflecting on the character or even the discretion of these missionaries. They were gentlemen of education and judgment, who in a noble spirit of self-denial devoted their lives to the task, not of converting the Armenians and other Oriental Christians, but of bettering their condition and diffusing among them religious knowledge, in the hope of dispelling, or at least of supplementing, the excessive ceremonialism and superstition to which the ancient Churches of the East are too prone. For this purpose they founded several colleges and schools in various parts of Anatolia, which, though open to all races, became practically Armenian institutions, because in most towns the great majority of Christians were Armenians. Somewhat later, in 1890, was founded in London the Anglo-Armenian Society, an institution which was equally unconnected with such societies as the Hintchak on the one hand and with the British Government on the other, though the list of members comprised several eminent Englishmen. Their object was to ameliorate the condition of Armenia, and to secure the introduction of the reforms promised by treaty. This laudable project was hampered by their invincible ignorance of the spirit and methods of the East. They invoked public opinion, the rights of Armenia, religious equality, and other excellent principles, which were understood in Turkey about as well as a body of British electors would understand a proposal to cure agricultural depression by a Hatt-i-Sherif.

A certain well-known proverb about good intentions is often misapplied, but unfortunately in the present case the really important point is not what were the objects of the missionaries and of the sympathisers of the Armenians in England, but what were the ideas, stupid and distorted as they may have been, which they inspired in the Turks. It is no use proving that red is a quite harmless colour, and that bulls ought not to be afraid of it.

The good position of the Armenians in Turkey had largely depended on the fact that they were thoroughly Oriental and devoid of that tincture of European culture common among Greeks and Slavs. But now this character was being destroyed: European education and European books were being introduced among them. Foreigners were talking of Armenia as they had once talked of Bulgaria. The Turks thought that there was clearly an intention to break up what remained of the Ottoman Empire and found an Armenian kingdom. This hostile feeling was aggravated by the tendency which prevailed in the same decade to accentuate the Sultan's position as Caliph. Previously this had been a respectable, accepted, but little-talked-of belief, much like the doctrine that the Queen is the head of the English Church. But now there was a continuous attempt to make it a vital reality, which kept before the minds of Moslims the idea that the Sultan was the head of all Islam on one side, as opposed to all Christians on the other. One other cause of discord must be mentioned. It is that the clergy of the old Gregorian Church were naturally ill-disposed to the missionaries, and were ready to assent to and support the Turkish idea that their schools and colleges were centres of disaffection.

Again I say that I have nothing but approval for the aims of the missionaries and of the friends of Armenia; but the Armenian massacres are not intelligible unless we understand that there are two sides to every question, and that things appear very different according as they are looked at from the East or West. " Onward, Christian soldiers, marching as to war," in English is a harmless hymn, suggestive of nothing worse than a mildly ritualistic procession; but I confess that the same words literally rendered into Turkish do sound like an appeal to Christians to rise against their Mahommedan masters, and I cannot be surprised that the Ottoman authorities found the hymn seditious and forbade it to be sung.

The first symptoms of the hatred and distrust of the Armenians which were growing among the Turks were seen in the increasing lawlessness and violence of the Kurds, who plundered and ravaged with absolute impunity. The pressure of certain foreign Embassies obliged the Porte to summon the famous bandit chief, Musa Bey, to Constantinople and to try him for his misdeeds; but he was triumphantly acquitted and treated with great respect. Naturally his example found many imitators.

In 1890 the Patriarch Ashikian presented a petition to the Porte, setting forth the grievances of the Armenian people and complaining of the violence to which they were subjected. He obtained no redress. On the contrary, the summer of the same year witnessed an event which may be regarded as the opening of hostilities between the Ottoman Government and the Armenian people. It was reported to the Sublime Porte that the Armenians of Erzerum had stored arms and ammunition in the principal church of that town for the purposes of a revolutionary outbreak. The church was searched by the troops and brutally dese-crated. Nothing suspicious was found in it, but popular passion was aroused; the Turks were alarmed, and the Armenians ready to defend their religion with their blood. The result was a conflict, in which about fifteen Armenians were killed and many wounded. Several foreign houses and missionary establishments were attacked. At the time this outbreak was called a massacre. Five years later so trivial a slaughter would hardly have attracted attention.

It was at the time of these disturbances at Erzerum that I first visited Armenia, travelling southwards from Kars. The Armenians of Russia were then discontented, and full of revolutionary talk, affecting to think that it was better to be under the capricious but lax government of the Porte than to submit to the minute and galling regu-lations imposed by Russian bureaucracy. The Turkish Armenians hardly shared this view. They were beginning to find the double yoke of Kurds and Turkish soldiers intolerable, and to form wild, vague aspirations towards autonomy.

Northern Armenia is one of the gloomiest and dreariest countries in the world. It may have some brief spell of tenderness and grace in the spring, which I have never seen, but in summer and winter alike it is hard, repulsive, and terrible. During the heat everything is baked to a dry, muddy yellow, from the spiky grass on the plains to the scanty brushwood on the mountains, which is hardly distinguishable from the rocks. A village is indicated by heaps of grey stones on a mountain side suggesting the remains of a landslip. These heaps are really the roofs of subterranean dwellings, for the inhabitants of the country are Troglodytes. Their houses are large burrows, lighted by a circular hole in the ceiling, and consisting of a family dwelling-room, into which neither Christians nor Moslims ever admit the stranger, and a stable in which the sheep, cattle, and horses of the owner are lodged. In this latter apartment is a small raised platform made of baked clay and surrounded by wooden lattice-work. This is the reception-room for guests, but the hospitality which it accords is not refreshing. The stench of the big animals and the attacks of the small ones render comfort impossible. The Armenian women show themselves little. They wear a sort of veil, and if they appear at meals do not sit down but wait on the men. A curious custom forbids an Armenian bride to speak to her husband's relations for some time after marriage, and it is said that this practice does much to ensure domestic tranquillity. Besides these human rabbit-warrens Northern Armenia has little architecture to show; but every now and then one sees a church of solid, simple masonry, devoid of ornament within or without, battered by the outrages of time and of Turkish soldiery and perhaps not unscathed by fire — unpoetic, unattractive, unsung, unpitied, almost uninteresting, but still crowned with the dignity of stubborn suffering and ages of martyrdom.

If Armenia is not a pleasant land in summer, it is still less so in winter. Every country which is periodically overwhelmed with snow must present a terrible monotony of whiteness, but in Russia and Siberia mankind have learnt, if not to conquer, at least to cope successfully with the all-pervading phenomenon. They have snow roads and sledges, well-warmed houses, suitable exercise, and food. But in Anatolia man lets himself be helplessly overwhelmed by the annual avalanche. The roads are blocked and life is at a standstill. There are no amusements, no resources, no means of getting about. The earth, the mountains, and the sky are all full of snow, and the human race sit huddled together like sheep in a pen trying to keep themselves warm.

It was in these desolate oppressed regions rather than in Constantinople that the discontent of the Armenians and the suspicions of the Turks first became serious. The Armenians of the capital were, it is true, more accessible to European ideas, but they were also wealthy and prosperous and apparently secure. It was not till later that the revolutionary committees attempted active measures in Europe. In the early nineties they worked chiefly upon the population of the provinces. Another society called the Troshak was formed, and a considerable number of delegates from both it and the Hintchak found their way into Asia Minor, and in many cases resorted to terrorism in order to force the country populations to adopt their cause. The irritation on the Turkish side became stronger, and acts of aggravating and malicious tyranny more frequent. Ecclesiastics were arrested, the firmans, or permissions, granted to Armenian schools were withdrawn, and all institutions which seemed to be connected with the Armenian race or name were systematically persecuted. In February 1893 the college at Marsovan was burnt; more and more Armenians were thrown into prison on more and more frivolous charges, and more and more terrible stories were circulated as to the horrors they endured.

With regard to these stories of torture, I think a certain amount of circumspect scepticism is not amiss. No doubt the interiors of Turkish prisons present most of the horrors which can be caused by brutality and neglect. No doubt educated and delicate persons are confined in the same rooms with the lowest ruffians, who are allowed to treat them as they choose. No doubt, too, such rough punishments as the bastinado are freely employed. This is all very bad, but still it does not prove the truth of the " hellish " and " unutterable " forms of torture of which the Turks are freely accused. These are often spoken of as being so terrible that the details cannot be given in print, but I believe them to be largely the invention of morbid and somewhat prurient brains. Medical testimony makes it certain that no human being could survive the tortures which some Armenians are said to have suffered without dying.

In the summer of 1894 took place an event of more importance for the Armenians than any yet described—the massacres of Sasun. Sasun, as already mentioned, is a mountainous district near Mush, inhabited by a peculiarly sturdy race of Armenians who were practically independent and allowed no Turkish functionaries to enter their villages. They paid no taxes to the Government, but maintained good relations with the Kurds by presenting them with an annual pecuniary contribution. Though their independence was certainly anomalous, it does not seem proved that they in any way formed a revolutionary centre; but it is alleged that some secret agents of the Armenian committees had been working in the district. In 1893 the local Ottoman officials called upon the inhabitants of Sasun to pay their taxes, but were informed in reply that the Kurds had taken all there was to get; the villagers were ready to pay taxes to the Porte if protected against the Kurds, but they had not enough for both. This was reasonable enough, but it did not please the Turks. When once their attention was called to the fact, they felt that the existence of an independent, untaxed Christian district was highly irregular;

but unfortunately they did not for a moment entertain the idea of ameliorating matters by keeping the Kurds in order and giving the Armenians a chance of paying their taxes. The Kurds were Mohammedans, whom the Porte was determined to regard as a bulwark of the empire. All Armenians were, in their estimation, of doubtful loyalty: these Armenians of Sasun had openly refused to obey orders. Therefore it was decided (it is well to use this impersonal formula, for we do not know who decided) to give them a lesson. Turkish troops and Kurds—among the latter some Moslim ecclesiastics, including the Sheikh of Zeilan—attacked Sasun, destroyed several villages, and massacred the inhabitants. The number of killed was at first stated as 8000, but the final report of the Commission of Inquiry reduced the figure to 900.

This Commission of Inquiry was appointed in consequence of the sensation created in Europe by the reports of the Sasun massacre. It consisted of Russian, French, and English Consular officials, besides Turkish functionaries, and the evidence which it received clearly demonstrated that the Ottoman authorities were responsible for the attack. The principle implied in this commission—that it was time for Europe to actively interest herself in the affairs of Armenia—was not allowed to drop, and the three Embassies who had sent delegates proceeded to prepare a scheme of reforms to be introduced into the Armenian vilayets. This scheme was altered many times to meet the objections of the Porte, and in its final form was open to severe criticism, as compromises generally are. It was sufficiently complicated and formidable in appearance to exasperate the Turks, but yet it gave the Armenians no really practical guarantees of better government. It was proposed to create a Governor-General for the six Armenian vilayets, to appoint Christians as adjuncts to Moslim functionaries, to restrict the license of the Hamidie troops and

of the nomad Kurds, to develop the various institutions of
local and municipal government so as to secure a representation of Christians as well as of Moslims, and to give the
right of supervision and interference to a commission sitting
at Constantinople and in communication with the Embassies.
Most of these so-called reforms existed already in the Ottoman statute-book, and had simply never been put into
practice. It was certain that the men who would now be
entrusted with their execution would continue to ignore
them, and had the Turks simply accepted the proposals of
the Powers, the condition of Armenia would probably have
remained unchanged, just as it remained unchanged by the
Treaty of Berlin. But fear and irritation prevented the
Porte from merely ignoring and evading the obnoxious
measures. It is said that when the Sultan read the
memorandum presented to him he observed, " This business will end in blood." Perhaps his Majesty was acting
on the transatlantic principle of " Don't prophesy unless
you know," for the result of the scheme of reforms was an
outbreak of massacres in the Armenian districts of Asia
Minor. That the responsibility for these massacres rested
with both the local authorities and the central Government
no impartial reader of the papers officially published can
doubt. But we should probably be doing an injustice if we
suppose, as is often done, that orders were issued for a
deliberate and organised slaughter of Armenians. The
Turks were alarmed. They believed that the Armenians,
people who lived in their midst, who were employed by the
Government as officials and by private persons as domestic
servants, were plotting against the Turkish Empire, and
were ready to assassinate individual Turks. These nefarious
schemes were now strengthened by the protection of at least
some European Powers, who urged the Porte to recognise
the Armenians as a special privileged race, and, according
to Turkish ideas, abetted and encouraged them in their

rebellious attitude. Perhaps their frame of mind will be more intelligible if we try to imagine what would be the feelings of Anglo-Indians if they supposed that the natives, under the influence of Russian intrigues, were preparing to repeat the horrors of the Mutiny. Probably the orders issued to the local Ottoman authorities warned them to be on their guard against any revolutionary movement of the Armenians, and, should there be any reason to apprehend one, to at once take the offensive.

Under diplomatic pressure the Sultan sanctioned the scheme of reforms in the autumn of 1895, but it was not officially published by the Turkish Government, and the arrangements made for executing it through the Commission sitting in Constantinople were, for any one who knew Turkey, obviously inadequate. But it mattered little what arrangements had been made for the execution, for the massacres seemed to have for object to so reduce the number of Armenians that it should be impossible to contend they were the predominant element in any district. The first blood was shed in Constantinople at the end of September on the occasion of a demonstration of Armenians in the streets. Other attacks of the Moslims on Armenians followed in rapid succession, without, as it would appear, any special cause. In the last three months of 1895 outbreaks occurred in some fifteen towns of Asia Minor, to say nothing of sporadic butchery in the villages. The most considerable carnage took place at Trebizonde, Erzerum, Diarbekir, Arabkir, Bitlis, Kaisariye, and Urfa. The number of victims in the cases of which detailed consular reports were forthcoming amounted to about 25,000, but it would probably be safe to double this figure if we include the slaughter which took place in the villages and remoter towns and of which no record was kept.

There were two remarkable features about these massacres. Firstly, they were executed with military precision.

Each lasted only a short time, generally twenty-four or forty-eight hours, and often began and ended with the sound of the trumpet. The authorities did not interfere, and in some cases encouraged the mob. The victims were only Gregorian Armenians; other Christians, and even Catholic Armenians, remaining as a rule untouched. Secondly, though the motive of the slaughter seems to have been clearly political and not religious fanaticism, the movement was anti-Christian in this sense that in many places Armenians were offered their lives if they would abjure Christianity, and after the bloodthirsty ebullition was over, persistent efforts were made to induce the villagers in various districts to accept Islam. From the Turkish point of view it was much the same whether an Armenian was killed or whether he embraced that faith. In either case he ceased to be an Armenian, and the sacred law punishes apostasy from Islam with death.

This destruction of human life passed unpunished, and in most countries excited strangely little comment. In England and the United States, indeed, it called forth expressions of indignation against the Ottoman Government and of sympathy with the sufferers. Meetings were held, and very considerable relief funds were raised. But in France, Austria, Germany, and most of the other European countries, both the press and public opinion seemed disinclined to attach any importance to the question, or even to believe what were later proved to be indisputable facts. In Russia Prince Lobanoff was not disposed to coerce or restrain the Sultan by any exercise of force, and no national sentiment urged him to abandon this negative attitude. The Russian people did not think of the Armenians as " little brothers."

So the winter of 1895–96 wore on. Destitution took the place of massacre. In whole districts the surviving population—chiefly widows and orphans—were in want of food, shelter, and raiment. Much difficulty was experienced in distributing the sums subscribed for the purpose of relieving this misery, and the authorities usually raised objection to the foundation of almshouses for the reception of fatherless children. Cold, hunger, and exposure greatly reduced the number of those who had survived the slaughter.

In the spring of 1896 a conflict broke out in Zeitun. This district was, like Sasun, a confederation of mountain villages, practically independent and possessed of arms, but controlled by a small Turkish garrison posted in a fort. After the frightful massacre which occurred in Urfa at the end of 1895, they doubtless feared they would be the next victims, and, resolving to anticipate an attack by the Turks, rose and besieged the garrison. They successfully repulsed the Ottoman force sent to reduce them, and the conflict was only terminated by the mediation of the British Embassy at Constantinople.

Meanwhile serious trouble arose in Crete, and emboldened the Armenian revolutionary committees, who were not unnaturally goaded to frenzy by the sufferings of their compatriots and the apathy of Europe. In June 1896 disturbances occurred at Van, apparently due to an attempt to stir up an insurrection there, and a couple of months later Constantinople itself was the scene of an extraordinary series of events which seem to have at least temporarily disposed of the Armenian question.

The Armenian colony in Constantinople is considerable. There is no census in Turkey, but it is variously reckoned at from 200,000 to 400,000 persons. It may be divided into two classes. First of all there is the trading community comprising not only bankers, money-changers, and considerable commercial houses, but also an enormous number of small merchants. One has only to observe the quantity of Armenian inscriptions in Pera and

Galata, and indeed everywhere except in the exclusively Mussulman quarters, to realise how large a proportion of the shops are owned by Armenians. The second class are commonly known as hammals, or porters. They are peasants from Asia Minor, who leave their families in the provinces and remain in the capital until they have amassed what they consider a sufficient sum of money and then they return home. The bad roads of Constantinople, in many instances impassable for carriages, and the primitive arrangements of the Turkish Custom-House, offer employment to a large number of these human beasts of burden. The Kurds, who are so often the enemies of the Armenians at home, are also their competitors and rivals in the carrying trade, and there is no love lost between the Christian and Mohammedan porters.

The Armenians are generally distributed through the European quarters of Pera and Galata, and are also found collected in compact communities in several places, notably Haskeui, on the Golden Horn, and Kum Kapu, on the southern slope of Stambul. This latter is in some ways the centre of the nation in Turkey, for in it are situate the Cathedral, Patriarchate, and other institutions of the community recognised by the Sublime Porte. It was only natural that the Armenian revolutionists, when determined to strike a final blow, should collect in Constantinople. They had a better chance of being concealed there than in the provinces, and of extorting concessions from the Turks by terrorism. A new revolutionary society was formed, called the Dashnaktsutiun, which appears to have been more violent in its methods and objects than any which had preceded it. Convinced that it was useless to either appeal to the humanity of the Powers, or to remind them of the obligations which they had assumed, the members of this society armed themselves with dynamite and firearms, and on August 26th suddenly attacked and captured the

Ottoman Bank in Galata, declaring that they would blow it up if their demands for the introduction of reforms in Armenia were not granted. The attempt proved a complete failure. The desperate conspirators who had captured the Bank by an audacious surprise about 1.0 P.M. left it quietly at midnight, having obtained no better terms than a promise of a safe passage to France. This sudden collapse was probably due to the fact that the leaders of the party were killed in a scuffle as they first entered the building.

But the matter did not end here. About 6 o'clock bands of Moslims, chiefly Kurds and Lazes, made their appearance, armed with iron bars and wooden clubs of a peculiar pattern, and throughout the night and the next day paraded the streets, destroying all the Gregorian Armenians they could find by smashing their heads. The massacre continued until about eight o'clock on the following evening. The victims were chiefly hammals, or porters, and, as in other cases, almost exclusively Gregorians, hardly any Catholics or other Christians being touched, and those few apparently by mistake. The troops and police did not attempt to stop the massacre, though they did not take part in it. It is estimated that about 6000 persons perished.

These events were a bolt from the blue for the Embassies in Constantinople, and, indeed, for all Europeans, but there is reason to think that they were not so much of a surprise to many of the Turks and Armenians interested. There was clearly a deliberate attempt on the part of the Armenian revolutionists to bring pressure upon Turkey and Europe by seizing the Ottoman Bank, and threatening to destroy its inmates. Whether that was the full extent of the programme is a matter of uncertainty. On the same day bombs were thrown near Galata Serai, and it seems to me an exceedingly plausible supposition that the Armenians had contemplated a series of attacks on different points of importance, including the Sublime Porte. The Turkish police, with their system of ubiquitous espionage, could not fail to be informed of these plans. Such of them as menaced Ottoman interests they nipped in the bud, but the attack on the Ottoman Bank was allowed to develop itself. They justly calculated that it would discredit the Armenians in the eyes of Europe, and if it succeeded it would merely blow up a pack of Christian clerks. And what did that matter? It is pretty certain that the Armenian community knew that something was likely to happen on the 26th of August. Many well-to-do families left Constantinople for the Islands, in the Gulf of Ismidt, on the morning of the fatal day, and it is probably not too much to say that there was a national conspiracy among the Armenians of Constantinople, a vague and ill-organised conspiracy, no doubt, but still a consciousness that a last and desperate effort was going to be made, and a hope that it would succeed. There can be equally little doubt that the Turks were prepared for acts of violence on the part of the Armenians. The Sopajis—that is, the organised mob armed with bludgeons — appeared about five hours after the Armenians attacked the Bank, and must have been got ready some time beforehand, for clearly they were not a spontaneous demonstration of the Turkish populace. The Ottoman authorities had had a very good notion of what was likely to happen, and had taken their measures accordingly. Probably their idea was not that they were going to slaughter Armenians, but that for the protection of the city it was necessary to enrol a special service of constables. In fact, the Turks thought that the whole Armenian people were combining against them, and they combined against the Armenians. It was a real outburst of national feeling, and, though individuals may have regretted the cruelty displayed by the rabble, no section of Turkish opinion sympathised with the Armenians. The

Liberals and young Turks were as ready to explain and excuse the carnage as the most fanatical Mollah.

This massacre attracted more attention than those of the preceding winter, for it took place in Europe, in the capital of the Turkish Empire, under the eyes of the representatives of the six Powers, a large part of whose time was occupied in treating the Armenian question. Yet it brought about no intervention and no punishment. The Embassies proved to the Sublime Porte that the Ottoman Government was responsible for what had occurred. The Porte simply denied the fact, and declined all responsibility. The revolts of the subject Christian races against the Turkish yoke have been generally successful, but in this case the tables were turned, and the Ottoman Government triumphed completely; and one reason why I have spoken of the Armenian question in a book devoted to Turkey in Europe is because this triumph has affected all the Turkish Empire, and not merely Asia. There can be no doubt that after the massacres, both those of 1895 and 1896, the Turks were alarmed at what they had done, and thought they would draw upon themselves the vengeance of Europe; but when they recognised that Europe was too indifferent, or too divided, to interfere, they felt correspondingly reassured and confident. Plots and revolts are of so common occurrence in Turkey that one must be prepared for them at all times; but the spectacle afforded by the Armenians certainly did much to keep the Balkans and Macedonia quiet. All classes of native Christians felt that neither Russia nor England could be depended upon to act as champions of Christianity unless it suited their other interests at the moment, and saw that it was useless to manufacture horrors, because the most terrible outrages might not succeed in attracting the attention of Europe.

Much blame has been thrown on England for abandoning the cause of the Armenians, and if that unhappy people feel that we have deceived and betrayed them, it can hardly be thought unnatural. But, for the honour of England, it must be remembered that we did not promise the Armenians reforms, as the criticisms of our policy often assume. In both the Treaty of Berlin and the Cyprus Convention it was the Porte who engaged to introduce reforms. No one engaged to force the Porte. At the present day most people with an adequate knowledge of the facts are probably agreed that it is useless to attempt to introduce reforms in Turkey (except in unobtrusive matters of detail) if they are to be executed by Turkish officials. Reform under foreign super-vision is another matter, but naturally is beset with inter-national complications. As long as improvements have to be executed by officials who are unanimous in hating all improvement, it matters very little what the details of such schemes may be: they must be doomed to failure in prac-tice. A country detached from Turkey, like Bulgaria, may change, but it is not clear that any act of forcible inter-vention, such as a Russian army on the Caucasian frontier, or a British fleet in the Sea of Marmora, could improve the administration of Asia Minor by Ottoman officials.

It is hard to see any hope for the Armenians politically, for, unlike Bulgaria, they cannot be detached from Turkey. If we call a certain Turkish district Armenia, we are forced to admit that the majority of the inhabitants of Armenia are not Armenians, and that the majority of Armenians do not live in Armenia. Besides, if it were possible to create an Armenian province in Northern Anatolia, where the Armenian population is densest, this would naturally en-counter the opposition of Russia, whose interests would be more threatened than those of Turkey by such a step. What effect the gradual opening up of Asia Minor may have on Armenians it is hard to say, but unless some future outburst of Mohammedan fury is provoked, it will probably be beneficial. The extension of railways can hardly fail to ultimately increase the security and good order of the country districts, and the Armenians are certain to profit by the growth of trade and civilisation, and become superior to the Turks and Kurds. The danger is that when that superiority is felt another outbreak may occur.

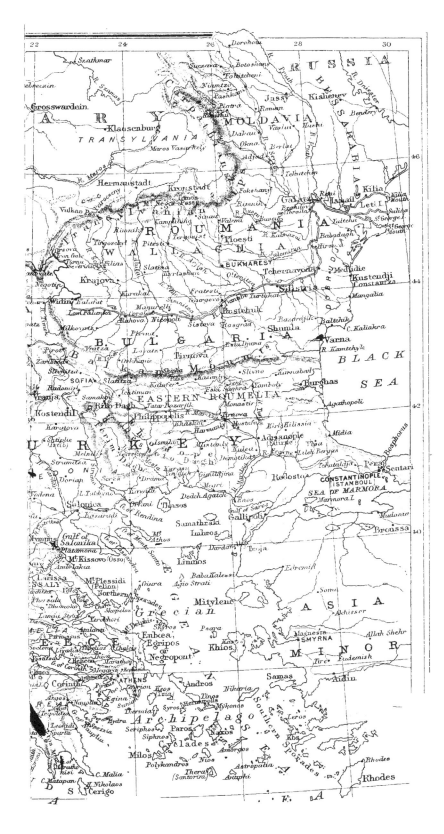

INDEX

A'A, application of title, 121 *note*
Abbaside dynasty, 21, 84, 87, 127
Abd-ul-Aziz, Sultan, 349
Abd-ul-Hamid II., Sultan, mosques of, 115 ; autocratic rule of, 130
Abdul Mejid, palace built by, 94 ; Christians conciliated by, 320
Acacius, Patriarch, 218, 223
Adrian II., Pope, 237
Aga, application of title, 121 *note*
Agathangelus, Patriarch, 278
Agatho, Pope, 227
Agriculture, Turkish fondness for, 95
Aivali, Greek colony at, 311
Alau-'d-din, Sultan, assisted by Erto-ghrul, 88 ; Mevlana at the court of, 197 ; story of Osman's present from, 198
Albania—
  Despotate of Epirus, 22, 48
  Dushan's lordship over, 48
  Geographical situation of, 58
  Independence of, after Dushan's death, 42
  Scenery of, 385
  Skanderbeg's rule over, 48-9 ; history of, from Skanderbeg to Mahmud II., 71-2
Albanian League, 407-8
Albanians—
  Arms, right of bearing, possessed by, 77, 386
  Bravery of, 24, 48
  Dervendji Pasha, office of, held by, 314, 402
  Distribution of, 388
  Disunion of, 24, 48, 408
  Family names, pride in, 120
  Feuds of, 330, 395-6
  Greece, in rural parts of, 300 ; Greeks massacred by, 315-16 ; share of, in Greek War of Independence, 329
  Hospitality of, 362, 398-9
  Illyrians the ancestors of, 24, 387
  Individuality of, 24, 298 *note*, 386
  Islam, conversions to, 72, 76, 383, 392, 401-2
  Language of, 388, 394, 419-21
  Literature of, inconsiderable, 393-4
  Old Servia occupied by, 275
  Physical characteristics of, 387

Albanians—*continued*
  Religion of (*see also above*, Islam), 390-2, 401 ; Catholics protected by Austria, 125, 392
  Treachery of, 395
  Turkish attitude towards, 434
  Turks served by, 383 ; Turkish attitude towards, 386, 406-8
  Unsubdued position of, 48, 150, 390-2
Alexander Couza of Roumania, 71, 280
—— Mavrocordato the Phanariot, 307
Alexandria, Patriarchate of, importance of, 216 ; curtailment of sphere of, 217 ; Bulgarian Church declared schismatic by, 285
Alexius Angelus, Emperor, 22
—— Comnenus, Emperor, quarrels with Crusaders, 21 ; seeks aid from the Pope, 244 ; persecutes Bogomils, 264-5, 364
Ali, Caliph, 194
Ali-Pasha of Janina, 72-3, 316-17, 401-6
Allah, signification of title, 167
Almanach à l'usage du Levant, 142-3
Alp Arslan, 21, 85
Ambelakia, village of, 334-5
Andronicus II., Emperor, the "Grand Company" hired by, 21 ; misgovernment of, 60 ; ecclesiastical policy of, 250-1
—— III., besieged in Salonica, 41 ; expedition of, against Albanians, 48 ; Barlaam sent to Rome by, 252
Angeli, Emperors, incapacity and misgovernment of, 21, 60 ; foreign settlers encouraged by, 123-4
Angels, Moslim belief in, 185
Anglican Church compared with Mohammedan, 195 ; with Orthodox, 232
Ani, ruins of, 424, 431
Antai (Slavs), 26
Anthimus, Patriarch, 277-8
Antioch, Patriarchate of, ancient existence of, 216-17 ; Bulgarian Church declared schismatic by, 285 ; Georgian Church formerly a dependency of, 289
Aphthartodocetism, 428
Arabic, influence of, on Turkish, 106-8
Arabs, Constantinople besieged by, 30, 227 ; traces of, in Crete, 335

461

THE END

Printed by BALLANTYNE, HANSON & CO.
Edinburgh & London